Thomas Mann's *The Magic Mountain*

Thomas Mann's *The Magic Mountain*:
A Reader's Guide

By

Rodney Symington

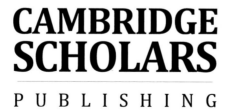

CAMBRIDGE
SCHOLARS
PUBLISHING

Thomas Mann's *The Magic Mountain*: A Reader's Guide,
by Rodney Symington

This book first published 2011. The present binding first published 2014.

Cambridge Scholars Publishing

12 Back Chapman Street, Newcastle upon Tyne, NE6 2XX, UK

British Library Cataloguing in Publication Data
A catalogue record for this book is available from the British Library

ISBN (10): 1-4438-5627-4, ISBN (13): 978-1-4438-5627-0

"The novel is the highest example of subtle interrelatedness that man has discovered."
—D.H. Lawrence

"One cannot read a book; one can only re-read it."
—Vladimir Nabokov

"Without recognition of death, how can there be any knowledge of it?"
—Buddhist saying

"All interest in disease and death is only another expression of interest in life."
—Thomas Mann

TABLE OF CONTENTS

INTRODUCTION

The Magic Mountain by Thomas Mann (1875−1955) is one of the premier works of fiction of the twentieth century. Although the novel is set in a specific time-period (1907−1914), it is far more than merely a novel about the seven years preceding the First World War. The setting—a tuberculosis sanatorium in the Swiss Alps—allows the author to bring together in one place people who represent not only various European countries, but also different views of life. In essence, the novel is a portrayal of the state of European civilization in the early twentieth century and a discussion of the fundamental philosophical choices available to people in the modern age. The ultimate questions of life and death assume a central role in the novel.

Alongside the historical context—both factual and philosophical—the novel also portrays a journey of self-discovery by an "ordinary" young man. In so doing, it implicitly invites the reader to participate vicariously in his intellectual and physical adventures, and to formulate a personal odyssey of the reader's own. The novel ends with a question that is an invitation to further thoughts and reflections.

The Magic Mountain underwent a long period of composition—one that was not foreseen by its author when he first conceived of the work. The occasion that gave rise to Thomas Mann's writing the story was a period of convalescence undertaken by his wife Katia. In March 1912 she traveled from their home in Munich to Davos in Switzerland, to be treated for what was thought to be tuberculosis. She remained there in the Wald-sanatorium from 12 March to 25 September, under the care of the sanatorium's director, Dr. Friedrich Jessen. Thomas Mann went to visit her from 15 May to 13 June 1912.

The impressions he gained from this visit gave him the idea of writing a humorous story about life in the sanatorium, as a kind of "grotesque counterpart" (as he called it) to the seriousness of his novella *Death in Venice*, which he had published in 1911. During his visit to his wife he had been examined by Dr. Jessen, and in recalling this episode in 1940 Thomas Mann wrote sardonically:

> "The head doctor [...] thumped me about, and with the greatest rapidity discovered a so-called moist spot in my lung. [...] The physician assured

me I should be acting very wisely to submit to a six-month cure up there, and if I had followed his advice, who knows, perhaps I would still be lying up there."

Waldsanatorium

100 m oberhalb Davos
Inmitteibar am Wald

Günstigste Besonrung
Bevorzugte Lage

Davos

Höchster   Höchste
Komfort   Hygiene

Privat-Appartements mit ei-
genem Bad, Toilette, Telefon.
Lichtsignale anstatt Glocken.
Fliessend Wasser in den
Südzimmern.
Röntgenkabinett.
Quarzlampe   Sonnenbad

Leitender Arzt:

Dr. F. JESSEN

Hausarzt: Dr. K. REHS

Näheres Prospekt

Advertisement for the Waldsanatorium

Mann's thoughts coalesced over the ensuing year (during which time he was also working on other projects), and he began writing the new "short story" in July 1913. However, as he wrote, the "short story" became longer and longer, so that by May 1915 he was referring to the work as a "novel."

The outbreak of the First World War in September 1914 presented Mann with the ending to the novel that he had been seeking, but it also interrupted his work on it. Although he continued writing the novel for various periods during 1915, the events of the day preoccupied his mind so much that in October 1915 he finally put the novel aside and began what was to become the *Reflections of a Non-Political Man* (published 1918)— and the writing of that long book caused a four-year hiatus in the composition of the novel.

In March 1919 Mann began thinking about the novel again, and read various materials with a view to incorporating them. On 20 April 1919 Mann wrote in his diary: "After a four-year interruption I began to write *The Magic Mountain* again." However, the War and its outcome had had a profound effect on him, and it was some time before he could find clarity about what he wanted to do with the already composed sections and where he wanted the novel to go. Thus it was not until more than five years later, on 27 September 1924, that he was able to write the last word "Finis" under the manuscript. It had taken him twelve years to complete it.

Tuberculosis

The tuberculosis bacterium has been present in the human population since antiquity, and the term "phthisis" (consumption) first appears in Greek literature. In the nineteenth century the disease we now know as tuberculosis was a plague that ravaged Europe and killed thousands of people.

At the turn of the 19th century everybody in Europe was at some point in their lives infected with tuberculosis. (Thus it is not surprising that in the novel Hans Castorp's lungs show evidence of an earlier infection.) In most cases there were no serious complications—some scarring, and natural immunization by the body,—but two variants were far more dangerous. Either the afflicted person suffered from "galloping TB" and died quickly, or the disease stayed with them for years or even decades, progressing very slowly and leading to shortness of breath, the coughing of blood—or even the eventual failure of the body's entire systems. Causes were thought to be heredity, evil spirits, and odors from foul sewage or swamplands, vapors and corruption within the body—including possibly an infection. Since the disease was simply not understood, treatment included all kinds of desperate measures, including hypnosis, purging, and blood-letting.

Not unexpectedly, society itself was greatly affected by the disease: for example, those who suffered from the disease were excluded from many occupations, and governments undertook widespread public health measures.

The introduction of the sanatorium cure provided the first step towards stemming the progress of the disease. Hermann Brehmer (1826–89), a Silesian botany student suffering from tuberculosis, was advised by his doctor to seek out a healthier climate. He travelled to the Himalayan Mountains where he could pursue his botanical studies while trying to rid himself of the disease. He returned home cured and began to study medicine. In 1854, he presented his doctoral dissertation bearing the optimistic title, *Tuberculosis is a Curable Disease*. In the same year, he built an institution in Görbersdorf in Lower Silesia (today: Sokolowsko in Poland) where, in the midst of fir trees, and with good nutrition, patients were exposed on their balconies to continuous fresh air. (Göbersdorf eventually became known as the Silesian Davos.) This method of treatment became the blueprint for the establishment of sanatoria all over the world, and was seen as a significant development in the battle against an insidious opponent.

In 1882, the German physician Robert Koch (1843–1910), who had previously isolated the anthrax bacillus in 1877, discovered a staining technique that enabled him to see the tuberculosis bacterium. This development raised the hope that the disease could be defeated.

However, despite the fact that the bacterium had been identified, the measures available to treat the disease were still quite limited. In general, social and sanitary conditions could be (and were) improved, and adequate nutrition was promoted to strengthen the body's defenses. Sanatoria provided a dual function: on the one hand they isolated the sick, the source of infection, from the general population, while on the other hand the enforced rest and a proper diet and the well-regulated hospital life assisted the healing process.

Accordingly, the actual results were modest: patients stayed in a sanatorium for three months on average (although doctors often tried to persuade them to stay for six to twelve months). At the beginning of the twentieth century up 70% of the patients who came to Davos with infectious tuberculosis died within ten years. (The sanatoria frequently attempted to hide the dying patients—for example, by moving them elsewhere—in order not to undermine the reputation of the resort as a place where people could be cured.) By 1930 and with improved treatment methods, the death rate was still 48%. Harsher critics of the system called the treatment ultimately useless.

Davos

Davos developed into a popular location for sanatoria in the late nineteenth century. Starting in the 1860s it had become a center for invalids and affluent hypochondriacs. It had been noted that residents of the high-alpine town (5000ft above sea-level) did not suffer from tuberculosis. The first lung patient came to the town in 1865, and the man who put Davos on the map, medically speaking, was Dr. Alexander Spengler who built his sanatorium there in 1867. It was Spengler who devised the resort's celebrated regimen for a "cure": every morning patients were taken out on to a south-facing wooden balcony on fur-covered rattan loungers to enjoy the sunshine and ice-cold air. This came to be known as "corpse rest" ("Kadaverruhe")—a term that has a direct bearing on the theme of death in *The Magic Mountain*.

Davos 1863

The high point of Davos's popularity was between 1900 and 1914. By 1912 30,000 patients from various nations were staying in the town's facilities. Davos was a truly international location—with five foreign consulates, an English Quarter, and countless clubs for foreign nationals. In first two decades of the twentieth century the medical diagnosis relied on observation, touching, tapping, and listening—but above all on the "expertise" of the physician in percussion and auscultation. (The medical procedures described in the novel reflect the practices current in the second decade of the 20th century.) Nowadays we know that these methods, that relied in any case on the mysterious "secret knowledge" of the physician, were highly dubious. Some visitors to Davos were very skeptical—including the mother of Katia Mann, Hedwig Pringsheim, who astutely perceived the questionable alliance of medicine and commerce and declared the entire enterprise to be "bogus." In fact, many years later when Katia Mann's original chest x-rays were re-examined, it was discovered that none of them showed any signs of tuberculosis. Thus *The Magic Mountain* arose, at least in part, out of an incorrect diagnosis.

All over Europe Davos advertised itself as the continent's leading "refuge for the healthy, the sick, and the recovering." In the 1920s and 1930s the popularity of the resort was at its peak, but in the 1940s the British developed penicillin, and almost overnight a successful treatment became available. On November 20, 1944, the antibiotic was administered for the first time to a critically ill TB-patient. The effect was almost immediate. The patient's advanced disease was visibly arrested, the bacteria disappeared from the sputum, and the result was a rapid recovery. Tuberculosis was no longer a mystery: it could be defeated. Thereafter the clinics had to change their strategy, and started taking asthma patients instead, but the number of clinics still declined drastically: from around thirty to four.

Tuberculosis and Art

It is not surprising that the widespread prevalence of the disease in the nineteenth century should have led to so many works of art that featured it. Artists variously viewed the disease as a romantic affliction that promised redemption, or alternatively, as a punishment for a less than virtuous life (for example, in the case of the consumptive prostitute). More progressive thinkers viewed the disease as a symbol of society's ills, and its sufferers as victims of social injustice.

In opera the consumptive heroine was an attractive figure because the audience could see the suffering of a beautiful woman wasting away, and her sexuality and her passion destroyed by a pernicious enemy. Thus in Verdi's *La Traviata* (1853) the heroine, Violetta, is a courtesan whose beauty is heightened by the progress of the disease.

But later operas took a less romanticized and more pragmatic view of the disease. In Offenbach's *The Tales of Hoffmann* (1881) the beautiful, but consumptive Antonia is treated by a quack doctor, Dr. Miracle. By portraying Antonia as a victim of a charlatan, Hoffmann was satirizing medical incompetence. Since the opera also linked Antonia's consumption to her mother's heredity as a possible cause of consumption (a popular belief before Koch's discovery of the bacillus), this seemed to absolve the patient from guilt or shame. A decade and a half later in Puccini's *La Bohème* (1896) tuberculosis was employed as social commentary: the opera features street artists living with poverty and disease. Mimi, a seamstress, loves a poor poet named Rodolfo. At first he loves her in return, but then he abandons her, because he fears he cannot provide for her and perhaps because he believes she will infect him with the disease.

In prose works also, such as Victor Hugo's *Les Misérables* (1862) and Tolstoy's *Anna Karenina* (1877), the progress and final stages of the disease were depicted graphically. This shift in the perception of the disease from the romantic to the realistic was accompanied by many "scientific" attempts to conquer the disease: vaccines and therapies, rest cures, tonics, various surgical invasions (some of which occur in *The Magic Mountain*), and a lot of quackery: for example, various surgeons experimented by packing the pleural cavity with fat, paraffin, and even ping-pong balls.

When the novel *The Magic Mountain* appeared, many in Davos were outraged by its depiction of their society, failing to understand that the town and its medical environment were intended as a metaphor for the state of European society before 1914. Among the novel's many detractors was one of the leading-lights of Davos, Dr. Karl Turban, the founder of the village's first tuberculosis sanatorium, who in his *Autobiography* (1935) predicted that: "This sensational novel, a dark distillation of a dark age, … will soon be forgotten."

Disease and illness

In 1913 Thomas Mann wrote to his brother Heinrich of "a sympathy with death that is deeply innate in me: I have always been intensely interested in decay." This fascination with decay and disease can be traced throughout Thomas Mann's works. Disease obviously plays a major role in the novel *The Magic Mountain*, too. For the patients at the sanatorium disease is a mark of honor, a confirmation of their élite status. Spurred on by Behrens, they are proud of their sickness and talk of the ability to acquire it as a "talent." As Hans Castorp remarks, anyone who had the honor of being healthy didn't count. The mountain air is "good for illness"—and the ambiguity is intentional: the ambience promotes both the progress of a disease and its cure. However, in the novel disease is explored in many ramifications. Hans Castorp is fascinated by it, and his acquaintance with and contemplation of it leads him into areas of emotion and intellect with which he had previously been unfamiliar. In pursuing these interests he breaks the fetters of tradition and places himself outside of the conventional bourgeois limits. Furthermore, he is troubled by the harsh reality (as opposed to the convenient myth of disease as an ennobling agent) that disease and stupidity may go hand in hand—and based on the overt evidence at the Berghof, disease for most people leads to destruction.

In "normal" society on the "Flatland" illness—that is, the state of being ill as a fundamental feature of humanity—is repressed. Thus Hans Castorp's real reason for coming to the Berghof Sanatorium is to discover the truth: namely, that he is ill, both physically and metaphysically. At first he rejects the idea—propounded by Dr. Krokowski—that he might be ill and does not subscribe to Krokowski's thesis that he has "never met a perfectly healthy person before." But the discovery of his "moist spot" is liberating for him and he takes pride in it. During the course of the novel the contemplation of disease leads him into the realms of passion, adventure and abandonment, until gradually he comes to realize the wisdom

of Krokowski's view, so that by the time Naphta arrives on the scene he is
ready to accept the latter's argument that "to be human was to be ill." The
entire novel is concerned with form and dissolution, the disciplined effort
needed to live a "conventional" life on the one hand, and the relaxing lure
of death on the other. How can we find meaning in life when the very
nature of it is decay and dissolution? Despite all the views and opinions
expressed in the novel, there is no one clear and convincing answer to that
ultimate question.

In an essay written at the time he was composing *The Magic Mountain*
Thomas Mann wrote: "An interest in death and illness, in the pathological,
in decay, is merely a kind of expression of an interest in life, in humanity,
as the humanistic faculty of medicine shows; anyone who is interested in
the organic, in life, that person is also interested in death; and it could well
be the theme of a *Bildungsroman* to show that the experience of death is,
in the final analysis, an experience of life and that it leads one to
humanity." This is, in essence, a summary of the "education" of Hans
Castorp in the novel.

The "polyphonic" novel and the leitmotif

In the literary novel the form of the work, as well as its content, is
intended to give us aesthetic pleasure. In the case of Thomas Mann, the
pleasure that we take in reading well-written prose is compounded and
extended by the way in which his prose endeavors also to imitate the
structure of music. Thomas Mann constructs his novel out of words and
phrases (leitmotifs) that recur time and again, but, just as happens in a
musical composition, with variations, not always in precisely the same
form. There is, of course, lots of text that does not consist of leitmotifs, but
all of it is directly related to the themes of the novel. In Thomas Mann's
works, nothing is there simply to fill out the page: every word has relevance to the central concerns of the work.

Thomas Mann's aim in *The Magic* Mountain was to write what he
called a "polyphonic" novel. What does that mean? Music is polyphonic,
in that multiple notes can be played at once. But writing consists of one
word after another, in a linear progression. Thus it is difficult to conceive
of how an author could possibly write a "polyphonic" novel: the ear can
hear more than one sound at once, but it is difficult for the eye to read
more than one word at once, especially for 700 pages.

However, by "polyphony" in the novel, Thomas Mann meant something slightly different from the polyphony of music. For him literary
polyphony was created by the interweaving of words and phrases (just like

musical themes or leitmotifs), like a symphony in prose. However, the "polyphony" arises only insofar as the reader remembers the words and phrases and leitmotifs and recognizes them as such. In the worst-case scenario, of course, the non-discerning reader would remember nothing and polyphony would never arise; whereas in the best-case scenario, the reader would remember *every* word. Thus this novel should be read as you would listen to a symphony: just as the musical themes are repeated throughout the movements of a symphony, so, too, in *The Magic Mountain* there is a complex structure of themes and verbal leitmotifs that form a dense web.

At many times throughout the novel the narrator reminds us of something that was said or that happened. But as well as the instances in which the narrator takes the trouble to remind the reader when an important idea was expressed earlier and by whom, or when a character did something in a particular situation, a great many of the leitmotifs in *The Magic Mountain* are repeated or reprised without narratorial comment, and thus it is up to readers to construct their own symphony out of them. The more allusions a reader recalls, the richer the symphony will be.

Thus Thomas Mann encouraged his readers to regard his novels as musical scores. He wrote, for example: "Judge what I have done, my works of art, as you will and must, but they were always good scores, one like the other; musicians have also loved them; Gustav Mahler, for example, loved them, and I have often wanted musicians as public judges."

Like a piece of music that contains so many strands that we cannot grasp them all at one listening, the polyphonic complexity of *The Magic Mountain* also cannot be apprehended in one reading. In order to encompass the full extent of the novel's rich interweaving of leitmotifs, we would ideally have to have the entire text in our brain and be able to recall every relevant line at will. The best reader would be the one who could recall all the references and leitmotifs and be able to see the relationship of everything to everything else. That is, of course, impossible for the average reader, just as the average listener cannot do it for a symphony either. But, as we listen to a favorite piece of music over and over again, and hear new aspects each time, so it is with *The Magic Mountain*: it is a novel that demands to be read and re-read many times, because the full complexity of its allusiveness can never be fully grasped. Every reading, and every discovery of new allusions and connections, increases our aesthetic pleasure.

This is what Thomas Mann himself said about this novel: "I believe that the peculiar construction of the book, its composition, results in a heightened and deepened pleasure for the reader if he goes through it a second time—just as one must be acquainted with a piece of music to enjoy it properly. Musical composition—I have already mentioned in connection with earlier works that the novel has always been for me a symphony, a work of counterpoint—a thematic fabric in which ideas play the part of musical motifs. This technique is applied to *The Magic Mountain* in the most complex and all-pervasive way. On that account you have my presumptuous suggestion to read it twice. Only then can one penetrate the associational musical complex of ideas. When the reader knows his thematic material, then he is in a position to interpret the symbolic and allusive formulae both forwards and backwards."

In *The Magic Mountain* the words connote associations (frequently erotic) with the ideas that underlie the surface structure of the novel: the pencil, thermometer, cigar, lying horizontally, x-ray pictures, Asiatic eyes, mushrooms, etc.—those are examples of "things" from every day in the sanatorium that at the same time relate to both the erotic sphere and the complex of ideas relating to the mysteries of life. Such objects are real and have a practical function, but each of them also has a more important significance on the symbolic level.

Because of the dense web of leitmotifs the novel exists simultaneously on two planes: the real and the symbolical. Thus the Berghof sanatorium and everything connected with it are described in realistic detail. But at the same time as the Berghof is a sanatorium, it is also a hotel, a prison, a monastery, a Siberian salt-mine, a barracks, a school (kindergarten), and a brothel. It is located on a magic mountain with echoes from Germanic myth, from Greek and Roman mythology, from opera, and from many other sources. In sum, it represents a multitude of possibilities that are intended to connote a wide range of associations in the reader's mind.

The perils of art

Now all of this musical invention is not merely an attempt to be clever. Thomas Mann was acutely aware of—and deeply concerned about—the dangers of pure aestheticism: that is, creating things that have beautiful form, but nothing else. He had developed his interest in literature at the end of the nineteenth century, when "art for art's sake" had been a very influential movement, and Thomas Mann's early works contain elements that show the influence of that style of art. He realized, however, that this approach to art had serious problems, such as the danger of becoming superficial and barren. The danger of "aestheticism" (i.e. beauty merely for the sake of beauty) was to remain in his conscience his whole life long, and he never completely overcame the fear that his art might be merely clever, and not at the same time significant. This was essentially the charge that Nietzsche had leveled at Wagner's music: that it was all sound and fury and had no real content—and while Thomas Mann adored Wagner's music, the doubts that Nietzsche had raised about it preyed on Thomas Mann's mind, and caused him to wonder if his own works might also be criticized in like manner.

This concern was but one element in the broader problem of the nature and status of the artist. Thomas Mann was never able to rid himself of the nagging fear that the artist was fundamentally a charlatan: a man who pulls the wool over the eyes of a gullible public, while knowing that what he is doing is essentially fraudulent. (And that gullible public applauds him loudly and heaps honors on him—which only makes him feel even guiltier.) Mann's early story *Tonio Kröger* (1903) portrayed a writer who was tormented by being "different" and outside of "normal" bourgeois society and who had a guilty conscience about being an artist and not fitting in: he finds it only right and proper, for example, that when he returns to his home town for a visit, he is suspected of being a criminal whom the police are seeking.

Mann's unfinished novel *The Confessions of Felix Krull, Confidence Trickster* (started in 1911, thus not long before Mann commenced writing *The Magic Mountain*) went one step further by implying that the other side of the coin was equally valid currency: it portrayed the criminal as a consummate artist. In one memorable scene, the young Felix is taken by his father to see a concert performer, Müller-Rosé. The latter appears on stage, in a glittering costume and with brilliant make-up, and he over-whelms his admiring, even swooning audience with his splendor. When, however, Felix and his father go down to the dressing-room after the performance, they see Müller-Rosé with one half of his face still encased in the make-up that made him look so impressive on stage, but the other half, without make-up, pallid and pock-marked, his eyes red and watery, and his back covered in seeping pustules. This was Thomas Mann's merciless metaphor for the real nature of the artist: the luminescent glitter on the outside hides the festering corruption beneath the mask.

Thus when Thomas Mann created the complex novels of his maturity, he was still troubled by nagging doubts about his art. In the case of *The Magic Mountain*, however, the aesthetic dimension—while providing the reader with pleasure in itself—is a vehicle for the expression of profound reflections about life. This is a novel of ideas, but they are couched in a host of metaphors that populate all aspects of life. The complex structure of the novel might thus be considered to reflect a metaphysical principle:

the victory of art over life—a fundamental idea that Mann found in the philosophy of Arthur Schopenhauer.

Schopenhauer, Nietzsche, and Wagner are the three major influences on Thomas Mann's view of life and art. Mann himself spoke of these three as the "triple star of eternally united spirits that shines powerfully in the German sky." But we must always bear in mind that Mann did not simply accept and adopt the ideas he found in the works of these men wholesale and without discrimination. On the contrary, he took from them only those elements that fitted in with his own understanding both of life and of art, and at all times his use of sources was highly selective.

Schopenhauer

Thomas Mann's reading of Schopenhauer introduced him to a world-view that confirmed his own. As he wrote to a correspondent (in respect of Schopenhauer): "We always find ourselves in books. Strange that our pleasure is always great and we declare the author to be a genius."

From Schopenhauer Mann absorbed the view that in life all things are in conflict, and that ultimately we have no power over our actions. Behind all this conflict Schopenhauer divined that there was a mysterious force that he called the "Will":

> Thus everywhere in nature we see conflict, struggle and the variations of victory, and furthermore we will more clearly recognize how the Will is essentially in conflict with itself. [...] We can observe this conflict through the whole of nature. [...] This struggle achieves its clearest manifestation in the animal world that exploits the plant world for its nourishment, and in which every animal becomes the prey and nourishment of another animal, [...] and where every animal can maintain its existence only by destroying that of another; thus the Will to Life constantly devours itself and becomes its own nourishment in different forms, all the way up to humanity which conquers all other living things and regards nature as a phenomenon for its own use; yet this same species [...] manifests in itself that inner conflict of the Will with the most terrible clarity, and becomes *homo homini lupus* [man the wolf].
> —Arthur Schopenhauer, *The World as Will and Representation* (Vol. 1, Book 2)

The Will asserts itself at all times, and we have no control over it. Our libido is a good example of the way in which the Will does with us what it wants. If we look, for example, at Hans Castorp's infatuation with Clavdia Chauchat, we see that he criticizes rationally any number of features that he observes (her slamming of doors, her slouched posture, the fact that she bites her nails and is "sick, listless, feverish, and worm-eaten deep inside")—and yet he cannot help falling in love with her. Like so many other people who love, he suffers—when Chauchat is at the Berghof, when she leaves, and when she returns. In this manner, the novel demonstrates the principle that the Will causes a man to fall in love—and to suffer as a consequence.

All the characters in the novel demonstrate their ultimate inability to counteract the Will. Joachim is intent on becoming cured of his illness and is highly disciplined and single-minded in pursuit of his goal. But even he is distracted from time to time by the physical attractions of the Russian girl, Marusya. Even the ultra-rationalist Settembrini, who always insists on proper manners and the formality of social intercourse, breaks down as Hans Castorp is leaving the Berghof: he uses the informal form of address and gives him a "Russian" kiss.

Is there then no salvation, no escape from the pernicious influence of the Will? No—and yes. The only way in which human beings can release themselves from the toils of the Will is by creating something that the Will cannot touch, namely, a work of art. Artistic creation may *temporarily* escape the power of the Will; the artist, by creating a work of art, is able to rise above the Will and demonstrate independence from it. Thus while *The Magic Mountain* may be viewed as exemplifying in its *content* the effect of Will on the characters and their behavior, the *novel itself* is a product that rises above the Will's power to dominate existence. Nevertheless, whereas the novel as an artistic creation rises above the Will, the content of the novel still reflects the Will's power—especially since the novel ends with the cataclysm of the First World War, which may be viewed as the ultimate manifestation of the Will.

One of the central questions of Thomas Mann research has remained unanswered: Is *The Magic Mountain* an affirmation of Schopenhauer's philosophy—that life is dominated by irrational forces—or a denial (i. e. an overcoming) of it? Is the complex structure of the novel—with its infinite connotations through the use of leitmotifs—a demonstration that art can, indeed, overcome irrational chaos, or is that artificial structure a confirmation of the emptiness of the world of forms that we construct? Ultimately, it is up to each reader to decide those questions.

Nietzsche

The title of Thomas Mann's novel is taken from a passage in Nietzsche's *The Birth of Tragedy*: "Now it is as if the Olympian magic mountain had opened before us and revealed its roots to us." But Nietzsche's influence on Thomas Mann and on this novel goes far deeper than merely borrowing a phrase for the novel's title.

Nietzsche's philosophy played a major role in Thomas Mann's view of life and art, and the influence of Nietzsche is all-pervasive in the novel. The latter's criticism of ethics and ideologies that rest on a belief in the divine finds its counterpart in the novel's search for answers to the important questions of life. Nietzsche's famous dictum: "God is dead" has to be read in the context of Nietzsche's view of Western religion and ethics. He perceived that in the late 19th century the increasing secularization of society was resulting in a loss of faith. "God is dead" meant nothing more than that people had lost their faith and that, as a result, the foundation of Western ethics had been demolished (although people in Nietzsche's day did not realize that fact—which led Nietzsche to affirm that his ideas were dynamite that would explode posthumously). Whereas in the past God (religion) had been the benchmark for answers to ethical questions, the loss of faith in God signified a loss of an ultimate reference-point for such answers. To whom or what do we turn for such answers now? Since Nietzsche's death the question has become increasingly relevant and acute, as he predicted it would become, and ethical issues—such as abortion, euthanasia, etc.—have since his day so often become the subject of political struggles.

Thus for Nietzsche, once the belief in the divine being was lost, the entire fabric of Western ethics became a sham, an empty façade behind which there was nothing of substance. This is reflected in the novel when Hans Castorp seeks for answers and hears nothing but a "hollow silence."

Furthermore, the novel's context of illness presupposes Nietzsche's assertion that all human beings are sick. Sickness is the normal state of human beings (cf. Samuel Beckett in his play *Endgame*: "You're on earth; there's no cure for that"). Sick people are more aware of what they have, and illness promotes introspection. An interest in degeneracy is essential to self-analysis: without a feeling of disharmony, human beings have nothing to analyze.

Nietzsche had recognized that the path towards health lies in recognizing decadence and overcoming it. Thus it is not wise to repress the signs of disease and death; rather one must acknowledge and face them. As Thomas Mann himself put it in 1925, not long after completing the novel: "One can come to appreciate life in two ways. The first way is robust and is entirely naïve, and knows nothing of death; the other way is familiar with death. I believe that it is only the latter that has any intellectual value. This is the way chosen by artists, poets and writers."

Another aspect of Nietzsche's philosophy that is embedded in the novel is the opposition between Apollo and Dionysus. Apollo, the sun-god, represents reason, enlightenment, progress—all the rational constructs that we enjoy in civilized society: laws, technology, ethical behavior, social manners, etc.; while Dionysus, on the other hand, represents all that endangers our rational world: the passions, the darker forces that lurk in the depths of our being, the world that we, as rational beings, attempt to repress. (These are the elements of human behavior that Freud described as "the dogs in the basement.") From time to time, these repressed elements rise to the surface and may threaten to destroy all the civilized aspects of life that we have struggled to construct. In fact, Dionysus *always* surfaces eventually, no matter how hard we try to deny his existence. (That is why the Greeks acknowledged the need to purge the body of Dionysian urges, by holding an annual festival that served to cleanse the body.) We strive and strive to create Apollo's world, but Dionysus always threatens to destroy it.

In *The Magic Mountain* Settembrini, as the champion of reason, enlightenment, and progress represents Apollo, while Clavdia Chauchat, and later Naphta, represent Dionysus. It is, of course, highly significant that Hans Castorp listens with his rational mind to Settembrini's arguments, but cannot prevent himself from being fatally attracted to Clavdia Chauchat and all that she represents. Likewise, Naphta—ugly, unlikable, even corrosive—expresses views about the world and human history that are closer to the truth than Settembrini's fine phrases, as Hans Castorp comes to realize.

Once again, as with the issue of Schopenhauer's presence in the novel, it will be up to the reader to decide whether or not the novel ultimately sides with Dionysus and destruction, or whether it offers the hope that Apollonian principle will survive and triumph.

On another level Nietzsche's influence can also be seen in the musical elements in the novel. Nietzsche viewed German culture as essentially one that was centered on music, and Thomas Mann also adopted this view. But the German cult of music is not without problems: in the novel Settembrini declares music to be "politically suspect." In its tendency to cloud the reason and to lead listeners to emotional extremes or lethargy, music stands in the way of progress and acts as both a soporific and escape from the obligations of bourgeois life. Furthermore, music has the capacity to enflame the emotions and to sway the listener towards irrational political or religious action. Nietzsche's condemnation of Wagner's music as a "narcotic art" certainly seems to apply to the effect that music has on Hans Castorp.

For Nietzsche the key concept for progress as an individual was the "conquest of the self" ("Selbstüberwindung")—a realization of the innate problems of the personality and a conscious victory over them. This becomes Hans Castorp's ultimate goal—and he achieves it while contemplating music.

Wagner

Wagner's music plays a comparatively small explicit role in *The Magic Mountain*; but Wagner's influence and his musical technique (i.e. the extensive use of the *leitmotif*), on the other hand, infuse the entire novel.

In the 1920s classical music was appreciated by a much larger portion of the populace than it is today, so that Thomas Mann could assume that his readers would understand most, if not all of the musical references in his novel. Similarly, as a devotee of Wagner's music himself, Thomas Mann could count on the fact that Wagner's importance to German culture would also resound in his readership.

Furthermore, the essence of Wagner's world-view and the implicit content of his works exert a profound influence on the entire novel. Thomas Mann's views on Wagner's music were strongly influenced by what Nietzsche had written about Wagner. Nietzsche, having been initially wildly enthusiastic about Wagner's music and a devoted disciple of the composer, eventually turned away from him and called him "a master of hypnotic tricks." For Thomas Mann, Wagner represents a world that runs counter to the expectations and conformism of bourgeois society. In Wagner Mann saw portrayed, among other things, the neglect of duty, eroticism, the fascination with death, and the metaphysics of Schopenhauer. In a word: Wagner is Romanticism, which stands diametrically opposed to the rational, enlightened attitude espoused by Settembrini. Hans Castorp's innate inclination to lethargy, loss of the perception of time, abandonment of duty and obligations, fascination with the erotic, with disease and death—all that derives ultimately from Thomas Mann's personal experience of Wagner's works.

Thomas Mann adored Wagner's music (he called Wagner "my strongest, most defining artistic experience"), but he was also concerned about what he perceived as its seditious intent: Wagner evokes a romanticized version of German history and encourages an unhealthy nostalgia for melancholy and death. His music seduces the listener into a mythical past that is infused with the powers of darkness. The ultimate motivation of Wagner's music is the death wish and the yearning for the grave that is a hallmark of the Romantic temperament. Wagner's music is unquestionably

Dionysian and leads us down the path to irrationality. Settembrini is undoubtedly right in his suspicions about the possible effect of music.

Romanticism

When we employ the term "Romanticism," we must be very careful not to use it in the loose sense (as so often happens nowadays) of something trivial. German Romanticism means something quite different and fairly specific. Broadly speaking, we can differentiate in German culture the set of values described by the term "Classicism," and those that come under the heading of "Romanticism." In the case of the former (whose primary representative for Thomas Mann, as for many Germans, was Johann Wolfgang von Goethe) the emphasis is on form, reason, harmony and balance; a positive outlook is stressed and the darker phenomena of life are consciously suppressed and rejected. Humans, in order to aspire to the highest ideals, must be prepared to renounce anything that might detract from that pursuit—including the passions that can endanger civilized behavior. (In the novel this attitude to life is represented by Settembrini.)

For the German Romantics, however, this view of life meant excluding from consideration many elements of our humanity that were indubitably there—and to suppress them meant to be less than whole. Thus the Romantics strived for universality, to encompass all that it means to be human. The emotions, dreams, the subconscious, the supernatural—all those phenomena are part of life, and to ignore or to seek to repress them was unhealthy and self-defeating. Literature could only be genuine if it portrayed the totality of human experience—including death.

Naturally, the "darker" side of human existence is the more interesting (the Devil has the best lines)—and provides the better material for literature, as Tolstoy's famous opening to his novel *Anna Karenina* recognizes: "All happy families are alike. Unhappy families are unhappy, each in its own way."

For Thomas Mann, German Romanticism had a perennial fascination, for two reasons. First, it had been a fundamental element of German culture since 1800, and had exerted a very powerful influence on German thinking and writing in all fields, including politics. "We are all its sons," he said on several occasions. Second, it placed Germans before a dilemma: should they venerate the ideals embodied in the works of the Classical writers such as Goethe, or should they adopt the "Romantic" view—with its concomitant dangers of excess? When the Nazis were on the verge of coming to power, Thomas Mann wrote: "The Germans must choose between Goethe and Wagner." By that he meant that the choice was between on the one hand self-restraint and reason, versus an involvement with the darker forces of existence on the other. Since Romanticism—or more accurately: the seductive dangers of Romanticism—are so deeply engrained in the German character, they must be overcome if one is to achieve a healthy view of life.

This was also Mann's own personal dilemma: while being by nature fascinated by and strongly attracted to the ideas of the German Romantics, he was intellectually fully aware of its dangers and therefore rationally drawn to Classical ideals. This personal struggle is also, in Mann's eyes a dilemma for the German nation—as his statement about Goethe and Wagner reveals. Thus in *The Magic Mountain* the struggle between the "classical" and the "romantic" views of life is transferred into a wider, general cultural context through the figure of Hans Castorp—with Chauchat, Krokowski and Naphta as embodiments of various aspects of the Romantic, and Settembrini and Joachim as their "adversaries."

Thus overcoming Romanticism means at the same time "overcoming oneself" ("Selbstüberwindung"), as already noted a central concept of Nietzsche's philosophy. In a speech on the occasion of Nietzsche's 80th birthday, Thomas Mann said: "This is what he represents for us: a friend of life, a visionary of a higher humanity, a leader into the future, a teacher for overcoming all those elements within us that oppose life and the future, namely: Romanticism."

Spengler

In 1919 Thomas Mann read Volume 1 of Oswald Spengler's *The Decline of the West*, (vol. 1 1918; vol. 2 1923). He called it "the book of the epoch" and compared it to his reading Schopenhauer for the first time. Spengler (1880–1936) saw history as cyclical, and his book enabled readers to view Germany's loss of the War as part of a larger historical process. Spengler theorized that Westerners were Faustian beings, and that were now living in the winter-time of the Faustian civilization,—a civilization where the populace constantly strives for the unattainable, making western man a proud but tragic figure, for while he strives and creates he secretly knows the actual goal will never be reached.

Spengler rejected Western democracy and the Weimar republic that had emerged after the First World War. He believed that individual desires should be subordinated to the will of the collective, and he called for a government of the élite with dictatorial powers. Spengler's two volumes contain much, much more, of course, but important for *The Magic Mountain* is the overall message of the work: a sense of cultural pessimism, of an era coming to an end.

Although Thomas Mann came to reject Spengler's theses not long after he had praised them so highly, they did find their way into the second half of the novel, for example, in the arguments between Settembrini and Naphta, where the author has placed some of Spengler's ideas into Naphta's mouth.

Sexuality

While working on the novel, Thomas Mann wrote: "*The Magic Mountain* will be the most sensual work that I have ever written, but in a detached style." To the casual reader, who witnesses no explicit sex in the novel, that may be hard to believe.

The Magic Mountain is set in a time when there was much more reticence about sex than there is today. Its portrayal of sex (as far as it is portrayed at all) is what we might call "old-fashioned." The Berghof is the site of numerous sexual liaisons, but none of them is a source of prurient interest for the narrator. There are certainly no graphic sex scenes, and the hints of sexual activity are always couched in vague and suggestive turns of phrase. The most significant sexual encounter in the novel (the hour that Castorp spends with Chauchat) is recounted by mere allusion.

But on a deeper level sex is always present in the novel. It runs like a thread throughout the text, but always with the implication that sex belongs to the realm of ideas that include lassitude, ethical freedom, disease, dissolution, and death. The chief preoccupation of the narrator is with the *nature* of sexuality in general and its influence on our psyche and actions. The erotic is everywhere in the novel, and by implication everywhere in life. In fact, Thomas Mann was correct in describing this novel as his "most sensual work," because in this novel almost every detail is eroticized: a pencil, a cigar, a thermometer, an x-ray picture, a deck-chair, etc.—all the real objects of daily life assume also a connoted metaphorical significance infused with sexuality.

One writer described *The Magic Mountain* as a "novel of forbidden love," by which he meant not only the heterosexual activities in the Berghof sanatorium, but also the veiled homosexual references throughout the text. Hans Castorp's love for Clavdia Chauchat reprises his adolescent homosexual attraction to Pribislav Hippe. She is small-breasted, narrow-hipped, like a young girl in her physical appearance. Furthermore, her other physical characteristics repeat Hans Castorp's memory of Hippe: the similarities extend to the blue-green eyes, the mouth, the voice, and the high cheek-bones. Chauchat's act of lending a pencil to Castorp rehearses his homoerotic experience in the schoolyard with Hippe. What is the nature of Hans Castorp's sexuality? Certainly, his sexual inclinations are somewhat ambiguous, and he is by no means alone is his being attracted to the androgynous Chauchat: after all, she has a husband, and both Behrens and Peeperkorn are drawn sexually to her.

But the veiled homosexuality goes further: the relationship between Hans Castorp and Joachim Ziemssen has definite homoerotic undertones, and the textual sexualization in the exchanges between Castorp and Behrens likewise reveal sexual ambiguities.

The intellectual duels between Settembrini and Naphta also have an erotic content, as Thomas Mann himself noted, being based, as he wrote, on "not only intellectual hatred, but also pedagogical rivalry (quasi-erotic)." Thomas Mann may have acquired this idea from his reading of Walt Whitman: in his copy of Whitman's works, he marked a passage in the Introduction that spoke of Whitman as a teacher possessing "something of that eros that is present in every leaning towards pedagogy."

The novel thus plays with the idea of bisexuality, not merely in the portrayal of the relationships. In nature there are many varieties of sexuality: flowers that reproduce themselves or that are bisexual. Does human sexuality also perhaps reflect such variety? Life is sexual—but what kind of sexuality is it? The novel seems to imply that sexual identities may be precarious and intrinsically unstable.

Allusiveness and modern myth

To say that *The Magic Mountain* is rich in allusions is an understatement. The novel abounds in allusions. This allusiveness is of two kinds: first, allusions to things outside of the novel—to classical myth, to Germanic myth, to literature, to music, to history, geology, medicine, and so on. Second, the entire novel is "self-referential," that is, it refers to itself time and time again. All of this is expressed in language that is, itself highly connotative and allusive: one critic described the novel as consisting of a tissue of "magic words with indefinitely ramified associations."

Thomas Mann's knowledge was deeply rooted in German culture, but he was also extremely well-read in Classical and European cultures. All of this knowledge permitted him two things: first, to indulge in a game of allusiveness that is both good-humored (for example, by referring to characters in the novel as mythological figures), and serious (in so far as those allusions emphasize the themes of the novel). And second, to draw parallels between the people and events at the Berghof sanatorium and figures and episodes from mythology—thus implying that the characters and events at the Berghof, though of our age, are mythical in nature.

The novel contains many allusions to both classical and Germanic myth. Krokowski and Behrens are called Minos and Rhadamanthus; Hans and Joachim are the Dioscuri, Castor and Pollux; the thermometer is Mercury; the people in the dining-hall "burst into Homeric laughter." The main protagonists in the novel are characterized both by their geographical origin and a mythological association. Germanic mythological sites, such as the Venusberg and the Brocken Mountain, permit the narrator to indulge in parallels that emphasize the timelessness of the events that occur in the novel.

There are also scores of literary and biblical allusions strewn throughout the text, and it would take an especially well-read reader (say someone like Thomas Mann) to spot them all.

Much of the allusiveness is playful and adds to the aesthetic pleasure of reading the novel. Despite all the serious themes that Thomas Mann addresses, and despite the formal style he adopts, *The Magic Mountain* is a novel infused with a great deal of humor, much of which occurs when the narrator draws allusive parallels.

All of this allusiveness is motivated by a very simple principle that Thomas Mann had been applying since he wrote *Death in Venice* (1911): Events of every day may be interpreted as mythical. In that story, Mann assures us, all the events actually occurred and he witnessed them. The genius of Thomas Mann resided in his ability to take everyday events (such as taking a gondola ride) and make out of them something highly symbolic and infuse them with mythological associations.

The conclusion he wants us to draw is that myth is not dead: we relive mythical events in our everyday lives. Mythology contains basic patterns of human behavior, and those patterns recur throughout history.

Number symbolism

The novel also indulges in number symbolism that is closely interwoven with the novel's allusiveness. Thomas Mann was fascinated by numbers, in particular by numbers that he considered significant. He wrote, for example, about the number 7 that it was "a good, handy figure in its way, picturesque, with a savor of the mythical; one might say that it is more filling to the spirit than a dull, academic half-dozen." The number symbolism of the novel influences both the structure and the content: there are at least sixty-one references to the number 7 in the novel. Among those references are the following:

The novel has seven chapters, and Volume 1 ends after seven months. The central sub-chapter "Snow" is the seventh section of Chapter Six. Hans Castorp meets seven major characters who have an influence on him. There are many characters with names of seven letters—and the name of Settembrini is based on the Italian for seven.

Hans Castorp is orphaned at the age of seven, when he has the important conversation with his grandfather, and seven of his forefathers had the christening cup before him. At 7 p.m. he sees day and moonlight. He leaves Hamburg in the seventh month (July) 1907 and arrives in Davos on August 7. He plans a visit of 21 days, but stays seven years.

Hans Castorp's room is number 34; Clavdia Chauchat's room is number 7. (She is 28 years old, at the most.) He exchanges looks with her seven times before she smiles at him, and has sex with her after having been at the Berghof sanatorium for seven months. There are seven tables in the dining-room, seven people sit at each table, and the evening meal is a 7 p.m. Frau Stöhr claims to be able to prepare 28 fish-sauces. The thermometer is to be kept in the mouth for seven minutes (the day's first measurement is at 7 a.m.), and the mail is distributed every seven days. Castorp orders 700 cigars from Bremen. He gets his first bill after seven days, and he has his first x-ray after seven weeks. Joachim returns to the Berghof in the seventh month, is assigned to room 28, and he dies at 7 p.m., when Castorp has been at the Berghof for 28 months.

Hans Castorp leaves the Berghof at 7 a.m., in order to go to the duel between Settembrini and Naphta. Peeperkorn and his guests play "Twenty-One." Seven people take the trip to the waterfall. In the First World War he marches for seven hours.

Such a dull listing of the occurrences of the number 7 is on the one hand somewhat tiresome, and the other hand tells us nothing about the reason for it and what it all means. The function of all of these references to the number seven is twofold: first, they divide up time, and they determine the situation of the characters in both time and space. And second, the figure 7 also symbolizes the magical nature of the Berghof environment in which Hans Castorp attempts to seek answers to the questions that trouble him.

The number seven figures prominently in the Bible (e.g. the seven days of Creation, the Seven Pillars of the House of Wisdom, seven days of the feast of Passover, seven loaves multiplied into seven baskets of surplus, etc., etc.). But the purpose of the number seven in the novel is not merely to create Biblical allusions; rather, it is to widen the allusiveness and carry the events onto the mythical level.

Likewise, at certain times (particularly in the Peeperkorn episodes) the numbers three and four play a significant symbolical role. The number three represents the Christian Trinity (Father, Son, and Holy Spirit), and since Peeperkorn is on one respect likened to a Christ figure, attaching the number three to his person is appropriate. Four, on the other hand, relates more to secular (non-religious) phenomena (cf. the four corners of the earth), and thus its occurrence points to the pagan aspects of Peeperkorn's character and actions.

As already noted above, for Thomas Mann, everyday phenomena contain within themselves the traces of mythical: thus a train journey is not merely a means of getting from one place to another, but also a meta-phorical odyssey that relates to all the odysseys in history. The number symbolism is therefore both a part of the aesthetic structure that is intended to give pleasure, and a fundamental element in the overall fabric of allusions that carries the novel's themes.

Irony

In a well-known book about Thomas Mann, the author (Erich Heller) called him "The Ironic German." Irony is a persistent feature of Thomas Mann's works. On the one hand, irony is a defense against pain and suffering: by relativizing and ironizing potentially painful events and experiences, their effect is dulled and the individual is protected against unpleasant emotions. Despite the irony that infuses the novel, there are some very moving scenes: the passing of Joachim, the second encounter of Castorp and Chauchat, and Peeperkorn's death.

Irony also implicitly reveals a view of life that recognizes life's uncertainty and unpredictability. In the face of the chaos of existence, what is the appropriate stance to take? Thomas Mann's answer is to adopt the ironical stance: In a world in which nothing can be taken for granted, the writer's attitude is to doubt the veracity and reliability of everything. He does not believe that we can possess the truth; thus the world is presented from different perspectives, none of which has absolute validity. The multiplicity of opinions presents us with a picture that is both enlightening and confusing: the wealth of viewpoints seems to thwart all attempts to find the truth, but in each of them there is a kernel of it. The ironical stance prevents a wholehearted acceptance of any fixed opinion.

The *Bildungsroman*

The *Bildungsroman* (novel of education) has had a long and much debated tradition in German literature since the late eighteenth century. The basic structure of a *Bildungsroman* shows the hero (it is usually a male, at least until more recent times) progressing by means of various experiences and adventures from being a callow and naïve youth, into becoming a mature and productive member of society. This type of novel was popular in the nineteenth century because it embodied the noble bourgeois ideal of education for life as a productive citizen. When we look at Thomas Mann's *The Magic Mountain*, however, we encounter a major problem. For while Hans Castorp is certainly "educated" at the Berghof, and while he has many experiences and "adventures," the question remains: What is he educated *for*? He returns to the Flatland to take part in the bloodbath of the First World War—and it is not even clear that he will survive (some commentators read the ending as signaling his death, although from a close reading of the text it is clear that the narrator leaves Castorp's fate uncertain.) We know that Thomas Mann, the eternal ironist, will (and does) relativize all the progress that Hans Castorp makes in the course of his "education" at the Berghof; and the novel ends with a question that expresses a noble hope for the future, not a plan of action.

Some commentators even doubt that Castorp makes any progress at all—although there is overwhelming evidence that he does. One need only look at the way in which he absorbs vocabulary and ideas from other people, or his constantly critical, even skeptical, assessment of what they say, or his growing fascination with the significance of music and what it means for his personal ethic. In the course of the novel he learns about philosophy, theology, botany, astronomy, anatomy, physiology, histology, physics, mathematics, chemistry, pathology, pharmacology, radiology, psychoanalysis, parapsychology, embryology, bacteriology, meteorology, political science, and music (but not literature). So is Castorp be the end of the novel "educated" and ready to become a productive member of society? In the nineteenth-century sense, certainly not, because he has rejected the bourgeois ethic that he had brought with him to the Berghof (and which provided him with no answers to the important questions of life). But there is no doubt that he has acquired a different, and more profound, understanding of existence. In the Berghof sanatorium he undergoes a process of transformation or heightening ("Steigerung") whereby his affinity for sickness and death leads him to a higher plane of existence that confirms the humanistic vision as the only true alternative.

From this it is clear that *The Magic Mountain* is not a conventional *Bildungsroman*. How could it be so in the first half of the twentieth century when millions of young men had been slaughtered senselessly on the battlefields of Europe? No, the message of Hans Castorp—and of the novel—is much more profound: he has a vision of a possible future, of a world in which death is both acknowledged and overcome, and of a world in which the natural destructive forces are tamed. It is a message that transcends the bourgeois concern with the work-ethic and productivity. Bourgeois society belongs to the realm of Apollo; during his stay at the Berghof Hans Castorp experiences the realm of Dionysus and gains insights into how to overcome it.

Here is Thomas Mann's own view of his hero: "Hans Castorp's story is the story of a 'heightening'. A simple hero in the hermetic feverish atmosphere of the magic mountain is made capable of moral, intellectual, sensual adventures of which he could never have dreamed before. His story is that of a heightening process; but also as a narrative it is the heightening process itself. It employs the methods of the realistic novel, but actually it is not one, for it constantly passes beyond realism. It heightens realism by symbolism and makes it a transparency for intellectual and ideal elements. The characters are all more to the reader than they seem; in effect they are nothing but exponents, representatives, emissaries from worlds, principalities, domains of the spirit."

Thomas Mann faced the difficulty of reconciling a "Bildungsroman," that leads upwards to personal fulfillment, with a historical novel (in this case leading downward to catastrophe). We may conclude therefore that *The Magic Mountain* manages to be two things at the same time: it is both a "Bildungsroman" itself, and a parody of the genre. It is a "Bildungsroman" for the modern age. Hans Castorp's quest is not an odyssey with the aim of becoming a productive member of society, but rather it is an investigation of the fundamental questions of existence with the aim of finding answers about the nature of life.

Hermes, Hermes Trismegistos, and the Hermetic

Throughout the novel Thomas Mann draws associations between the modern world of the Berghof and mythology. Thus the sanatorium is the realm of the dead, with the flag of Hermes flying in front of the building. From the mercury thermometer to the coffin-like gramophone, symbols of death abound. The Berghof world is presented to us as "hermetic," that is, as a closed, self-contained system. The illusion is created that life at the Berghof is like being on a distant island: people may arrive or leave, but once there, they interact with one another as if they were the only people on earth (in fact, as if there were no earth). The normal parameters of time and place do not apply. Thus it is that the narrator can frequently refer to Hans Castorp's "hermetic pedagogy."

Hermes

In Classical Mythology Hermes (his Greek name; in Roman mythology he is called Mercury) was the son of Zeus and Maia. Hermes was very popular with the Greeks, and he was given by them all the frailties and virtues of man that they admired most: intelligent, cunning, lovable, and mischievous. He was also a thief and began his career early in life: his first act was to steal the cows of Apollo; then he invented the lyre which he gave as a gift to that god, receiving in exchange the shepherd's crook that eventually evolved into the caduceus (a rod with two intertwining snakes). Over time he acquired many attributes: thus he appears as the official herald of the gods, conductor of the souls of the dead to the Underworld (Hades), guardian of orators, of travelers, of thieves, and the inventor of the alphabet, of music, of astronomy, weights and measures (since he was the god of merchants and of commerce). He is the nomadic god, whose winged sandals transport him everywhere with the speed of wind, as he delivers the messages of the gods. He is normally portrayed also wearing a broad-brimmed hat (a *petassus*) which also has wings on either side, and carrying a staff or a caduceus. He is the god of wanderers and travelers and the patron of all those circulating in the streets or on the paths and tried always to keep them on the right track. Thus one finds the *hermae* or mileposts on the roads or at street corners and road junctions. Moreover, Hermes was the god of youth with symbols such as the phallus, the goat, the boar, and the ram, and also helped people overcome illness.

He has a special association with the night, as at night the dead are under way, and thus he is also the god of dreams, both bringing them and waking up the sleeper. His staff is seen as magical and even phallic. He is often associated with Aphrodite (the goddess of love). He is a divine rogue and thief, and his characteristics make him the god of youth and education. The Roman god Mercury was similar to the Greek god: he was cunning and entertaining, chameleon-like, part-animal and part-god.

The figure of Hermes Trismegistos arose through the merger of the Greek god Hermes with the Egyptian god Thoth. The name Trismegistos, which means thrice-greatest Hermes, is the title given by the Greeks to the Egyptian god Thoth or Tehuti, a lord of wisdom and learning. He became the legendary author of works on alchemy, astrology, and magic, and is the alleged teacher of the magical system known as Hermetism of which high magic and alchemy were considered to be twin branches. He was reputed to be able through magic to seal vessels, giving rise to the term "hermetic" (airtight).

During the Middle Ages and the Renaissance, the writings attributed to Hermes Trismegistos known as *Hermetica* were popular among alchemists. The "hermetic tradition" therefore refers to alchemy, magic, astrology and related subjects. The texts are usually divided in two categories the "philosophical" and "technical" hermetica. The former deals mainly with issues of philosophy, and the latter with magic, potions and alchemy. Among other things there are spells to protect objects by means of magic; hence the origin of the term "hermetically sealed." The invention of the thermometer is also ascribed to him.

Time

The Magic Mountain is a novel about time in two senses. First, it is set in the historical time-period 1907−14, but the historical events of those years form a somewhat distant background to the happenings at the Berghof sanatorium. Only as the First World War approaches do political developments have an increasing impact on the residents.

More important, however, than everyday events is the portrayal of the nature of European society and culture in that period. The characters embody the dilemmas facing human beings in the first decade and a half of the twentieth century. The novel depicts those dilemmas—moral and philosophical—and shows various possibilities of coming to terms with them.

Second, time itself—the passage and the perception of time—is a theme of the novel. The "problematic" nature of time is alluded to on the first page of the novel, and discussions of time occur frequently throughout the book.

The subjectivity of the perception of time is repeatedly emphasized. The first three weeks of Hans Castorp's stay at the Berghof take as long to narrate as the last five years. Chapter Four describes seventeen days, while Chapter Five covers six and a half months, Chapter Six a year and nine months, and Chapter Seven four years and eight months. The increasingly long periods of time covered by the narrative reflect the hero's progressive loss of a sense of time, until he reaches the point where time "stands still." It is only appropriate that in the hermetic nature of the Berghof environment the experience of time would also different from conventional measurement. The loss of a sense of time accords with the susceptibility to the idea of lethargy and the dissolution of form.

Confusing categories

The Berghof is a hospital and a hotel, but on the metaphorical level it is also the Underworld, a school, a barracks, a lunatic asylum, a brothel and a prison (like prisoners, its inmates are hermetically sealed off from the outside world). The patients are undergoing a cure, but they are addressed as delinquents and ordered around like soldiers or criminals.

The world is turned on its head and the normal categories are confused. "Service" and "duty" mean obeying the orders relating to the rest-cure; "desertion" means leaving the Berghof uncured and without permission, as Joachim does; climbing up to the level of the Berghof (5000 ft.) is descending into the Underworld. Everything is something else: laziness is learning, living is dying, love is disease, music is death, Clavdia is Pribislav.

"Up here" and "down there" are more than merely geographical terms: they express different views of life. "Down there" on the "Flatland" implies the acceptance of conventional bourgeois morality, a belief in the ethic of work and duty, and an adherence to the Western idea of technology and "progress."

"Up here" at the Berghof is a world removed from reality, a place where time stands still and all the conventional ideas are thrown into doubt, where people are excused because of illness and therefore permitted to behave in ways that would be rejected in normal society. Idleness, a concept that is anathema "down below," is a central element of the cure.

Conventional concepts of seasons and the weather" are unreliable. The seasons "get all mixed up, so to speak, and pay no attention to the calendar."

Nor is there any stability in the identity and political stances of the major protagonists. Settembrini is a strong and committed advocate of Enlightenment, rationality, progress, and democracy; but he also harbors a profound dislike for Russians, a fear that Europe could be racially in decline, and a deep-seated hatred for Austria which he wishes to see destroyed. He wishes to eliminate suffering, class conflict, and war, and as a Freemason he belongs to a world-wide movement of like-minded individuals exemplifying the liberal values of an enlightened society. But, as Naphta points out, Settembrini's Freemasons had their origins in a distant past where the Eleusian mysteries and aphrodisiacal secrets abounded and that the movement's origins were terroristic and anti-liberal. So what is the real nature of the movement today?

Naphta is a walking cornucopia of contradictions: A Jew who becomes a Jesuit, an advocate of violence, torture, and communism. An ascetic who likes luxury, a proponent of terror who shoots himself, a detractor of rationalism who argues with strict logic, a learned man who derides science, a Catholic who commits suicide. Every description and definition of a person with a particular view of reality implicitly signifies a limitation of the infinite complexity of reality. At the same time, parody and irony undermine the seriousness of the characters and their moralistic-didactic intentions.

The Major Characters

From the opening lines of *The Magic Mountain* it is clear that this novel is about a journey undertaken by a young man from Hamburg. It is not merely a physical journey, but also metaphorical one. We are to follow him through seven crucial years of his life.

Hans Castorp appears on the scene as a 23-year old apprentice naval engineer who is seeking an answer to the meaning of life and who harbors serious doubts—at this stage mostly vague—about the values of the bourgeois society in which he has grown up. The initial indications that he is uncomfortable with his chosen profession are quickly reinforced by a multitude of new impressions at the Berghof sanatorium that undermine his values and expose him to a wealth of alternative viewpoints. In particular, he learns that freedom from restraint and the pursuit of *eros* are pleasurable experiences; but at the same time they lead into dangerous realms where decay, dissolution, and death must be confronted. The darker side of life has its fascinations, but he who surrenders to it must also find a way to move beyond its magnetic charms to a more mature outlook on life.

His progress can be measured by the way in which he synthesizes the knowledge he gains—critically evaluating it and weighing it in the balance—into conclusions that are completely his own. His search for meaning and his doubts about the bourgeois order lead, once he arrives at the Berghof, to a total alienation from bourgeois values. The various influences to which he is subjected and the experiences that he undergoes lead him to an independent view of life, achieved through reflection (a process that in the novel is called "playing king"). The naïve young man who leaves Hamburg, becomes the mature adult (with a beard) whose final position is the vision of a hopeful future for himself and for humankind—a vision that is ironically undermined, however, by the catastrophe of the First World War.

During his seven-year stay at the Berghof Hans Castorp is influenced by the seven major characters who surround him.

His cousin Joachim is the least complex of these. He represents the unquestioning acceptance of bourgeois values, the belief in order and self-discipline, the obligation to be loyal and perform one's duty, and the single-minded focus on the goal of service. However, even the most disciplined and single-minded individual is not immune from the intrusions of the Will: Joachim has adopted the Berghof habits of shrugging and not wearing a hat; and his studying of Russian ("that rather boneless language") and his attraction to the ample-bosomed Marusya represent cracks in his hard shell of committed devotion to duty.

Hofrat Behrens his outward appearance is based on the figure of Dr. Friedrich Jessen who was chief doctor in the Waldsanatorium where Mann's wife Katia spent some time. Behrens's jocular manner of speaking in university fraternity jargon, his flowery and colorful language, and his constant air of affability disguise the fact that he is deeply melancholic and harbors a number of secrets that are only hinted at. As is the case with all the characters in the novel, Behrens's character is undercut by the narrator's irony: the chief doctor is himself sick.

Edhin Krokowski is an ambivalent figure because on the one hand he represents the darker side of the mind—elements of life to which Hans Castorp is attracted—while on the other hand the author undermines his significance with irony and satire. The physical description of Krokowski suggests a somewhat sinister, even devilish appearance, and both his name and his "drawl of a foreign accent" align him with the East. While incorporating Freudian theories in Krokowski's lectures, the author at the same time clearly does not accept them wholeheartedly. Krokowski has important things to say about the relationship between illness and love, but the narrator's reservations are revealed by his implicit criticism of all-too-enthusiastic disciples of Krokowski's (i.e. Freud's) theories.

According to Thomas Mann, the figure of Ludovico Settembrini was based only on "slight associations" with any actual human beings. It is known that Thomas Mann spent some time in 1909 in a clinic in Zurich where he met an Italian writer, Paolo Enrico Zendrini and that Settembrini is also based two other figures: Giuseppe Mazzini, whose works he quotes, and Giosuè Carducci, whom he reveres. He also expresses opinions that Thomas Mann ascribed to those (such as his brother Heinrich) who thought, that "civilization" was the highest good. Thus Settembrini represents the positive ideals of the Enlightenment (humanism, demo-cracy, tolerance, and human rights); he is the man of letters, the represent-ative of Western civilization, and the embodiment of morality and political virtue. Thomas Mann affirmed that Settembrini is "sometimes a mouth-piece for the author, but by no means the author himself."

The fact that Settembrini always wears the same threadbare clothes and is himself sick is, however, an ironic comment on his philosophy of life: the ideas are old and familiar—even shop-worn nowadays. Furthermore, there is a paradox in Settembrini's attempts to "educate" Hans Castorp and to preserve the latter's "flatland"-identity: these attempts represent a diminution of the endless variety of reality.

Clavdia Chauchat unlocks an essential and repressed component of Hans Castorp's psyche: a feeling that love and death are somehow associated. She represents the East, the loss of individuality, anarchy, and dissolution, the attraction of death and the mystery of the flesh. Chauchat's feline characteristics are noted often, her last name is derived from the French *chaud chat* (Eng., *hot cat*). She is connected throughout with phallic symbols. After her departure her influence on Hans Castorp wanes somewhat (without ever entirely disappearing), as he progresses to his own mature view of existence.

Leo Naphta is described as ugly, and he *has* to be ugly, because he embodies the ugly side of life. He represents the forces of decay, of radicalism and extremism. He brilliantly criticizes Settembrini's values and ethics and shows them to be empty. (Naphta has all the best arguments and is right: i.e. life is nasty, brutish and short.) Hans Castorp tries to classify Naphta politically and comes to the conclusion that he is just as revolutionary as Settembrini—not in liberal, but in a conservative way. So he decides that Naphta is a "revolutionary of conservation." In the end, however, Castorp sides with Settembrini, based on the latter's underlying benevolence and humanism.

Pieter Peeperkorn's late appearance in the novel puts all the other characters in the shade. As a dominant and domineering personality he is a complex amalgam of both holy and pagan characteristics. On the one hand, he is portrayed (and portrays himself) as a Christ-like figure of suffering. On the other hand, his bacchanalian life-style associates him with the pagan god Dionysus. As an embodiment of pure "life" he demonstrates the inadequacy of the intellect of Settembrini and Naphta. But ironically he is himself inadequate: malarial fever and impotence undermine his status, and his suicide is an "abdication" (Chauchat's word) in the face of life's challenges.

Thomas Mann's Sources

In his mature novels Thomas Mann relied on a multitude of sources for material. In *The Magic Mountain* the range of topics dealt with is large: philosophy, theology, botany, astronomy, anatomy, physiology, histology, physics, mathematics, chemistry, pathology, pharmacology, radiology, psychoanalysis, parapsychology, biology, anatomy, embryology, bacteriology, meteorology, political science, and music. While some on Mann's knowledge about these subjects (e.g. music) had been acquired during his life, for the writing of the novel he consulted a broad range of secondary works. In all of his reading, however, he was looking for facts and ideas that would support the major themes of the novel, and in absorbing material from his many sources he always filtered it through his artistic prism. Thus the studies of Hans Castorp into biology and anatomy are derived from books that Thomas Mann consulted, but the information is re-worked and presented in a manner that blends it into the novel's web of themes. Similarly, the debates between Settembrini and Naphta are based in large measure on works that Mann read during the composition of the novel, but from each of these works he selected those aspects that would be in accordance with the views of one or the other of those figures.

Over the decades since the novel appeared, scholars have uncovered many of the works that Thomas Mann consulted. A list of all of Thomas Mann's sources for this novel takes up eight pages. However, for an understanding and appreciation of the novel, a knowledge of and familiarity with these sources is not necessary.

We do need to take note of the fact that the use of sources—direct or indirect—points to an important aspect of Thomas Mann's work: the myriad of hidden quotations and allusions, and the reworking of the texts of other writers is a tacit admission by the author that as a writer he is both a compiler and a creator.

The Commentary

This commentary is based on the translation by John E. Woods (New York: Vintage International, 1995). Some readers may be more familiar with the original translation of H.T. Lowe-Porter (first published in 1928), which until the publication of Woods's version was the only means by which non-German speaking readers in the English-speaking world could encounter the novel. H.T. Lowe-Porter was for many years Thomas Mann's official translator and, despite her limitations, her achievement deserves appropriate recognition: in making Thomas Mann's major works available to English-speaking readers as he published them, she performed a great service and facilitated the spread of his name outside of Germany.

But the many years that have passed since her translations have appeared have revealed their inadequacy. In the decades since the publication of *The Magic Mountain*, for example, scholarship has discovered a multitude of aspects of which readers in the 1920's were unaware, and close comparisons of the original text with H.T. Lowe-Porter's translation have revealed its many inaccuracies and infelicities, its omissions and additions. The translation of a dense and complex 800-page novel is a daunting task, and we should not expect that the first attempt would ever survive subsequent reading and analysis.

So now it is time to move on: the newer, far more acceptable translation by John E. Woods is likely to be the standard text for many decades to come. Even though a few quibbles can be expressed with this translation, it is definitely a great step forward—it is complete, and it is for the most part accurate, fluent, and contemporary—, and thus it is to be hoped that it will enable many more thousands of readers to gain access to one of the representative works of German literature and one of the key cultural artifacts of the twentieth century.

Readers of German may be familiar with Michael Neumann's German commentary to *The Magic Mountain* (2002), prepared and published as a companion volume to the official critical edition of Thomas Mann's works. (For publication details, see Bibliography.) However, this present commentary, being aimed at the non-German-speaking reader, has somewhat different aims from those of Neumann's commentary. The latter contains a large number of references to Thomas Mann's own works (and letters and diaries), as well as manifold indications of the sources that

Thomas Mann may have used, along with parallels to the works of other authors. Neumann also points out misprints and variations between the different editions. As such, Neumann's Commentary is really aimed at the *scholar*, and many of the allusions in the novel are simply explained factually, with little attempt at interpretation.

Another book of commentary, also in German, is Daniela Langer's *Thomas Mann* Der Zauberberg *Erläuterungen und Dokumente* (Reclam 2009). While it contains much useful information—including interpretive commentary—it is accessible only to the reader of German.

This present Commentary, however, is intended for the English-speaking *reader*. Consequently, it attempts to guide the reader through the novel, not only explaining words, phrases, and references as an aid to comprehension, but also providing relevant commentary where necessary to enable the reader to gain as much understanding and pleasure as possible from reading the novel. Thus the many references to Thomas Mann's sources, the relationship of passages in *The Magic Mountain* to his other works, the occurrence of phrases in other contexts—either before or after the publication of the novel—, etc. are omitted, since they are not an aid to comprehension for the reader who wishes to extract full reading pleasure from the novel. It is assumed, for example, that the reader of the English translation would not be particularly interested in knowing that Thomas Mann's description of the snowstorm in the sub-chapter *Snow* was influenced by descriptions of similar scenes he found in the works of Adalbert Stifter, Hans Christian Andersen, and Knut Hamsun. The aim of this commentary is to aid the reader in understanding the content and form of the novel, not to list all the sources that Thomas Man used (although it must be added that sometimes a knowledge of the sources can help in comprehending Mann's ideas). This Commentary therefore contains very few references to the works of other authors that Thomas Mann consulted; rather it attempts to provide the reader with enough explanatory comment to fully understand the text and extract enjoyment from it.

Some readers may find some of the explanatory notes too elementary, but the author strove to explain all those items that he felt might need explanation—without being able to determine the level of knowledge that each reader might bring to the novel. *All* foreign words are translated, even at the risk of insulting the knowledge of some readers.

It is impossible to comment on everything in *The Magic Mountain*—to do so would require several volumes of commentary—and each commentator would, no doubt, select different aspects of the novel to elucidate. Thus a commentary of this nature, while striving to present the reader with information that will enable the reader to reach his or her own conclusions, is inevitably also influenced by the personal views of the commentator. A commentary is also an interpretation, and it should not be expected that every reader will agree with every viewpoint expressed here. However, this commentary has the modest goal of introducing the English-speaking reader to one of the great works of Western literature and of increasing that reader's pleasure in engaging in a personal debate with the work.

Many of the notes and comments that follow rely on research done by many other scholars and commentators, a few of whose works will be found cited in the Bibliography. It would have been impractical to footnote the hundreds of secondary sources used in this Commentary; thus all I can do is extend a general acknowledgement to all the many Thomas Mann scholars and the helpful staff of the Thomas Mann Archive who have vicariously contributed to this book. In conducting the research for this book over more than two decades I enjoyed the support and hospitality of Dr. Armin Arnold (†) and Dr. Ingrid Schuster-Arnold in various locations in Switzerland, and of Frau Valerie Schwitter in Davos.

THE COMMENTARY

All the notes that follow refer to Thomas Mann, *The Magic Mountain*, transl. John E. Woods (New York: Vintage, 1996).

The Magic Mountain

The title of the novel connotes a wide variety of things. It arouses associations with a range of myths, legends, and works of art. According to Germanic legend, after the advent of Christianity to Germany the heathen goddess of love took refuge in the mountain known as the "Hörselberg," which was located near Eisenach, Thuringia. The original title of Mann's work was "The enchanted Mountain" ("Der verzauberte Berg"), which connotes both the Hörselberg and the "Venusberg" of the legend of Tannhäuser (and Wagner's opera of the same name, too; see note to p. 83, l. 17). In the legendary account Tannhäuser, a knight and poet, comes to the Venusberg (also in Eisenach), the subterranean home of Venus, and spends a year there worshipping the goddess. Wagner's immediate inspiration was a ballad by Heinrich Heine (1799–1856), in which the hero goes to the Venusberg and spends seven years there. "The Magic Mountain" is thus a place of forgetfulness where time stands still, removed from the normal world of bourgeois values of work, reason, and progress.

(xi) *Foreword*

The word "Foreword," although it is a conventional heading in English, fails to convey the intentionally ambiguous connotation of the German word used by Thomas Mann: "Vorsatz." The latter has multiple meanings, all of which the author wishes to exploit. The word is not commonly used in German to mean "Foreword," but it does imply something of that kind. More important, it is used in a musical context to signify "Prelude"—and since music will play a major role in the novel, both as a theme and as a structural element, we can assume that Thomas Mann wished this connotation to resound in the reader's mind. In addition, the word signifies an "intention"—which indicates what the author has in store for his hero.

l. 7   *patina of history*: the phrase points to the historical nature of the world to be described. The events of the novel are, of course, "historical"; but there is also a touch of irony here, because although the *events* may be in the distant past, the more important metaphysical issues are topical.

l. 16   *around the sun*: the style here is deliberately archaic—as it also is in the next paragraph (cf. l. 24: "back then, long ago, in the old days of the world"). Such expressions are intended to connect the novel with mythological time.

l. 22   *certain turning point*: the novel ends in 1914 with the outbreak of World War I, and thus the phrase is indicative of Thomas Mann's personal views about the significance of WWI in political, social and cultural terms: the war heralded the end of one era and the beginning of another. On another level it is possible to interpret this phrase as having much wider significance: the crisis of Western civilization. Thus when the Foreword speaks of "the Great War, with whose beginnings so many things began *whose beginnings, it seems, have not yet ceased*" (p. xi, ll. 25f.; emphasis added), the implication is that the crisis has continued after the War and continues still. Since the War stands as the ultimate metaphor for the destructive nature of humanity—and since all other manifestations of human aggression and destructiveness culminate in that apocalyptic event—the ultimate question posed by the novel is this: How can human civilization break out of that pattern of destructiveness and create a create a future society based on positive values?

l. 25   *the Great War*: the First World War.

(**xii**) l. 7 *short on diversion or long on boredom*: a leitmotif that will be used by Hans Castorp himself (cf. p. 83, l. 24 & p. 534, ll. 22f.).

l. 12   *seven days*: an early invocation of the number symbolism that infuses the novel—even connoting perhaps the Creation. Writing the novel is itself an act of creation.

(3) Chapter One

Arrival

The first chapter serves the function not merely of getting Hans Castorp to Davos and the Berghof sanatorium; it also summarizes and foretells the entire course of the novel. The journey itself—in particular, the train journey from Landquart to Davos—is a metaphorical summary of what the next seven years will bring. Castorp's first experiences at the Berghof hint what will befall him, ironically comment on his naïveté and lack of self-knowledge, and demonstrate that, despite his overt statements, his innate nature is, in fact, drawn away from Hamburg and all that that city symbolizes and towards the Berghof and its contrary values.

l. 1   *An ordinary young man*: The author frequently emphasizes the point that Hans Castorp is ordinary—and in one sense he is: he is a typical, middle-class young man who has completed his education and embarked on his career. However, he is also assailed by doubts about his chosen profession and about life in general. He is looking for meaning and, as we are told later, all he has heard in response to his question about the meaning of life is "a hollow silence." In the course of the novel he becomes uncommonly receptive to all kinds of ideas and influences. Thus this opening description of Hans Castorp might be considered ironic: How "ordinary" is Hans Castorp really?

l. 2   *Hamburg*: Hamburg is an important port city in North Germany, situated on the River Elbe. Hans Castorp's origins in Hamburg are significant, because for Thomas Mann North Germany embodies the typical bourgeois ethic of hard work and economic progress.

l. 2   *Davos-Platz in the canton of Graubünden*: Davos lies in the Alps in the canton of Graubünden, in the eastern part Switzerland. The town consists officially of two parts: Davos-Dorf and Davos-Platz. Graubünden is a large canton, situated in the south-eastern part of Switzerland, adjoining Italy, Austria and Liechtenstein (see maps).

Graubünden in Switzerland

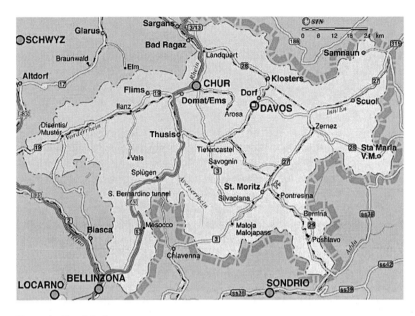

Davos in Graubünden

l. 4   *It is a long trip*: the description of Hans Castorp's journey from
Hamburg to Davos is, like every other description in the novel, intended to
be both realistic and metaphorical. In its metaphorical dimension it connotes the adventures—intellectual, spiritual and emotional—that Hans
Castorp will encounter in the course of his stay at the Berghof sanatorium.

l. 7   *Swabia's sea*: an alternative name for Lake Constance, which
lies between the German province of Swabia and Switzerland (see map).
The characterization of the inland lake as a "sea" intensifies the impression that Hans Castorp's journey is more onerous than it really is. The idea
also connotes an association with an odyssey.

ll. 7f. *across its skipping waves ... abysses once thought unfathomable*: this is another attempt to enhance the mythical implications. Both
in the *Odyssey* and the *Aeniad* one crosses the sea to reach the Underworld. These geographical features are no longer strictly mythical, because
they are now "fathomable" (i.e. measurable): the world is no longer
governed by myth, but traces remain (see also note to p. 13, l. 26f.).
Among the novel's many allusions to mythology, Hans Castorp's journey
to the Berghof sanatorium is likened to a journey to the Underworld.

l. 10 *Rorschach*: having traveled by train from Hamburg to Lake
Constance, Castorp takes a boat across to Rorschach on the Swiss side.

While we are not told where he embarks on the German side, it was probably the town of Friedrichshafen. (A more direct route would be to travel Hamburg–Zurich–Landquart by train, but this route is fictionally necessary in order to connote the mythical associations.)

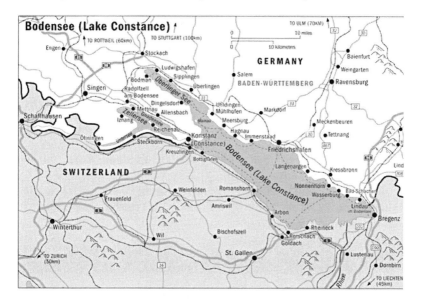

Lake Constance

l. 15   *the real adventure begins*: the phrase and the rest of the paragraph indicate metaphorically the nature of Castorp's undertaking: he is embarking on a serious adventure into dangerous regions (both physical and metaphysical) where he has never been before.

l. 20   *Hans Castorp*: Hans, the abbreviated form of Johannes (John), is a common German first name. It also connotes associations with Grimm's fairy tale "Lucky Hans," in which the simple-minded hero is tricked out of his money—and with the biblical John. The family name contains a common North-German component ("-torp").

(4) l. 3   *Ocean Steamships*: the fact that this book "now lay neglected, the cover dirtied by soot" (p. 4, l. 4) is an early indication that Castorp has already begun to lose interest in his chosen profession.

l. 6   *Two days of travel…*: this paragraph contains a number of allusions that hint that Hans Castorp has already loosened the bonds that connect him to his "duties, interests, worries and prospects" (l. 8). Although his journey has only taken two days he feels separated "far more

than he had dreamed possible" (ll. 8f.) from his accustomed existence, and
his future is predicted by suggesting that such an individual finds himself
"in a free and pristine state" (l. 14f.) and that he might even become "a
vagabond" (l. 16). In addition, these comments allude to Wagner's *Tannhäuser* who is informed on his arrival at the Venusberg that "here space
becomes time." Thomas Mann once described Hans Castorp as a "seeker
of the Holy Grail"—which arouses associations with the legend of
Parsifal, who sought the Holy Grail, and about whom Wagner also wrote
an opera.

ll. 13ff. *Space, like time, gives birth to forgetfulness ... vagabond*: a
major theme of the novel is the conflict between duty and lassitude.
Castorp's ingrained work-ethic competes with his innate inclination to
idleness. This theme finds expression in many ways in the novel: for
example, through the opposing characters of Settembrini (who represents,
reason, enlightenment, order, and progress) and Chauchat (who embodies
emotion, mystery [sex], and disorder).

l. 17   *Lethe*: in Greek mythology, Lethe is one of the several rivers of
Hades. Drinking from the river Lethe ("oblivion") caused complete forgetfulness. Some ancient Greeks believed that souls were made to drink from
the river before being reincarnated, so they would not remember their past
lives. Thus the reference in the novel is imbued with implications for Hans
Castorp: although the process is not immediate, he, too, will come to
"forget" his past life and to detach himself from it.

ll. 19f. *He had not planned to take this trip so seriously*: There is
irony here insofar as Hans Castorp has no idea at this moment about how
wrong his assumptions are: he has embarked on a journey that will transform his existence. One has only to read carefully the vocabulary used in
order to comprehend the symbolical implications of the text: "present
circumstances demanded his full attention" (this is a simple train journey);
these are "regions whose air he had never breathed before" (i.e. he has
never been to Davos, but he has also never been subjected to the
influences he is about to encounter); he is entering "extreme regions"
(Davos is only 5000 feet above sea-level); and, moreover, he "wished he
had already reached his goal" (his journey will last seven years).

On the one hand, the account of the train-journey from Landquart to
Davos is completely realistic and accurate (i.e. the narrator describes it just
as it existed, and you can still take that journey today), but on the other
hand this description of it in the novel also serves as a metaphorical
summary of what is to befall Castorp in the next seven years. His
intellectual and spiritual journey will take him along perilous paths, he will
enter "tunnels" and be confused, he will feel as if he has emerged

backwards out of them, he will be petrified by "precipitous abysses" (into which he could very well plunge) and awed by "mountainous vistas" that promise a glimpse of truth—but also frustrated because the snow-capped peaks (of insight and truth) are suddenly covered by cloud.

Thus the details of the train journey need to be read with an eye on their symbolical implications: "a narrow pass," "a deep ravine," "pitch-black tunnels," "vast chasms," "views closed again," "new passes," "confusing your sense of direction," "magnificent vistas," "a world of ineffable, phantasmagoric Alpine peaks," "a slight attack of dizziness and nausea," etc.—the entire account is intended to be read on two levels at once: the realistic train journey is also a fanciful, poetic mirror of the hero's future life. (Cf. Hans Castorp's words on p. 486, ll. 5f.: "I have passed on with Naphta and Settembrini into these dangerous mountains.")

l. 32   *a brown ulster*: a long loose overcoat made of heavy material.

l. 32   *but no hat of any sort*: these little details are telling: convention in normal bourgeois society at this time would require the wearing of a hat, and the fact that Joachim is not wearing one is indicative of his having been influenced by the ambience of the sanatorium and having in this respect discarded bourgeois convention—even though he is striving to return to bourgeois society as soon as possible.

l. 35   *But I'm not there yet*: Hans Castorp's objection has a second, metaphorical meaning: a subconscious sense that his personal journey has only just begun.

l. 35   *Dumbfounded*: Castorp's disorientation has already started.

(6) ll. 4f.   *they had always avoided calling one another by their first names*: indicative of the formality of social intercourse at the time, even between close relatives. We are presented in this novel with a world quite different from our own—a world in which there is much more reserve and where formal manners are strictly observed. Nevertheless, the relationship between Hans and Joachim is a close one, but it is based in large measure on an unspoken affection: the silences between them are often as important as their conversations. See also note to p. 30, ll. 1f.

ll. 13f.   *International Sanatorium Berghof*: the "Berghof Sanatorium" is a fictional place, composed of the elements of several sanatoria in Davos (and elsewhere) that Thomas Mann had seen. His wife, Katia, had stayed at the Waldsanatorium (which had only 25 beds), and no doubt the descriptions of the interior rooms of the Berghof are derived from that institution. But the exterior description of the sanatorium in the novel owes its origin to the Sanatorium Valbella, the façade of which permitted the author to hint at mythological allusions (see picture overleaf).

Sanatorium Valbella

l. 16   *The man had an obvious limp*: he has a hint of the Devil about him (cf. Settembrini, p. 237, l. 24: "That limping little devil"), thus associating the Berghof with the Underworld.

l. 17   *a war veteran...*: Hans Castorp's naïve question reveals his ignorance about life in Davos. Joachim's reply is somewhat sarcastic: the "war" that the porter has fought is with some form of serious illness—i.e. bone-tuberculosis. (In an earlier version of this scene Joachim informed Hans that the porter had had tuberculosis.)

l. 40   *a weary, indeed sad expression*: an early hint of Joachim's eventual fate.

(7) l. 5   *Acclimatize yourself first...*: this is unwitting irony by Joachim: as Hans will discover, "acclimatizing" himself to his new environment (intellectual as well as physical) will be an insoluble problem. Castorp will come to use the phrase: "one gets used to not getting used" (cf. p. 237, l. 37).

ll. 6f.   *You'll see quite a few new sights here...*: "new things" would be a more accurate translation. Joachim again unwittingly indicates the significant changes that Hans Castorp is going to experience. See also l. 23: "A man changes a lot of his ideas here"—words that will certainly apply in Hans Castorp's case.

ll. 21f.   *Three weeks are the same as a day to them*: Biblical allusion: cf. *Psalms* 90.4, which in the German Bible reads: "For a thousand years are to you [God] as the day that passed yesterday."

l. 33   *How learned you've become*: ironic, because it is Castorp who will eventually become far more learned than Joachim.

l. 36   *a nonchalant, but somehow vehement shrug*: the shrug of the shoulders is a recurrent motif that connotes a different attitude to life by those at the Berghof: resigned, stoical, and accepting (cf. p. 9, l. 27; p. 13, l. 21f.; p. 70, ll. 15f,; p. 144, l, 20, etc.).

l. 39   *a curved, flattened bottle...*: this is the so-called Blue Henry ("We even have a name for it, a kind of nickname..."; cf. p. 76, l. 9), a device invented in 1889 to enable tubercular patients to discharge their spittle into a flask made of blue glass, rather than into a handkerchief—or even onto the pavement, as some used to do. Since tuberculosis is transmitted by way of the sputum, from 1900 onwards all tubercular patients in Davos had to carry one of these bottles.

(8) l. 3   *You think so, do you?*: Joachim's indifference towards the splendid scenery is caused both by his having been there so long, but also by his desire to return to the "Flatland" and his duties as a soldier.

ll. 8ff.   *elongated building...*: the description of the Berghof Sanatorium's façade is meant to conjure up a lung itself (cf. l. 11: "as pockmarked and porous as a sponge"). See picture of the International Sanatorium Valbella, p. 44.

ll. 29ff.   *Schwarzhorn, Scaletta-Gletscher, Piz Michel, Tinzenhorn*: mountains near Davos.

ll. 32f.   *they're always snow-covered*: hints at Hans Castorp's future adventure (and near death) in the *Snow* sub-chapter (Ch. 6; pp. 460ff.). (In the German text the mountains are covered "in eternal snow"—a phrase that has wider implications.)

l. 39   *Yes, it was quite a climb. Certainly had me scared...*: unwittingly ironic words, since the physical anxiety that Hans Castorp experienced is suggestive of his intellectual and spiritual adventures to come—and of which he does not yet know.

(9) l. 10   *You are talking so strangely*: another indication of the changes that life "up here" effects on the residents.

ll. 19f.   *Schatzalp*: one of the major mountains in Davos. It was the location of the highest sanatorium, 300 meters above the Berghof—the only other sanatorium that is named in the novel (see picture overleaf).

ll. 20f.   *transport the bodies down by bobsled*: this reflection of the common practice of hiding the dead from the living is also the first hint of the central theme of the novel: death.

ll. 32f.   *They make special note of his services in the brochure*: this is unlikely, as in 1907 psychoanalysis was still in its infancy and associated in the popular mind with mental illness.

l. 33   *He dissects the patients' psyches*: the use of the unusual, and more graphic German word ("Seelenzergliederung" = literally, dissecting souls), instead of the more common Greek word "psychoanalysis" is intended to cast ironic doubt on the activity.

Davos, Schatzalp & Schatzalp Sanatorium (upper middle) 1903

l. 34   *Dissects their psyches?*: Castorp's abrupt rejection of Krok-owski here contrasts ironically with his later attendance at Krokowski's lectures and his private sessions with him (cf. p. 362, ll. 2f.). This initial reaction is reconfirmed when he first meets Krokowski and refuses the latter's offer of treatment, "almost stepping back" (p. 16, l. 36). He first has to open himself up to aspects of life with which he is not yet familiar.

Room 34

(10)   *Room 34*: Hans Castorp's room number relates to the number symbolism of the novel (cf. "Introduction," pp. 21f.).

l. 7   *Taking their rest cure*: a significant element of the "cure" was to lie in the cold mountain air—five times a day.

l. 23   *Do they feed you properly up here?*: more unwittingly ironic words. Life at the Berghof, as Castorp will discover, revolves around mealtimes (five per day; cf. note to p. 74, l. 10). Eating well was one of the recommended measures, since most tuberculosis patients lost weight and wasted away. Also, one should note that Hans Castorp has already acquired the "different" manner of speaking: he has already absorbed and now produces the phrase "up here." One of the great subtleties of the novel is the way in which Castorp absorbs ideas and vocabulary from those around him and later often reproduces them as his own creations.

l. 30   *Some balloon-shaped objects*: oxygen for dying patients. Hans Castorp meets symbols of death as soon as he arrives.

ll. 34f. *I'm on your right, and on your left is a Russian couple*: Castorp is symbolically located between duty and order (Joachim), and license and disorder (the Russian couple). He is the "man of the middle"— a position that Thomas Mann considered to be Germany's situation in Europe. Castorp, the engineer, has come to visit his cousin, the dedicated army officer, but he is about to be introduced to an aspect of life that he has so far blocked out: sex.

l. 35   *they're rather slovenly and loud...*: Castorp will soon discover that for himself.

(11) l. 7   *distant dance music*: popular music is associated in the novel with superficial relationships or "questionable" (i.e. sexual) activities, and this early hint foreshadows the unmistakable noises Castorp will soon hear from the neighboring room of the Russian couple.

ll. 7f. *Joachim had thoughtfully placed a few wildflowers...*: cf. p. 202, ll. 15f., where Joachim places flowers at Hans Castorp's table-setting; & p. 362, ll. 25ff. where Hans Castorp collects similar flowers for his botanical studies.

l. 9   *in their second bloom*: the translation is not quite correct. The meaning is: flowers that had been found after the hay had been harvested and the grass had started to grow again.

ll. 11f. *I'll have no trouble putting up here for a week or two*: much of what Castorp says in these early pages is unwittingly ironic. As time goes on, he will willingly stay longer and longer in the Berghof.

ll. 14f. *Behrens told me...*: indicative of the matter-of-fact attitude to death at the Berghof. Cf. also l. 20 where Joachim speaks somewhat cavalierly of "first-class hemorrhages."

l. 22   *formalin*: formaldehyde in liquid form; used for disinfecting.

l. 28   *methyl aldehyde*: another name for formaldehyde. This is an early hint of Castorp's future extensive scientific studies.

l. 40   *Maria Mancini*: a brand of cigar (made in Honduras, and named after one of Louis XIV's mistresses), whose name was appropriate for Thomas Mann's purposes. The cigar is an example of the manner in which in Thomas Mann's mature works an everyday object assumes a significance that is both extensive and profound. First, the cigar is a sexual symbol (indubitably phallic). It is associated with the thermometer, which Behrens calls a "mercury cigar" (cf. p. 45, l. 25)—and mercury was used to treat venereal disease. Hans Castorp's innate "sickness" has existed from birth, and his enjoyment of smoking as a young man in Hamburg is a sign that he is predestined to become a patient in the Berghof sanatorium. His liking for the cigar is a precursor of his love for Clavdia. It is only fitting then that he will exchange cigars with Behrens—as they "exchange" Clavdia. See also later notes to pp. 249, ll. 21ff.

The cigar also symbolizes Castorp's anti-bourgeois inclinations and his dislike of work. It is associated with Chauchat's chewing of her fingernails, with formlessness, and death. Smoking a cigar is like lying by the ocean, a submission of the self to the pleasures of nothingness. It distinguishes those who do not subscribe to bourgeois morality from those who do. Castorp's fluctuating responses to smoking his favorite cigar at the Berghof reflect his process of acclimatization (or lack of it).

MARIA MANCINI   Beste Zusammenstellung feinster Sumatra-Havana-
Selloritas   Gewächse, als Nachtisch-Cigarre hervorragend geeignet;
                   große elegante Form, 15¹⁄₄ cm lang, in Kisten von 50 Stück.
                   Siehe Musterkiste Nr. 15, Seite 87.

Preis M 450. –
pro Mille

Maria Mancini

ll. 41ff.   *getting through customs…*: the original makes it clear that the customs inspection was friendly, not that Castorp was smuggling.

(12) l. 4   *August*: Seven years before the events that caused the outbreak of the First World War.

ll. 6f.   *my face feels awfully flushed*: the "new" atmosphere of the Berghof has already had an effect on Hans Castorp. The hot cheeks are a physical manifestation of the overheated state of his being—a state that persists for a long time to come (cf. p. 236, ll. 1ff.).

ll. 11f.   *Some people never get used to it*: among them will be Castorp. Cf. note to p. 7, l. 5.

ll. 23f.   *a terrible mush of decomposing material*: a recurrent image (leitmotif) in the novel. The word "dissolution" ("Auflösung") as a principle of life occurs ten times in the novel. The scene prepares the reader for Hans Castorp's researches about the connection between the body and illness in the sub-chapter *Research* (cf. pp. 271ff.). This image also recurs at the end when Hans Castorp is tramping through the "squishy mire" (p. 704, l. 1) in the First World War.

l. 26   *your born horseman*: the Austrian is, in fact, an amateur rider in horse-races who owns his own horse.

ll. 37f. *It's as if you were looking right down inside...*: Castorp's innate fascination with dissolution and death emerges involuntarily in this conversation. This later becomes one of his major preoccupations, but it clearly excites him here as he enters the restaurant and "his eyes ... had taken on a glint of nervous excitement" (p. 13, l. 3)—a leitmotif that will recur (cf. p. 236, l. 2). The act of "looking into someone" becomes one of his major experiences (cf. *My God, I See It*, pp. 201 ff.).

l. 38   *the mucus and the slime*: a major theme of the novel is the relationship between form and formlessness. Without its skeletal structure the body would collapse; and so it is with life in general: form and structure are bastions against formlessness—which is the ultimate fate of all living things. Inside the body the human being is full of sludge, held together by bones. Form and beauty are merely an illusion (note the implications of this for the form of this novel). Thus the slime inside the Austrian horseman stands as a symbol for the "slime" that lurks behind all aspects of life—and it points forward to the end of the novel where Hans Castorp has to slog through the slime of the First World War (cf. p. 705, l. 18: "the soggy ... earth," where the translation, however, loses the direct verbal association of the original).

(13) l. 3   *a glint of nervous excitement*: the first hint of death has excited Hans Castorp.

In the Restaurant

l. 9   *Things could get very lively in the restaurant*: hints at later events, notably on Walpurgis Night (cf. pp. 316 ff.), and Peeperkorn's wild party (*Vingt et un*, p. 546 ff.).

ll. 21f.   *gave his new, uncharacteristic shrug*: "new" and "uncharacteristic" only if Joachim is still considered from the point of view of the "Flatland."

l. 25   *table lamp with a red shade*: the red lamp is a leitmotif that runs throughout the novel. It has mostly erotic connotations.

ll. 26f. *clasped his freshly washed hands together...*: the novel plays with idea of the transfer of qualities—here the implication that the religious inclinations of Castorp's forefathers finds expression in the secularized act of rubbing his hands in anticipation of the meal. Indications of this process of secularization range from the "skipping waves" of Lake Constance (cf. note to p. 3, ll. 8f.) to Naphta's father's profession of village butcher, a task he carries out with "a solemnity recalling ancient times when the slaughtering of animals had indeed been the duty of priests" (p. 432, ll. 33f.).

l. 32   *Gruaud Larose*: distinguished French red Bordeaux wine.

(14) ll. 12ff.   *a break in the everlasting ... monotony*: Joachim touches here on the nature of time spent at the sanatorium, and prepares Hans Castorp for his own experience of time and reflections about it.

ll. 18f.   *this is no life...*: Joachim utters these words with frustration as is shown both by the following phrase: "shaking his head and reaching again for his glass," and by the fact that these words are recalled much later as having been said "out of pure disgust" (cf. p. 534, l. 23).

l. 30   *plans for making the Elbe more navigable*: the idea was developed into a general plan for the expansion of Hamburg harbor that was approved in 1908.

l. 36   *he at once abandoned the topic...*: an early indication of Castorp's distancing himself from his life in Hamburg—and from the values it embodies.

(15) l. 2   *Frau Stöhr*: the name connotes several things: it is close to the name of a fish ("Stör" = sturgeon)—and it is appropriate, therefore, that she should later claim to be able to prepare "a total of twenty-eight different fish sauces" (p. 81, l. 27ff.). Her name also implies "stören" (disturb), which she certainly does when she utters one of her howlers, and it also allows the narrator frequently to add the epithet "mulish" or "stubborn" ("störrisch") to her utterances.

l. 3   *Cannstatt*: Bad Cannstatt, near Stuttgart, location of Europe's largest mineral spas.

ll. 3ff.   *the most illiterate person...*: it is ironic that Hans Castorp would look down on Frau Stöhr's ignorance, when he himself makes mistakes similar to hers (e.g. with Settembrini's name [p. 55, l. 35]; confusing Rhadamanthus with Radames [p. 192, l. 15]; calling Marusya "Mazurka" [p. 70, l. 25]; his ignorance of the Lisbon earthquake [p. 246, l. 23]; his not recognizing quotes from Goethe's *Faust* [p. 322, ll. 6ff.]; and his mistaking Lilith for "Lilli" [p. 322, l. 16]).

l. 4   *"decentfiction"*: Frau Stöhr's mangling of "disinfection."

l. 5   *"eighty camp"*: Krokowski is Behrens's assistant, hence his "aide-de-camp."

ll. 25f.   *did they serve porter here*: a heavy, dark-brown beer that Hans Castorp has been drinking since Dr. Heidekind prescribed it for him as a somewhat anemic child (see p. 28, l. 35ff.).

(16) ll. 3ff.   *He was about thirty-five years old...*: the physical description of Krokowski ("dark, glowing eyes, black eyebrows, a rather long beard ... a black ... business suit and black open-worked shoes") suggests a somewhat sinister, even devilish appearance. Both his name and his "drawl of a foreign accent" (l. 15) align him with the East. The portrayal of Krokowski is intended to be, in part, a satire of psychoanalysis. Thomas Mann was aware that his portrayal of psychoanalysis in the novel contained equal parts of seriousness and satire, but he commented: "That doesn't hurt."

ll. 27f.   *I have never met a perfectly healthy person before*: cf. Krokowski's later assertion that being human and healthy is incompatible (p. 188, ll. 28ff.).

ll. 36   *No, no, thanks just the same*: Castorp's hasty rejection of treatment (accompanied by an involuntary physical confirmation—"almost stepping back") is ironic in the light of the already existing state of his health: he has "moist spot" on his lung, although he doesn't yet know it.

(17) ll. 5f.   *He never had got round to a last cigar…*: i.e. at the end of the evening, as planned. The process of Castorp's loosening his ties to the "Flatland" is slow and subtle, but inexorable.

l. 27   *deathbed*: the fact that Hans Castorp thinks this thought is a foreshadowing of his "sympathy with death."

ll. 28ff.   *he began to dream…*: the nature of these dreams points to Hans Castorp's loss of certainty: after only a short while at the Berghof Sanatorium he has already lost his bearings, both physical and metaphysical. The deconstruction of his "normal" world has already begun. Furthermore, these confused dreams implicitly also point to the uncertainty and unreliability of our conscious reality.

l. 30   *Joachim Ziemssen … riding down a steep slope on a bobsled*: another indication of Joachim's eventual fate.

Chapter Two

This chapter serves the two-fold function of grounding Hans Castorp's acquired values in the long and honored tradition of his family, and of demonstrating that his inherited view of life does not provide him with the answers he seeks. Hans Castorp becomes familiar with death at an early age, as within a short span of time he loses his mother, father, and grandfather. All this is narrated in one short chapter, which emphasizes the impact of these experiences on him. The funeral ceremony is "sadly beautiful" (p. 26, l. 22), and he recognizes that death is partly a serene final event, but also one that masks the ugly fact of physical decay. These early events plant the seeds of his later fascination with death.

Furthermore, the family observances he describes are the bastions erected by civilization against the emptiness and meaninglessness of existence. (Here the influence of Nietzsche's view of Western ethics is apparent.) Despite all the ceremonies and all the formalities observed by his forefathers, Castorp's ultimate question to the universe is met with a "hollow silence." This "apprenticeship" prepares him for the journey to Davos: he is already highly susceptible (having found no answers) and will have little trouble in releasing himself from the professional and family bonds that he instinctively perceives as empty ritual.

The Baptismal Bowl/Grandfather in His Two Forms

(18) l. 8   *a fit of laughter*...: the motif connecting laughter and death recurs in the sub-chapter *Dance of Death*, cf. pp. 300, l. 22f. & p. 301, ll. 21ff.

l. 16   *pneumonia*: since both Hans Castorp's father and grandfather (cf. p. 25, l. 20) die of pneumonia (a lung infection), tubercular problems obviously run in the family. As Hans Castorp will discover later, somewhere in his past in Hamburg he, too, had a lung infection that left a scar.

ll. 20f.   *Saint Catherine's Church*: one of the five principal historic churches of Hamburg. The base of its spire, dating from the 13th century, is the oldest building preserved in the city. It is situated on an island near what was formerly the southern boundary of the medieval city, opposite the historic harbor area. It traditionally served as the church of seamen.

l. 21   *with a view to the botanical gardens*: a view that the dead could scarcely appreciate.

ll. 24f.   *Hans Lorenz Castorp*: in his copy of Oswald Spengler's *Downfall of the West* Mann marked the following passage: "... the belief among primitive peoples that the soul of the grandfather returns in the soul of the grandson. Hence comes the common practice of giving the grandson the name of the grandfather, which with its mystical power once again gives physical form to the grandfather's soul." Beside this passage Mann wrote: "H.C!" Thus he intends there to be a close association between Hans Castorp and his grandfather, hence their identical first names.

(19) l. 15   *batiste necktie*: fine, soft-sheer linen with a plain weave. The necktie, a leitmotif that weaves through the novel, assumes an important symbolic significance for Hans Castorp (see next note).

(20) ll. 3f.   *there was something about it that found approval*...: the necktie symbolizes tradition and discipline. Hans Lorenz Castorp belongs firmly in the nineteenth century, testifying to the solidity of the past. The ruff that the grandfather wears has, however, an ambivalent significance: on the one hand it symbolizes the stability of life based on firm foundations; yet in time it becomes a necessary support for the old man's head as he ages and loses control of his physical functions. The ruff, therefore, comes to represent the attempt to stave off degeneration and death.

ll. 30ff.   *the china cabinet*: all of these objects evoke the past.

l. 34   *daguerreotypes*: first form of photographs. The process allowed images to be formed on the surface of a silver plate through the use of heated mercury.

l. 39   *a heavily tarnished, round silver bowl*: according to Thomas Mann himself, a symbol of history and death.

(21) ll. 15f. *There were seven names in all now*: number symbolism.

l. 23   *he would listen to the great-great-great*: the translation loses unfortunately the important sound of the original ("Ur-Ur-Ur-Ur," pronounced "oor") that is much more evocative, since it is "that somber sound of the crypt" (l. 24), and is intended to connote death. This is one of Hans Castorp's key experiences as a boy and renders him susceptible later to developing his "sympathy with death."

ll. 28f. *Saint Catherine's Church*: see note to p. 18, l. 20.

l. 29   *Saint Michael's*: one of Hamburg's five main Protestant churches and the most famous church in the city.

ll. 30ff. *where as you walked...*: this is an early intimation of an attitude and action that Hans Castorp will adopt in later scenes of death, cf. p. 287, ll. 30ff., p. 296, l. 16, p. 304, l. 24, & p. 337, l. 8.

l. 42   *And it will soon be eight years now...*: i.e., Hans Castorp is seven years old in this scene. The description of the use of the baptismal bowl that follows underscores the sense of history and continuity in the family: not only Hans Castorp's father forty-four years ago, but also his grandfather seventy-five years ago were baptized using this same bowl and the same words were spoken. At the mystical age of seven Hans is now made aware of his lineage and his place in an unbroken tradition.

(22) l. 2   *Saint Jacob's*: church named after the protective patron of all Hamburg churches.

ll. 13ff. *almost got himself shot...*: In the 19th century the city of Hamburg was one of the most powerful fortresses east of the Rhine. After being freed from Napoleonic rule by advancing Cossacks and other allied troops, it was once more occupied by Marshal Davout's French XIII Corps on 28 May 1813. The French forces remained in the city until May 1814.

ll. 16ff. *seventy-five years ago...*: the baptismal bowl and the ceremonial activities connected with it symbolize the traditions and stability, not only of the Castorp family, but also of bourgeois life in general.

l. 24   *a familiar feeling stole over him...*: the consciousness of belonging to an age-old tradition; he is a part of both past and present.

ll. 34f. *this may possibly have had its basis ... in sympathy*: confirmation of the close connection between Hans Castorp and his grandfather.

(23) l. 2 *member of a Reformed parish*: The reformed evangelical churches in Germany had their origin in the Reformation of the 16th century, and most of them followed Martin Luther's teaching: both churches and services are characterized by extreme simplicity and strict adherence to the Bible.

l. 3 *an advocate of restricting qualifications for those who govern…*: a leitmotif of Castorp's sojourn at the Berghof will be the phrase "playing king" (see note to p. 383, ll. 34f.)—an attempt on his part to "take stock" of all that has been happening to him. A verbal allusion to that later activity occurs here (unfortunately lost in the translation). Castorp's grandfather's belief that only certain people are capable of governing is paralleled later by Hans Castorp's ability to "govern" himself by taking stock of the state of his soul.

ll. 23f. *their exclusively positive stamp, immune to all discussion or analysis*: these early experiences of Hans Castorp make a deep impression on him and accompany him through his later life, without being subjected to critical scrutiny, as so many of his other experiences are.

ll. 24f. *As noted, mutual sympathy was at work here…*: cf. note to p. 18, ll. 23f.

ll. 36f. *to prop his chin in the way that so pleased little Hans*: the attitude of Senator Hans Lorenz Castorp symbolizes a central issue of the novel: the attempt by the bourgeois world to control by rational behavior the increasing loss of control over the body.

(24) l. 12 *the Esplanade*: a wide, elegant street in Hamburg, commissioned to be built by the city (1827–30) on the model of the famous boulevard Unter den Linden in Berlin (see picture opposite).

l. 30 *a wide, starched, heavily pleated ruff*: another leitmotif, symbolical of sternness and rigidity. The ruff remains for Hans Castorp a symbol of fortitude in the face of life's inevitable progress towards death. He cites the symbol with this significance in a much later conversation with Naphta and Settembrini (cf. p. 372, l. 11).

l. 32 *batiste jabot*: white linen cascade of frills down the front of a shirt.

ll. 36f. *images of the Late Middle Ages and the Spanish Netherlands*: evoking religious and intellectual rigidity and strict morality. In the novel two camps are drawn against each other: on the one side is Spanish-Medieval-Catholic-Jesuitical rigidity and strictness (here represented by North-German patricians with their strict adherence to tradition and resistance to change), and on the other side, Russian-Asian licentiousness (embodied in Clavdia Chauchat). For Hans Castorp the painting of his grandfather is symbolical of a conservative attitude to life and a refusal to let death have dominion. It plays a major role later when he formulates his own attitude to life and death (cf. p. 290, ll. 1ff.).

Esplanade, Hamburg

(25) l. 9   *the Spanish ruff*: the leitmotifs of necktie, stiff collar, and Spanish ruff are all connected. Cf. note above to l. 30.

ll. 39f.   *interim stage … the form appropriate to him*: for the grandfather life was but an "interim stage," and the finality of death is more appropriate for a man so wedded to tradition and opposed to change. Cf. also p. 36, l. 24: "his authentic and true form."

(26) ll. 4f.   *Hans Castorp's mind and senses … his senses in particular*: the repetition emphasizes the strong impression that these deaths make on him. This early experience of death stays with him, and during his time at the Berghof sanatorium these early experiences will resurface as he contemplates the serious questions of life and death. The vocabulary here—"really quite familiar" (i.e. with death), "the look of knowledgeable experience," "now he remembered it [i.e. death] … in every precise, piercing, and incomparable detail"—reinforces the significance of these childhood experiences. Cf. also p. 107, ll. 22ff. where he feels "in my element somehow" when talking to Tous-les-deux.

l. 30   *Thorvaldsen's Christ*: Bertel Thorvaldsen (1770–1844), a Danish sculptor who enjoyed wide renown in the nineteenth century. He completed the statues of Christ and the Apostles for the Cathedral Church of Our Lady in Copenhagen from 1821 to 1824 (see picture overleaf).

ll. 36ff.   *the masses of flowers…*: flowers at a funeral serve both to beautify the scene and to mask any unpleasant odors. But this tradition also glosses over the reality of death. Hans Castorp will learn that the open acceptance of death is essential to a genuine examination of life.

Thorwaldsen's Christ

ll. 40f. *to make people forget it...*: the young Castorp is aware of the manner in which society attempts to gloss over the harsh reality of death. This early experience is, once again, an important factor in Hans Castorp's later pursuit of knowledge about the relationship between life and death. The use of the word "indecent" (l. 39) points to his later studies in the sub-chapter *Research*.

(27) l. 14f. a *shadow of respectability darkened his face*: the servant's reaction to something he perceives as inappropriate has its parallel in Castorp's reaction to the behavior of the Russian couple in the next room at the Berghof (cf. 36 ff.: *The Shadow of Respectability*). The person who draws a veil over unpleasant events is evading them. In time Hans Castorp will learn to face the unpleasant aspects of life and to remain open to them.

At the Tienappels'/Hans Castorp's Moral State

The two sub-chapters about Hans Castorp's family establish that their world is stable and based on tradition; its members are conscious of time and history. Thus his staying the Berghof sanatorium is, in the first instance, a radical break with family tradition. But this sub-chapter also introduces the fundamental issue that subconsciously motivates all of Hans Castorp's future behavior: his search for meaning in life.

Harvestehuder Weg

(28) l. 12   *Harvestehuder Weg*: elegant boulevard in Hamburg.

l. 21   *a gray seaman's beard*: the beard begins by the temples and leaves the upper lip and the chin free (i.e. shaven).

l. 29   *roast beef with tomato ketchup*: not an apparent lapse in taste, but a common combination at this time.

ll. 36   *a nice daily glass of porter*: see note to p.15, ll. 25f. This "medicinal" beverage remains one of Hans Castorp's preferences—even at breakfast.

(29) ll. 3f.   *his proclivity to "doze"*: Castorp's early inclinations point forward to his later receptivity for the ideas embodied in the figure of Chauchat. His glass of porter, the sea, his cigar, and music—all put him in the state of daydreaming. Cf. also p. 101, ll. 22ff.: "who could spend long hours doing nothing in particular." On the metaphorical level, the cigar and the ocean imply the same fundamental attitude to life: the ocean is a metaphysical sphere, symbol of infinity and of the dissolution of space and time.

l. 8   *Uhlenhorst Boathouse*: Uhlenhorst is on the Eastern bank of the Outer Alster, one of two artificial lakes in Hamburg that were formed by damming the river Alster, a tributary of the river Elbe. Before the Second World War the Boathouse was a popular destination for outings; it was destroyed in the War and never rebuilt (see picture overleaf.)

Uhlenhorst Boathouse

l. 9   *listening to music*: the role of music in Hans Castorp's life progresses from his sitting over a drink while listening to light music to his fascination with certain major musical works that embody for him some fundamental truths (cf. *Fullness of Harmony*, 626 ff.).

l. 12   *just a hint of Platt*: i.e. Hamburg dialect.

(30) ll. 1f.   *Ziemssen—Joachim Ziemssen*: confirmation of the fact that Hans does not normally address Joachim by his first name (cf. note to p. 6, ll. 4ff.).

l. 2   *the pavilion on the Alster*: a famous café situated on the Inner Alster, the smaller artificial lake (cf. p. 29, l. 8; see picture opposite).

l. 5   *that he dearly and truly loved living well*: Castorp's enjoyment of life is a fundamental element of his character that will move from this early self-indulgence to more profound experiences at the Berghof.

ll. 16f.   *that no one in the empire except residents of Hamburg knew how to iron*: Hamburg and its upper-middle class culture is portrayed as the epitome of the bourgeois life-style—an important preparation for Hans Castorp's eventual rejection of it. The "empire" is the German Reich before 1918.

ll. 21f.   *his teeth*: the imperfection of Castorp's teeth hints at the imperfection of his health in general and his tenuous hold on life. Thomas Mann's frequently gives the characters in his works physical imperfections as indicators of existential weaknesses.

l. 24   *the impression of a certain slackness*: all of Castorp's later behavior is predicted by his youthful imperfections.

Pavilion on the Alster

ll. 24f. *his posture at the dinner table was excellent*: and it will remain so until he fully absorbs the atmosphere of the Berghof and succumbs to its culture of lassitude. (Cf. p. 226, ll. 9ff., where he experiments with letting his back go limp at table, in imitation of Chauchat's posture.)

ll. 25f. *He would politely turn his erect upper body...*: another sign of his good bourgeois upbringing. Cf. p. 74, ll. 36f.: "turning his whole upper body."

ll. 30f. *a Russian cigarette...*: his predilection for a *Russian* cigarette is an early and subtle hint of his innate proclivities: the enjoyment of something "eastern"—and, of course, the Russian cigarette evokes Chauchat. (Note also that despite his bourgeois ethic he acquires these cigarettes illegally.) The fact he is already a smoker when living in Hamburg is a sign that he is susceptible to the attractions of the Berghof. Smoking is an irrational act, showing opposition to the rationality of middle-class society. It is the drug of those who conform to middle-class values but need some kind of compensation to survive.

l. 32ff. *Maria Mancini*: see note to p. 11, l. 39. The description of the cigar's taste—"whose spicy toxins blended so satisfyingly with those of his coffee"—create the association with Pieter Peeperkorn, the coffee-planter who poisons himself, and whom Castorp will not meet for several years yet.

(31) l. 2 *"mediocre"*: the translator has struggled to find an appropriate English equivalent for the German "mittelmässig." The word "mediocre" generally has a slightly more negative connotation than the German original. Perhaps a better word would be "average" (i.e. middling); cf. the opening sentence of Chapter I, p. 3, l.1: "An ordinary young man." However, the German word also connotes another aspect of

Hans Castorp's position in the world: the narrator wants to portray him as being "in the middle," between extremes, as a representative of German culture, in the middle between Europe and Asia. Hans Castorp is also "in the middle" in other respects: he is torn between the obligations of bourgeois life and the attractions of death; and he also suffers a clearly sexual conflict between heterosexual and homosexual love.

l. 5   *a more general significance*: the narrator wishes to portray Hans Castorp as a *representative* character: he stands in the middle, surrounded by manifold other characters who have an influence on him. He is the representative German in the European panoply at the Berghof. Cf. also the opening lines of the novel: "The story of Hans Castorp that we intend to tell here—*not for his sake*" (p. xi, ll. 1f., emphasis added).

l. 6   *a modern secondary school*: he has, in fact, attended a school where the focus is on scientific and technical subjects ("Realgymnasium"); in other words, he has not received a humanistic education (a defect that Settembrini will attempt to correct).

ll. 13ff.   *A human being lives out not only his personal life…*: an indication that the narrator wishes the work also to be understood as a novel of the age: it is a portrayal (among other things) of Europe before the First World War, and the experiences of the individual Hans Castorp, the questions he asks, the answers he seeks, are those of the entire age. Beyond that, however, the broader question is also being posed: "What is the meaning of life?" Hans Castorp is a child of his age, and his doubts about his work are accompanied by the question: What is the point of it?

ll. 26f.   *if the times respond with a hollow silence*: one of the most significant motifs of the novel, and a major motivator for Castorp's pursuit of knowledge. This is one of the key paragraphs of the novel, and it summarizes the modern dilemma: the search for meaning in a world that offers none. Hans Castorp has grown up in a society in which he has failed to discover a sense of purpose, and his stay at the Berghof will provide him with the opportunity to explore various avenues on his search for meaning. Castorp embodies the modern condition that was summarized by Nietzsche: In a world without faith where can we find meaning?

ll. 30   *a crippling effect*: the lack of meaning can be not only physically enervating, it can even incline one to sickness. In effect, metaphysical emptiness manifests itself in organic disease. There is thus an implication here that Hans Castorp's sickness, diagnosed by Behrens at the Berghof sanatorium, is, in fact, psychosomatic.

ll. 33f.   *his own times may provide no satisfactory answer…*: the repetition of the themes underscores the importance of this paragraph. The age can provide no answer to the question of the meaning of life—and this, in turn, leads to physical illness. The two issues are crucial for Hans Castorp's development.

(32) ll. 5   *his report card in his freshman year*: a misleading translation. In fact, the word in the German text states that Hans Castorp had to perform one year of military service—which was at his own expense—after which he received his "report card," whereupon he would have been released from further service (that normally lasted two to three years) in order to pursue higher studies.

ll. 9f.   *when it was finally decided*: Castorp's decision to become an engineer is presented impersonally—i.e. he didn't really make the decision himself—and this indicates his half-hearted relationship to the profession.

ll. 16f.   *Hansa ... Blohm and Voss*: the latter was (and still is) a German shipbuilding company with a long history. A vessel named *Hansa* was launched in 1899.

ll. 22   *would make a good painter of seascapes*: another indication that Castorp is not completely suited—or committed—to becoming an engineer. In Thomas Mann's fictional world successful business-people are totally single-minded; if a businessman has even a hint of an interest in something artistic or philosophical, the business is doomed to fail.

(33) ll. 6f.   *as Hans Castorp had remarked rather patronizingly*: Castorp's slight disdain for Joachim's choice of profession because it involved no "serious brainwork or stress" reveals an element of nascent intellectual snobbery (which ironic, since at this point he is still "ordinary" himself), but also points to his future development.

l.7   *he had the greatest respect for work*: an inevitable result of his upbringing, although his innate disposition is opposed to the idea: cf. "he did tire easily" (l. 7) and p. 57, ll. 13ff. when Settembrini says that "all labor truly deserving of the name is difficult, is it not" and Castorp replies: "Devil knows that's right."

l. 8   *he found that he did tire easily*: another indication of his innate predilection for indolence. The next paragraph (ll. 9ff.) expounds in some detail Castorp's dilemma: work is a central concept in his view of life, something that was never brought into question. However, his nature is opposed to work ("it did not agree with him"; l. 19) and in his heart of hearts he does not really *believe* in the value of work.

ll. 9ff.   *Which brings us back...*: Thomas Mann considered this paragraph to be extremely important. He indicated in his diary (12 June 1919) that it was his intention to depict the ethical situation of a young man in the period before the First World War: "the ethical difference between capitalism and socialism is minimal, because both consider *work* to be the highest principle, the absolute. ... [T]he bourgeois world knows no higher value than work, and this ethical principle is made official by socialism." Socialism is just as "godless" as capitalism, "for work is not divine." The argument of this paragraph emphasizes how the bourgeois work-ethic is indoctrinated into people and it portrays Hans Castorp's innate nature as rebelling against this ethic.

ll. 10f.   *the damage inflicted by the times...*: the central issues of the novel are broached here for third time in the space of two pages. (Cf. also ll. 28–29: "first his mind, and through it his body.")

ll. 21ff.   *when time passed easily...*: these lines already indicate Hans Castorp's innate predilection for lethargy which will become a defining factor of his life at the Berghof.

ll. 34f.   *work was simply something that stood in the way of the unencumbered enjoyment of a Maria Mancini*: the themes of the novel (here: work versus idleness) are presented throughout in the form of contradictory motifs.

ll. 36f.   *He was not attracted to military service himself*: Castorp's "inner nature" is opposed to the idea of duty: "Something deep within him resisted the idea."

(34) ll. 2f.   *the habit of drinking porter...*: the alcohol slows down his mental processes.

ll. 7f.   *were not as good as his watercolor depiction*: another hint that he has chosen the wrong profession.

ll. 13f.   *his sleepy, young patrician face*: the adjective "sleepy" ironically detracts from his patrician image.

l. 18   *a self-governing city-state*: the "self-governing" of the city of Hamburg—the epitome of the bourgeois ethic—will be contrasted with Hans Castorp's "self-governing" (the same word is used) during his time at the Berghof.

ll. 29f.   *his resemblance to his grandfather was undeniable*: cf. note to p. 18, ll. 23f.

ll. 31f.   *but so was the opposite...*: an early indication of Hans Castorp's possible break with his inherited values.

l. 34   *turn out to be a go-getter*: he will, indeed—for this is the term that Director Behrens will use to describe him, although the leitmotif is lost in the translation (cf. p. 262, ll. 37f.).

ll. 35f.   *as footloose as a Jew...*: the narrator's prejudice is a reflection of his times.

(35) l. 2   *Hans Castorp, being an unwritten page*: this is a "novel of education" ("Bildungsroman"—see "Introduction," pp. 24f.); thus Hans Castorp's life is yet to be written.

ll. 4f. *twenty-three years old*: the translation silently solves a problem in the original where the text states that Hans Castorp is "in his twenty-third year." That would mean that here he would be twenty-two, but on page 83, l. 37 (just a few days later) he says he is "in my twenty-fourth year … That is, I'll be twenty-four soon." The error probably arose from the fact that Thomas Mann changed his mind at least twice about how old he wanted Hans Castorp to be.

l. 5   *Danzig Polytechnic*: The Technical University of Danzig (now called the Gdansk University of Technology).

l. 6   *Braunschweig*: city located in Central Germany north of the Harz Mountains.

l. 7   *Karlsruhe*: city in Southwest Germany near the French border.

ll. 10f. *And that point, his life took the following turn*: the translation omits an important phrase: "for the moment"—which is narratorial irony, since (as the narrator well knows) Castorp's life is about to change not for the moment, but forever.

ll. 15f. *Nordeney or Wyk on the island of Föhr*: Nordeney and Föhr are islands in the North Sea off the northwest coast of Germany, part of the archipelago that extends along the German and Dutch North Sea coastline. Nordeney is the largest of the East Friesian islands, and Wyk is the only town on the island of Föhr in the North Friesian group.

l. 22   *sensible barometric pressure*: a leitmotif for the unwillingness of the "sensible" bourgeois to travel to places with unusual conditions. Cf. p. 420, l. 26.

l. 27   *He had always been susceptible to bronchitis…*: i.e. as a psychosomatic manifestation of his doubts about the meaning of life.

l. 41   *the last week of July*: it has to be the seventh month, of course.

(36) Chapter Three

The Shadow of Respectability

The title of this section gains leitmotivic force through its occurrence whenever something unpleasant is repressed. Initially (as in this chapter) Hans Castorp's middle-class sensibility is offended by the shameless behavior of his neighbors: his reaction is to blot it out. As the novel progresses, however, he learns that the activities he attempts to ignore or deny are a natural part of life and the "shadowing" will eventually become a vehicle for his own pleasant fantasies.

(36) l. 10   *by the light of reasonable day*: Hans Castorp's disorientation at finding himself in a totally different world is corrected (at least to begin with) by his re-assertion of the power of reason. As the atmosphere of the Berghof increasingly infects his being, however, the "light of reasonable day" will weaken.

l. 21   *Somewhere morning music was playing*: what begins as "background music" gradually in the course of the novel assumes more and more significance for Castorp. Music becomes one of the defining experiences of his life.

ll. 24ff.   *Hans Castorp loved music with all his heart*: the motif of music connotes the entire corpus of Castorp's inclinations to idleness, lassitude and the "darker" (Dionysian) side of life. The effect of music (and porter) on him (Cf. p. 37, l. 1: "profoundly calming, numbing, and 'doze'-inducing") stands in stark contrast to reason and enlightenment (the Apollonian side), represented by Settembrini. Music suspends his critical faculty and opens the door to his subconscious mind and releases those elements that his upbringing had repressed. It is also associated with his "sympathy with death." The fact that Castorp's natural inclination is revealed here will be significant in the later struggle for his mind and soul.

(37) l. 5   *short-stemmed, starlike gentians*: deep-blue flowers; the first hint of his later fascination with blue flowers (see p. 117, ll. 5ff.).

l. 11f.   *a snake-entwined caduceus*: a slight mistranslation, as the German uses the word "Schlangenstab" (literally: "snake-staff"), which is not a caduceus, but the staff of Asclepius, the Greek god of medicine and healing. Strictly speaking, the caduceus is a herald's staff, not a symbol of medicine. In classical mythology the caduceus with two snakes was carried by the messenger Hermes (cf. "Introduction," pp. 25f.): as a symbol of the medical profession the staff has *one* snake wound around it. The snake, however, also has allusions to sex (Chauchat) and poison (Peeperkorn).

Staff of Asclepius

Eleonore Duse

ll. 21f.   *a famous tragedian*: the Italian actress Eleonore Duse (1858–1924). The reference connotes tragedy and death.

ll. 23f.   *the rhythm of march music in the distance*: the lady in black walks to the rhythm of the march music without even realizing it. It is, in effect, a funeral march, evoking thereby the image of death before we even know that the lady is Tous-les-deux whose two sons are deathly ill. The association of music and death is a leitmotif that weaves its way through the novel to its final paragraph that describes the First World War as "the wicked dance" (p. 706, l. 12). The march music symbolizes—and foretells—Hans Castorp's innate fascination with death, his "sympathy with death," as he will call it later. It also hints at the subchapter *Danse Macabre* (301 ff.), in which he and Joachim pay visits to moribund patients. As a symbol of war the military march also points to Hans Castorp's future on the battlefield and his possible fate.

ll. 40f.   *a shadow of respectability*: the repetition of the same phrase that had occurred in relation to death (p. 27, l. 14) places sex in the same context. Sex and death (in French: "l'amour et la mort"; Mann found the same idea expressed in Walt Whitman's poems) are among the phenomena that in polite, bourgeois society are suppressed and avoided. Castorp's revulsion at the noises from the neighboring room is both an expression of his upbringing and his lack of personal development: sex has not yet registered in his life. The leitmotif follows him throughout the novel and recurs significantly in the sub-chapter *Snow* where a handsome boy looks towards a terrible scene of child murder "without so much as a frown"— and the original uses the verbal form of the same word employed here (cf. p. 484, l. 16).

(38) ll. 9f. *a waltz was stuck up in the distance*: the music that accompanies the love-making of the "bad" Russian couple in the neighboring room is a banal waltz tune—the kind of music that Hans Castorp throughout the novel associates with the lower classes and cheap emotions (in this regard, he is definitely a snob). The waltz, associated by Castorp with superficiality and vulgarity, is an appropriate accompaniment to the activities next door.

ll. 11f. *Hans Castorp stood ... and listened against his best intentions*: despite his disapproval of the behavior next door, he listens nevertheless—trapped by his own fascination with activities that do not accord with his bourgeois morality. On the one hand, he—like a typical bourgeois of his time—strongly disapproves of such behavior and is judgmental; on the other hand, against his rational judgment he is a voyeur, ensnared by the Will (see "Introduction" re Schopenhauer, pp. 12f.).

ll. 16ff. *But in broad daylight ... After all, they are ill*: Castorp's naïveté is the occasion for a good deal of humor in the novel. Here he intimates that the Russian couple has gone beyond the bounds of decency in having sex "in broad daylight," but the fact that they are having sex at an "unusual time" can be ascribed to their being sick. Decent, healthy, bourgeois people have sex at night, in the dark.

ll. 22f. *I wonder if I shall see these people later*: with his good middle-class upbringing he will be more embarrassed than they will be.

ll. 25f. *the flush...*: the motif cleverly conflates Castorp's embarrassment at what he hears next door with the immediate physical effect that his arrival at the Berghof has had on him. The physical change in his appearance points to the altered psychological circumstances.

(39) *Breakfast*

l. 4 *ulster*: see note to p. 5, l. 32.

l. 4 *the outline of the flat bottle*: for sputum, cf. note to p. 7, l. 39.

l. 5 *He wasn't wearing a hat today, either*: an indication of Joachim's concession to Berghof laxity. Down on the "Flatland" the wearing of a hat is *de rigeur* for people of Hans's and Joachim's class.

l. 8 *not soundproof*: i.e. he could hear his neighbors.

l. 11 *Tous-les-deux*: both of them.

l. 16 *poisoned*: the word is used as a leitmotif throughout the novel, together with its antonym: "detoxified" (free of poison; "entgiftet"), and it often has metaphorical force (i.e. "poisoned" in the sense of "infected by ideas").

l. 29 *tous les deux*: see note to l. 11.

l. 35   *his eyes took on yesterday's look…*: the small physical changes that place as soon as Hans Castorp arrives in Davos hint at his psychical state: his dissatisfaction with his life "down there."

ll. 36f.   *shone with the same glint…*: cf. p. 13, l. 3.

(40) l. 7   *tous les deux*: see note to p. 39, l. 11.

l. 8   *Joachim cast him a gentle glance…*: throughout the novel subtle details hint at Joachim's less-than-perfect military attitude. Despite his repeated avowals that he is focused solely on his cure and his desire to return to military duty, he, too, has been "infected" by the atmosphere at the Berghof sanatorium which has undermined his stern resolve.

l. 11   *walking-stick, coat, and hat—the latter out of obstinacy…*: Castorp's decision is all the more ironic precisely because he is *not* "all too definite in his own civilized habits" (l. 11f.). His world was susceptible to crumbling before his arrival, and in the very short time he has been at the Berghof the indications that his world is changing irreversibly and forever have begun to manifest themselves.

l. 26   *tous les deux*: see note to p. 39, l. 11.

ll. 28ff.   *don't want to make the acquaintance…*: repressing the unpleasant and avoiding disagreeable aspects of reality. By the end of the novel he will take his place at the table where they currently sit.

ll. 34f.   *they are barbarians…*: Joachim places Russians in the same camp as Settembrini does.

(41) l. 9   *There were seven tables*: part of the number symbolism of the novel. (Seven persons sit at each table.) In the course of the seven years he spends at the Berghof, Hans Castorp will send a year at each of the seven tables—until he finally ends up at the "bad" Russian table. (For a discussion of the number-symbolism, see "Introduction," pp. 21f.) First breakfast is at 8 a.m., and second breakfast at 11 a.m.; lunch is at 1 p.m., tea at 4 p.m., and dinner at 7 p.m.

ll. 18f.   *Frau Stöhr…*: see note to p. 15, l. 2. The original also makes a pun about her name here, describing her as "störrisch" which means "mulish."

l. 22   *marmalade*: "jams" would be more accurate.

(43) ll. 33f.   *A door … had banged shut*: this is the first "encounter" between Castorp and Chauchat. The motif of the banging door illustrates the contrast between Castorp's rigid middle-class code ("a noise that Hans Castorp absolutely could not tolerate"; l. 36) and Chauchat's *laissez-faire* attitude to life: she comes late to breakfast and lets the door slam. His reaction is ironically exaggerated (he reacts "angrily"—the word in German is even stronger ["wütend" = in a rage]), because it will be the person who causes his anger (Chauchat) whom he will eventually come to love and who will be instrumental in his rejection of the bourgeois ethic. Her action typifies what she represents: she is a free spirit who rejects the moral order of conventional society.

(44) l. 36   *There's something so civilian ... about you*: Behrens's initial description of Castorp sticks to the latter throughout the novel; cf. p. 47, l. 15, p. 346, l. 1, p. 365, l. 34, & p. 519, l. 36.

l. 37   *You would be a better patient than he*: prophetic words.

l. 40   *Myrmidon*: in Homer's *Iliad* the Myrmidons were the soldiers commanded by Achilles against the Trojans—thus brave and courageous.

(45) l. 6   *There's no shortage of ladies*: a foretaste of things to come for Castorp.

l. 7   *Many of them are quite picturesque—viewed externally at least*: This seemingly innocent and jocular remark hints at future developments: Castorp's infatuation with Clavdia Chauchat and his acquisition of the x-ray of her tubercular chest (he will even find her diseased interior "picturesque"). The epithet Behrens uses in German ("malerisch") is derived from "Maler" (painter); appropriate since he has painted a portrait of Chauchat—a fact that Castorp does not know at this point.

l. 8   *But* you'll *have to improve your color...*: Behrens uses the French loan-word "Couleur," which lends his advice the suggestion that Castorp may make the acquaintance of a French woman.

l. 9   *The golden tree of life is green*: quotation from Goethe's *Faust: Part 1*, l. 1717–18, uttered to a naïve student by Mephistopheles (the servant of the Devil) in the guise of an academic. The play *Faust* by Germany's most famous writer, Johann Wolfgang von Goethe (1749–1832) plays a major role in the novel: quotations from the play abound, and one of the play's central scenes, "Walpurgis Night," serves a structural function in the sub-chapter *Walpurgis Night* (pp. 316ff.). Other references to Goethe also occur in the novel.

ll. 12   *pulled an eyelid down...*: a typical action by Behrens when meeting a prospective patient; cf. p. 426, l. 31, when Hans's uncle James Tienappel comes to visit.

l. 17   *sine pecunia*: without cost. This is one of many phrases that Castorp digests and reproduces later (cf. p. 58, l. 38 & p. 323, l. 36). This absorption of vocabulary constitutes a major feature of his education.

l. 20   *tuberculosis pulmonum*: pulmonary tuberculosis. Behrens's advice to Castorp to behave during his three-week stay as if he were a patient is, of course, ironic, because, in fact, he already is one.

l. 20   *build up your protein a little*: deeply ironic words, as Hans Castorp will find at Joachim's deathbed, where his protein emerges in the form of tears (cf. p. 528, l. 30).

l. 23f. *do get on with your promenade*: the German word used here (and frequently throughout the novel) is "Lustwandel," which, while meaning "stroll," also connotes the word "pleasure." (While "Lust" in German is not the English "lust," the German word "Wollust" is.) Thus something sexual is connoted—a connotation that is continued when Behrens immediately thereafter refers the thermometer as a "mercury cigar." The connection of cigar, thermometer, and pencil (all of which have sexual connotations) is repeatedly exploited in the novel (see also note to p. 11, l. 40). The pencil and the thermometer have the same color.

l. 25   *mercury cigar*: Behrens's jocular term for the thermometer. For its implications and connection to the real cigar, see note to p. 11, l. 40. N.B. in the German original Behrens calls it a "quicksilver cigar"—and quicksilver was once used as a cure for venereal disease, an infection that connotes more than the merely physical. Castorp's "infection" (i.e. his obsession with Chauchat) will lead him into metaphysical adventures.

l. 26   *Conscientiously doing one's duty*: Behrens's exhortation to Joachim touches on the nexus of motifs that have to do with "duty." Joachim is determined to do his "duty" to his cure—so that he can get better and leave for the "Flatland" in order to perform his real duty as an officer. The novel exploits this ambiguity repeatedly.

(45) *Teasing/Viaticum/Interrupted Merriment*

Viaticum: the Christian Eucharist given to a person close to death.

(46) l. 28   *our promenade*: Castorp uses the same word that Behrens had just employed ("Lustwandel"; see note to p. 45, l. 23). Castorp has already absorbed Behrens's vocabulary.

l. 28   *being a zealot*: another word used by Behrens, cf. p. 45, l. 2. In the original Behrens uses a jocular term ("Biereifer") that implies enthusiasm brought on by alcohol. It is not a word that, given Hans Castorp's upbringing, one would expect him to use.

ll. 33f.   *the best part of life*: echoes of *Ecclesiastes* 3: 22: "…there is nothing better, than that a man should rejoice in his own works; for that is his portion." However, that smoking a cigar is "the best part of life" is surely, on the surface, an exaggeration. The deeper meaning is that a life without the obligation to work is preferable.

(47) l. 2   *if a man has a good cigar*: for Castorp the cigar symbolizes his withdrawal from the constraints of duty and activity—as his comparison with lying by the sea demonstrates ("you don't need anything else—no work, no other amusements"). Smoking symbolizes a predilection for freedom and lethargy. Thomas Mann described smoking as "a metaphysical act, like sleeping, lying by the ocean, or lying on the balcony of an alpine sanatorium."

ll. 7f.   *Even polar explorers*: of which Castorp is one, since he, too, has come to the region of snow and ice with his supply of cigars.

l. 13   *All the same, it's a sign of a rather weak will*: Joachim's criticism of Hans Castorp is unwittingly also an insightful analysis of the latter's fundamental character: he is not a confirmed adherent of the bourgeois ethic of work and duty.

l. 14   *you're a civilian*: Joachim, adapting Behrens's description of Castorp (cf. p. 44, l. 36) ascribes his cousin to the healthy—and therefore not "in the service" (of the cure).

l. 22   *sine pecunia*: he has remembered the term from his conversation with Behrens (cf. p. 45, l. 17).

l. 25   *build up my protein*: cf. note to p. 45, l. 20.

ll. 31f.   *But he did not look back*: conforming to the usual reserve between the cousins, so as not to embarrass Joachim.

(48) l. 38   *Pneumothorax*: a medical procedure in which gas is pumped into the lung. Artificial pneumothorax became a widespread form of treatment. Under medical supervision a lung would be artificially collapsed then refilled. It was hoped that it would somehow rest the infected lung. In some instances ribs were removed and this allowed pressure to be taken off the infected lung—a procedure that even Behrens carries out later (cf. p. 149, l. 15 & p. 170, l. 38).

(49) l. 10   *the caseated lobes of the lung*: caseation is the transformation of tissue into a soft cheese-like mass, as happens in tuberculosis.

l. 21   *because she can whistle...*: if an opening was present from which gas could escape, the patient "whistled" from time to time.

l. 36   *associate member*: the translation loses the jocularity of the original, in which Hans Castorp uses a word ("Konkneipant") that could have come from Behrens's lips. It implies an associate member of a student society where drinking is a major activity.

(50) l. 5   *they're so* free: Joachim broaches the novel's theme of sickness as a means to freedom (one that will be developed later by Chauchat). Sickness releases one from the obligations of life ("things are serious only down below in real life")—a lesson that Hans, as Joachim points out to him, will "come to understand ... in due time" (l. 10f.). It is, however, Joachim who, because of his limitations and his concentration on his bourgeois duty, fails to comprehend that the metaphysical issues of "sickness and death" are far more serious that anything "down below in real life," and it is Hans who will come to understand that in far greater measure than his cousin ever could.

l. 6   *they're young*: tuberculosis attacked young people above all.

l. 15   *this doesn't taste good*: another sign of his breaking his bonds with the "Flatland." Later he will come to enjoy a different brand of cigar.

(51) l. 5   *he demanded to know other things*: this curiosity is an integral part of his "sympathy with death." The secrecy surrounding death in the Berghof sanatorium parallels the similar phenomenon that Castorp observed when growing up in Hamburg.

ll. 17f.   *quite a bit is happening backstage*: the translation is correct, but loses the ambiguity of the original's "behind the curtains"—with its metaphorical connections to the "veils" that are present at other times.

ll. 19f.   *But recently ... it must have been eight weeks ago*: Hans Castorp's objection ("you can't call it recently") is ironic, as his own perception of time—and, in particular, of what "recent" means—changes radically in the course of the novel. Here Hans objects to Joachim's use of the adverb "recently" to refer to eight weeks ago; but much later in the novel, he himself will speak of "a hundred and twenty years" ago as "recently" (p. 364, l. 18), and immediately thereafter he will claim that "three thousand years seem fairly recent" (p. 364, l. 23).

l. 27   *Viaticum*: see note to p. 45. However, Joachim here equates the word with "extreme unction," which it is not. The latter is the sacrament of "last rites" administered to a dying person.

l. 39   *glockenspiel*: musical instrument of the percussion family. It is similar to the xylophone, in that it has tuned bars laid out in a fashion resembling a piano keyboard. But whereas the xylophone's bars are wooden, the glockenspiel's are metal.

Glockenspiel

l. 39   *turkish-style military band*: following European encounters with Turkish armies, Turkish military music had had an influence on European military music since the eighteenth century—an influence that even extended to the world of opera and concert-hall music (cf. Mozart's opera *The Abduction from the Seraglio* [1782]).

(52) ll. 14f.   *You see, a man should always wear a hat!*: Castorp's sense of the proper bourgeois decorum asserts itself in the context of the freedom from the normal rituals enjoyed at the Berghof. If Joachim had been wearing a hat, in accordance with the bourgeois ethic, he would have been able to raise it in order to show respect and politeness.

l. 20   *the little Hujus girls' room, number twenty-eight*: even a trivial fact retains the number symbolism (four times seven). But there is a further—and far more ominous—irony in the fact that when Joachim returns to the Berghof sanatorium, he will be assigned this room and die there (cf. p. 493, l. 25).

(53) l. 17   *crossing his ankles*: this detail, together with the hat and the stick, evoke the image of Hermes, messenger of the gods and himself god of travelers, merchants and thieves. Hermes (cf. picture p. 26) was also known in mythology as the guide who led dead souls to the Underworld. But there is yet another association intended by the author: We know from Thomas Mann himself that he is quoting here an essay by Gotthold Ephraim Lessing *How the Ancients Portrayed Death,* in which Lessing affirmed (incorrectly) that Thanatos (Death) was likewise portrayed with his ankles crossed and leaning on a stick. Thus for all his advocacy of enlightenment and freedom and progress Settembrini is still associated with death, and his positive humanism is ironically undermined by his symbolic associations.

l. 32   *Hans Castorp slapped his thigh with one hand*: Castorp performs this action on several occasions (cf. p. 111, l. 27): it indicates his youthful self-confidence.

(54) *Satana*

Satana: Satan. Settembrini is Satan—but with a difference. He is not the traditional Satan, but rather a modern, enlightened figure who campaigns (like his model Carducci; cf. note to p. 56, l. 41) against superstition and obscurantism and for clarity and reason (cf. text p. 57, ll. 23ff.).

l. 21   *in two wide arcs...*: suggestive of horns and therefore associating Settembrini with the Devil.

ll. 22ff.   *His outfit*: the description of Settembrini's appearance is both an excellent example of Thomas Mann's realistic-symbolical style and an ironic commentary on Settembrini's philosophy. His clothing is flamboyant ("loose trousers in a pastel-yellow check..."), but shows clear signs of wear ("rough from frequent laundering")—all of which parallels his ideas. Although the principles he expounds to Hans Castorp are striking in their humanity, they are somewhat shop-worn (i.e. obsolete).

Like their author's clothing, the ideas are a "mixture of shabbiness and charm." There is, of course, a further irony in the fact that Settembrini is an advocate of progress and a man of action—yet he is sick and confined to a sanatorium. Cf. also p. 366, ll. 38ff.

l. 24   *petersham*: a rough, heavy, knotted wool cloth used for men's coats.

l. 35   *An organ-grinder!*: Castorp's skepticism vis-à-vis Settembrini is established immediately. As much as Castorp will be attracted to Settembrini both as a man and as a mentor, he will always retain a healthy critical distance about what Settembrini preaches to him. This critical attitude is an important factor in his progress: while he is always receptive to Settembrini's ideas, he also maintains at all times a certain independence of mind. In addition, the figure of the organ-grinder evokes the image of someone mechanically playing the same tunes over and over again.

(55) l. 2   *Settembrini*: The name clearly plays on the number 7, but other associations are also connoted. There has been speculation about the same name in Italian being used in Venice to describe homosexuals: the unmarried Settembrini may harbor a homoerotic tendency towards his student. Settembrini's yellow, checkered trousers and yellow shoes may be further indications of his inclinations. The important thing to remember here is that the name is meant to connote a wide range of associations.

ll. 14ff.   *And with and easy, felicitous wave...*: throughout the novel Settembrini accompanies his words with theatrical gestures, as if to indicate that the effect he wishes to convey is as important as the content of his words. The gestures serve to undermine his credibility.

l. 16f   *One could in fact forget completely...*: an allusion to Davos as the realm of the dead.

ll. 29f.   *Minos und Rhadamanthus*: guardians of the Underworld. Minos, the son of Zeus and Europa, was the King of the Underworld. Rhadamanthus was Minos's brother who ruled Tartarus, the realm of criminals (with implications for the patients at the Berghof). In the speeches that follow, Settembrini plays with the motifs of the Underworld in applying them to the Berghof which is the "realm of the shades" (p. 56, l. 1) and its inmates "creatures who have fallen to great depths" (p. 56, ll. 7f.). These motifs permit Thomas Mann also to raise the mere facts (the Berghof and its patients) from the everyday into the mythico-psychological realm. In comparing Castorp to Odysseus—and in suggesting that Castorp is only a guest in the Underworld—Settembrini is characterizing Castorp's own personal Odyssey that started when he left Hamburg. The parallel with the Odyssey will give Settembrini (and the narrator) other opportunities in the course of the novel to compare Hans

Castorp's "journey" to an odyssey. The Berghof sanatorium and its doctors are frequently categorized in mythological terms: cf. "imp of Satan" (p. 94, l. 31), "prince of shades" (p. 465, ll. 26f.).

Note: The appellation "Rhadamanthus" for Behrens will recur many times throughout the novel. In order not to burden the commentary with every such reference, this will be the only entry for that name.

l. 35   *Herr Septem-*: Settembrini's name suggests both "September" and "seven" (Latin: septem), and the naïve Hans Castorp makes the unwitting error. The association of Settembrini's name with "September" implies that his ideas are aging; it is, of course, ironic that it is his "student" who implies this—even before the teacher has commenced his "lessons."

ll. 38f.   *I am not sick at all*: irony—he is sick, but does not yet know it.

ll. 41f.   *you are merely stopping over, as it were*: the verb used in the original German ("hospitieren") implies a student visiting lectures as a guest—which will be shown to be appropriate as Hans Castorp begins his "studies" at the Berghof, especially as Settembrini hopes to make Castorp into *his* student. (The verb and the noun derived from it ["Hospitant"] recur several times in the novel in different contexts.)

(56) l. 1   *Odysseus in the realm of the shades*: In Book XI of Homer's *Odyssey* the hero Odysseus visits Hades (the Underworld), where he converses with the shades of famous dead figures, his mother, and others. This is an important, if obtuse, observation: Settembrini is the first to inform us that Hans Castorp has embarked on a spiritual journey. Hans Castorp will later repeat more of Odysseus's adventures when he visits (metaphorically) the island of Circe and communes with the pigs (cf. p. 243, ll. 35ff. and p. 325, l. 12ff.). Note also that the reference to the "realm of the shades" associates the Berghof's residents with dead people—an image that is pursued throughout the novel in various contexts (cf. p. 311, ll. 2f.)—to the very end of the novel where Hans Castorp is referred to as "seeing shadows as things" (p. 699, l. 36), and even the narrator is merely a shade by the roadside (p. 703, l. 23).

ll. 1f.   *How bold of you…*: cf. *Odyssey* 11, V. 475f.: "Resourceful Odysseus, … what a bold man you are … How can you dare to come/ down into Hades' home, the dwelling place/for the mindless dead, shades of worn-out men?"

ll. 7f.   *creatures who have fallen to great depths*: also meant in the moral sense—thus acknowledging that the Berghof is a place where sickness, sexuality and death are intermingled.

l. 8   *lieutenant*: Settembrini repeatedly exaggerates the military or social standing of Joachim and Hans. Joachim is not yet an officer, and

Hans is not yet an engineer. Cf. later when Joachim returns to the Berghof as a lieutenant, and Settembrini calls him "capitano" (cf. p. 497, l. 7).

l. 26   *O dio*: Oh, God.

l. 29   *Our smallest unit of time is the month*: a concept that Hans Castorp absorbs and repeats in his letter home on p. 221, l. 20.

l. 30   *shades*: i.e. the dead—since Settembrini has described the Berghof as the Underworld.

l. 37   *shipbuilder*: we are not told precisely what Hans Castorp told Settembrini ("provided the information," ll. 35f.), but Settembrini's reaction is significant. He immediately sees Hans as a man of progress, and his approval is probably reinforced by his belief, as a Freemason, in the symbolism of structures.

l. 41   *Carducci*: Giosuè Carducci (1836–1907), a leading Italian poet, famous for his provocative *Inno a Satana* (*Hymn to Satan,* 1863), in which he praised the rebellious spirit of reason as the driving force of life and progress. He won the Nobel Prize for Literature in 1906 and died in February 1907, thus Settembrini's obituary would have appeared about six months before the date of this conversation.

Giosué Carducci

(57) ll. 6f.   *I sat at his feet in Bologna*: Carducci became Professor of Italian Literature in Bologna in 1860.

l. 8   *shipbuilder*: Settembrini repeatedly inflates Castorp's qualifications to make him seem more important—and more representative of a
view of life that Settembrini approves of (see following note).

ll. 10f.   *the representative of a whole world of labor and practical
genius*: Settembrini represents the world of reason, enlightenment, order,
duty, technology, etc. and thus he sets great hopes on Hans Castorp as a
member of that world.

ll. 13f.   *all labor truly deserving...*: Settembrini unwittingly describes
Hans Castorp's own view of work.

ll. 15f.   *it came from the heart*: Castorp's doubts about his chosen
profession keep on surfacing.

l. 19   *my great teacher once wrote a hymn to him*: Carducci's *Hymn
to Satan* praises Satan as the rebellious spirit that has promoted freedom,
reason and progress—the major factors in human history.

l. 21   *sung on certain festive occasions*: in particular, by Freemasons
who sang it with great enthusiasm. Freemasonry will play a major role in
the novel when Naphta arrives on the scene (*Someone Else*, pp. 362 ff.).

l. 22   *O salute...*: the penultimate line of the fifty in Carducci's hymn.
It means: "Hail, O Satan, O rebellion, O avenging power of reason!" (In
the original there is no "O" at the beginning.)

l. 26   *the other one*: unwittingly ironic words from Settembrini, for
Castorp has, indeed, unconsciously already given this "other devil" his
little finger: this second devil—who inclines humans to inactivity and
sloth—will eventually take far more of Castorp than merely a little finger.
In addition, Castorp reveals even at this early point in the novel that he is
not at all inclined to Settembrini's world by indicating that he does not like
work (p. 58, ll. 8ff.) and is a cigar-smoker (p. 58, ll. 19ff.), a habit that
Settembrini detests (p. 58, l. 26ff.).

l. 39   *homo humanus*: the concept derives from Ancient Roman
culture. The civilized *homo humanus* was regarded as a product of Roman
socialization and philosophy, and was concerned with good conduct and
scholarship. (The opposite was *homo barbarus*.) In describing himself as a
"humanist," Settembrini is stressing both his adherence to the principles of
human dignity and well-being and to the ideals of a humanistic education,
that is: ancient languages and classical culture.

l. 40   *such ingenious matters*: Settembrini makes a pun on the word
"engineer" (cf. l. 35: "Someone must show some wit").

(58) l. 6   *one might truly lose all heart*: He has, of course, already lost
his courage, although he is not aware of that.

ll. 10f.   *I only feel really healthy when I am doing nothing at all*: a
frank admission of his innate inclination.

l. 13   *a little confused*: indeed, he is confused—but not just because everything about the Berghof is new to him: he is confused about his life in general. The epithet "confused" remains with him for a long time.

l. 19   *I'm feeling somewhat uneasy*: another sign that changes are under way.

l. 29f.   *He is a devotee of your vice*: i.e. smoking cigars. Cf. the later exchanges between Hans Castorp and Behrens on the topic of cigars (p. 249, ll. 19ff.).

l. 33   *I have my vices, too*: since, apart from whistling at and ogling girls (cf. p. 370, ll. 13f.), it is not clear what vices Settembrini has, the statement may be meant ironically.

l. 38   *sine pecunia*: from having heard the expression from Behrens (p. 45, l. 17), then having first repeated it as having come from Behrens (p. 47, l. 22), Castorp now uses it as his own.

(59) ll. 2f.   *I am the man who catches birds*: Settembrini cites Papageno's aria from Mozart's *The Magic Flute* (1791). Settembrini is referring to Behrens's practice of snaring new patients. (Thomas Mann had experienced this personally during his visit to his wife in 1912, cf. "Introduction," pp. 1f.) The mention of The *Magic Flute* here is also a veiled allusion to Settembrini's allegiance to Freemasonry: the opera's connection to Freemasonry has long been the subject of speculation and debate. (Settembrini's suspicions about music [cf. p. 111, ll. 19ff.] do not prevent him from alluding to it if the reference helps his argument.)

l. 5   *a devil of a fellow*: the original is less complimentary, using a word ("Satanskerl") with more negative connotations (e.g. evil-doer).

l. 13   *From the house of the von Mylendonks*: see note to l. 17 below.

l. 14   *She differs from the Medici Venus*: marble copy, from the first century B.C., of an original bronze Greek sculpture. At one time or another the sculpture was ascribed to various Greek sculptors, including Praxiteles, whose name will recur obliquely later in Hans Castorp's conversation with Behrens about Chauchat's portrait in Behrens's apartment (cf. note to p. 257, ll. 6f.). The term used to describe this pose is "Venus pudica": the unclothed female keeps one hand covering her private parts (see picture overleaf). Krokowski will speak later of the "impudency of matter" and the "impudicus" mushroom (cf. p. 358, l. 40).

l. 17   *Adriatica*: abbess of the convent Dietikirchen in Bonn in the thirteenth century. Also the name of the wife of St. Alexius: on their wedding-night he was so anxious about his spiritual well-being, left the house and never came back.

Venus de Medici

l. 20 *It has an absolutely medieval ring*: it is part of the playfulness of the novel that the Berghof sanatorium is likened, among other things, to a monastery/convent and its inmates to monks/nuns. Cf. also p. 378, ll. 36ff. where Hans Castorp remembers this conversation.

ll. 21f. *there is much that has a 'medieval ring' to it*: an early hint that Naphta will be arriving much later.

l. 25 *He paints in oils*: this fact will assume great significance for Hans Castorp sometime later (cf. pp. 252 ff.).

l. 28 *the abbess of a cloister*: factually true.

ll. 35f. *the brightest sword that reason has*: Settembrini's speech summarizes his rhetorical principles in the pursuit of enlightenment.

l. 36 *the powers of darkness and ugliness*: an early hint of the later arrival of Naphta and his view of life.

l. 38 *Petrarch*: Francesco Petrarca (1304–1374), regarded as the "Father of Modernity," because he attempted to renew Mediaeval Latin, using the model of Cicero's prose, which was characterized by a combination of clarity and eloquence and became one of the standards by which all other Latin prose is judged. It is only natural, therefore, that Settembrini would hail him as a precursor of enlightenment and progress.

(60) l. 3f. *'to the right, which leads to the walls of mightiest Dis'*: quote from Virgil's *Aeneid*, 6, V. 541. "Dis" (later assimilated into the figure of the god Pluto) is the Roman god of the Underworld that corresponds to the Greek "Hades." (Settembrini again draws a parallel between the Berghof and the Underworld.) Pluto's palace was in Elysium, which was located in the Underworld. Thus when Hans Castorp embarks on his *Snow*-adventure and decides to take a path to the right (cf. p. 469, l. 33), he is entering a favorable part of the Underworld, in contrast to the place that Rhadamanthus (Behrens) rules: Tartaros, where the dead reside.

l. 4   *Virgil*: Publius Virgilius Maro (70–19 BC), author of the *Aeneid*, which until the 18th century was regarded as the greatest of all the ancient epics. In Dante's *Divine Comedy* the author makes Virgil his guide through the first two parts of the work ("Inferno" and "Purgatory"). For the nine circles of "Paradise" Beatrice is his guide (because Virgil, as a non-Christian may not enter Paradise), and later Settembrini will imply that Chauchat is Castorp's Beatrice (cf. note to p. 510, l. 12). The hidden irony here lies in the fact that Settembrini is praising Virgil as the ideal guide, while unwittingly also referring to Castorp's future "guide," namely Chauchat. In classical Latin the form "Vergil" is preferred, but Settembrini uses the form "Virgil" that was adopted after the fifth century and became associated in the Middle Ages with the Latin word "virga" (magic wand), as Virgil was considered to be a magician.

ll. 11f.   *'her flashing eye in the slippery light'*: cf. Settembrini's earlier admission of his "vices" (cf. p. 58, l. 32). The "quote" appears to be invented.

l. 14   *What a windbag*: Hans Castorp's later affection for Settembrini is always tempered by this initial impression of the man.

l. 17   *Hofrat*: honorific title awarded to people for meritorious service.

ll. 20f.   *every inch a* Hofrat: Settembrini's way of implying that Behrens is motivated by mercenary interests—to the detriment of his moral standards (cf. next note).

l. 22   *the inventor of the summer season*: until the 20th century Davos was frequented only in the winter as a place to seek a cure. Patients left when the snow melted, as it was believed to be harmful to remain in the town (cf. l. 36).

l. 40   *Fiume*: at that time (1907) an independent seaport in Croatia, governed from Budapest and Hungary's only international port. Nowadays it is called Rijeka.

(61) l. 2   *celebrissimo*: literally: the most famous; thus "His Excellency."

l. 6   *'the vine's gladdening gift'*: wine.

l. 8   *phthisis*: earlier term for consumptive disease, especially tuberculosis.

l. 8   *cirrhosis*: chronic liver disease (commonly caused by alcoholism).

ll. 22f.   *the judges of the dead*: reference to Settembrini's characterization of Behrens and Krokowski as Minos and Rhadamanthus (see note to p. 55, l. 29f.).

ll. 37f.   *the delicate symbolism of his garb*: it is ironic that Settembrini would point this out, as his own garb is equally symbolic.

ll. 38f.   *his particular specialty is the night*: Settembrini, the man of the Enlightenment, looks askance at anything unclear or dark. Cf. also the narrator's later comments: "His [Krokowski's] field of study had always been concerned with those dark, vast regions of the human soul that are called the subconscious" (p. 644, ll. 30ff.).

l. 39   *The man has but one thought in his head....*: Krokowski's Freudian view of the connection between illness and sexuality—amplified in his weekly lectures (see pp. 122 ff.). Settembrini here is satirizing the Freudian reduction of neuroses to sexual disorders.

(62) l. 4   *I'm not all that rash about forming opinions...*: but he was in respect of Settembrini.

l. 6   *Form opinions!*: Settembrini's view of life is governed by the belief that criticism leads to progress—hence the "pedagogic streak" of the humanist.

l. 18   *in abstracto*: in the abstract.

ll. 22f.   *a small room with a view to the rear*: the size of Settembrini's room and its location ironically undermine his philosophy.

l. 29   *Well, you see*: he means: that explains it, i.e. writers never have any money (Thomas Mann's little joke).

l. 29   *Is he seriously ill, then?*: the simple dialogue has metaphorical implications: Settembrini's ideas are likewise less than robust.

ll. 36f.   *Do you often spend time with him?*: despite his reservations Castorp is clearly fascinated with Settembrini.

(63) *Clarity of Mind*

l. 3   *filled with mercury*: the original's "quicksilver" widens the connotations.

l. 6   *a tuniclike jacket*: in the German the jacket is said to be of Polish origin, thus hinting at Joachim's subconscious inclination towards the East and what it represents.

l. 7   *he was learning Russian*: although the superficial reason Joachim gives for studying Russian that it will be "of use in his career," the activity represents a symbolic weakening of his resolve—also indicated by his attraction to the Russian girl Marusya (cf. p. 66, ll. 29ff.).

l. 24   *Joachim raised seven fingers*: number symbolism.

ll. 27ff.   *when you pay close attention to it...*: the cousins' first extended discussion of time.

(64) l. 1   *He was not at all used to philosophizing*: Castorp's nascent philosophical curiosity finds increasing expression in his new environment ("yet felt some urge to do so"; ll. 1f.).

l. 15   *we measure time with space...*: an allusion to Wagner's opera *Tannhäuser* (cf. note to p. 4, l. 6).

ll. 19f.   *I think being up here with us is getting to you*: unwittingly ironic and true words from Joachim.

l. 21   *bending the tip of his nose...*: Castorp as a figure of fun. His "naïveté" leads him into many a comic situation.

(65) ll. 14f.   *he could not remember ... a more comfortable lounge chair*: a foretaste of future experiences that run counter to the work-ethic. The "horizontal" position points to love and death. (Cf. "If they're for sale up here, I'll take one back to Hamburg with me, they're simply heavenly"; ll. 38f.)

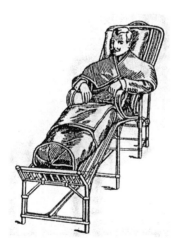

The lounge chair

l. 39   *they're simply heavenly*: more accurately: "when you lie on them, you think you are in heaven"—with much wider metaphorical connotations (e.g. death).

(66) ll. 1f.   *The room glistened with white...*: it was believed that milk helped the cure.

l. 9   *Kulmbach beer*: brewed in Kulmbach (Northern Bavaria), a strong "bock" (lager) beer.

ll. 35f.   *Joachim would lower his eyes…*: the lowering of the eyes (or looking away) is a repeated motif in the novel, and it betokens the presence of strong emotions that the person wishes to conceal. Joachim's attraction to the Russian girl, Marusya, undermines his avowed devotion to his military duty. She represents for Joachim what Clavdia Chauchat signifies for Hans Castorp: even in Joachim's case, the emotions (Dionysus) overcome reason (Apollo).

(67) ll. 19f.   *the glass door on his left slammed shut*: Castorp's failure to turn around is caused by his "breakfast beer."

(68) ll. 1f.   *in meek embarrassment*: in the German their behavior vis-à-vis Krokowski is described as "chaste"—a word that becomes a major motif in his lectures.

ll. 7ff.   *When is the next rest cure … I wish I were lying in my splendid lounge chair again right now*: cf. p. 65, ll. 37ff. The lure of the horizontal (i.e. love and death) is irresistible.

One Word Too Many

l. 14   *dinner*: lunch is meant. The meals at the Berghof are two breakfasts (8 a.m. & 11 a.m.), dinner (1 p.m.), tea (4 p.m.), and supper (7 p.m.). Throughout, the translator uses "dinner" when referring to the midday meal, which was the largest meal of the day.

l. 18   *Little Schiahorn, the Green Towers, and Dorfberg*: a group of mountains near Davos.

(69) ll. 8ff.   *it turned out that he had forgotten...*: a common problem from which he suffers, most significantly after his enlightening vision in the sub-chapter *Snow* (cf. p. 489, ll. 4ff.).

l. 24   *too much for a visitor*: Settembrini had described Hans Castorp as merely "stopping over" ("hospitieren"; cf. p. 55, l. 41f.). Hans Castorp here describes himself with the noun derived from that verb ("Hospitant"): he has absorbed Settembrini's word and now uses it as a noun. His use of the word is, of course, ironic, for he will stay far longer than he suspects. The word becomes a leitmotif that recurs throughout the novel.

ll. 24ff.   *If I only knew … why my heart keeps pounding the whole time*: Hans Castorp's conversations with his cousin—first about the nature of time and now about the body—are clear indications of his philosophical curiosity.

ll. 33ff.   *a dead body*: Castorp's reflections here anticipate Settembrini's conclusions later (p. 98)—a sign of Castorp's independence of mind and developing philosophical sense: he is thinking more and more about the processes of life and of the connection between life and death.

ll. 39f.   *perhaps revenging himself*: cf. p. 51, l. 39.

(70) ll. 14f. *in a quivering voice*: Joachim is as unwilling to discuss the topics of illness and death as Castorp is keen to do so.

ll. 15f.   *To which Hans Castorp merely gave a shrug*: an action, as the narrator tells us, that he has acquired (overnight) from Joachim.

l. 25   *Mazurka*: Castorp's mispronouncing of names is a source of humor in the novel (cf. note to p. 15, ll. 3ff.). The mazurka is a Polish dance in three-four time.

l. 35   *Joachim's tanned face...*: Castorp's little joke about Marusya's ample chest is the "one word too many" referred to in the title of this subchapter; it touches a sensitive spot and Joachim is embarrassed. This episode illustrates a frequent occurrence in the novel: the two cousins understand each other very well and whenever an embarrassing topic arises, silence ensues.

(71) l. 29   *We're the horizontals*: the "horizontal" position is typical not only for the tubercular observing the rest-cure, but also the lethargic, as well as the moribund (and the connection with sex and death is also implied). Cf. later when a character dies and is "placed in a permanent horizontal position" (p. 441, l. 35).

l. 35   *petits chevaux*: gambling game with a mechanism that moves toy horses and riders around a track; popular in casinos and hotels.

But of Course—a Female!

(72) ll. 16f.   *so he lay there for a while*: the pleasure of lying in the horizontal position outweighs the obligation to get dressed for lunch.

l. 20   *He hated unpunctuality*: not surprising in a military man, but it is a trait that he shares with Behrens, cf. p. 173, ll. 32f.

(73) l. 4   *fragrant with orange perfume*: oranges were symbols of love, and courtesans would sprinkle their sheets with orange perfume.

(74) l. 7   *"cosmological salon"*: in the German Frau Stöhr says "cosmic salon," instead of "cosmetic." She means a "beauty salon."

l. 10   *The dinner*: "lunch" (cf. note to p. 68, l. 14).

l. 11   *six courses*: if you count them—and assume that "cheese and fruit" are one course—there are seven courses.

l. 38   *a girl really*: the German is even more explicit: "a young girl"—which underlines the youthful appearance of Chauchat and brings her physically closer to Hippe.

(75) ll. 1f.   *she walked soundlessly, with a peculiar slinking gait*: the description of Chauchat—seen through the eyes of Hans Castorp—includes the major motifs that define her essence (e.g. "slinking"). It is only fitting that Madame Chauchat should slink like a cat—or a snake.

ll. 16f.   *Hans Castorp only surmised all this, however...*: Castorp's perception of Chauchat is intuitive, i.e. he senses what she represents even before he has examined her closely (but the amount of detail is nevertheless remarkable).

l. 22   *her broad cheekbones and narrow eyes ... a vague memory*: the first hint of Castorp's synchronous mingling of Chauchat with Pribislav Hippe. His memory is stirred several times again: cf. p. 82, l. 32, p. 84, ll. 35f., & p. 88, ll. 40ff.—the last occasion a dream that brings him close to the realization of whom she reminds him and looks forward to his borrowing a pencil from her on Walpurgis Night.

(76) l. 9   *have a talk with his Blue Henry*: see note to p. 7, l. 39.

l. 26   *red traces of blood*: a physical symptom of his inner unease.

Herr Albin

l. 34   *caduceus*: see note to p. 37, ll. 11f.

(78) ll. 39f.   *Gala-Peter*: a milk chocolate, invented by D. Peter (1836 –1919), produced by Nestlé and advertised as "the best milk chocolate in the world."

l. 40   *Lindt nougats*: Lindt is a Swiss chocolate manufacturer.

(79) ll. 7f.   *his sophomore year*: in fact, it was the sixth year of High School: German Schools used to count up from six (youngest) to one (oldest). Thus Hans Castorp had to repeat a year comparatively late in his high-school studies. See also p. 32, l. 2: "...he did indeed have to repeat a class or two."

ll. 13ff.   *although honor had its advantages...*: Another step forward in Hans Castorp's emancipation from the strictures of bourgeois life. He can see that true freedom consists in not worrying about the consequences of one's actions (a lesson that will be reinforced by Clavdia Chauchat), and this insight leads to his being "terrified by a sense of dissolute sweetness that set his heart pounding even faster for a while." Castorp's reflections on honor and shame reveal his increasing distance from the values of the "Flatland" and his innate predilection for the "irrational" side of life. The process is internal (he does nothing that he is not already predisposed to doing), and the external events merely offer him the opportunity for self-analysis and self-development.

Satana Makes Shameful Suggestions

ll. 31f.   *anyone who had the honor of being healthy didn't count...*: Castorp feels a little hurt that Krokowski doesn't come to visit him—at least he would have liked to be asked—but his claim to be healthy is, once again, unwittingly ironic, since he now *wants* to belong to the recognized clientele of the Berghof.

(80) ll. 7ff.   *The man should be disciplined ... Gross insubordination*: Joachim's military outlook on life reflects also the idea of the cure as a period of duty and strict obedience.

(81) l. 1   *zwieback*: literally: twice-baked. A sweet bread enriched with eggs, sliced and toasted.

l. 11   *Hans Castorp felt chilled and shivered badly*: it will take him a while to get used to the cold temperatures (i.e. he is not yet acclimatized physically), but he will in time adapt totally.

ll. 16f.   *Kulmbach beer*: see note to p. 66, l. 9.

ll. 27f.   *twenty-eight different sauces for fish*: four times seven.

(82) l. 5   *a stereoscopic viewer*: a "stereoscope" was a device with two eye-pieces. The viewer looked into the eye-pieces and saw a three-dimensional image that was actually composed of two images side by side.

ll. 7f.   *a long, tube-like kaleidoscope...*: a tube containing brightly colored objects and a set of mirrors that reflects them as they move, forming a varying succession of colors and patterns.

ll. 10f.   *a little rotating drum...*: also known as a "zoetrope," a device that produces the illusion of moving pictures by means of a rapid succession of still pictures; invented in 1834 by William George Horner.

l. 32   *She reminds me of something, but I really can't say what*: Hippe is one again evoked—but at this stage Castorp can only say that he is reminded of some*thing*.

ll. 34f.   *the "Wedding March" from* A Midsummer Night's Dream: The reference is to Felix Mendelssohn's incidental music to the play, composed for a production in 1843. This may seem to be a trivial detail, but in the context of the associations connoted by all the motifs of the novel, we can interpret this motif, too, as a playful reference by the narrator to Castorp's nascent involvement with Chauchat. Also, in the course of this day he has gradually slipped into a dream-like state, for which the beer, the cigar, and other objective elements are responsible.

(83) l. 9 *I took you for an organ-grinder*: Castorp's ingenuousness is a constant source of humor.

l. 17 *cozy resort*: in the original Settembrini describes the Berghof as a "Lustort," a word that connotes both a place of pleasure and a more subtle allusion to Wagner's opera *Tannhäuser and the Singers' Contest at the Wartburg*. As the opera opens, Tannhäuser is held at the Venusberg (in the vicinity of Eisenach, Thuringia) a willing captive through his love for Venus. Tannhäuser eventually escapes from the spell of Venus (i.e. sexual pleasure) and finds himself at the Wartburg (see picture opposite), where a singers' competition on the subject of "love's awakening" is to be held. The German medieval poet-singers ("minnesingers") conventionally sang of chaste love, but Tannhäuser sings the praises of physical love, thus causing outrage, and he returns to the Venusberg. Key themes of the opera are the struggle between sacred and profane love, and redemption through love. This allusion looks forward to Hans Castorp's contemplation of an aria from the opera in the sub-chapter *Fullness of Harmony* (cf. note to p. 632, ll. 5ff.). The term ("Lustort") also connects to Behrens's description of the cousins' walk as a "Lustwandel" (cf. note to p. 45, l. 23f.).

ll. 19f. *as I have been told...*: by Joachim, cf. p. 71, l. 29.

l. 24 *Diverting and dull*: a leitmotivic play on words ("kurzweilig und langweilig") that is untranslatable. It first occurred in the *Foreword* (cf. p. xii, l. 7) and will occur many times in the novel (for example, cf. p. 186, ll. 8f., p. 534, l. 22, & p. 706, ll. 3f., where the phrase is translated in a slightly different form).

l. 26 *hustle and bustle*: the same expression he had used on p. 69, l. 37.

l. 29 *almost as if I had grown older and wiser*: the process of Castorp's becoming "wiser," has, as we have seen, already commenced: his reflections on various topics have already brought him new insights.

l. 33 *Hans Castorp didn't know!*: Castorp's confusion about his age is an indication of his disorientation since arriving at the Berghof.

ll. 36f. *I'm in my twenty-fourth year*: see note to p. 35, ll. 4f.

(84) ll. 14f. *earlier that morning*: cf. p. 56, l. 14.

ll. 25f. *Since your stay here appears not to be good for you...*: in the original Settembrini shows himself concerned for Castorp's "spiritual" (not "mental") well-being. He has already perceived that Castorp has been captivated by those aspects of the Berghof environment that he (Settembrini) condemns. His advice to Castorp to leave the Berghof forthwith is an attempt to "save" him from the deleterious influences to which he is being subjected.

The Wartburg

ll. 30ff.   *You mean I should leave?...*: Hans Castorp's reaction is ironic, since he had just raised the possibility himself when talking to Joachim, cf. p. 80, ll. 21ff.

ll. 31f.   *But no...*: Castorp's refusal is accompanied by a casual glance in the direction of Chauchat, which subconsciously evokes Hippe again and reinforces his desire to stay.

l. 35   *what or who is it she reminds me of?*: the clever phrasing of this question invokes both the personages (Chauchat and Hippe) and what they represent (the opposite of reason).

l. 41   *it would be quite counter to reason*: Castorp's use of Settembrini's own weapon (reason) against him is a clear indicator of his intellectual independence. Castorp continues to maintain a skeptical attitude towards the Italian's opinions.

(85) l. 19   *'silent sister'*: a thermometer with no scale (introduced in 1896). After taking a patient's temperature, the doctor slips a metal tube with a scale over the thermometer (see illustration overleaf.)

(86) l. 3   *It tasted like paste, like coal*: the decreasing pleasure Castorp gets from smoking Maria Mancini cigar is another indicator of his detachment from his previous life.

ll. 4f.   *he watched Joachim get ready...*: Joachim's Polish jacket, Russian grammar, and thermometer all connote his susceptibility to Marusya. His clever technique of wrapping himself in his blankets—so that he finally looks like a mummy—connotes his eventual death.

l. 18   *You'll learn how, too*: prophetic words.

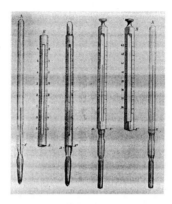

The Silent Sister

l. 22   *I'm not going to lie out on my balcony at night...*: little does he know what his future will bring. See, for example, p. 267, ll. 14ff.

l. 33   *flagrante delicto*: "caught in the act."

ll. 35f.   *it would be no disgrace to heat the place*: Hans Castorp's complains here, but disagrees when Settembrini utters the same complaint the next day, cf. p. 93, ll. 30f.

(87) l. 10   *the civilized ritual...*: his nocturnal preparations for bed—emphasizing order and routine—contrast with the unfettered and troubling nature of the dreams he is about to have.

l. 15   *the American woman's death-pillow*: the gratuitous mention of the previous occupant of the bed undermines Hans Castorp's careful "ritual."

l. 31   *the expression on Joachim's face...*: see p. 70, l. 35f. Hans Castorp divines that Joachim's attraction to Marusya bodes no good for his future—hence Castorp's attempt to forget what he had seen "out of both dismay and tact" (l. 30f.) The fact that he "understood ... saw through it" (l. 34) emphasizes the significance of his insight.

l. 38   *an insipid ... operetta melody*: the music, which Castorp also whistles, is an appropriate accompaniment to the noises he hears from the next room.

(88) ll. 18ff.   *But with it came dreams...*: in these dreams various experiences that Hans Castorp has had so far intermingle with each other.

ll. 20ff. *Director Behrens ... his knees slightly bent...*: in his dream Hans Castorp conflates the image of Behrens with that of Tous-les-deux, cf. p. 37, l. 16.

ll. 24f.   *he was wearing glasses...*: another melding, this time of an adolescent at the next table in the dining-room, cf. p. 74, ll. 22 ff.

ll. 26f.   *extended two fingers ... and pulled down Hans Castorp's eyelid*: as he had done when they first met, cf. p. 45, ll. 11 ff.

ll. 29f.   *won't be stingy…*: cf. Settembrini, p. 55, l. 32: "They're not stingy, you know…"

l. 31   *promenade*: the same word ("Lustwandel") that Behrens had originally used (cf. p. 45, l. 23f.).

ll. 38f.   *to wipe away sweat or tears*: cf. p. 74, ll. 27f., the adolescent at the next table again.

ll. 40ff.   *And now as he dreamed on…*: Castorp's dream expresses both his memories of the past (Hippe) and his fears of the present (Krokowski and psychoanalysis). In his dream he connects Hippe and Chauchat for the first time, but the insight evaporates.

(89) l. 1   *borrow a drawing pencil*: a central motif that will play a role later; cf. pp. 120, ll. 5ff. and pp. 326, ll. 39ff. The German text uses the French loan-word "Crayon"—see note to p. 120, ll. 24f.

ll. 22f.   *You bother me…*: awake, Hans Castorp assures Settembrini that he does not bother him (cf. p. 191, ll. 16f.: "You're not disturbing me in the least"—and in German the same verb is used in both places). The unconscious reaction of the dream is clearly more trustworthy—as is Hans Castorp's later description of him as a "bothersome person" (p. 237, l. 12).

(90) ll. 1ff.   *her hand…*: the rational perception that Madame Chauchat's hand is far from beautiful is irrelevant in the face of desire. Despite all of his rational reservations about Madame Chauchat's physical appearance, Hans Castorp is still captivated by her.

ll. 4ff.   *that sense of dissolute sweetness…*: Castorp's dream allows him the freedom to indulge his innermost phantasies and express the inclinations that in his waking state are held in check by reason and decorum. This paragraph repeats the ideas expressed at the end of the sub-chapter *Herr Albin*: "…how it must be when one is finally free of the pressures honor brings and one can endlessly enjoy the unbounded advantages of disgrace" (p. 79, ll. 15ff.). Hans Castorp's fascination with Herr Albin's antics indicates his subconscious belief that the Berghof could be the location for experiences unthinkable on the Flatland.

(91) Chapter Four

In the course of this chapter Hans Castorp becomes more and more attracted to the Berghof, until he is diagnosed with "a moist spot" in his lungs and becomes a full-fledged patient.

A Necessary Purchase

(91) l. 4   *as a visiting guest*: the word used is the leitmotivic "Hospitant" (cf. note to p. 55, l. 41f.).

ll. 9ff.   *sheer washable blouses ... diaphanous clothes*: a foretaste of what is to come: Chauchat's diaphanous sleeves will fascinate and captivate Hans Castorp (cf. p. 126, ll. 25ff.).

l. 14   *luster wool*: made of a warp of cotton and a filling of wool, as in mohair or alpaca.

l. 22   *the full extent of his wardrobe*: a metaphor for Settembrini's philosophy.

l. 25   *It was just after dinner*: "lunch." Cf. note to p. 74, l. 10.

(92) l. 42   *What a pretty mess!*: the original—literally: "That's a lovely confusion!"—refers ironically to Hans Castorp's person as much as it does to the weather. The unreliability of the weather reflects the philosophical uncertainty of life at the Berghof.

(93) l.5   *felt somewhat frightened by the idea*: because it metaphorically denotes death.

ll. 9f.   *I'd feel as if I were planning...*: ironic words, since that will soon come to pass.

l. 14f.   *the English quarter*: the area around the "Promenade," where the Hotel d'Angleterre (cf. note to p. 309, l. 14) was located, especially after the construction of a church in 1883 for the English congregation.

l. 28   *their wretched overseers*: the image ("ruler, lord") is part of Settembrini's characterization of the Berghof as (among other things) a prison (cf. Rhadamanthus, p. 55, ll. 29f.).

(95) l. 5   *tramontana*: literally: "cross-mountain," i.e. a northerly wind that blows across the Alps and the Apennines towards the coast.

ll. 15f.   *uomo litterato*: man of letters, literary man.

l. 16   *Boccaccio*: Giovanni Boccaccio (1313–75), author of *The Decameron*.

l. 17   *Haparanda*: seaport in Sweden on the Gulf of Bothnia.

l. 17   *Kraków*: former capital of Poland on the river Vistula.

l. 18   *Padua*: city in north-eastern Italy, not far from Venice.

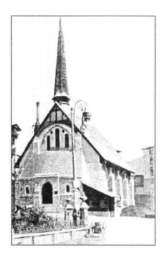

English Church, Davos

l. 20   *in the most elegant Tuscan prose*: the Tuscan poets Petrarch and Dante Alighieri created a standard for modern Italian.

l. 21   *idioma gentile*: gracious manner of speech. *L'idioma gentile* was the title of a style-book written by Edmondo di Amicis, who died in 1908.

l. 23   *after Virgil's models*: in Virgil's *Eclogues* the shepherds of Arcadia reflect on life and the human condition, against the backdrop of green pastures, orchards and fields with plump sheep—in a golden age when human beings lived in harmony with nature. Similarly, in his *Georgics* Virgil described the agricultural conditions under which humanity could live peaceful and productive lives.

l. 31   *Hofrat*: see note to p. 60, l. 17.

l. 31   *an imp of Satan*: i.e. a servant of the devil, appropriate for a place that Settembrini considers to be Hell. Cf. note to p. 59, l. 5.

ll. 32f.   *our shameless father confessor*: Krokowski stands for every-thing counter to Settembrini's view of life and everything that he opposes: the mysteries of the psyche, the inexplicable in human behavior (cf. also "monkish excesses"). The phrase "father confessor" also implies that for some of his patients Krokowski fulfils a quasi-religious role.

(95) ll. 16ff.   *sick and stupid*: Castorp's musings on the relationship between illness and stupidity are further evidence of his intellectual pro-gress. These thoughts anticipate those of Naphta later, cf. p. 456, ll. 35ff.

l. 39   *Sapristi*: Good gracious!

l. 41 *you would have to be less healthy than you give the appearance of being*: unbeknownst to all of them—Settembrini, Joachim, Castorp himself—the latter is, indeed, less healthy than he looks.

(96) l. 14 *Placet experiri*: it is pleasant to experiment. Cf. the narrator's comment on p. 153, ll. 30 ff.: "But he was willing to let himself be influenced, in the sense that it was pleasant to experiment..." This becomes one of the most important lessons that Hans Castorp learns from Settembrini. The pleasure in examining different ideas and subjecting them to critical scrutiny is a central pedagogical principle. Experiment-ation and the heightening of his consciousness are two primary elements of Hans Castorp's progress. It is, however, ironic that in following Settem-brini's advice, Castorp will distance himself from the Italian's views.

ll. 17ff. *I fear the presence of a tendency*: Settembrini astutely per-ceives Castorp's innate predilection for the "darker" side of life and begins his "campaign" to save him. However, all of Settembrini's attempts to promote a "healthy" view of life in Hans Castorp—a commitment to work, progress and enlightenment—are doomed from the start to failure, because his philosophy of life represents a narrow viewpoint that ignores or represses those aspects of life to which Hans Castorp is attracted.

ll. 29f. *such a view is itself a sickness, or leads to it*: Settembrini attempts to warn Castorp of the danger of regarding illness as something honorable. For Settembrini, the view expounded by Castorp that illness "has something more or less venerable about it" (p. 95, l. 22) must be flatly rejected. Such an attitude, in his opinion, signals a return to an age before reason and civilization, and age of superstition ("it comes from an era of superstitious contrition"—ll. 30f.), fear and chaos. The vehemence of Settembrini's response reveals both his passionate advocacy of reason and enlightenment, and his fear that reason has not yet won the day against the forces of darkness. With these remarks Settembrini is drawing the battle-lines between himself and Chauchat, and (later) himself and Naphta. In fact, Settembrini's remarks here are an unwittingly ironic reflection (in advance) of precisely what Naphta will say when he arrives at the Berghof, even to the repetition of the same vocabulary. Settembrini's assertion that the human soul is involved in a battle with the forces of unreason and darkness is not only a warning to Hans Castorp, but it is also a signal to the reader that this battle will be waged in the course of the novel. Settembrini's exhortation to Hans Castorp to regard work in the service of progress as the bastion against the darker forces of existence has already been undermined by Hans Castorp's demonstrated doubts about his chosen profession and his obvious innate inclination to lassitude.

l. 38   *earthly labor*: the greatest manifestation of reason on earth is represented by work—for the benefit of humanity. This is the reason why Settembrini was so encouraged on learning Hans Castorp's profession, as he could see in Castorp an ally in his battle for reason and progress.

(97) l. 8   *Backsliding*: a return to the Dark Ages represents for Settembrini the end of humanity. The word becomes a leitmotif that recurs in connection with Hans Castorp's intellectual growth. In the figure of Castorp the battle is waged between reason and progress on the one hand, and unreason, freedom and sloth on the other (cf. Naphta). The term is crucial element in Hans Castorp's conclusions about life at the end of the sub-chapter *Fullness of Harmony* (cf. p. 642, ll. 40ff.).

l. 12   *various names*: the two terms to which Settembrini is obliquely referring are not immediately obvious. He seems to be referring in the first instance to the psychoanalytic interpretation, as practiced by Freud in his *Leonardo da Vinci and a Memory of His Childhood* (1910), and in the second instance to "conservative reaction" (which will be Naphta's fundamental position). Settembrini finds them to be so worthless, that they may be dispensed with.

l. 17   *and you along with it*: Castorp's somewhat exploratory reflections on the relationship between illness and stupidity represent for Settembrini the offering of his little finger to the devil. Settembrini's fear that Castorp might fall totally victim to the "devil" of irrationality and darkness is justified: Castorp has already started down that slippery path.

l. 24   *an aberration*: for Settembrini there is nothing noble in sickness. While one may sympathize with the individual who is sick, the very concept of sickness is repulsive to the world of reason.

ll. 31f.   *the real tragedy begins*: tragedy ensues when Nature makes the harmony of the personality impossible. The combination of a noble mind with a sickly body is tragic (cf. Settembrini himself).

l. 35   *Leopardi*: Giacomo Leopardi (1798–1837), greatest Italian poet since Petrarch (and editor of the latter's works), who was sickly his whole short life. His fundamentally pessimistic view of life was compensated by writing about the themes of youth, beauty and love in strict classical form.

(98) ll. 17f.   *a human being who lives as an invalid*: a body without spirit (mind) is for Settembrini a denial of humanity.

ll. 21f.   *you said something very similar*…: Joachim remembers Castorp's earlier remarks (p. 69, ll. 27ff.), but Castorp claims not to remember them. While Joachim is factually accurate about Castorp's earlier reflections, they did not contain the philosophical conclusions that Settembrini draws.

ll. 30f.   *temporarily experimenting*: Settembrini captures very aptly the nature of Castorp's experiences at the Berghof: he is engaged in philosophical experiments.

l. 31   *a page where everything has already been written*: if Settembrini is correct, that Castorp's "soul" contains potentially all that is good and bad, then he is fully conscious of the battle that is ahead of him: the influences that might potentially draw Castorp away from him and reason are, as Settembrini well knows, present in full measure at the Berghof (hence his earlier advice to Castorp to leave forthwith).

l. 33   *appealing inks*: the meaning is actually "invisible ink" which reveals itself when warmed or otherwise treated.

ll. 33f.   *the educator's task*: leaves no doubt that Settembrini sees himself as the mentor whose task it is to lead Castorp down the correct path. Note, however, that Settembrini's repeated urging of Castorp to return home and become an engineer signifies not a widening of philosophical perspective and life-experience, but a narrowing of them.

l. 36   *adopting a lighter tone*: informs us that Settembrini's earlier remarks were made in an insistent, serious manner.

(99) l. 2   *placet experiri*: see note to p. 96, l. 14.

ll. 10f.   *You have to be awfully careful*: Castorp's independence of mind and philosophical caution asserts itself whenever he is engaged by Settembrini.

l. 23   *Settembrini should have said...*: Castorp's critical acumen is not blunted by Settembrini's mellifluous manner of speech.

l. 35   *He hacks away at everything around him*: Castorp's conclusions about Settembrini's critical style are somewhat unfair—it is, for example, surely an exaggeration to say that Settembrini's analysis "makes things rather untidy and disorderly" (the word in the German is "degenerate").

ll. 39f.   *respect for people in general*: Joachim defends Settembrini by reminding his cousin that Settembrini's aim is the improvement of humanity as a whole.

ll. 42f.   *something rigorous*: the epithet that Castorp applies to Settembrini is ironical, since the same word will apply later to Settembrini's adversary Naphta. Castorp is correct in his perception that Settembrini attempts to exercise control, and his intuition that the Italian disapproves of Castorp's having purchased the blankets for the "rest cure" is also accurate: Settembrini cannot accept that Castorp might actually be staying at the Berghof for longer than originally planned.

(100) *Excursus on the Sense of Time*

ll. 24ff. *Only a few old veterans*: the translation attempts to capture the connotation of "service" in the original ("Altgediente"). "Service" to the cure is described with a word borrowed from military parlance.

ll. 27f. *a natural predisposition*: i.e. for the horizontal life-style and all that it symbolizes.

(101) ll. 6f. Ocean Steamships … *lay trembling*: underlining the conflict between his newly adopted life-style and the old.

ll. 10f. *the comfortable position furnished by the lounge chair:...:* another example of Castorp's liking for the "horizontal position."

l. 12 *difficult to analyze*: the verb "analyze" will pursue Hans Castorp as a leitmotif through the novel. Much as he strives to distance himself from Krokowski's psychoanalytic suggestions, time and again aspects of his character and facets of life that cannot be approached or explained by the power of reason come to the surface. This is the case here with the mysterious attraction of the lounge chair: his enjoyment of the experience has its roots in his natural tendency to lassitude and. ultimately in his "sympathy with death"—a realm that he has not yet explored.

ll. 16f. *nothing could possibly have offered more humane benefits*: the choice of the word "humane" ironically undermines the world of Settembrini for whom the seductive comfort of the "rest cure" is the very antithesis of what he would understand by "humane." In essence, the enjoyment of the lounge chair is "contrary to reason" (as Settembrini would say), but as it is a part of being human, it belongs in the realm of humanity. Here again we see how Hans Castorp emancipates himself from his humanistic pedagogue.

l. 29 *the stereoscopic viewer*: see note to p. 82, l. 5.

l. 29 *the kaleidoscopic tube*: see note to p. 82, l. 7f.

ll. 29f. *the cinematographic drum*: see note to p. 82, l. 10.

(103) ll. 12ff. *I've always found it odd...*: Hans Castorp's own experience at the Berghof has caused him to come to agree with Joachim (cf. p. 14, ll. 16ff.) and Settembrini (p. 56, ll. 26ff.).

He Tries Out His Conversational French

The title of this sub-chapter is ironic, as Castorp's "conversation" is no more than one sentence (nine words), for which he asks Joachim's confirmation afterwards that it was correct. However, this initial sally into French is a foretaste of his surprising and sudden fluency in that language in the sub-chapter *Walpurgis Nigh*t (329 ff.).

(104) ll. 6f. *Hans Castorp had to learn at every step*...: the process of his education continues—absorbing new experiences and reflecting about them, developing both his power of perception and his critical faculties.

l. 11   *the evening of his arrival*: cf. p. 10, l. 30.

l. 16   *moribundi*: the dying (Latin plural).

ll. 22f. *our summer season*...: cf. note to p. 60, l. 22.

l. 28   *the crème de la crème*: literally: "the cream of the cream," i.e. the very best, the élite.

l. 30   *just for educational purposes*: the translation flattens out an important reference. In the original Behrens tells Castorp that observing the "crème de la crème" he would "do something for [his] education." Since these visitors "leap ... about on planks tied to their feet" (i.e. skis), this amounts to Behrens encouraging Castorp to pursue skiing—which he does, with significant consequences for Castorp's "education" (cf. sub-chapter *Snow*, pp. 460ff.).

l. 33   *eminently amorous*: Behrens hints once again at Castorp's future. In the original the word translated as "amorous" is "gallant"— which recurs at the beginning of the sub-chapter *Walpurgis Night* in a direct quote from Goethe's *Faust* (cf. p. 316, l. 28).

l. 34   *moribundus*: a dying person (Latin).

l. 35   *fiascoes*: the word has the secondary meaning of "flask" or "bottle"—hence Behrens is making a pun.

l. 36   *joining his ancestors by noon*: "ancestors" is the translation for the original "ad penates" (Latin) in the novel, which evokes the Roman gods of hearth and home who were called Lares and Penates. Behrens uses the names again on p. 178, l. 21. Castorp absorbs the phrase and uses it on p. 290, l. 35 in a conversation with Joachim—during which he recalls this event with Behrens.

(105) l. 1 *moribundus*: see note to p. 104, l. 34.

ll. 6f.   *Hans Castorp instinctively tried to make the same ... eyes*: This imitation occurs at the precise moment that he bumps into Chauchat. This chance and humorous episode connotes the connection of Chauchat with death ("l'amour et la mort").

l. 13   *soundlessly, supplely*: the alliteration aptly conveys the quality of Chauchat's movement. The epithets used to describe Chauchat are not only her leitmotifs, they also connote her "cat-like" qualities.

l. 33   *Coburg*: city in Bavaria, until 1918 the capital of the Duchy of Saxe-Coburg-Gotha. Albert of Saxe-Coburg-Gotha married Queen Victoria of Great Britain in 1840.

(107) ll. 11f. *Tous les dé*...: mispronunciation for "tous les deux" (= both of them). Both of them, sir. Both of them, you know.

ll. 13f.   *Je le sais, madame ... Et je le regrette beaucoup*: I know, madame, and I deeply regret it.

l. 18   *Merci*: Thank you.

ll. 23f.   *I can handle people like that very nicely*: Castorp's naïve self-confidence contains the deeper truth that he does, indeed, innately understand the nature of death.

l. 29   *I feel in my element somehow*: further confirmation of his inclination towards death.

ll. 34f.   *Don't you love to look at coffins?*: Castorp's remarks may be somewhat callow and ingenuous, but they represent the beginning of his later more mature reflections on death. The coffin in this speech will recur as the "coffin" of the record player (in *Fullness of Harmony*, pp. 626 ff.) where his mature reflections on life and death find expression. The description of a coffin as "an absolutely lovely piece of furniture" connects it directly to the record player (p. 627, ll. 15ff.).

(108) *Politically Suspect*

l. 9   *a band concert*: the German text speaks of "Kurmusik," which means both music that is played at a spa and (literally) "music that cures." The kind of music typically played at such a Sunday band concert would be light and harmless, therefore possibly "therapeutic."

l. 25   *lace peignoir*: properly speaking, a peignoir is a loose dressing-gown (e.g. worn while combing the hair); here it means an elegant morning-gown.

l. 29   *Königsberg*: the capital of East Prussia until 1945 (now called Kaliningrad).

l. 39   *scowled ... and blushed*: Castorp's discomfort as the appearance of the Russian couple is only one example of various features of the Berghof that cause him to turn red with embarrassment.

(109) l. 20   *A Midsummernight's Dream*: see note to p. 82, ll. 34f.

l. 38   *Dazed from the beer and the music...*: Castorp's reaction to music underscores further his tendency to formlessness. The effect of music on Hans Castorp, especially in the first half of the novel, is intox-icating—and in this respect Settembrini's assertion that music cripples the critical faculty is correct. Later in the novel (notably in the sub-chapter *Fullness of Harmony*, pp. 626ff.) one piece of music (the "Lindenbaum" —"The Linden Tree") assumes a profoundly pedagogical function that leads Castorp to significant insights about life.

(110) l. 34   *your harmonious state*: Settembrini's words are intended ironically.

l. 35   *Hans Castorp ordered his facial expression*: Settembrini's appearance causes Castorp—on more than one occasion—to "bring himself together" and to return to the Italian's world of reason and enlightenment.

(111) l. 2   *I am merely a visitor, much as you play the full-time visitor*: Settembrini uses the same word ("hospitieren") as on his first meeting with Hans Castorp (cf. p. 55, ll. 41f.).

ll. 19f.   *It is not true clarity...*: Settembrini represents the view of the strict rationalist that music dulls the senses, fogs the reason, and leads the listener into a world of illusions (cf. "I read that at once from your face as I arrived just now," p. 111, ll. 34f.). Hence his conclusion that music is "dangerous" (p. 111, l. 21), because it is a medium that inhibits progress by inducing reverie and impeding activity. Music "enslaves" the listener, is the work of the Devil, has the same effect as "opiates" (p. 112, l. 29), and leads to "quietism" (p. 111, l. 25). (These arguments reflect Nietzsche's criticism of Wagner's music as a "narcotic art" and "an opiate.") Quietism is a Christian philosophy that swept through France, Italy and Spain during the 17th century, but had much earlier origins. The mystics known as Quietists insist on intellectual stillness and interior passivity as essential conditions of perfection.

l. 27   *slapping his knee*: Castorp's frequent gesture that indicates both his enthusiasm and his naïveté (cf. p. 53, l. 32). In this case he is both surprised by Settembrini's remarks and skeptical of them.

ll. 33ff.   *And for you in particular...*: Settembrini has divined Castorp's inclination from afar ("I read that at once from your face"); cf. also p. 110, l. 36: "Hans Castorp ordered his facial expression." Music is "dangerous" for Castorp because it will lead him away from Settembrini's world of reason and clarity.

ll. 38f.   *I find it much more difficult...*: the process of "acclimatization" is more than merely physical: it is also philosophical and spiritual.

(112) ll. 1ff.   *It seems to me, however...*: these comments by Joachim about music and the passage of time are unusual for a man who is usually sparse of word and not given to reflection. Much later—after Joachim's death—the narrator comments that they represent "a certain alchemistic enhancement of his own character" (cf. p. 532, ll. 38f.).

l. 13   *seven minutes*: part of Thomas Mann's little game with the reader. Those who understand the author's game and who grasp the allusiveness of the text may feel some degree of aesthetic satisfaction in being part of the select group who "belong."

ll. 27f. *If it were to numb us…*: Settembrini's objects to music because it may dull the senses and inhibit action and progress. This is what happens when Castorp listens to music—and Settembrini even uses the same word the narrator had already used: "numb" (cf. p. 37, l. 1: "numbing"); thus Settembrini has once again drawn the battle-lines.

ll. 30f. *slavish inertia*: the word "slavish" will become a key word in Settembrini's debates with Naphta.

l. 33 *politically suspect*: by this he simply means that music does not contribute to human progress in the sense of positive activity for the purpose of furthering enlightenment.

ll. 34f. *Hans Castorp listened, too…*: Castorp's lack of attention to Settembrini's words and the ease with which he is distracted are indications of his rejection of Settembrini's views: Castorp retains his independence, especially where music is concerned.

ll. 34ff. *Hans Castorp … was unable to follow the argument*: another sign that he does not agree with Settembrini.

(113) l. 3 *The band was playing a polka*: the music is appropriate in the context: popular music is associated with "normal" relations between men and women.

Hippe

ll. 11f. *Clavadel, Flüelatal, Klosters*: places near Davos.

l. 20 *a light duster*: a long coat.

l. 20 *no hat*: one of the leitmotifs that indicate allegiance to the Berghof environment (cf. notes to p. 5, l. 32 & p. 39, l. 5).

l. 23 *rather boneless language*: associates the Russian language with the lack of form; thus the Russian language also plays a role as a leitmotif of formlessness throughout the novel.

ll. 33f. *Reminded him of something else…*: Cf. p. 70, ll. 33ff. where Joachim reacts to Hans Castorp's mention of Marusya's ample chest. Joachim's obvious attraction to Marusya is the occasion not only for hints of his lack of total devotion to the "service," but also allows the narrator to produce a humorous episode: Castorp is closely observing Joachim's reaction to Marusya and perceives that his cousin's gaze is anything but "military," and when Joachim comes to his senses and looks at Castorp, the latter quickly looks up at the sky.

(114) l. 11 *chaudfroid*: literally: warm-cold (French); chicken in gelée.

l. 17 *visitor*: the leitmotif "Hospitant" is used by the narrator (cf. note to p. 55, l. 41f.).

ll. 22f. *Love as a Force Conducive to Illness*: an appropriate topic in view of Hans Castorp's development at the Berghof.

l. 42 *We'll see if I'm not a new man when I get back*: Castorp will, indeed, be a different man when he gets back from his walk.

(115) ll. 23ff. *early morning air ... that evoked no memories*: Castorp is about to experience an ironic reversal of that thought.

l. 34 *handbooks of sport and business clubs*: a misleading mistranslation. The original ("Kommers- und Turnliederbücher") means "student and gymnastic club song-books." ("Kommers" does not mean "commerce"; rather, it comes from the Latin word "commercium" which was a traditional academic feast celebrated at universities in most Middle and Eastern European countries.) Student song-books were (and still are) very popular, and they were frequently used at social occasions of student clubs (in Thomas Mann's day there were also dueling student societies). The "gymnastic clubs" (whose function was more political and social than sporting) arose from the nationalistic gymnastic clubs founded by Friedrich Jahn (known as "the father of gymnastics") in 1811 and thereafter to foster national spirit and oppose the occupation of Prussia by Napoleon.

ll. 36f. [Verses]: the two lines are from the fourth verse of a popular student song that praises the old values of loyalty and virtue. (Verse: Matthias Claudius 1772; music: Albert Methfessel 1811.) The two lines quoted are particularly appropriate, as they touch on central issues in the novel (love, intoxication, virtue).

(116) l. 3 *well-rounded vowels of opera singers*: some commentators have seen a parody of Wagner here: the hero climbing a mountain and singing "with theatrical gestures" (l. 5) is reminiscent of scenes in Wagner's *The Ring of the Nibelung*.

l. 4 *fantasizing*: a too literal translation. In a musical context the verb in the original ("fantasieren") means "to improvise."

l. 14 *his neck was twitching so violently*: the connection with his grandfather is made explicit (cf. p. 23, ll. 34 ff.).

(117) ll. 4f. *the ground about was blue...*: the plant is the ranunculus, a major leitmotif of the novel. This plant, particularly in its blue form (which does not actually occur around Davos), is of crucial symbolical significance for the novel—and specifically for Hans Castorp's reflections about life. The bisexual nature of the flower relates to the connection between Hippe and Chauchat, and it lends special significance to the place where the memory of Hippe first occurred. He will repeatedly come back to this place—"his favorite spot" (p. 380, l. 34)—"now and then" (p. 380, l. 24), but only when Joachim is "tied up" (p. 380, ll. 31f.)—in other words, in secret. The leitmotif of the blue flower recurs on p. 358, ll. 1ff., where Castorp stresses its bisexual nature; p. 380, ll. 14ff.; p. 380, ll. 14ff.; p. 413, l. 35; & p. 417, l. 23.

The blue flower is a central symbol of German Romanticism, representing desire, love, and the yearning for the infinite. In the novel *Heinrich von Ofterdingen* (unfinished, publ. 1802) by Novalis (pseudonym for Georg Friedrich Philipp, Freiherr von Hardenberg, 1772–1801), the eponymous hero looks at the blue flower and dreams of his future love. In a similar manner, Hans Castorp looks at the blue ranunculus and dreams of Hippe—who is for him a precursor of his future love. The blue flower reflects the blue in the eyes of both Hippe and Chauchat (cf. p. 118, l. 17), and in the case of these two figures, looking into their eyes Castorp sees vague, distant vistas that hold a promise of something undefined: the intimation of a fulfillment, the satisfaction of an unformulated yearning—similar to the Romantic yearning expressed in the symbol of the blue flower. The blue color of distant mountains and of the deep snow arouse similar associations. The entire complex of motifs points to Hans Castorp's "yearning" for knowledge of life and his "sympathy with death."

ll. 28f.   *A dream filled with more recent impressions*: cf. pp. 88, ll. 40ff.

(118) l. 7   *Hippe*: Polish for "sickle"—and thus connected with death (after the conventional image of Death holding a sickle). The Slavic origin of Hippe and his similarity to Chauchat connects both of them with the realm of the "East" and its connotations in the novel: freedom, lassitude, love, and death. Castorp's attraction to Hippe as a young boy prepares his emotional development at the Berghof.

ll. 7ff.   *Pribislav*: the Polish pronunciation of the "r" as "sh" connects Hippe with Chauchat.

l. 14   *Mecklenburg*: North-German area east of the river Elbe, home to a mixture of settlers of both German and West-Slavic origin.

l. 16   *Slavic-Wendish*: although the geographical area described by these racial adjectives is somewhat vague—located somewhere in the East of Germany pre-1914—their intention is to associate Hippe with the "East" and therefore with Chauchat and the issues attaching to her.

l. 17   *But his eyes*: Hippe has the same colored eyes as Chauchat—blue-grey or grey-blue—and they are recalled by the color of the ranunculus. The fact that they recall the color of distant mountains further underscores the mystery of all the associations connoted by Hippe and Chauchat. The eyes are also narrow, hinting at something Asiatic.

l. 23   *the Kirghiz*: a widespread Asiatic tribe found in Turkey, Russia and Mongolia. Hippe's features suggest something Mongolian, hence his nickname (and his prominent cheekbones associate him with Chauchat [cf.

p. 143, 1. 27], who also has "khirgiz eyes," cf. p. 143, ll. 32f.). The purpose of this association is to indicate Hans Castorp's innate inclination towards the "East"—i.e. the spiritual world embodied by Chauchat that opposes the Western bourgeois ethic. Although Hippe is not of Asian extraction (let alone Kirghiz), he becomes a symbol of Asia in Hans Castorp's mind. His "Kirghiz eyes" remind Hans of distant mountains—but there are no mountains in Mecklenburg from where Hippe hails.

1. 33   *that husky ... voice*: a recurring leitmotif (cf. p. 120, 1. 22) that connects Hippe with Chauchat (cf. p. 327, ll. 26f.).

ll. 38f.   *a veiled dusky look*: this characterization of Hippe's eyes is identical to that of Chauchat (cf. p. 143, 1. 32f.), and evokes the mystery of their associations. The phrase "veiled dusky look" is an important leitmotif that relates to the mysterious power of love.

ll. 41f.   *It could not be called friendship...*: however, his "relation-ship" with Chauchat is based on even less contact.

(120) ll. 24f.   *And he pulled a pencil from his pocket*: the German text subtly replaces here the German word for "pencil" with the French loan-word "Crayon"—thus evoking a connection with Chauchat and eroticism.

ll. 26f.   *As he explained its simple mechanism...*: there are undertones of sexuality here: Castorp takes Hippe's pencil (= phallus) in his hand and does with it what Hippe tells him to do. The scene is repeated with Chauchat on p. 327, ll. 41ff. This dream-scene is followed by Hans Castorp's attendance at Krokowski's lecture "Love as a Force Conducive to Illness" (cf. p. 123, ll. 31ff.).

(121) 1. 3   *long, intimate relationship*: the translation is a little mis-leading. The original speaks (literally) of "the intimate intercourse with Hippe." The word "intercourse" in German means both everyday contact and sexual relations.

1. 17   *Is that why I have been so intrigued by her?*: The plausibility of Castorp's interest in Chauchat deriving from his memory of Hippe is not undermined by the reverse (i.e. that he was attracted to Hippe because he was interested in Chauchat). The point here is that he is predisposed to be attracted to the *type* that they represent, and thus also the corpus of ideas and attitudes that they embody. (The association of an earlier figure with a later love is a common device in German Romantic literature.)

(122) ll. 4f.   *Dépêchez-vous, monsieur ... La conférence de Monsieur Krokowski vient de commence*r: Hurry up, sir! Mr. Krokowski's lecture has just begun.

Analysis

The title of this sub-chapter is intended to be understood ironically. Krokowski's lecture is an ironic discourse on Freud's theory of the libido.

(122) ll. 32ff. *Frau Chauchat sat in a limp slouch...*: her posture implies her embodiment of "Eastern" attitudes and mentality.

(123) ll. 2f. *Frau Chauchat's careless posture*: the ideas that have been flowing into Castorp's mind are now coalescing into a corpus that brings him face to face with a view of life contrary to his former existence in Hamburg. Two things should be noted here. First, it is Castorp himself who draws all the necessary conclusions from his encounters. This is an important step in his "education" at the Berghof. Second, the conclusions he draws, while occasioned by external factors (e.g. Chauchat and her behavior) merely highlight aspects of his character that have always been present as potential. At this stage (during Krokowski's lecture) he is still confused and seeking clarity, but he has made significant progress, both by conscious and unconscious means, towards bringing the ideas symbolized by Chauchat and Hippe into focus. She will eventually lead him to conclude that love and death are in some way connected.

ll. 4f. *that same license Herr Albin had praised*: cf. p. 78, ll. 31 ff.

l. 31 *And what was Dr. Krokowski talking about?*: The following remarks by Krokowski are based on Freud's "Three Treatises on Sexual Theory" (1905). Thomas Mann does not cite them slavishly, but adapts them to fit in with the novel's themes.

(124) l. 15 *lingual and labial consonants*: only in the case of the pronunciation of the German word "Liebe" (love).

(125) ll. 1ff. *Logic demanded it...*: this paragraph is based on Freud's essay, where he argues that the sexual instinct has to fight against the resistance of moral powers such as shame and disgust. The latter are instrumental in keeping the sexual drive within bounds.

l. 25 *a Pyrrhic victory*: a victory gained at too great a cost. Named after King Pyrrhus of Epirus gained such a victory over the Romans in 279 BC at the battle of Asculum in Apulia.

ll. 28f. *in transmuted, unrecognizable form*: Krokowski's remarks apply to Castorp's state, although he may not yet be aware of it.

(126) l. 3 *illness was merely transformed love*: with direct application to Castorp. The idea is taken from Freud's essay where he states that the conflict between the sexual drive and the attempt to control it leads to illness. Krokowski's remarks, however, go one step further, and the author is satirizing him by placing such an extreme conclusion in his mouth.

l. 24   *corrective bourgeois forces*: Castorp has to overcome these before he can commit himself to Chauchat. After contemplating her arm in its sleeve of gauze, there are in respect of it no barriers any more.

l. 25   *But this arm was more beautiful...*: and it becomes a focal point of his obsession, cf. p. 319, ll. 26ff. & p. 322, ll. 4f.

(127) ll. 10ff.   *for a man to be interested in a sick woman...*: since Frau Chauchat is sick, Castorp assumes that she cannot have children; thus any affection for her would be the same as being attracted to Pribislav Hippe: i.e. homosexual. Despite Hans Castorp's rejection of the comparison as "stupid" (l. 13), the homosexual component is definitely present.

l. 18   *like Jesus on the cross*: Krokowski's appearance and words lend him a messianic dimension: psychoanalysis as religion—a religion through which he attempts to gain control over his patients.

l. 21   *Come unto me...*: cf. *Matthew* 11: 28: "Come unto me, all ye that labor and are heavy laden, and I will give you rest."

l. 36   *like a swarm of rats behind the Pied Piper*: the legend tells of an infestation of rats in the town of Hamelin. The Pied Piper promised to rid the town of the rats—which he did, leading them into the River Weser by playing his pipe, where they drowned. But the town refused to pay him the agreed fee—so later he returned and lured the children of the town into a cave and they were never seen again. In German the word "Rattenfänger" (rat catcher) now means a person who seduces the populace.

(128) l. 2   *he flinched*: once again Castorp is caught "napping"—his mind is on Chauchat when Joachim approaches and catches him off guard. (In the original he flinches "nervously.")

ll. 9f.   *Hans Castorp said nothing about it*: a sign of how deeply it has affected him? Certainly, it has given him much food for thought.

Doubts and Considerations

(128) l. 18   *psychological therapy...*: cf. note to p. 9, ll. 32f.

(129) ll. 17f.   *Above and behind him stood invisible forces ... an associate of those higher powers*: these terms add to the aura of mythology surrounding the Berghof. In the original the word "those" does not occur (it speaks merely of "higher powers"), which renders the phrase more mysterious and suggestive. Not only is Behrens subject to a higher authority (in the form of the owners of the sanatorium), but also to the "higher powers" that govern existence.

(130) l. 9   *also shared their sufferings*: Behrens is himself sick, and therefore better able to empathize with and treat his patients. The narrator asks: Can such a doctor, himself sick, really be as interested in combating illness as a healthy man would be?

l. 14   *guide and healer*: the two words used in the original connote also wider associations that go beyond the merely medical—for example, the German word "Heiland" can mean "healer," but its most common meaning is "savior."

l. 31   *auscultation*: technical term for listening to the internal sounds of the body (usually by means of a stethoscope).

ll. 36f.   *of whom Settembrini had spoken so scornfully*: cf. p. 59, ll. 13ff.

(131) ll. 8ff.   *the well-lit basement of the building...*: the topography of the Berghof is such that the "basement," where the doctor's offices are located, is still above ground. The description is intended to be understood symbolically: the doctors are situated between life and death.

l. 40   *Behind her ... it was much darker*: Krokowski's offices are "downstairs" and wreathed in twilight, as is only appropriate. The entire aura of Krokowski (his appearance, the location of offices, the twilight) connotes associations with Hades.

(132) *Table Talk*

ll. 4f.   *the grandfatherly tremor*: Hans Castorp's lack of physical control is not caused by senility (as in the case of his grandfather); rather it is an indication that his world of bourgeois stability has been shaken to its foundations by his recent experiences. His tremor has psychical causes— cf. l. 23 "was also the expression of an inner excitement."

ll. 28ff.   *Madame Chauchat almost always came late for meals*: this paragraph, that describes the development of Castorp's reaction to Chauchat's late arrivals in the dining-room and her banging of the door, is another example of the inherently comic—even farcical—nature of his behavior. One can understand his initial annoyance at her actions, but his obsession with her entrance—"with fidgeting feet" (and the German says that he "*couldn't* keep his feet still" [emphasis added])—quickly becomes comical. His disapproving look, sometimes accompanied by a muttered curse, gradually metamorphoses into guilt and shame that he is equally to blame for her actions. This is not the reaction of a mature individual.

(133) ll. 12f.   *bond ... that ... had moved to a higher plane*: there is, of course, no "bond" between Castorp and Chauchat. (The German uses the word "relationship.") So to talk of a "higher plane" is nonsense.

(134) l. 5   *Königsberg*: see note to p. 108, l. 29. However, it is not true that the city was located "not at all that far from the Russian border," so Hans Castorp is grasping at straws to see a connection between Chauchat and Russia on that basis.

ll. 19f. *She has a maiden name, a Russian one…*: Frau Chauchat's origins are a little vague. More important, however, is her spiritual connection to Russia and the "East."

l. 25   *a little basket for her keys*: if Frau Chauchat were a "normal" housewife who wore a wedding ring, she would also have a basket in which to keep the keys of the household, in order to maintain control over them.

l. 38   *the tremor of his head*: the talk about Chauchat causes him to lose control; cf. note to p. 132, ll. 4f.

l. 41   *Daghestan*: in the North Caucasus, the southernmost part of Imperial Russia. Chauchat's husband is French, but he works for the Russian government in the colony of Daghestan—an oil-producing region. Some commentators have viewed this as a veiled reference to the competition for oil between European nations at this time.

Daghestan

(135) l. 23   *his wobbling head*: his criticism of Frau Chauchat is a ploy to hide his real state: he is deeply unsettled by his attraction to her.

l. 26   *I would not trust her out of my sight*: more accurately: "I wouldn't trust her an inch." As the narrator remarks ("That was how he worked it sometimes"; l. 30), this is merely a ploy by Castorp to find out more about Chauchat.

ll. 29f.   *With a cunning that was actually foreign to him...*: In fact, on many occasions in the novel Castorp behaves in a cunning manner. Cf. the number of times that Castorp plots ways to meet Chauchat.

ll. 36f. *You did dream about lovely Minka...*: another example of Castorp's "cunning": if anyone is likely to dream of Chauchat, it is sure Castorp himself. (The narrator confirms that this was once again an example of Castorp's "unnatural cunning" [p. 136, l. 26], but the frequency of these occasions renders the narrator's disclaimer ironic.)

(137) l. 12   *English quarter*: see note to p. 93, l. 14f.

ll. 30f.   *He hummed a little song*: the song that he has heard somewhere before and that he now finds "inside himself" is directly applicable to Chauchat. The fact that he is about to voice the third and fourth lines (obviously relating to Chauchat) which are well known to him indicates the subconscious process that is taking place. His reaction to his own behavior is a combination of his "old" manners ("austere") and his growing new attitude ("melancholy"). Although he concludes that the tune is "tasteless and insipidly sentimental," and only appropriate to a conventional affair on the "Flatland," the fact remains that it has in his mind been connected unconsciously with Chauchat. In wishing to reject this fact after the event Castorp is endeavoring to raise his "relationship" with Chauchat on to a higher plane (i.e. more elevated than a conventional episode "down below"). The humor of the situation lies in the fact that there is no relationship at all and that his conscious and overt comments about her have so far all been negative. The unconscious process, however, has been continuing unabated, and the involuntary emergence of the song—which he clearly relates to her—is an indication of this. The song, in fact, becomes a leitmotif that is mentioned whenever Castorp wishes to contrast his love for Chauchat with the (in his view) more superficial type of love down on the "Flatland" (cf. p. 226, ll. 21f. & p. 336, l. 17).

ll. 35ff.   *'How oft it thrills me...'*: lines from a song by Czech composer Franz Bendel (1833–1874) that was very popular at that time. The emergence of this "gentle bit of nonsense" (l. 34) is another example of how music gives expression to Castorp's subconscious desires, but it is also ironic that he who despises such superficial tunes as belonging to the Flatland and who scorns the "love" that they express and symbolize, would nevertheless conjure up such a song involuntarily when thinking of Chauchat. Indeed, even though he considers the words to be inappropriate, "he knew of nothing more suitable to replace them with" (p. 138, ll. 13f.).

(138) ll. 9f. *the word "relationship" must be credited to Hans Castorp*: not quite true; the word had been used by the narrator earlier (cf. note to p. 133, l. 12f.) in relation to Castorp and Chauchat (the verbal parallel is lost in the translation). In any case, what has happened so far is entirely inside Castorp's head (and heart): there is no real relationship.

Growing Anxiety. Two Grandfathers and a Twilight Boat Ride

l. 34 *Schatzalp*: see note to p. 9, ll. 19f.

(139) ll. 6f. *felt his days were full enough*: preoccupied with Chauchat.

ll. 13f. *the initial refreshment of his sense of time...*: cf. p. 102, pp. 6ff.

l. 22 *'how oft it thrills me'*: see note to p. 137, ll. 35ff..

ll. 24ff. *It was impossible for Madame Chauchat...*: Hans Castorp's "relationship" to Chauchat reveals a young man who is clearly very immature and naïve ("ordinary"), and his behavior towards her is at times farcical and even uncivil. The fact that he is fully aware that his behavior is unreasonable ("irrational") cannot prevent him from behaving the way he does: he is driven to approach her, one way or the other (this is an example of Schopenhauer's "Will" in action). We should also be aware that the narrator is enjoying himself immensely as he describes Castorp's antics. The detailed description of Castorp's attempts to catch Chauchat's eye, his "sensing" that she is looking at him, his deliberate avoidance of her gaze, his jumping up to save her napkin from falling to the floor—all these things, we are asked to believe, take place across a distance of eight yards (p. 140, ll. 14f.).

(140) l. 4 *the Kirghiz eyes*: the same as Hippe's, cf. p. 118, l. 23.

l. 18 *she scowls*: the original German uses the leitmotivic phrase "with a darkened look" ("verfinstert") which recalls Hans Castorp's own look when he heard the amorous antics of the Russian couple in the next room. Frau Chauchat's annoyance at losing her napkin is described in exaggerated terms by the narrator in order to exploit further the "relationship" between her and Castorp. The use of the leitmotivic phrase associates her reaction to dropping her napkin with Castorp's reaction to the inappropriate behavior of his "bad" Russian neighbors.

l. 28 *a negative form*: Chauchat's avoidance of Castorp (all because she almost dropped her napkin and blamed him) is to him evidence that they have a relationship.

l. 39 *other reasons of regimen...*: presumably Joachim wishes to avoid the unhealthy preoccupation with persons Russian.

ll. 41ff.   *whatever the aim of his desires…*: the conscious struggle in Castorp's mind is between his awareness that he is attracted to Chauchat and the knowledge that he cannot possibly approve of her in a formal, social way. His upbringing and all the values he has brought with him from Hamburg cause him consciously to reject all that she stands for socially. The grandson of Hans Lorenz Castorp (the narrator's use of this manner of describing Hans Castorp here underlines the traditions and social values the latter embodies and that Hans Castorp shares—see note to p. 18, ll. 23f.) can have nothing to do formally and socially with a person who in almost every respect flouts the social conventions of the world in which Castorp grew up. However, when the narrator informs us that "deep chasms separated her existence from his" (p. 141, ll. 14f.), that is not intended to be understood only on the superficial level of social convention, but also (and primarily) it indicates the abyss between the whole corpus of metaphysical values underlying her world-view compared to the one he has inherited and with which he has been indoctrinated. His arrogance about the superiority of his attitude to hers stems not from his nature, but rather from the inherent arrogance of the culture in which he was raised (cf. "a more general and traditional sort," p. 141, ll. 17f.)—a feeling of superiority, however, that is ironically undermined by the description of "the drowsy look in his eyes" (p.141, l. 18): in Thomas Mann's fictional world men of conviction do not have any doubts at all and look at the world unambiguously.

The final self-justification for Castorp's attitude is that this is merely a "a vacation adventure" (p. 141, l. 33), that would never be approved by any man of reason (i.e. Castorp himself), and that in any case he could not possibly get involved with her in an sense at all because she is sick—and the exaggerated manner in which he describes her ("sick, listless, feverish, and worm-eaten deep inside," p. 141, ll. 35f.) ironically undermines his conscious rejection of her. In fact, he (consciously) relates her questionable mode of existence ("the dubious nature of her whole being," p. 141, l. 37) directly to her sickness. This is all a mere rationalization that is belied by his irresistible subconscious attraction to her and what she represents.

(141) l. 40   *for better or worse*: Castorp has ostensibly rejected any social contact with Chauchat, yet as much as he pretends to keep his "relationship" with her on a conscious level, he knows that his attraction to her has another dimension—the emotional. This is underscored by his conclusion that his "tender relationship" (p. 142, l. 3; another exaggeration) to Chauchat constitutes the real purpose of his stay at the Berghof. He is not aware, of course, of the irony of this conclusion since the "real purpose" of his stay at the Berghof will be to expose himself to the alternative set of values that Chauchat represents.

(142) l. 20 *he made a point of being late himself*: Castorp's antics are once again a source of humor.

l. 27 *room 7*: Chauchat's room, one floor beneath Castorp's room. Her room number is the sum of the figures in his: 34.

(143) l. 15 *this meeting had a powerful effect*: the encounter is also intended to be understood metaphorically—in other words, Castorp's close confrontation is not simply with Chauchat's face, but with all that she represents. This is underscored by the fact that he becomes aware of the significance of the meeting "only when it was all over" (p. 143, l. 16). In other words, he reflects upon this and draws conclusions from it. The detailed analysis of Chauchat's head and face (p. 143, ll. 17ff.) is improbable on the basis of a brief encounter, but it is significant because of its transferred metaphorical meaning: it is the "features" that the face represents that make such a deep impression on him. The translation here fails to convey the deliberate ambiguity of the original: Thomas Mann cleverly uses the ambiguous word "Bildung" which does mean the structure of the face (its features), but also the "culture" that it represents. We are told by the narrator that this "Bildung," although it is "foreign," had long been familiar to him ("familiar to him for so long now," p. 143, l. 22): her face—and especially her eyes (cf. "magical")—remind him of Pribislav Hippe, and the narrator uses the same vocabulary to describe the two characters ("Kirghiz-shaped eyes," "bluish-gray or grayish-blue like distant mountains," "a veiled dusky look," p. 143, ll. 32f.; cf. p. 118, ll. 17f., 36f., 38f.).

(144) l. 5 *It was thrilling in every sense of the word*...: The emotions and memories that Chauchat's face has stirred up in Castorp cause him deep anxiety: he senses that a realm has been awakened within him that endangers all the breeding and education that has brought with him to the Berghof. (The narrator's word in German is "erschütternd" which means "shattering.") His fear is intensified by the knowledge that what is happening to him is inevitable or inescapable ("as if he were locked up together with something inevitable or inescapable," p. 144, ll. 10f.), and he feels the urgent need for help ("a search for help … advice and support," p. 144, ll. 14ff.). Furthermore, he thinks of "various people" to whom he might turn for help and support (p. 144, l. 16)—Joachim, Behrens, and Settembrini. The encounter with Chauchat and his reaction to it represent a major upheaval in his life. Things will never be the same again. In the hermetic world of the Berghof sanatorium the elements are in place to produce a major reaction.

ll. 7f.   *that suffocating feeling...*: cf. p. 142, ll. 6f.

ll. 18   *Joachim ... whose eyes had taken on such a sad expression...*: this and Joachim's frequent shrugs are increasingly strong signs of his eventual fate.

l. 21   *Blue Henry*: see note to p. 7, l. 39.

(145) ll. 14ff.   *Joachim's good example ... had a dubious side as well*: if Joachim's devotion to the cure has an element of doubt for Castorp, what could that be, if not the latter's doubt about the purpose of being cured at all?

l. 20   *strange and perverse*: one might expect that it would be life at the Berghof that would be described in this manner. Hans Castorp's alienation from life down on the "Flatland" proceeds apace.

l. 22   *turning himself into a veritable mummy*: the image is intended to evoke death in the context of the novel's wider discussion of idleness, sickness and death.

l. 31   *sine pecunia*: see note to p. 45, l. 17.

ll. 33f.   *The Magic Flute*: cf. note to p. 59, ll. 2f.

ll. 37f.   *a restive longing for paternal authority*: in travelling to the Berghof Castorp has been compelled to brave the new adventures and experiences alone, which for an "ordinary young man" is a daunting and unsettling proposition. His innate need for fatherly advice is a sign that he has not yet matured into a fully independent adult.

(146) ll. 18f.   *naysayer, windbag, and* homo humanus: the three terms used by Castorp to characterize Settembrini are significant, since they reveal Castorp's problematical relationship with the Italian. The fact that Settembrini appears repeatedly in Castorp's "exceedingly vivid dreams" (p. 146, l. 23), as a figure to be repressed, reveals what is taking place in Castorp's mind when he is asleep; he is clearly dreaming of Chauchat, and his conscience (in the guise of Settembrini) interferes with his dreams. In his waking life, Castorp is less inclined to dismiss Settembrini as a pest: on the contrary, we are told that he listens to him "eagerly, but cautiously and attentively, too" (p. 146, ll. 38f.)—in other words: receptive, but critical.

l. 36   *Placet experiri*: see note to p. 96, l. 14.

l. 37   *homo humanus*: see note to p. 57, l. 39.

(147) ll. 5f.   *with his ankles crossed*: as they had been when Hans Castorp first met him, cf. p. 54, l. 17.

l. 11   *I beg admission to this noble circle*: another allusion to Wagner's *Tannhäuser*. Wolfram (one of the minnesingers) stands in contrast to Tannhäuser as the opposite of Venus, so Settembrini represents the antipode of Chauchat. Cf. p. 632, ll. 5–6, where Wolfram's aria is quoted. Re *Tannhäuser*, see note to p. 83, l. 17.

ll. 20f. *with graveyard blossoms on her cheeks*: purple blotches on the cheeks that were a sign of advanced tuberculosis.

l. 21 *Transylvania*: a region in the central part of Romania. The German word for Transylvania was "Siebenbürgen," after the colonization of the area by the so-called "Siebenbürgen Saxons" in the Middle Ages. (The origin of the name "Siebenbürgen" remains a mystery.) The translation loses the play on the number seven ("sieben").

l. 24 *hastily vacated the primroses*: she means "vacated the premises."

ll. 33ff. *the tortures of Tantalus*: Frau Stöhr confuses Tantalus with Sisyphus. The former was punished for his misdeeds by being tantalized. He was hanged forever from a tree in Tartarus afflicted with tormenting thirst and hunger. Under him was a pool of water, but when he stooped to drink from it, the pool would sink from sight. The tree above him was laden with several kinds of fruit, but when he reached up, the wind blew the branches away. Sisyphus was condemned for ever to push huge boulder up a hill, only to watch it roll back down, and to repeat this throughout eternity.

l. 36 *a little variety*: Settembrini makes gentle fun of Frau Stöhr (without her being aware of it, of course) by complimenting her on giving Tantalus some variety in his punishment: for a change he gets to push the boulder up the hill.

l. 40 *doppelgänger*: a double.

l. 40 *astral bodies*: invisible spirit bodies that contain the soul.

(148) l. 1 *reticule*: she means, of course, ridicule.

l. 11 *cinematographo*: early form of cinema.

ll. 13f. *some sort of meringues*: the original uses the word "Baisers" that means both meringues and kisses. Settembrini thus exploits the double-entendre.

l. 21 *Cannstatt*: see note to p. 15, l. 3.

ll. 23f. *you partook of these meringues in the company of a gentleman*: since Settembrini again uses the word "Baisers" the ambiguity is highly suggestive.

l. 30 *foamy meringues*: the original contains no word "foamy," but is even more suggestive: "… your spiritual part was having fun in the company of Captain Miklosch and his "Baisers" (meringues/kisses)."

(149) l. 5 *in Baccho et ceteris*: Settembrini's quotation in Latin is truncated: he replaces the second half of the quotation by the words "et ceteris" ("et cetera")—and in so doing he hides the fact that the last word should be "Venere," that is to say: Venus. The person referred to, Anton Schneermann, has been over-indulging himself in wine (Bacchus) and love (Venus). Throughout the novel associations are drawn between the Magic Mountain ("Zauberberg") and the Venusberg (see notes to p. 83, l. 17 & 632, l. 5).

ll. 15f. *a rib resection*: a procedure in which ribs are removed in order to permit better access to the lungs to treat them.

l. 19   *Mytilene*: capital city of the Greek island of Lesbos.

l. 22   *Friedrichshafen*: Friedrichshafen is a town on the northern side of Lake Constance in southern Germany, near the borders with Switzerland and Austria. It was most likely from here that Hans Castorp took ship to cross Lake Constance at the beginning of his odyssey (cf. note to p. 3, l. 10).

ll. 31f.   *Cautious, attentive, puzzled, but willing to let himself be influenced*: The two words "cautious, attentive" represent a leitmotif (more accurately: "attentively examining"; cf. p. 146, ll. 38f.). This leitmotif characterizes Castorp's attitude to everything that Settembrini says. Castorp is open being influenced by the Italian and is happy to listen to the Italian who opens for him a strange new world ("a strange and very new world," p. 149, l. 33). It is the attitude of a person who wishes to learn, to be introduced to new ideas and experiences, but who will retain an attitude of critical objectivity and reach his own conclusions.

ll. 34ff.   *his grandfather who had been a lawyer in Milan...*: Settembrini's grandfather would have been alive in the period when Milan and Northern Italy was controlled by Austria in the middle of the nineteenth century. The Austrian Field Marshall Radetzky was forced to withdraw from the city temporarily. However, after defeating Italian forces at Custoza on July 24, 1848, he was able to reassert Austrian control over Milan and northern Italy. Italian nationalists, championed by the Kingdom of Sardinia, called for the removal of Austria in the interest of Italian unification. Sardinia and France formed an alliance and defeated Austria at the Battle of Solferino in 1859, after which Milan and the rest of Lombardy were incorporated into the Kingdom of Sardinia, which soon gained control of most of Italy and in 1861 was rechristened as the Kingdom of Italy. The characteristics of Settembrini's grandfather are closely based on the figure of the Italian freedom-fighter Guiseppe Mazzini (1813–76).

(150) l. 1   *Austria and the Holy Alliance*: The Holy Alliance was a coalition of Russia, Austria, and Prussia, created in 1815, at the behest of Tsar Alexander I of Russia, signed by the three powers in Vienna on September 26, 1815. Ostensibly, it was to instill the Christian values of justice, love and peace in European political life, but in practice the Austrian Minister, Prince Metternich, made it a bastion against democratic movements.

l. 4 *Carbonaro*: the Carbonari (literally: "charcoal burners") were secret revolutionary societies founded in early 19th-century Italy (mainly in Naples), to resist the Napoleonic occupation. Later, their goals were patriotic and liberal (opposed to conservative regimes), and they played an important role in the early years of Italian nationalism. They were also Freemasons (which bound them closer together), with whom Settembrini himself is allied.

ll. 22f. *patriotic feelings ... established order*: a typical German inclination that would come naturally to Hans and Joachim because of their upbringing and political education. Cf. note to p. 175, ll. 25f.

l. 30   *Turin*: in 1821 the Carbonari led an uprising in Turin that led to the abdication of King Victor Emmanuel I (1759–1824).

l. 31   *Prince Metternich*: 1773–1859, the most important diplomat of his era, dominated Austrian (and European politics) from 1815–1848.

ll. 32f.   *in Spain ... the Hellenic peoples*: in the nineteenth century Spain was a country in turmoil. It was occupied by the French under Napoleon from 1808 to 1814, and a brutal "war of independence" was waged against the occupiers that led to an emergent Spanish nationalism. An era of reaction against the liberal ideas associated with revolutionary France followed the war, personified by the rule of Ferdinand VII and—to a lesser extent—his daughter Isabella II. A series of civil wars then broke out, pitting Spanish liberals and then republicans against conservatives, culminating in the Carlist Wars (1833–1876). The Ottomans ruled Greece until the early 19th century. On March 25, 1821, the Greeks rebelled and declared their independence, but did not achieve it until 1829.

l. 39   *Milan*: see note to p. 149, l. 35.

(151) l. 14   *the form appropriate to him—the Spanish ruff*: Hans Lorenz Castorp clung to tradition and his ruff was a bastion against decay and death; but at the same time in its rigid form the ruff also symbolizes death. The two grandfathers signify two different views of the world: Hans's grandfather clung to the past; Settembrini's wanted to overthrow the past/present and create a new world.

ll. 18f.   *he honestly did attempt...*: Castorp's open-mindedness and his reflecting about what he has learned indicate the process of education that is taking place within him.

ll. 22f. *he saw him round his lips...*: in English one does not round one's lips to form the syllable "great," but one does so in German for the word "Ur" in the original (cf. note to p. 21, l. 23).

l. 25   *the tricolor*: the flag of Italy (with vertical bands of green, white, and red).

l. 38   *yes, those were two worlds...*: Hans Castorp's reflections about the two grandfathers demonstrate considerable awareness of and perspicacity towards the historical, political, and philosophical differences between them. Once again the key word in his reflections is "casting a critical eye" (p. 151, l. 41)—and the word used in the original is "prüfend," which the narrator had already used on p. 149, l. 31 ("aufmerksam prüfend"; in the translation: "cautious"). This critical attitude towards Settembrini's ideas had already been apparent earlier: cf. p. 146, ll. 38ff. ("eagerly, but cautiously and attentively, too").

l. 41   *casting a critical eye*: Hans Castorp assumes a position in the middle, viewing both sides critically—the location that the narrator reserves for him throughout the novel.

ll. 41ff.   *it seemed to him ...*: the memory of his strange boat trip at twilight offers Castorp a metaphor for the two worlds represented by Hans Lorenz Castorp and Giuseppe Settembrini. The paragraph illustrates Thomas Mann's double-layered style: this is the realistic description of a boat-trip, but at the same time the account is intended also to be read symbolically. In the West the sun shines and there is daylight (Apollo, Settembrini, enlightenment), while in the East the moon can be seen (Dionysus, Chauchat, night). Significant here is that the scene ends in darkness: the sun disappears and Castorp is left looking at the night sky. Metaphorically, he is prepared for the "darker" side of life represented by Chauchat.

(152) l. 31   *given the palm*: i.e. the symbol of victory.

l. 37   *helping humankind reach moral perfection*: for Settembrini, technology is a means to an end. Insofar as technology improves the material lot of humanity it can contribute to the real aims of life: bringing nations closer together (p. 153, l. 1), achieving peace, and eliminating suffering.

(153) l. 10   *Technology and morality*: Settembrini has once more caused Castorp to expand his thinking, for Castorp had never before connected technology with morality.

l. 14   *the great French Revolution*: for Settembrini the French Revolution (1789) represents the first attempt to enshrine the equality and unity of humankind in a nation's constitution.

l. 19   *July Revolution in Paris*: the three days at the end of July 1830, when the people rose up and deposed the autocratic King Charles X (1757–1836).

l. 22   *Hans Castorp could not help banging his hand on the table*: a typical reaction when he is excited about a new idea (cf. pp. 53, l. 32 & p. 111, l. 27). However, he takes Settembrini's comparison of the three days of the July Revolution in 1830 with the six days of creation with more than a grain of salt: after further reflection he even finds it "absolutely offensive" (p. 153, l. 29).

ll. 30f.   *It was pleasant to experiment*: Hans Castorp has adopted Settembrini's suggestion ("placet experiri"; cf. note to p. 96, l. 14)—which will be his attitude for the rest of the novel.

l. 39   *Hans Castorp knew why he listened to Herr Settembrini...*: Hans Castorp's "reasons" for listening to Settembrini are now no longer based on a curiosity to hear his views, but rather on duty, politeness, and on the fact that he doesn't have to take them seriously. He describes himself as a visitor (using the same word as before: "Hospitant"; see note to p. 55, l. 41) who will be able to escape without taking a position. He has already left Settembrini's rationalist fold and moved to the Chauchat camp.

l. 41   *visitor*: he uses the leitmotif "Hospitant" (cf. note to p. 55, ll. 41f.).

(154) l. 4   *the qualms of conscience...*: Castorp listens to Settembrini knowing full well that in his own mind, Chauchat is in the background.

ll. 9f.   *two principles were locked in combat...*: this speech outlines Settembrini's view of the world—and the essential struggle in the novel. Settembrini's division of the "world" into the Asiatic principle and the European is, in essence, the dualism that Thomas Mann employs in the structure of the novel. The elements that Settembrini lists as being typical of each category are the same elements that compete in and for Hans Castorp's mind and soul.

ll. 22f.   *when monarchies and religions would at last collapse*: Settembrini is an unrepentant republican and atheist.

l. 24   *an eighteenth century*: i.e. a century of rationalism and enlightenment.

l. 24   *a 1789*: i.e. a revolution such as the one in France that had overthrown a feudal monarchy.

l. 28   *a new Holy Alliance*: See note to p. 150, l.1. The monarchs of the three countries involved, Russia, Austria and Prussia, (cf. "that thrice-infamous alliance") used this alliance to band together in order to prevent revolutionary influence (especially from the French Revolution) from entering these nations. The old Alliance stood against democracy, revolution, and secularism. Settembrini's vision is, of course, of a new Alliance that would be secular, democratic, and republican.

l. 32f.   *the Asiatic principle of bondage and obduracy*: as we shall later learn, this is the world-view of Settembrini's opponent Naphta. Before the latter even appears on the scene, his world-view is rejected.

ll. 33f.   *in Vienna*: Settembrini's attack on Vienna is motivated both by historical resentment ("to avenge past wrongs") and by the belief that the Hapsburgs (it is 1907 and they still rule the Austro-Hungarian Empire from Vienna) continue to represent the forces of reaction endangering his vision for the future. Settembrini's views about East and West are, in fact, quite quixotic: he equates Vienna with Asia (as exemplifying the "principle of bondage and obduracy" [ll. 32f.]), but ignores the fact that "Asia," in the form of the Turks, was defeated and turned back from Vienna in 1683, thereby permitting the "West" (i.e. Europe) to develop the set of enlightened ideas that he champions. For all his talk of pacifism Settembrini harbors deep-seated resentments against Austria. His national-ism proves to have deeper roots than his pacifism. The influence of Schopenhauer's philosophy can be seen in the implicit thesis that human beings are essentially warlike, and all nations are perpetually in compet-ition with each other. The natural condition of humanity is a fight with teeth and nails. "Civilization" is but a thin veneer on the surface: war reveals the truth about humankind.

l. 38   *He did not like it, in fact*: just as Settembrini's flirtation with a passing girl had upset Castorp during his first encounter with the Italian (cf. p. 60, ll. 7ff.), so do Settembrini's comments about Austria. We are told that he made such comments frequently ("every time it reappeared," ll. 38f.), and that Castorp closes at such times his otherwise open mind ("did not feel he was required to pay any regard," p. 155, l. 3). Castorp is now at the point of inviting Settembrini to expound on his ideas whenever they meet ("he would ask he Italian to expound on his ideas," p. 155, ll. 7f.), but the latter's animadversions about Austria are outside the boundary of topics on which Castorp is willing to be influenced ("they lay beyond the limits…," p. 155, l. 4). It is highly ironic, of course, that the rationalist democrat, Settembrini, should utter such bellicose and intolerant tirades.

(155) l. 18   *the importance of form*: a central theme of the novel is the matter of form. For Settembrini, the issue is simple: reason, enlighten-ment, progress, democracy, and justice are all based on form, and a cultivation of form is an indication that one desires to further the nobility of humankind. A lack of form, however,—which characterizes, for example, the Middle Ages (and which will be the position of Naphta when he arrives on the scene), mired in superstition and enmity—indicates a lack of respect for humanity. The theme of "form" and "formlessness" infuses the novel from start to finish and goes well beyond Settembrini's concrete and historically determined views. For Thomas Mann, form and its counterpart are central issues—if not *the* central issue—of life and art, pertaining to the nature of life itself and the struggle against dissolution and death. If art, following Schopenhauer, is a bastion against the meaninglessness of existence, what is the relationship of the *form* of art (in this case, the novel) to the ultimate *formlessness* of life itself that ends in death and dissolution? Is not such a relationship deeply ironic? In the endeavor to grasp the nature of life itself (which is a progression towards formlessness) how can a work of art—a work of form—be the appropriate medium? There is an ultimate irony in the fact that an artist (in this case, Thomas Mann) attempts to capture the essence of existence (formlessness) in its opposite (form). This dilemma is particularly acute in a work of art such as the *Magic Mountain* which, with its highly complex web of motifs, is a work of intricate form, but whose ultimate message is concerned with decay, dissolution, and death. One is therefore justified in viewing *The Magic Mountain* as an example of Schopenhauer's belief that only a work of art can *temporarily* postpone the victory of the Will whose blind purpose is the destruction of life itself.

l. 24   *Prometheus*: created Man in the image of the gods and then stole fire from the gods and gave it to Man. Zeus was enraged because the giving of fire began an era of enlightenment for Man, and he had Prometheus carried to Mount Caucasus, where an eagle pecked at his liver every night; it grew back each day and each night the eagle ate it again.

l. 25   *Satana, Carducci*: see note to p. 56, l. 41.

ll. 26f.   *that old enemy of the church*: Carducci's political views were consistently opposed to Christianity generally and the secular power of the Catholic Church in particular.

l. 28   *Manzoni*: Alessandro Manzoni (1785–1873), Italian poet and novelist, published his *Sacred Hymns* 1815–1822.

l. 29   *the shadowy moonshine of the* Romanticismo: the objection is to the conventional type of "romantic" poetry that depicts scenes of moonlight and shadows.

l. 30   *Luna, that pallid nun of heaven*: paraphrase of a line by Carducci—critical of "moonlight poetry."

l. 30   *Per Bacco*: an Italian exclamation of approbation.

l. 32   *Dante*: Dante Alighieri (1265–1321), one of the greatest Italian poets, author of *The Divine Comedy*.

ll. 35f.   *the sickly and mystagogic shadow of Beatrice*: In *The Divine Comedy* Beatrice is Dante's guide through Paradise. Dante had met Beatrice when he was nine and she eight years of age, and she became for him the deal embodiment of love, although he probably saw her only twice. ("Mystagogic" means "pertaining to the interpretation of mysteries.")

l. 36   *donna gentile e pietosa*: gentle and sympathetic lady. The phrase is a composite from two different lines of Dante's poem *The New Life* (1293). In fact, Dante did not apply the phrase to Beatrice, but rather to the woman in *The New Life* who comforted Dante after the death of Beatrice.

l. 39   *from the best of sources*: i.e. Settembrini.

(156) ll. 10f.   *learn in what way literature...*: Hans Castorp knows almost nothing about literature, and what little he learns comes from Settembrini.

l. 12   *Brunetto Latini*: 1210–1294, Florentine philosopher, scholar, and statesman, friend and counsellor of Dante, who placed him in *The Divine Comedy* in the seventh circle of Hell, among the sodomites. Many scholars have thus concluded that Latini was homosexual.

ll. 15f.   *how to speak and the fine art...*: words that Hans Castorp remembers and reproduces to himself (in an ironic manner) after Chauchat's departure (cf. p. 348. ll. 32f.).

ll. 27f.   *two hundred years ago ... you had a poet...*: Settembrini is referring to Christian Fürchtegott Gellert (1715–69) who held the view that a person's handwriting pointed to that person's character and circum- stances. Settembrini's characterization of Gellert as "a fine old confab- ulator" is a humorous and belittling comment that seems to be lost on Castorp.

(157) l. 1   *Young Hans Castorp...*: Castorp's thirst for knowledge is, as always, accompanied by critical awareness. These comments by Settem- brini are received by Castorp as yet another "experiment" (l. 2) in a long series. Settembrini's remarks are subjected, as always, to "testing" (p. 157, l. 8) once he has digested them. The process of reflection is a fundamental feature of all of his experiences at the Berghof. He attempts at all times to be scrupulously fair to the Italian and his ideas (cf. p. 157, l. 13) and struggles to resist his instinctive inclination to reject out of hand what he hears. In case there should be any doubt at all about the origin of Castorp's own philosophical inclinations, we are told once again that they arise from deep within his nature ("had always been there naturally and from the start," p. 157, l. 16f.—"from the start" means before he met Settembrini). Out of politeness and fairness Castorp listens to Settembrini and is open to being influenced (the leitmotif occurs again here: "was prepared to be influenced by them," p. 157, ll. 24f.), but when he reflects on what he has heard—as he always does—his own personal views and inclinations go "in the *opposite* direction" to that of the Italian (p. 157, ll. 26f., and the italics are in the original). The aftermath of his encounters with Settembrini is not only contained in his waking thoughts, but also in his *dreams* (p. 157, l. 26), and the narrator opines that Castorp's careful listening to Settembrini's pontifications is merely to assuage his conscience, to make him feel free of guilt in giving rein to those thoughts and feelings that go in the opposite direction. These inclinations are all concentrated in the figure of Clavdia Chauchat (with the repetition of his previous description of her: "listless, worm-eaten, Kirghiz-eyed," p. 157, ll. 33f.; cf. p. 141, ll. 35f.).

l. 12   *because he was "bothering" him*: cf. note to p. 89, ll. 22f.

l. 20   *What a piece of work is man*: cf. Psalm 8, verse 4: "What is man, that thou art mindful of him?" There is an echo of the second half of the biblical verse towards the end of this paragraph (l. 34) when we are told that Hans Castorp "thought" of Chauchat: Thomas Mann uses the Bible's word: "was mindful of." This last paragraph summarizes Hans Castorp's divided personality: he listens with his rational mind to Herr Settembrini, but his natural inclination always leans toward the world represented by Chauchat.

ll. 37ff.   *that boat on the lake in Holstein...*: see note to p. 151, ll. 41ff. "Eastern sky," "moonlit night," and "a web of mist" all point metaphorically to Chauchat and the Asiatic principle.

The Thermometer

The word "thermometer" is always intended to connote multiple associations (e.g. illness, eroticism, and death).

(158) l. 5   *the priceless benefits of his stay*: both real and metaphorical, of course. He has yet to reap the "benefits" that will be the outcome of his seven years at the Berghof.

l. 12   *visitor*: "Hospitant" in the original (cf. notes to pp. 55, l. 41f., p. 69, l. 24, p.111, l. 2, p. 153, l. 41).

ll. 21f.   *less than ten thousand Marks a year*: Castorp's calculation of the cost of staying at the Berghof for one year is intended to be an ironic prediction of his impending future.

l. 34   *the result of preparation*: Hans Castorp worked out the calculations one evening on paper. The narrator roguishly tells us that Castorp had calculated that his cousin, or "anyone just in general" (p. 159, l. 3) could live off 12 000 francs a year—and that "just for the fun of it" (p. 159, ll. 4f.) he had realized that he, too, could afford to live there. Notice also Joachim's ironic comment: "And how generous of you to figure up the charges by the year, too" (p. 158, ll. 24f.). The decision to stay has already been taken, albeit subconsciously.

ll. 36f.   *he had begun taking it in the evenings now, too...*: i.e. as if he were already a full-time resident.

(159) l. 8   *And so three had passed*: This entire paragraph is infused with the numbers three and seven (cf. "third and last week" [l. 10]; "fortnightly band concerts" [l. 12]; "twenty-one days" [l. 21]; "seven minutes" [l. 35f.], etc.).

l. 11   *On the coming Sunday*: Castorp's consciousness of the bi-weekly concerts and bi-weekly lectures by Krokowski indicate the (unconscious) significance of these events for him. (The magical number seven is present here, too.) Music, even "popular" music, attracts him already, in anticipation of its profound influence on him as the novel progresses. Krokowski's lectures, in like manner, have taken their place in his "experiments" and the ideas in those lectures will leave a deep impression on him. Also present at those lectures, of course, will be Chauchat, whose life and being embody much of their message. The importance of these two events for him is underlined by our being told that he reminded both himself and his cousin of their schedule ("so he said to himself and to Joachim," p. 159, l. 14).

ll. 27f.   *Settembrini had said*: on p. 56, l. 29.

ll. 29f.   *as Director Behrens had put it*: cf. p. 104. ll. 25f.: "just dropping by."

ll. 40ff.   *in the service of transportation technology which brought nations closer together*: the phrase is an adaptation of what Settembrini had said earlier (cf. p. 152, ll. 37ff.). It will recur (slightly varied) in Hans Castorp's later conversation with Chauchat (cf. p. 601, ll. 30f.) and in the sub-chapter *Fullness of Harmony* (cf. p. 634, l. 4), in reference to the Suez Canal and Verdi's opera *Aida*. It is ironic that Castorp would use it here, because he is in the process of distancing himself from this goal.

(160) ll. 2f.   *he seriously doubted he would be able to leave...*: Castorp's doubts about being able to leave Joachim "alone" at the sana-torium are also unconsciously motivated by his desire to stay for his own good reasons.

ll. 7f.   *Given his natural tact and delicacy...*: apart from the irony of the phrase itself (tact and delicacy are not Castorp's most reliable qualities), his reluctance to talk about his departure has more to do with his desire to stay than to avoid offending Joachim.

ll. 17f.   *I don't have the feeling...*: Castorp will continue to reflect about the ideas to which he is subjected at the Berghof, and thus his remark is ironically truer than he even suspects. Not only has he not "acclimatized" himself, but all the physical signs of discomfort are still present (nose-bleeds, hot face, heart palpitations; p. 160, ll. 20ff.). His statement that is will take much longer "to get used to all these new impressions" ("new" is the translator's addition) is an ironic prediction of both the immediate future and the next seven years.

ll. 20ff.   *But from time to time...*: the physical discomforts are outward signs of inner processes.

ll. 24ff.   *It takes longer ... build up protein*: This is a restatement of what Behrens had said on p. 45, ll. 19f. Hans Castorp's desire to produce protein is ironic: later, when he stands at Joachim's deathbed, he produces more protein (in his tears) than he wants (cf. p. 528, l. 30).

ll. 27f.   *it was definitely a mistake...*: Castorp's subconscious wish to remain at the Berghof is coming to the fore. He is even aware that he *could* have spent more time there if he had chosen to. His experiences have been so enervating, he feels the need for a holiday to recover from his holiday. The delicious irony of the final sentence of this paragraph: "there's this catarrh I've caught" reveals the psychosomatic basis for his ailment (p. 160, ll. 31f.).

(161) l. 12   *the most agreeable state of affairs*: the horizontal position belongs to the complex of motifs that stand for idleness, lassitude, freedom, and death (cf. pp. 65, ll. 13f., 68, ll. 8f., 71, ll. 29f., 101, ll. 9ff., 195, ll. 2f., 328, ll. 39f.).

l. 14   *some writer and Carbonaro*: i.e. Settembrini. The description is disdainful, which demonstrates Hans Castorp's reservations about his self-appointed mentor. He is already irresistibly attracted to the "horizontal life."

ll. 24ff.   *music*: he has been subjected to music "almost every evening, for at least an hour" (p. 161, l. 24). But more important, the pieces of music that are mentioned: *Carmen, Il Trovatore, Der Freischütz* (and they are, of course, carefully chosen by the narrator) will have a symbolical bearing on his life. *Carmen* will become one of his central musical experiences, and he will interpret the events of the opera in a manner that makes him into the tragic hero, Don José, and Chauchat into Carmen. *Il Trovatore* also tells the story of an unhappy hero, gypsies, and a love triangle (all of which also relate to Castorp and Chauchat). In *Der Freischütz* the hero sells his soul to the Devil—and on Walpurgis Night (pp. 316 ff.) Castorp will, in Settembrini's eyes at least, throw in his lot with the forces of darkness. The remainder of the musical pieces that are mentioned connote various aspects of his life also: waltzes (the orderly nature of his conventional existence), marches (his cousin's life), and Mazurkas (a playful connotation of Marusya, but also of Chauchat).

ll. 35f.   *Russian grammar*: Joachim's interest in the Russian language and his attraction to Marusya undermine his devotion to duty and "Western" values (cf. note to p. 63, l. 7).

l. 36   *left* Ocean Steamships *lying*: the lure of music is stronger than that of duty.

l. 37   *with ardent interest*: the music makes a profound impression on Hans Castorp, even though it consists only of excerpts heard from afar. He looks "with contentment into the transparent depths of its structure" (p. 161, l. 38) and is so captivated by the melodies from time to time that he recalls with "nothing but hostility" (p. 161, ll. 39f.) Settembrini's opposition to music.

ll. 40f.   *Settembrini's opinions about music*: cf. p. 110, ll. 39ff.

(162) l. 1f.   *Grandfather Giuseppe's slogan..*: cf. p. 153, ll. 20f.

l. 13   *a truly delightful state of affairs*: the culmination of his thoughts about the "evening rest cure" (l. 13) and his life in general at the Berghof.

l. 14   *visitor*: "Hospitant" again (cf. note to p. 69, l. 24).

l. 24   *reçus*: recognized.

l. 30   *It's better not to get sick here*: unless you have tuberculosis, nobody shows sympathy for any other kind of "normal" illness.

(163) ll. 9ff.   *on me dit que vous avez pris froid, ich höre, Sie sind erkältet, vy, kazhetsya, prostudilis*: I hear you have caught a cold. (French, German, Russian.)

l. 13f.   *he's gone and eaten bean salad*: before being anesthetized one should not have eaten anything for a number of hours, to avoid the risk of food or liquid being regurgitated and entering the lungs.

l. 26   *Her watery-blue, bloodshot eyes*: similar to those of Behrens (cf. p. 44, l. 19). Her physical appearance—like so many of Thomas Mann's characters—is far from attractive.

l. 34   *twenty-four*: see note to p. 35, ll. 4ff.

(164) l. 1f.   *they come from an infection ... susceptible*: Nurse Mylendonk has accurately diagnosed Hans Castorp's nature: she describes him as "happily receptive" to an infection.

l. 9   *Formamint*: trade name for an antiseptic throat tablet containing formaldehyde. Hans Castorp's room has been fumigated before his arrival with "formalin"—liquid formaldehyde (cf. p. 11, l. 22).

l. 27   *I'm healthy*: this is the second time Hans Castorp has affirmed this: cf. p. 16, l. 24.

l. 34   *It will last you a lifetime*: the original is somewhat more ambiguous: "That is something for your life…"

l. 41   *mercury*: the original uses "quicksilver," which broadens the connotations (cf. note to p. 45, l. 25).

(165) ll. 1f.   *I'll take this one…*: While the purchase of a thermometer might seem innocuous, in this context it connotes further psychological dimensions. Hans Castorp's choice of the more expensive thermometer might on the surface be explained by his social standing, but the mere acquisition of the thermometer is yet another step in his inevitable attachment to the Berghof: he has "acquired" another tie binding him to the sanatorium—and an attachment also to all that the thermometer symbolizes: i.e. the erotic sphere.

l. 5   *important procurements*: the nurse continues to indicate Hans Castorp's fate.

l. 8   *mercury*: "quicksilver" in the original (cf. note to p. 45, l. 25).

l. 10   *Mercury*: see note to p. 45, l. 25.

l. 39   *silent sister*: see note to p. 85, l. 19.

(166) l. 8   *Brämenbühl*: mountain near Davos (correct spelling: Brämabüel).

l. 11   *Alteinwand*: mountain near Davos.

l. 20   *on little cat's feet*: there is no reason to speak of the passage of time in this way—unless the reference to a cat's feet is intended to conjure up Chauchat, whose view of life includes a cavalier attitude to time.

l. 38   *what sort of infection*: we know what kind it is: a psycho-somatic indicator of his desire to stay at the Berghof. His entire being has been "susceptible" (l. 37), and he has remembered (and adopts) the word Nurse Mylendonk used, which in German is even stronger: "happily receptive." His delight at discovering that he has a temperature stems both from the conscious joy of being sick and therefore "belonging," and the subconscious sensation of having something in common with Chauchat.

l. 40   *Pneumothorax*: see note to p. 48, l. 38.

(167) ll. 8ff.   *Settembrini with his republic and his beautiful style*: two leitmotifs that characterize Settembrini throughout the novel. Castorp's negative attitude towards Settembrini here (cf. "despised") stems from his predilection for illness over health. The original speaks, significantly, of Castorp's despising Settembrini's two defining elements *while* examining the thermometer—the unconscious implications of the latter (eros, Chauchat, etc.) override the conscious expression of noble sentiments.

ll. 20f.   *Now and then he smiled…*: we can divine the reason for his smile (he is happy that he is sick), and the person he is smiling at ("at someone," l. 21) can only be Chauchat.

(168) ll. 1f.   *It was point seven*: Castorp insists on having the highest reading recognized. (The translation converts the Celsius readings of the original into Fahrenheit; there is no number symbolism in the original.)

ll. 11f. *Yours is acute, but harmless*: in the topsy-turvy world of the Berghof the normal standards do not apply. Thus one can have a high temperature (as Castorp does), but it is "harmless"—i.e. not life-threatening. The genuine patients, however, have such a high temperature as a matter of course, and they are fighting for their lives.

l. 26   *twiddle-twaddle*: the word he had just described as sounding "ghastly and bizarre" (p. 163, l. 37f.) and "gruesome" (p. 164, l. 4) when uttered by Nurse Mylendonk.

(169) ll. 14f. *Mr. Visitor has a little temp himself*: Frau Stöhr's distortion of "temperature" (in the original she attempts to appear learned by saying that Hans Castorp has "Tempus," which means "time"). "Mr. Visitor" in German also suggests a discreet visitor to a lady.

l. 16   *gay blade*: the teasing of Hans Castorp both by the teacher ("sowing his oats," l. 11) and by Frau Stöhr ("a temp," "gay blade") imply that his temperature has risen because of an amorous adventure. In fact, they are closer to the mark than they could imagine.

ll. 27f. *my case is the most harmless imaginable*: having exploited to the full his new-found status as a sick person, Castorp now pretends that his illness is minor. The irony of his disclaimer, however, lies in the fact that he does not know really how sick he is and that he is about to discover the truth.

ll. 28f. *my eyes are watery*: in the original the line connotes both the Martin Luther's translation of the Bible (*John* 11: 35) and a poem by Goethe (cf. note to p. 45, l. 9), "The King of Thule" ("Der König in Thule") who loves one woman devotedly until his death. The phrase will recur several times (cf. p. 672, l. 18, when the ghost of Joachim appears: "the tears came to his eyes"—although repetition of the leitmotif is lost in the translation.

(170) l. 38   *rib resections*: cf. note to p. 149, ll. 15f.

l. 41   *mortis causa*: with the prospect of death.

(171) l. 7   *Tears are not allowed in public here*: this is said by the man whose eyes are always watery (cf. p. 44, l. 19).

(171) l. 1   *bon appétit*: French equivalent of "enjoy your meal."

l. 3   *basic physiology*: Hans Castorp will learn more about physiology in the sub-chapter *Research* (cf. pp. 263ff.).

l. 7f. *I should perhaps form my opinions more*: Castorp's confused reflections about critical judgment reveal the battle between Settembrini's attempts to "educate" him and the pull from Chauchat. While attempting to view a matter critically, "things creep in" (l. 10)—more accurately: "something gets in the way." That "something" is the influence of Chauchat; and the principles espoused by Settembrini suddenly seem "absurd" (l. 12; more accurately: "tasteless," "insipid"). Joachim looks at Castorp with bemused puzzlement.

(173) l. 13 *things become quite informal*: the imaginary remarks by Chauchat are phrased in the informal second person—a form that would be used only between close friends (especially in this era). Hans Castorp will use the excuse of Mardi Gras to speak to her in the informal form (cf. p. 326, l. 41).

ll. 42f. *Un poco più presto, Signori!*: A little faster, gentlemen! The phrase is used in music, not normally in everyday speech.

(174) l. 9 *report card*: in his typically jocular manner Behrens describes Joachim's temperature chart using a word ("Konduite") that refers to a superior's report on the performance of an officer.

ll. 22ff. *Still on the lambent side ... Still toxic*: the original has "illuminated," which may imply "intoxicated"; cf. p. 179, ll. 13ff. where Behrens explains that the toxins released during tuberculosis can intoxicate the patient. See also note to p. 176, l. 6. These phrases register with Hans Castorp and are included in his reflections about Joachim a few minutes later, cf. p. 175, l. 32.

ll. 23f. *"Of late" meant in the last four weeks*: in the German original the leitmotivic word "recently" is used. The narrator's comment *en passant* continues the novel's discourse on the use of the word "recent" and the nature of time (cf. pp. 51, ll. 21ff., 364, ll. 20ff., 535, ll. 22ff., & p. 700, l. 41).

l. 29 *hilum*: depression where the blood vessels and nerves enter the lung.

l. 31 *auscultation*: see note to p. 130, l. 31.

(175) ll. 14f. *vesicular*: indicating the presence of small blisters.

ll. 26f. *he always was concerned about his body*: Joachim's interest in the body is aimed towards physical health, in order to perform his military duty; whereas Castorp's interest in the body is sparked by his fascination with sickness and its effects. As the novel progresses, Castorp's interest in the body (especially Chauchat's body) intensifies.

ll. 32f. *He's lambent...*: all expressions he has just heard Behrens use (cf. p. 174, ll. 22f.).

ll. 34 *Apollo Belvedere*: marble statue, a Roman copy of a Greek original, rediscovered in 1495 and regarded as epitomizing the ideal of classical male beauty. See picture opposite.

ll. 36ff. *Illness makes people even more physical...*: a reflection that Castorp will pursue during his researches (cf. p. 280, ll. 40ff.).

Apollo Belvedere

(176) l. 6   *lambent*: literally "radiant." Behrens actually says "tipsy," which is his jocular way of referring to a tubercular infection. He means here that Joachim is still quite ill. Cf. note to p. 174, l. 22.

l. 9   *a prison ship ... Siberian salt mine*: the original speaks of a "Bagno"—an eighteenth century French prison for serious offenders that was located in seaports (where the prisoners had to work).

(177) l. 8   *praeter-propter*: literally: approximate, more or less. Behrens's meaning is not completely clear—which, given his eccentric mode of speaking, is not surprising. He probably means: "The situation looks more or less like this…"

l. 9   *the first time…*: p. 44, ll. 12ff.

l. 11   *secretly one of the locals*: Behrens's medical diagnosis of Hans Castorp also implies the latter's spiritual inclinations.

l. 16   *the seductions of mere curiosity*: Behrens's jocular comment once again hits the nail on the head.

l. 25   *a priori*: literally "from what comes before"; i.e. the fact that Joachim was ill leads to the inference that Hans Castorp must be ill, too

l. 36   *He died of pneumonia…*: Castorp's medical inheritance of a suspect lung stretches back through his father to his grandfather.

ll. 40f.   *And your heart pounds sometimes? Has only started of late?*: Behrens's diagnosis refers not just to Hans Castorp's physical state, but also to his emotional condition.

(178) ll. 10f.   *You are an old patient, Castorp*: Castorp has suffered an infection at some time in the past, without its having been diagnosed. The statement also has a metaphorical implication.

l. 19   *Aeolus's bellows*: jocular metaphor for "lung." Aeolus, god of the winds, lived on the island of Aeolia and was visited by Odysseus and his crew. The god gave Odysseus a west wind to carry them home; but he also gave him other winds in a magic bag, the crew opened the bag before they got home—and the winds therein drove them back to Aeolia (cf. *Odyssey*, Book X). In Virgil's *Aeneid* Aeneas was stranded with Dido because of the Aeolian winds.

l. 21   *lares and penates*: see note to p. 104, l. 36.

l. 32   *a moist spot*: the phrase becomes one of Hans Castorp's personal leitmotifs.

ll. 33f.   *the whole pulmonary lobe…*: words that Hans Castorp takes in and reproduces later, cf. p. 183, ll. 6ff. & p. 244, ll. 15f.

(179) l. 5 *there's the air up here*: Behrens's explanation of the effect of the air on dormant illnesses is also intended to be understood metaphorically: Castorp's dormant inclination to the "Chauchat syndrome" has been awakened also by the atmosphere of the Berghof. Castorp will absorb this knowledge and reproduce it a few days later (cf. p.192, ll. 27f.).

l. 8   *and your catarrh…*: as we saw, Castorp's changed metabolism was apparent from the moment of his arrival, as was his "mental metabolism." The catarrh is simply the physical manifestation of an interior process.

ll. 10f.   *and not because of any catarrh*: Behrens also intimates that Castorp's "illness" is more than merely physical.

ll. 20f.   *a case like yours is not healed just like that*: Castorp's "case" will take seven years—and even then may not be considered "cured."

ll. 25f.   *A citizen's first duty is to stay calm*: a common saying. After the defeat of the Prussians by Napoleon in 1806 at the battles of Jena and Auerstadt, the Prussian Minister announced: "The King has lost a battle. At this time calm is the first duty of the citizen."

l. 36   *a hearty handshake*: the gesture represents Hans Castorp's official reception both as a patient at the Berghof sanatorium and as an adherent of the world that Krokowski represents.

Chapter Five

Eternal Soup and Sudden Clarity

This sub-chapter represents a turning-point in Hans Castorp's life in several respects. From having been a guest at the sanatorium, he now becomes a patient. Where previously time was important (in so far as he had come for just three weeks), time will now be "frozen," so to speak, and his sense of time will gradually become uncertain (until it no longer matters). But on a more profound metaphorical and metaphysical level this chapter also represents his "rebirth"—as a human being who will be subjected to all the significant influences that will ultimately form him.

(180) l. 5   *twenty-one days at the height of summer*: the seemingly unnecessary repetition of the length of Hans Castorp's planned stay permits the narrator to indulge in yet more number symbolism.

l. 18   *impounded by fate*: fate has decreed that Hans Castorp will come to Davos and stay a while to continue his education; his earlier illness prepared him for this experience.

(181) l. 1   *an abiding now*: Hans Castorp's staying in bed is a metaphor for the transformation in his perception of time: from being a visitor for a planned three-week stay, he has become a patient in a location where time stands still. We have moved from the world of reality to that of mythology.

ll. 9f.   *we want to avoid paradoxes*: this has to be understood ironically: in fact, Castorp's entire world is built up on paradoxes.

l. 22   *the wild laughter of triumph...*: as he lies in bed Castorp's emotions run the gamut from triumph to terror: he is ecstatic that he has been ordered by Behrens to remain at the Berghof, but in his ecstasy his conscience also asserts itself and causes his heart to palpitate. The struggle between the demands of the "flatland" (reason, progress, technology, Settembrini) and the attractions of being "up here" (freedom, love, death, Chauchat) takes place within him.

l. 40   *Not yet*: Castorp will postpone as long as possible informing his relatives that he is not coming home at the appointed time. The evasive phrase indicates his guilty conscience.

(182) l. 20   *just dropping by for a visit*: he uses Behrens's term, cf. p. 104, l. 26.

ll. 26f.   *I've never really felt all that splendidly healthy*: Castorp's present state had its beginning many years ago, and he has been psychologically predisposed to it for a long time. This is, of course, an attempt to rationalize his situation.

ll. 31f. *Behrens at least dropped a hint...*: cf. p. 177, ll. 24f. Hans Castorp's observation shows that he was listening keenly to Behrens.

l. 33 *how I've always felt about it all...*: Castorp's reflections about his earlier years bring into the open feelings that he has had since he was young. This sentence indicates Castorp's growing self-analysis which will become an essential element in his personal growth.

l. 36 *We were speaking about the same thing here not long ago*: cf. p. 107, ll. 22 ff.

ll. 39f. *Requiescat in pace*: rest in peace. Castorp's inclination for the church is a manifestation of his sympathy with death (cf. "that's the loveliest phrase"; l. 40).

(183) ll. 1f. *having understood something about illness from the start*: his mind has suddenly become clear about his innate inclinations, and the veneer of bourgeois orderliness and duty has been breached. From now on the attractions of Chauchat (and all that she represents) will override the dictates of an ever-weakening conscience.

ll. 7f. *the whole pulmonary lobe would have gone...*: Hans Castorp repeats Behrens's prognosis, cf. p. 178, ll. 33f.

ll. 23f. *Who knows whether anything worth mentioning will even show up*: more irony, as the x-ray photograph of his chest will, in fact, not simply bring to the fore the evidence that he has "a moist spot" (cf. Behrens's "findings corresponded to his expectations" [p. 215, ll. 33f.]), but will also provide, in a metaphorical sense, the proof that in his nature he belongs to Chauchat's world.

(184) l. 12 *the fortnightly Sunday concert*: now Castorp allows himself to be captivated by the music ("a blurry look") and counters the memory of Settembrini's criticisms with a shrug of the shoulders ("a mental shrug," p.184, l. 17)—a gesture he has acquired from Joachim (cf. p. 7, l. 36; p. 70, ll. 15ff. & p. 144, ll. 20f.) and that is a typical feature of those who "belong" at the Berghof. His emancipation from the influence of the Italian proceeds apace.

l. 20 *he had Joachim provide him with a report*: Castorp's insisting on hearing all the news is not only mildly humorous, it also reveals his desire to participate fully in the life of the sanatorium. After all, he is no longer merely a visitor, he is paying full price for everything—and should therefore enjoy all the rights of a *bona fide* patient.

l. 21 *the lace peignoirs*: the kind of dress that Chauchat had been wearing at breakfast on the first Sunday (cf. note to p. 108, l. 25).

ll. 25f. *Dr. Krokowski's lecture*: the German uses the word "Conférence," which at this time could also mean an announcement at a cabaret or variety show. The intended irony is obvious.

ll. 26f. *Hans Castorp ... insisted on hearing details*: his interest in the content of Krokowski's lectures reveals his subconscious fascination with their topic, despite his "rational" rejection of the doctor's ideas. Joachim's reaction is typical: he is reluctant to talk about such matters—and the two cousins avoid such topics in their conversations (l. 28f.).

ll. 31f. *Here I lie, paying full price...*: his justification for insisting on hearing about the content of Krokowski's latest lecture is humorous: he equates the lecture with all the other medical services he is receiving.

ll. 38f. *Fare thee well...*: cf. p. 116, 25f. The association in Castorp's mind of Krokowski's lecture and the walk during which he had recollected the Hippe-experience is significant.

(185) l. 1 *And so Krokowski spoke about 'love' again, did he?*: the topic is one that interests him keenly, as it concerns his memory of Hippe, his fascination with Chauchat, and his subconscious desire to explore the irrational world of love and sickness.

ll. 8ff. *he was selling basic chemistry today*: the information that Castorp drags out of Joachim has direct application to his own case. The idea that sexual arousal has a chemical basis derives from Freud.

l. 23 *stories about love potions*: a leitmotif that will play a significant role later (cf. *Walpurgis Night*, pp. 316 ff.). The allusion is to the medieval legend of Tristan and Isolde. In the original story Tristan is sent by King Mark of Cornwall, to accompany the latter's bride, Isolde, back from Ireland. Isolde's mother entrusts her maid with a love-potion that she is to give to Isolde just before she disembarks and sees King Mark—for the potion will cause her to fall in love with the first man she sees. During the sea-journey, however, Isolde's maid mistakenly gives Isolde the love-potion prematurely—and Tristan is the first man the latter sees after drinking it. Although Isolde marries King Mark, she and Tristan cannot relinquish each other, and they find ways to be together. (Thereafter, the legend has various endings.) Thomas Mann was also familiar with Richard Wagner's opera, *Tristan and Isolde*, in which at the end the two lovers die a "Liebestod"—they are united in death. All of this, of course, has subconscious relevance for Hans Castorp in his "relationship" with Chauchat.

ll. 28f. *And the evening and the morning were the third day...*: the phrase has biblical overtones.

ll. 38f. *the supervising physician had found him very anemic*: cf. p. 45, l. 10.

(186) l. 5 *our adventurer felt he had put things in general good order*: Castorp (the "adventurer") is getting his life organized the way he wants it to be. At least the narrator is clear about Hans Castorp's situation.

l. 8f. *neither diverting nor boring*: a leitmotif of time that runs throughout the novel, cf. notes to p. xii, l. 7 & p. 83, l. 23.

l. 16 *seven o'clock temperature*: number symbolism: the thermometer is held in the mouth for seven minutes at seven o'clock.

(187) l. 7 *not on a restricted diet*: i.e. the diet of a sick patient. (To be on "short commons" means to receive a small allowance of food.) There is still the pretense that he is not really sick. This is one of those paradoxes that narrator claimed to wish to avoid (cf. p. 181, l. 10).

l. 10 *the six-course Berghof dinner*: this is lunch, the main meal of the day (cf. note to p. 68, l. 14).

ll. 18f. *tailor's son who dined from a magic table*: the reference is to a fairy-tale by the Brothers Grimm in which a tailor's son is given a magic table that fills with food when he says "Table, be set."

ll. 20ff. *And no sooner had he finished eating…*: the discussion about the passage of time in this paragraph plays with the numbers three and four (i.e. seven).

ll. 35f. *the apostrophe was Dr. Krokowski*: the translation is a little misleading. The "apostrophe" in German primarily means quotation marks, but it can also mean a person holding a formal speech. Thus the rest cure is given final emphasis by the appearance of Dr. Krokowski at the end of it.

(188) ll. 1f. *materialized…*: Krokowski is portrayed (ironically) as both a messianic figure and a satanic one—so it is only appropriate that he "appears" mysteriously.

ll. 9ff. *materialized out of thin air … two-pronged beard … yellowish teeth*: the portrayal of Krokowski and his arrival suggests something devilish.

l. 18 *comrade*: the word may well make "Hans Castorp feel uneasy": it implies a closer association than Castorp would rationally want at this time.

ll. 22f. *it was a mistake at the time*: Krokowski's disclaimer is, of course, ironic: Castorp was already "sick" on the night of his arrival at the Berghof.

ll. 26f. *my intentions were … more philosophical*: and he was right. Krokowski's theories fit Hans Castorp's case perfectly; in fact, the latter shares those views. The former's opinion that "human being" and "perfect health" are not consonant would find Castorp's agreement; while the doctor's final statement: "Organic factors are always secondary" (p. 188) applies to the patient to whom he is talking. As much as Hans Castorp initially rejected Krokowski's view that physical illness has a psychological basis, it is one of the more subtle aspects of the novel that Castorp moves from rejection of to fascination with Krokowski's view—and does indeed exemplify it in his own being. This will culminate eventually in his visiting Krokowski for consultations (cf. p. 361, ll. 37ff.).

l. 36   *And Hans Castorp had flinched*: he realizes that his own case has just been described.

(189) l. 8   *with an apostrophe*: repeating the thought of p. 187, l. 35f. and further emphasizing the importance of the rest cure and of Dr. Krokowski role. (In the German the verb "apostrophize" is used, which also connotes formal praise.)

l. 19   *if you had thoughts in your head*: no doubt of Clavdia Chauchat —especially when we read below of his reaction when Settembrini enters his room and switches the light on.

l. 19   *orbis pictus*: literally: the world in pictures. Originally, this was an illustrated textbook for children (the first was published in Nuremberg in 1658); later any textbook with pictures. The irony here lies in the fact that soon Castorp will have another illustration on his nightstand: the x-ray of Chauchat's chest—which will be, in fact, a symbol of Castorp's psychological "world."

l. 27   *There was evening—and there had just been morning*: biblical overtones, cf. *Genesis* 1, 13 & 18.

ll. 37f.   *all of a sudden the room was dazzlingly bright*: it is appropriate that Settembrini—the representative of the Enlightenment—should switch on the light when entering Hans Castorp's darkened room. Castorp's reaction to seeing Settembrini: "recognized him … and blushed" (p. 190, l. 35) stems from the fact that he has been dreaming of Chauchat and feels embarrassed and guilty when Settembrini enters—a fact that is explicitly confirmed only later on p. 203, ll. 12ff. This episode and Settembrini's action become an important leitmotif, cf. also p. 322, ll. 22ff.; p. 348, ll. 35f.; p. 404, ll. 1f.; & p. 603, ll. 31ff.

(190) l. 12   *Joachim replied curtly in the negative, his eyes lowered*: Castorp's inquiry is aimed at discovering if Chauchat is still at the Berghof, and Joachim, well aware of the reason for Castorp's question, looks away to avoid embarrassment.

l. 24   *Ecco! ... Poveretto!*: Well now! … you poor fellow!

l. 28   *why 'poveretto'*: Castorp does not regard himself as an object of pity—on the contrary.

l. 28   *Here he sits...*: Castorp understands the irony of Settembrini's situation: he wants to change the world, but he is unable to do so because he is confined to a sanatorium. Castorp's reaction to Settembrini's comment on his (Castorp's) condition shows a further step towards independence ("He shouldn't be so arrogant about pitying me," p. 190, l. 30f.).

l. 35   *Hans Castorp recognized him now, and blushed*: His explanation of the darkened room is weak: "I was simply too lazy to turn on the light" (p. 191, l. 18). The real reason he blushes is given on p. 203. ll. 10ff., when he admits he had been thinking of Chauchat before Settembrini entered.

(191) ll. 2f.   *waving one small hand...*: cf. p. 156, ll. 40f.

l. 11   *refectory*: the dining-room in a monastery. Monastic vocabulary occurs in the novel to indicate the hermetic isolation of the Berghof and the patients' obligation to devote themselves to the service of the cure.

l. 26   *our dining hall*: the use of the possessive adjective ("our") is significant: a sign that Castorp now feels that he belongs—a fact that does not escape Settembrini (cf. ll. 32–33).

ll. 31f.   *pious monk ... novitiate ... vows*: all of these words suggest that Hans Castorp is just beginning his "service" to the "order."

ll. 33ff.   *not that I want to cast any aspersions on your masculinity...*: but that is, in fact, what he does: the uncertainty of Hans Castorp's sexuality (i.e. his attraction to both Hippe and Chauchat) is further underlined by Settembrini's comments.

ll. 37f.   *a certain flood of sentimentality*: Settembrini himself has been the center of speculation (cf. note to p. 55, l. 2).

(192) l. 8f.   *how many months has the Director saddled you with?*: Settembrini uses the same verb he used when they first met—a verb that implies a prison sentence (cf. p. 55, l. 29f.).

l. 11   *You were very cocky with your answers that day*: Castorp had merely corrected Settembrini's false assumption that he was a patient (cf. p. 55, ll. 38ff.).

l. 15   *Radames*: Castorp's slip is ironic: later (in *Fullness of Harmony*, pp. 633–36) while listening to Verdi's *Aida*, he will imagine himself as the Egyptian general Radames, entombed with his beloved Aida, the enemy prisoner he loves.

l. 18   *Minos and Rhadamanthus*: cf. note to p. 55, ll. 29f..

l. 19   *Carducci*: see note to p. 56, l. 41.

l. 20   *we shall leave* him *out of this*: Settembrini objects to Castorp's invocation of Carducci (a model of reason and enlightenment) in the context of illness.

ll. 25f.   *Fräulein Kleefeld had just whistled...*: cf. p. 48, ll. 13f.

ll. 27ff.   *the air here is good not only for* fighting off *illness, but it's also good* for *it*: a piece of knowledge that Castorp heard from the lips of Behrens (p. 179, ll. 5ff.) and now repeats as his own, using almost the identical words. During the rest of Hans Castorp's conversation with Settembrini he uses words and phrases that he has heard and absorbed from his various contacts with people at the Berghof.

ll. 28f. *Which is probably necessary in the end...*: unwittingly insightful words from Hans Castorp. If he is to be "cured"—that is, achieve insights into his state of being, his search for answers, and his "sympathy with death"—his hidden questions need to be brought to the fore and answered. Hence, the use of the word "eruption" (l. 38) is appropriate.

(193) l. 5 *Behrens says now with a shrug*: the gesture that is typical of Berghof residents.

l. 13 *the girl who went for a swim*: cf. p. 85, ll. 7ff.

l. 14 *silent sister*: see note to p. 85, l. 19.

ll. 14f. *Always something new*: more accurately, Castorp says: "one never finishes learning"—with double-entendre: he still has a lot to learn in every respect.

l. 15 *My own case is still quite uncertain*: both in the medical and spiritual-philosophical sense.

l. 26 *Madonna, the photographic plate*: the connection of the name of Mary to the photographic plate foreshadows Hans Castorp's adoration of Chauchat's x-ray photograph.

l. 29 *phthisis*: see note to p. 61, l.8.

l. 30 *coccus*: a micro-organism (usually a bacterium) whose overall shape is spherical or nearly spherical.

l. 33 *I don't think I'm that far along just yet*: perhaps not, but he is certainly developing a profound fascination with death. Settembrini's remarks about the "Madonna" and "death" point ironically to Hans Castorp's interest in "l'amour et la mort."

l. 35 *you are a dyed-in-the-wool critic...*: Castorp's frankness towards Settembrini stems from his new status—he has "found" himself, so to speak, and can address the Italian from a position of self-confidence.

l. 35f. *You don't even believe in exact science*: unwittingly ironic words from the mouth of Castorp. Much later Settembrini will charge Naphta with not believing in the truth of objective science (cf. p. 390, ll. 28ff.).

l. 39 *Yes, unfortunately, I am rather ill*: Settembrini's admission is a telling commentary on the irony of his situation: all his splendid speeches about equality, democracy and the brotherhood of Man are ironically undermined by his physical infirmity. Krokowski's doubts that "human being" and "perfect health" can ever be "made to rhyme" (p. 188, ll. 29f.) apply equally to Settembrini.

(194) ll. 1f. *he had dumbfounded him...*: Hans Castorp's two questions have revealed the fragility of Settembrini's world-view. The nobility of the Italian's philosophy is undermined by the reality of his condition: while preaching health, Settembrini is deathly ill.

ll. 23f. *People are generally detached...*: Settembrini describes them literally as "phlegmatic"—i.e. reserved and taciturn—an opinion with which Hans Castorp agrees.

ll. 27f. *Detached and energetic*: the two adjectives summarize Thomas Mann's view of the people in the area where he grew up (in North Germany), in particular the middle-class burghers who formed he social circle in which his family moved. Sparse of word and energetic in business, they were the engine of commercial success—and the very antithesis of the philosophizing or artistic type who question life.

ll. 30f. *we shall all make your good uncle's acquaintance*: prophetic words. Despite Castorp's denial ("Wild horses wouldn't get him here!" l. 34), his uncle James Tienappel will come to the Berghof much later to find out what is going on with his nephew (pp. 420 ff.)—and be so shocked at what he sees that he runs away.

ll. 36f. *He'd be in an awful mess*: that is precisely what happens to Tienappel.

(195) l. 16 *homo humanus*: Castorp uses Settembrini's own term to describe him (cf. p. 57, l. 39).

l. 23 *that means hard, cold*: Hans Castorp's negative characterization of the life he has left behind shows both his critical awareness of the nature of his former environment and his emancipation from it. Note also that Castorp has busied himself with these thoughts repeatedly "in one form or another for the past few days" (p. 196, l. 24).

l. 25 *Lying and watching from a distance...*: the "horizontal position" is both a vantage point and an expression of the opposing philosophy.

l. 33 *life's shirkers*: i.e. those who do not subscribe to the bourgeois ethic, yet live in bourgeois society. This is, in fact, an ironic comment on Castorp himself.

l. 34 *proof of a certain alienation*: Settembrini's fear is that Castorp's attitude—as much as he admits the criticism is justified—may lead him to be totally alienated from his former environment. Settembrini has, indeed, deduced what has happened to Castorp. The superficial temptations of the Berghof ("flirting and taking his temperature," p. 195, l. 40) against which Settembrini warns Castorp are, in fact, what he has been indulging in.

l. 37 *to be lost to life*: Hans Castorp will use a similar phrase later, but in a poetic variation ("to be lost to the world"; cf. p. 584, l. 27). It is ironic that Settembrini should use the phrase as a warning, but that Castorp will employ it as an accurate description of his situation.

(196) l. 10 *You people down here lack the basic concepts*: the irony in Settembrini's words lies in the fact that he means them as a warning to Castorp, whereas they are, in Castorp's mind, true. The Berghof is for him already his "home" (p. 196, ll. 20f.), and the word used in the German is "Heimat," which implies one's spiritual, as well as physical home.

l. 16 *he would stay on and find a lady friend...*: precisely what happens to Castorp.

l. 18 *Hans Castorp had apparently only been half listening*: because he is no longer open to such influences by Settembrini—and in any case his thoughts have been in another realm recently. (Cf. also: "as if gazing into the distance" [ll. 19f.], and "His laugh came a little late" [l. 20].)

ll. 24f. *a person probably needs a rather thick skin...*: Castorp has been thinking a lot ("for the last few days," p. 196, l. 24) about the nature of the society and the people he has left behind, and it is clear from his comments in this conversation with Settembrini that he rejects that world. In fact, he states that he always felt uncomfortable ("I never found it all that natural," p. 196, ll. 28), and ascribes that to his "unconscious tendency to illness" (p. 196, l. 30). Reflecting back on his life "down there," he is categorizing himself as an outsider.

l. 31 *I heard those old spots myself*: Castorp's self-analysis is assuming the air of a self-fulfilling prophecy: "I always had doubts about the world in which I was brought up, and now I see that they were caused by my natural inclination towards sickness—which was confirmed when I heard my own lungs."

(197) ll. 3f. *early and repeated contacts with death*: Settembrini defines Castorp's attitude to death—with which Castorp agrees ("Precisely," p. 197, l. 7)—as a precursor to his sermon on the appropriate position to assume vis-à-vis death. The choice is between recognizing that death is an inevitable component of life ("life's holy prerequisite," p. 197, ll. 18f.) and honoring it, and the view that death is something separate and divorced from life, "an independent spiritual power" (p. 197, l. 27) with its own attractions. In chastising anyone who is inclined to "sympathize" with death ("the most abominable confusion of the human mind," p. 197, ll. 29f.), Settembrini is unwittingly employing the very term ("sympathy") that will become a central concern of Castorp during his stay at the Berghof. This is one of the most serious sermons Settembrini has delivered to Castorp—because in Settembrini's mind the issue is central to life itself. However, his moralizing attempt to convince Castorp is ironically weakened before he even begins by the narrator's mention of one detail: "Finally he opened his black eyes—those organ-grinder eyes" (p. 197, l. 14f.), words that undermine the message before it is spoken. This conversation also outlines the choice that faces Castorp: either to accept the humanist's view of death as something to be accepted as inevitable, but not to be honored, and the opposing view that death is attractive, fascinating even. The struggle between those two camps is a major theme of the novel.

ll. 22f. *The ancients decorated their sarcophagi...*: this fact registers with Hans Castorp and he repeats it during his visit to Behrens's apartment (p. 258, ll. 17ff.) and in a conversation with Settembrini and Naphta (p. 450, ll. 4f.).

ll. 28ff.   *death is a very depraved force...*: a conclusion to which Hans Castorp will also come in the sub-chapter *Snow* (cf. p. 487, ll. 26ff.).

l. 32   *He was very serious...*: Settembrini is fully aware that this is a decisive moment and that the topic he has just addressed is the most significant issue in Hans Castorp's life.

(198) l. 1   *a great deal of childish sullenness in his silence*: Castorp is aware that he has been lectured to and his reaction is that of a stubborn child. His drumming on the comforter (p. 197, ll. 40f.) reveals his annoyance.

ll. 4f.   *we once had a similar dispute...*: cf. p. 95, ll. 6ff.

l. 9f.   *you appeared not all that reluctant*: aware that he has perhaps run up against Castorp's stubbornness, Settembrini attempts to persuade Castorp to regard his remarks about death in the wider context of Castorp's intellectual experiments and to avoid taking prematurely a rigid position.

ll. 11f.   *its tendency to experiment..*: i.e. *placet experiri*; cf. note to 96, l. 14.

ll. 18f.   *play a corrective role*: a word that Hans Castorp will also immediately adopt as his own (cf. p. 199, l. 10).

l. 26   *"Quite* sine pecunia," *Herr Settembrini quoted*: the phrase has gone from Behrens to Castorp to Settembrini. This is an instance of the Italian's having learned something from Castorp.

l. 30f.   *He blushed when he caught sight of the Italian*: presumably because he has just seen Marusya and was thinking about her on his way back to the room, and like Castorp he has a guilty conscience when he is thinking of his love-interest and sees Settembrini.

(199) l. 3   *I think I might almost want to stay feverish indefinitely*: ironic words again: he will remain "feverish" for a long time to come.

ll. 13f.   *if I had run into him down in the flatlands*: Castorp believes that the atmosphere of the Berghof has made him receptive to ideas such as those of Settembrini and that "down below" he wouldn't even have understood them.

ll. 29f. *varied and lively dreams...*: Hans Castorp dreams a lot, and his dreams mingle all the impressions he has perceived at the Berghof—which gives him further food for thought on the following day (cf. ll. 30f.).

l. 34 *the objects in his room ... emerging from under a veil of gray*: also meant in the metaphorical sense: "things' in general are becoming clearer to Castorp.

l. 40 *Hans Castorp had not brought a calendar*: loss of the awareness of time is a frequently mentioned feature of life at the Berghof.

(**200**) l. 29 *Arise, go thy way, my good man*: cf. the biblical injunction of Jesus to the sick: "Arise, take up thy bed, and go into thine house" (cf. *Matthew* 9: 5; *Mark* 2: 9; *Luke* 5: 23). The verb used in German is "wandeln," which is ambiguous, as it means both to "go" and to "change." There is a further irony in this phrase: whereas in the Bible it is employed to signify that the man is cured, here it enjoins Castorp to re-enter the world of the Berghof as a sick man in need of a cure.

l. 30 *portrait of your interior*: that is, an x-ray. This points forward to Hans Castorp's acquisition of Chauchat's "inner portrait" (cf. p. 343, ll. 32ff.).

(201) *"My God, I See It"*

The translation, striving to be idiomatic, adds an extra word to the title ("it"), which dilutes some of the deliberate ambiguity of the original. The German the title: "My God, I see" ("Mein Gott, ich sehe!") indicates not just the physical act of seeing, but also connotes the achievement of insight. The expression "My God" becomes a leitmotivic expression that Hans Castorp uses at moments of intense insight: cf. when day-dreaming about Chauchat's body (p. 203, l. 27), seeing Joachim's body in the x-ray machine (p. 215, l. 14), seeing Clavdia's naked arm on Walpurgis Night (p. 319, l. 30 & p. 320, l. 2)], and twice when speaking French and admitting his love to her (p. 334, l. 15 & p. 337, l. 28, where the leitmotivic function of the expression is lost by the translation ("good God"). Although it is an everyday expression, its use also has an inevitably religious connotation.

l. 14 *Hans Castorp's case was hardly severe enough...*: his "case" may not seem medically urgent or important, but it has growing significance for him in its philosophical dimension.

ll. 22f. *considered inferior*: in the original they are "looked at over the shoulder" (a sign of disparagement), which is how Chauchat will look at Hans Castorp (cf. p. 202, ll. 34f.).

l. 31 *an inborn respect for law and order of every sort*: the Berghof has its own unwritten "rules" concerning status and an unstated hierarchy of patients—Castorp being near the bottom: he is "still low on the ladder" (p. 202, l. 8). His "inborn respect" for rules derives, no doubt, from his upbringing, but it is a little strange that he would apply this principle to life at the Berghof where the rules (such as they exist) are anything but conventional. All this is meant to be taken, of course, in a mildly humorous way.

ll. 31f. *When in Rome...*: When in Rome, do as the Romans do—i.e. Hans Castorp accepts and conforms to the conventions of the Berghof environment, no matter how strange they may seem to him, out of his "inborn respect for law and order of every sort."

l. 36 *cicerone*: strictly speaking: a guide who explains antiquities to sightseers. Here Joachim's superior knowledge of the Berghof and its culture is meant.

(202) l. 8 *he was still low on the ladder*: in the original: "a person of the lower grades"—with more ambiguity about his status in life generally.

l. 15 *a few flowers*: as he had done on Castorp's arrival (cf. p. 11, ll. 7ff.).

l. 21 *they were oblivious to the intervening time*: time is "frozen" in the hermetic world of the Berghof.

ll. 33ff. *her narrow eyes had rested on him...*: this episode (and the following glance over the shoulder) is narrated in the Subjunctive Mood—which implies that Castorp is not completely sure about his perceptions.

ll. 34f. *looked back over her shoulder*: the same image as used to express disparagement earlier (cf. p. 201, ll. 22f.). Hans Castorp is also not sure whether or not it is a "mark of disdain" (ll. 38f.)—the same word being used in both locations in the original.

l. 35 *the same smile he had seen three weeks before*: cf. p. 173, l. 11.

(203) l. 5 *Kirghiz-eyed*: see note to p. 118, l. 23.

l. 6 *his infatuation*: we are asked to believe that Castorp's obsession with Chauchat is of a higher order than any "normal" love-affair on the Flatland, for which the popular song might be an appropriate accompaniment. The "infatuation" is, of course, one-sided, and the "considerable progress" (l. 9) his "affair" has made is entirely in his own mind.

l. 8 *"how oft it thrills me"*: German folk song.

l. 11 *the early dawn slowly unveil...*: Castorp phantasizes about Chauchat in the twilight of his room both in the morning and the evening.

The image of twilight at both dawn and dusk connotes the earlier leitmotif of throwing of veil over the unpleasant or the immodest (cf. note to p. 37, ll. 40f.)—but here Castorp takes pleasure is conjuring up images that relate to sexual attraction.

l. 13   *set the room ablaze with light*: cf. p. 189, ll. 37f.

l. 21   *the terrifying bliss of these visions and images*: the contradiction (happy, but terrifying) arises from the struggle within him between the ecstatic feelings occasioned by dreaming about Chauchat, the moral doubts stemming from his upbringing ("qualms of conscience"; l. 21), and the frightening knowledge that those feelings are leading him towards aspects of life that stand in direct contradiction to all he has known so far: i.e. idleness, lassitude, irresponsibility, sickness, and death. This realization is all the more frightening because he, Castorp, is now "officially" ("according to medical dictum," ll. 32f.) one of the sick—and hence "in her camp" so to speak, whether he likes it or not.

ll. 30f.   *the illness that accentuated...*: cf. 280, ll. 40 ff. where Hans Castorp's researches lead him to see the connection between disease and the body.

ll. 35f.   *As if they were not social creatures at all*: Hans Castorp interprets both Chauchat's behavior towards him and their "relationship" as being outside of all social conventions and necessities—which, in its turn, implies that the ultimate meaning of this experience takes it beyond social mores into a much higher and deeper world. In the face of the realization that there is an entire emotional and philosophical world represented by the physical presence of Chauchat—a world that "normal" society refuses to acknowledge exists—Castorp is moving towards the Nietzschean view that conventional social morality is both a sham and a brittle defense against the true nature of existence. This realization represents a major step forward in his "education."

l. 38   *that day down in the examination room*: cf. p. 175, ll. 37 ff.

(204) l. 2   *waited to have a picture taken of his interior*: the actual procedure also has metaphorical implications.

l. 12   *this proximity*: the presence and example of Joachim (together with the latter's watchfulness—"its supervisory aspect," l. 13) causes Castorp both to assuage his conscience about being at the Berghof (his "service" to the cure is a substitute for being back at work, ll. 8f.) and to suppress his natural inclination—which would have been to have approached Chauchat in some perhaps reckless way ("kept him from overt actions and blind adventures," ll. 13f.). Joachim's restraint and self-control vis-à-vis Marusya is also an example to Castorp.

l. 20   *borrowing a pencil*: not merely a reference back to Hippe (cf. p. 120, ll. 19ff.), but also with obviously sexual connotations—and a hint of what is to come when he borrows a pencil from Chauchat (cf. p. 326, ll. 41ff.).

l. 28   *Grandfather Castorp's chin-propping method*: cf. p. 20, ll. 1f.

l. 32   *What would a woman like her do with children?*: Castorp had had similar thoughts earlier; cf. p. 127, ll. 5ff. These thoughts add to the question of what kind of sexuality is involved here.

l. 39   *twenty-eight*: four times seven.

(206) l. 4   *Hans Castorp took his temperature…*: the gossip fed to him by Fräulein Engelhart (chiefly in respect of the news that Behrens has been painting a portrait of Chauchat) causes his temperature to rise sharply.

l. 13   *twiddle-twaddle*: an expression he acquired from nurse Mylendonk (cf. p. 163, l. 6 & p. 164, l. 28). N.B. Castorp ascribes to Behrens his own inclinations and motives with regard to Chauchat.

l. 24   *Mannheim*: German city situated at the confluence of the rivers Rhine and Neckar.

ll. 27f.   *"Wedding March" from* A Midsummer Night's Dream: the musical references in the novel all relate to or connote love.

l. 31   *Platz*: cf. note to p. 3, l. 2.

(207) l. 17   *he did explore all the feelings…*: this, too, belongs to his education.

ll. 24ff.   *Hans Castorp's x-ray examination…*: the following scene is full of double-entendres and ironic ambiguities. Castorp is going to be "illuminated" (one of the meanings of the German verb), his "descent" to the x-ray room implies a move towards Hades, his "organic interior" is going to be revealed for the first time, and the x-ray room is bathed in "semi-darkness," just as in Krokowski's "analytical chamber."

(208) ll. 18f.   *just as it did in Dr. Krokowski's analytical chamber*: he had had a glimpse inside earlier, cf. p. 131, l. 40.

l. 25   *It was Clavdia Chauchat…*: the reaction of both Castorp and Joachim is remarkable.

l. 38   *crossed one leg lightly over the other*: cf. p. 210, l. 24: "had again lightly crossed one leg over the other"; and p. 328, l. 41: "she managed to cross one leg over the other."

ll. 40f.   *her Pribislav eyes*: cf. p. 75, l. 22 & p. 118, l. 17.

(209) ll. 7f.   *It was the voice Hans Castorp already knew*: Chauchat's voice sounds like Hippe's.

l. 15   *a sense of superiority*: the superiority of the native speaker—although he also experiences "humble delight" (l. 16) at the same time.

ll. 36f.   *Hans Castorp had himself showed off...*: cf. p. 56, ll. 24f.

l. 39   *despite the magazine...*: Joachim is trying to hide.

ll. 41f.   *a polite social conversation*: Joachim's civilized exchange with Chauchat is contrasted, in Castorp's mind, with the adventures he would undertake with her. The hyperbolic style of his musings is not merely intended to make gentle fun of him, but also to indicate that his "adventures" would be not merely sexual, but would extend into the realm of existential danger ([a] "savage, profound, terrible secret," p. 210, l. 1).

(210) ll. 12f.   *It did not bother him that she had turned to Joachim...*: Hans Castorp's rationalization of the situation ascribes to Chauchat the deliberate intention of talking to Joachim because she is fully aware of Castorp's feelings for her.

ll. 22f.   *his grandfather's chin-propping pose*: i.e. in order to preserve form; to avoid the outward display of inner turmoil.

l. 28   *not at all broad in the hips*: adding to her boyish appearance.

l. 33   *the small breasts of a young girl*: also bringing Chauchat close to Hippe and to an anodyne appearance.

l. 39   *the shadow of respectability*: there are still topics that Castorp would rather repress; imagining Chauchat's insides is one of them. The leitmotif first occurred on p. 27, l. 14 in the reaction of Fiete the servant to something he perceives as inappropriate, and it had its parallel in Castorp's reaction to the behavior of the Russian couple in the next room at the Berghof sanatorium (cf. p. 37, ll. 40f.).

(211) ll. 6f.   *perhaps even in French*: anticipating his later conversation with her on Walpurgis Night (cf. pp. 327 ff.).

ll. 15f.   *the adventures of the last ten minutes*: hardly anything has happened—but in Hans Castorp's mind the situation has been perilous.

l. 39   *sorcerer's laboratory*: more accurately: "witches' pharmacy"—an allusion to Goethe's *Faust*, where the hero is rejuvenated by a magic potion in the Witches' Kitchen.

(212) ll. 4f.   *our Dioskuri boys...*: Behrens makes a joke by naming the cousins after Castor (cf. Castorp) and Pollux, the twin gods born out of the union of Leda and the swan (the disguise assumed by Jupiter). Helen of Troy was their sister. After Paris had abducted Helen, Castor and Pollux went in search of her. Thus Behrens's reference connotes the cousins' attraction to feminine charms. After the death of Castor, he was permitted to spend the day in Olympus with Pollux, while at night they reversed roles and Castor descended with his brother to the Underworld. Castor and Pollux became a synonym for inseparable friends—and thus an appropriate metaphor for Hans and Joachim.

ll. 6f.   *I believe you're afraid to reveal your insides to us, Castorp...*:
now that Castorp knows about the contact between Behrens and Chauchat,
the Hofrat's words assume an added dimension of meaning. If only the
Hofrat knew what Castorp was inwardly thinking!

ll. 8f.   *Have you seen my private gallery?*: although Behrens is
referring to his collection of x-rays, the phrase points the reader (and Hans
Castorp) in the direction of Behrens's other private gallery of his own
paintings.

l. 15   *the skeleton*: a leitmotif that will assume central importance not
only in the rest of this sub-chapter, but also in the sub-chapter *Research*
(cf. p. 275, ll. 30ff.). N.B. Castorp's reaction, l. 16: "Very interesting."

l. 18   *illuminated anatomy*: this is, of course, an x-ray procedure (i.e.
with invisible rays), but for the purposes of metaphor images of "light"
occur throughout this sub-chapter. Thus here the Hofrat uses a word that
implies "light rays" ("Lichtanatomie"), and earlier (p. 210, l. 37) Castorp
had imagined not just "rays," but "light rays" turned on Chauchat.

l. 19   *This is a female arm*: it is almost as if Behrens knows that
Castorp is obsessed with Chauchat's arm. Behrens's gratuitous comment:
"the kind they hug you with on intimate occasions" (p. 212, ll. 9f.) is
another ironic dagger into Castorp's heart. The original speaks of "a little
hour" (Schäferstündchen = a lover's tryst)—which will be, in fact, all the
intimate time Hans Castorp spends with Chauchat.

(213) ll. 1f.   *Joachim expelled his breath ... It was over*: a forecast of
Joachim's ultimate end; cf. his death, p. 528, l. 20: "it was over."

l. 3   *Next culprit*: the word belongs to Behrens's humorous
characterization of the Berghof as a penal institution.

l. 4   *You'll get a free copy*: so will Chauchat—and she will give it to
Castorp.

l. 5   *the secrets of your bosom*: the secrets of Castorp's "bosom" are
known to the reader (and the narrator)—and he will see the "secrets" of
Chauchat's bosom when she gives him her x-ray.

l. 7   *the technician was changing plates*: connects with the changing
of gramophone records, where death is also conjured up (cf. p. 635, ll.
11ff.).

l. 9   *Hug the panel. Imagine it's something else...*: Behrens is
irrepressible in his double-entendres.

l. 10   *sweet bliss*: ditto.

ll. 22f.   *a red-globed light*: the red light (which has already been
mentioned [p. 212, l. 40], and is switched on again [p. 214, ll. 5f.]) is a
recurring leitmotif. The image recurs during Castorp's researches (cf. p.

270, ll. 11f.) and in the séance scene (cf. p. 664, ll. 3 & 8, p. 667, ll. 35f. & p. 669, l. 30). Its presence connotes the erotic.

l. 29   *like a cat's*: i.e. like Chauchat.

ll. 32f.   *we first have to ban any rousing daylight scenes…*: the process is metaphorically necessary because Hans Castorp is going to be looking into his grave (cf. p. 215, l. 38).

l. 34   *Of course*: said, apparently, in a sober voice, but spoken from the heart.

ll. 36f.   *We first have to let darkness wash over our eyes…*: as Castorp has already done many times.

l. 41   *That's oxygen that you scent…*: oxygen does not give off a scent.

(214) l. 2   *Let the exorcism begin*: shades of the later séance (cf. pp. 644 ff.). This procedure is an actual viewing of the body, as opposed to the taking of a photograph which was done earlier (cf. p. 212, ll. 24ff.).

l. 5   *the little red light*: ever-present when the body is being observed (cf. note to p. 270, l. 11f.). The x-ray scene and the later séance have many parallels.

l. 12   *my lad*: in the original Behrens uses a word ("Jüngling) that is ambiguous and can imply that Castorp is a "new boy." This is, in fact, the case, as he is about to learn about death and the grave.

l. 20   *peered into the void of Joachim Ziemssen's skeleton*: the key leitmotif of the skeleton indicates that the form of the human body would collapse and dissolve if it were not supported by the structure of the bones. Cf. note to p. 12, l. 38.

ll. 34f.   *Joachim's diaphragm … rose*: various medical authorities have pointed out Thomas Mann's error here: it should say that the diaphragm *falls*.

l. 37   *hilum*: a depression in an organ where the blood vessels and nerves enter.

ll. 38f.   *the toxins that make him so tipsy*: cf. note to p. 174, l. 22.

(215) l. 11   *Joachim's sepulchral form…*: the medical terms point to Joachim's eventual fate.

ll. 11f.   *his bare scaffolding*: Hans Castorp uses the same metaphor in describing the body in his later researches, cf. p. 273, ll. 4ff.

l. 12   *His gaunt* memento mori: remember that you are mortal (Latin). A forewarning of Joachim's fate.

l. 12f.   *He was filled with both reverence and terror*: reverence at the view of life he is witnessing; and terror because it has serious implications (i.e. Joachim's death, cf. ll. 14ff.).

l. 14 *My God, I see it!*: see note to p. 201. The act of seeing implies here much more than the concrete image: it also connotes the knowledge of the fate of the human form, the inevitable dissolution of the body, and death. Verbs of seeing occur many times in this scene.

l. 20f. *it did not really mean anything...*: on the contrary, it signals Joachim's death.

l. 26 *doubts about whether it was permissible...*: in a letter to a correspondent, Thomas Mann called this scene "impermissible," revealing its sensitive dimensions in his mind.

l. 28 *piety*: a key word in Castorp's world.

l. 35 *fluoroscope*: in its simplest form, a fluoroscope consists of an x-ray source and fluorescent screen between which a patient is placed.

l. 38 *he saw his own grave*: an image that commenced when he heard the cough of the Austrian horseman, cf. p. 12, l. 36.

l. 40 *decomposed, expunged, dissolved*: a key leitmotif; dissolution is one of life's processes (cf. note to p. 12, ll. 23f.).

(216) ll. 6ff. *he understood that he would die... when listening to music*: this major insight is accompanied by the reaction he has when listening to music. Music and death are indissolubly connected in Castorp's life (cf. p. 109, ll. 38 ff.).

l. 14 *The ceiling lamp went on*: as when Settembrini entered Castorp's room (p. 189, ll. 36ff.), the contemplation of the darker side of life is interrupted by enlightenment.

l. 20 *bronchi*: the passages that convey air into the lungs.

Freedom

(216) ll. 28ff. *seven weeks... seven days*: the nature of the experience of time and the use of the number 7 (with its allusion to the seven days of Creation) lend the story the aura of myth.

l. 34 *unnaturally brief and ... unnaturally long*: the typical effect of the suspension of time in the hermetic world of the Berghof.

(217) l. 12 *cozy resort*: cf. note to p. 83, l. 17. The German word ("Lustort") conjures up similar associations to those connoted by Behrens when he described the cousins' walk as a "Lustwandel." See note to p. 45, l. 23f.; cf. also p. 217, ll. 27 & 30, where Settembrini repeats the word: for him the Berghof embodies all the vices that human beings should avoid.

ll. 20f. *Not even a dog...*: A hidden quotation from Goethe's play *Faust*. In his monolog that opens the play, Faust, despairing of ever being able to know anything important, declaims: "No dog would want to continue living like this."

ll. 32f.   *Beware of the irony that flourishes here*: for Settembrini, irony only has one valid function: as a rhetorical device to promote rational argument and progress. An ironical attitude to existence is not only antithetical to progress, it is destructive and sinful—cf. "it becomes a source of depravity, a barrier to civilization, a squalid flirtation with inertia, nihilism, and vice" (p. 217, ll. 35ff.). This solemn warning also constitutes Thomas Mann's criticism of himself: in his works he used irony much more widely than merely as a rhetorical device (see "Introduction," p. 23).

(218) l. 1   *his stay up here had made his mind receptive*: Castorp is fully aware of what the atmosphere of the Berghof means for his personal development: he has become far more receptive and open to new ideas than he ever would have been on the Flatland.

ll. 2f.   *in terms of sympathy which perhaps is the more telling factor*: not only where intellectual matters are concerned is Castorp more receptive, but also in respect of the more intuitive areas of life—i.e. those represented by Chauchat.

l. 6f.   *his own perceptive powers had advanced*: Hans Castorp is aware that both his "education" is proceeding at the Berghof, but also that his critical faculties are being developed at the same time. It is, of course, ironic that Settembrini's attempts to educate Castorp result in the latter's becoming more critically perceptive; cf. also ll. 14ff.: "Such is the ingratitude of immature youth…"

l. 9   *almost the same way he talks about music*: Castorp's reflections about Settembrini's sermons are both critical and progressive: he is able to sense that Settembrini's remarks are motivated by the same fundamental concern: clarity and reason. On the other hand, his critical faculty rejects a simplistic view of irony and sees his way to clear to a concept of irony that is much more ambivalent ("But if 'no healthy mind can for a moment doubt its purpose', what sort of irony is that" [p. 218, ll. 11f.]).

l. 10   *politically suspect*: cf. p. 112, l. 33.

ll. 17f.   *to put his insubordination into words*: in all his dealings with Settembrini and the latter's ideas Castorp lets himself be guided by his own instincts. While being open to the Italian's sermonizing, he remains unconvinced that the Italian is right. However, he has so far only made some halting attempts to formulate his own position (e.g. in his remarks about the relationship between sickness and stupidity; see note to p. 95, ll.16ff.). Here, too, he is reluctant to risk formulating his own response (because he is clearly still not confident enough of himself and is apprehensive about the Italian's possible reaction) and contents himself with disapproving of Settembrini's criticism of Hermine Kleefeld which he *wants* to believe was wrong "for other reasons" (p. 218, l. 20).

l. 25   *Leopardi*: cf. note to p. 97, l. 35.

ll. 26f.   *what about our good schoolmaster himself?*: Castorp hits the nail on the head: he perceives the irony that Settembrini, the voluble advocate of enlightenment, reason and progress is sick. This exchange between Castorp and Settembrini constitutes a further step in Castorp's progress *away* from the Italian. Although his disagreement the Italian is confined openly to a relatively minor matter (Settembrini's criticism of Kleefeld), his inner thoughts reveal his total disapproval.

l. 27   *Carducci*: see note to p. 56, l. 41.

l. 37   *Grazie tanto*: many thanks.

ll. 40f.   *I despise paradoxes*: of course he does: the man of reason only wants clarity.

(219) l. 2   *quietism*: cf. note to p. 111, l. 19f.

ll. 3f.   *I also notice that you are coming to the defence of illness yet again*: cf. p. 95, ll. 22f.

ll. 5f.   *some of the things that Dr. Krokowski lectures about on Mondays*: cf. p. 188, ll. 33–34.

ll. 6f.   *illness to be a secondary phenomenon*: Hans Castorp has progressed from rejecting Krokowski's ideas to being receptive to them.

l. 15   *Analysis is good as a tool of enlightenment and civilization*: Settembrini's positions are always clear and simple (if not simplistic).

l. 20   *Analysis can be very unappetizing*: i.e. not approved by Settembrini and his positivistic philosophy. Hans Castorp assimilates these ideas and reproduces their negative side both when talking to Behrens about the body (p. 262, ll. 11f.) and in his conversation in French with Chauchat (p. 337, l. 34, where the translation fails to retain the verbal parallel of the word "anatomy" in the original).

l. 23   *Well roared, lion*: Shakespeare, *A Midsummer Night's Dream*, Act V, Scene 1, l. 249. The line is a common saying in everyday German.

l. 28   *you've scaled to that level, too*: implying that Castorp has acquired a new level of insight. (In the original the word, here translated by "level," is "Station"—which suggests even a "station of the cross.")

l. 35   *The imp of Satan!*: see note to p. 94, l. 31. Cf. also note to p. 58, l. 26.

(220) ll. 10f.   *Assume our positions*: the original is more ambiguous, implying also the assumption of battle-positions.

l. 17   *Parthians and Scythians*: The Parthian Empire (approx. 3 BC to 3 AD) stretched across modern-day Ukraine and Southern Russia, and the Scythian Empire encompassed present-day Iran, Iraq, Afghanistan,

Pakistan, and lands around the Persian Gulf. For the Ancient Greeks any people living east of the Rhine were "Scythians," and for both the Greeks and Romans the word meant "barbarians." That is, of course, how Settembrini also means it.

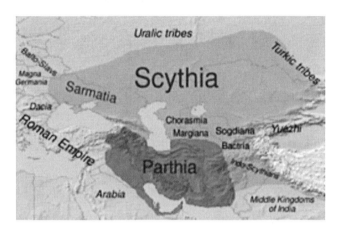

Parthia and Scythia

l. 19   *Russians, male and female*: in the original Settembrini responds to Castorp's question: "You mean Russians?" (using the masculine plural), by saying: "And Russian women"—an obvious dig at Castorp's infatuation with Chauchat (cf. Settembrini's "tightening ... at the corner of his mouth," ll. 19f.), as Castorp himself acknowledges in his next thought: "No doubt, he had meant something by that" (l. 21).

l. 29   *quibbler*: Hans Castorp's derogatory term for Settembrini will be used by the latter to describe Hans Castorp later (cf. p. 247, l. 31).

(222) ll. 1f.   *It established Hans Castorp's* freedom: "freedom" is a key word for Castorp, and it is clearly significant here in that it is italicized. It is also ironic that his view of freedom—as a personal odyssey—is quite different from the political significance that Settembrini gives the word. It includes lethargy, the "unbounded advantages of disgrace" (cf. p. 79, l. 17), his love for Clavdia Chauchat, his fascination with the body and with illness, and his "sympathy with death."

ll. 5f.   *a sense that had little to do with the meaning Settembrini attached to the word*: cf. p. 151, ll. 1ff.

l. 11   *Mercury climbed to one hundred degrees*: a sign of his emotional turmoil.

ll. 20f. *the alien scaffold*: a leitmotif (cf. p. 215, ll. 11f.) that relates to the skeleton as a fundamental structure that preserves form. Cf. also Hans Castorp's study of anatomy in the sub-chapter *Research*, p. 273, ll. 4ff.

ll. 20f. *the analytical pit*: he had had a glimpse into the grave earlier in the x-ray room, and will have more such insights in the future.

Mercury's Moods

l. 23 *no outward signs*: the German speaks of "signs and fires" ("Zeichen und Feuermale"). The summer solstice was (and still is) celebrated by the lighting of fires on the mountains tops.

ll. 25ff. *Real time knows no turning-points…*: this sentence is full of subtle allusions to the new age that dawned with the beginning of the First World War. Since that date signaled for Thomas Mann the end of an era (and thus the beginning of a new one), he employs an ambiguous German word ("Säkulum") that can mean either century or era, and underscores the implications with hints of war: "trumpet fanfares … cannons" (using an archaic, biblical word for "trumpets").

(223) ll. 20f. *hybrid Alpine alders…*: these trees do not, in fact, drop their needles, but they suit Thomas Mann's purpose in that they have both male and female blossoms on the same stem.

ll. 26f. *wildflowers*: the mention of the "bushy columbine" (line 27–28) masks the fact that this is the aquilegia of the ranunculus family—the blue flower that is the key flower in Hans Castorp's world (cf. note to p. 117, l. 4).

l. 32 *an icy shiver in the midst of fever*: a recurring leitmotif of the novel is the contrast between heat and cold (see next note.)

l. 39 *omelette en surprise*: now known as Baked Alaska, a dessert made of ice cream placed in a pie dish lined with slices of sponge cake and topped with meringue. The entire dessert is then placed in an extremely hot oven for just long enough to firm the meringue (see picture opposite). This is an appropriate metaphor for the state that Hans Castorp is in (both now and later). We are told that "he often made such comments … like a man who is chilled and feverish at the same time" (ll. 41ff.).

(224) l. 20 *lace peignoir*: cf. notes to p. 108, l. 25 & p. 184, 22.

l. 28 *a form of depravity*: Hans Castorp quotes Settembrini on the "misuse" of irony, p. 217. l. 35—but with obvious reservations. Castorp's use of the word "depravity" in the course of the novel reveals both his emancipation from Settembrini and the development of his own thinking. In his conversation with Chauchat on Walpurgis Night he uses the word more objectively: "The body, love and death, are simply one and the same.

Because the body is sickness and depravity" (p. 336, ll. 40f.), and by the time he listens to the music of Debussy he even embraces the word as something positive: "It was depravity with the best of consciences" (p. 637, ll. 13f.).

Omelette en surprise

ll. 29f.   *views ... on "illness and despair"*: see p. 96, ll. 28ff.

ll. 40f.   *her illness was ... of a moral nature*: Castorp is reflecting critically on what has transpired and is reaching some significant conclusions. Far from condemning Madame Chauchat for her behavior (as Settembrini would do), he now ascribes her behavior and her illness to the same source: her "moral nature," by which he means her view of life and everything she stands for. He has overcome his earlier disdain for her behavior ("back when he...," p. 225, l. 6), and rejects Settembrini's strictures against her and what she stands for ("Hans Castorp had almost totally renounced such feelings," p. 225, ll. 12–13)—although the word "almost" shows that he does still have some lingering doubts. This is a crucial step forward for him: he now accepts Chauchat's attitude to life as valid—which is but a short step from his accepting it also as a possible attitude for himself to adopt.

(225) ll. 8f.   *he had his Maria Mancinis*: chewing his cigars is equivalent to Chauchat's chewing her fingernails. Castorp and Chauchat have something in common.

l. 14   *Parthians and Scythians*: see note to p. 220, l. 17.

ll. 17f. *a boneless language...*: the Russian language (already described by this epithet on p. 113, l. 23) is connected with a lack of structure, thus connoting the formless world-view that Chauchat embodies. Much of this paragraph deals with formlessness and its connection to the rejection of conventional bourgeois morality.

ll. 18f.   *the one Director Behrens had described recently*: cf. p. 171, ll. 1f.

l. 30   *he could shrug off...*: the shrug is the act of indifference adopted by long-term residents of the Berghof. The act is symbolical of an attitude that stands in contrast to the conventional formalities of the bourgeois world; cf. p. 226, ll. 14f.

ll. 30f. *the world republic and beautiful style*: cf. note to p. 167, l. 8f.

ll. 31f. *especially coolly*: there is a nice touch of irony here. Although Settembrini gives the appearance of being intellectually superior and supremely rational (in the German he is "sober"), his body contradicts him, as it is "feverish and tipsy"—the latter is the word that was used by Behrens to describe the tubercular Joachim (cf. p. 214, l. 39).

l. 33   *Parthians and Scythians*: see note to p. 220, l. 17.

ll. 35ff. *he had himself begun to understand...*: N.B. it is a process of comprehension, not sudden enlightenment.

l. 39   *it was all over with such rigor*: Hans Castorp means that his initial condemnation of Frau Chauchat (that stemmed from his "rigor"— i.e. his strict upbringing) is suddenly replaced by fascination and even a growing acceptance.

ll. 41ff. *But what sort of dubious experience...*: why human beings behave in such a way is a mystery.

(226) l. 8f. *he began to experiment on his own...*: the wording here is the same as *placet experiri*. In other words, he is now pursuing experiments in respect of his attraction to Chauchat and her mode of existence

ll. 14f. *the shrug with which Joachim had greeted him*: cf. p. 7, l. 36.

ll. 21f. *not the ... melancholy found in our little song*: cf. p. 137, ll. 31ff. This is not a mere infatuation or a conventional love-affair. As the rest of this paragraph makes clear, Hans Castorp's attraction to Clavdia Chauchat is closely tied to his fascination with the non-rational aspects of existence and his yearning for answers to the meaning of life.

l. 23   *a fusion of frost and heat*: cf. *omelette en surprise*, p. 223, l. 39.

ll. 29ff. *her careless body...*: the connection between illness and the body—cf. p. 175, l. 36f. & p. 203, l. 30f.—is a topic he will study intensively in the sub-chapter *Research* (cf. p. 271ff.).

l. 33   *the terrifying and infinitely seductive dream...*: the lack of an answer in the bourgeois world to the question of the meaning of life leads to the dream of something else: another world-view that is at the same time both attractive and frightening.

l. 35   *hollow silence*: the repetition of the starting-point of Hans Castorp's questioning of life's purpose, cf. p. 31, ll. 26f.

l. 39   *meaning and purpose of life*: cf., p. 31, ll. 13 ff.

(227) l. 15 *merci*: thank you.

l. 15   *this perfectly conventional courtesy*: yes, but in Castorp's case the motivation is also more than mere courtesy.

l. 26   *some healthy little goose*: cf. p. 138, ll. 3ff. A love-affair on the "Flatland" would not have entailed the dangers attendant upon falling in love with Chauchat. The latter brings him face to face with the most profound questions which—this is the implication—a conventional bourgeois love-affair "down below" would never do.

l. 36   *dazzling red light*: the red light has an erotic connotation.

(228) ll. 19   *Joachim was keeping his eyes directed at his plate*: Joachim's typical behavior when faced with an action by his cousin that embarrasses him (cf. also p. 229, l. 39).

(229) l. 9   *Max and Moritz*: title of and main characters from an illustrated story (publ. 1865, in verse) by German humorist Wilhelm Busch. Every German child is familiar with Max and Moritz.

l. 31   *that day*: cf. p. 48, ll. 11ff.

l. 36   *pneumothorax*: cf. note to p. 48, l. 38.

l. 39   *with his eyes cast down*: cf. p. 228, l. 19.

(230) l. 20   *some healthy nitwit*: the original uses the parallel masculine term to "little goose" (cf. p. 227, l. 26).

l. 23   *a model pupil in the school of life*: he wishes now to be viewed by Chauchat as anything but a model citizen.

l. 25   *a shallow three-week visitor*: he uses the word "Hospitant" (see note to p. 69, l. 24).

l. 26   *But had he not taken vows…*: cf. p. 191, ll. 31f. The acceptance of Hans Castorp as a patient is equated with entering a monastery.

ll. 38f.   *The sun and the waning moon both stood…*: cf. p. 152, ll. 1ff. At the end of that sub-chapter (p. 157, ll. 33ff.) Clavdia Chauchat is conjured up—and she is in the background here, too.

ll. 41f.   *the forest path beyond the bench beside the water trough*: this is where Castorp first met Settembrini. His walking further now is symbolical: he has progressed *beyond* Settembrini's influence.

(231) l. 6   *they strolled off bareheaded*: the symbolic act represents a further step away from Castorp's earlier life.

ll. 6f.   *since taking vows*: another reference to the monastic act of entering the service of the cure, cf. p. 230, l. 26.

ll. 24f.   *he certainly could not allow him to march ahead alone*: the tensions here are manifold: Joachim's attachment to his cousin, their inseparability, the inappropriateness of Hans Castorp's approaching (and maybe talking to) Chauchat alone, and Joachim's determination not to let something like that happen. The entire scene is quite comical, with Castorp rushing ahead and Joachim struggling to keep up.

l. 35   *between slope above and drop-off below*: just as during the initial train-journey up to Davos, the geography implies symbolically the dimension of adventure and danger.

(232) l. 6   *It was the longed-for release*: the German ("Erlösung") implies even redemption and salvation.

l. 7   *On winged heels*: allusion to Hermes who is usually portrayed with wings on his heels (see picture on p. 26).

l. 9   *Joachim ... who went on staring in silence...*: embarrassed, but avoiding confrontation.

ll. 12f.   *as asking a total stranger for a pencil*: recalling Hans Castorp and Hippe (p. 120, ll. 19ff.) and looking forward to Walpurgis Night (p. 326, ll. 41ff.).

ll. 17f.   *the other reason why Joachim had turned his head away*: because Castorp's pursuit of Chauchat is the opposite of "honorable" (in Joachim's world-view) and a rejection of the bourgeois morality to which Joachim subscribes.

l. 19   *trace-kicking*: this is a leitmotif that had been used first by the narrator on p. 34, l. 34, in speculating about Hans Castorp's future, and that also comes later out of Behrens's mouth (cf. p. 262, l. 37f.).

l. 20   *No man in the flatlands could have been happier*: repeating the image of the "goose" or the "nitwit" down in the Flatland (cf. p. 227, l. 26 & p. 230, l. 20).

l. 22   *some healthy little goose*: cf. p. 227, l. 26.

ll. 28f.   *Maybe they'll play that aria from 'Carmen'*: the aria from *Carmen* that Hans Castorp cites is Don José's famous declaration of his love for Carmen ("La fleur que tu m'avais jetée"—The flower you threw to me). It will become one of Castorp's favorite recordings (cf. *Fullness of Harmony*, pp. 637–39), and he will see himself as Don José and Chauchat as Carmen. This reference to *Carmen* has sprung from Chauchat's simple act of acknowledging him with a nod and a "good morning." What is going on in his subconscious mind? The translation is a little misleading here, because Hans Castorp is familiar with the standard *German* translation of the aria which deviates from the original French text that the translator quotes here. However, the German text is also appropriate to his own case: "Here, safely next to my heart,/see the flower you gave me that morning,/leafless, faded in the air of the prison,/but still retaining its sweet aroma.// Oh, how anxiously those dark hours/passed for my closed eyes!/ Intoxicated by the aroma I lay there/and in the dark night I saw your image." That image recurs on other "dark nights": for example, as he lies in his darkened room just before Settembrini enters and switches on the light (cf. p. 189, ll. 37ff.) and at the end of the sub-chapter *Research* where

Castorp's study of anatomy leads him to conjure up Chauchat's "hot and tender" embrace (cf. p. 281, ll. 29ff.). Until the explicit descriptions of his favorite recordings in *Fullness of Harmony* (pp. 630ff.), music reveals Hans Castorp's inclinations on an unconscious level (and even in that sub-chapter, the unconscious also plays a major role).

Encyclopedia

(233) l. 1   *Herr Settembrini's innuendoes*: cf. p. 220, ll. 19ff.

l. 17   *as a certain gentleman...*: Settembrini, of course; see p. 195, ll. 38ff.

ll. 33ff.   *These were the kinds of suits...*: This long and rather obtuse disquisition about love at the Berghof propounds the view that the kind of "love" that is promoted by the Berghof atmosphere is of a different quality from that encountered "down below." The ambience of the Berghof reveals an aspect of life of which Castorp was not aware before coming here ("he had understood it very inadequately down in the flatlands, had actually been in a state of innocent ignorance" (p. 234, ll. 17ff.). The reaction of patients (e.g. Joachim, Castorp himself) is not to go red in the face (as one would expect of "normal" people), but to go pale (cf. p. 234, l. 30 & 33)—with the implication that the knowledge they have gained has opened a door to the soul (and to life) that offers a new and terrifying vista ("the ever-intensifying accent on shock and indescribable adventure," (p. 234, l. 22–23) of something irresistible but at the same time indefinable. It is this irresistible, but indefinable element that lures Castorp onwards.

(234) l. 21   *My God!*: see note to p. 201.

(235) ll. 20ff. Castorp increasingly makes a fool of himself by unabashedly demonstrating his infatuation with Chauchat.

l. 24   *schadenfreude*: taking pleasure in someone else's discomfort.

l. 36   *a man in a highly lambent state*: radiant, illuminated; cf. p. 174, ll. 22ff. This is, in fact, a leitmotif that relates to the "illuminated" state of the Freemasons. The order was founded in the late 18th century as a rational alternative to the irrational thinking of some Freemason groups. It was organized on military-Jesuitical principles. Naphta will call Settembrini "a good *illuminatus*" (p. 455, l. 16). See also the sub-chapter *A Good Soldier* (p. 489 ff.) where these ideas are developed.

l. 39   *the young man with the saltcellar fingernail*: cf. p. 109, l. 26.

(236) ll. 1ff.   *the same flush on his cheeks...*: the immediate effect of the Berghof atmosphere on Hans Castorp, and his reaction to hearing the cough of the Austrian horseman (i.e. a death rattle; cf. p.13, l. 3), are both related to his contemplation of Chauchat. In other words, the three realms are connected: the rarified atmosphere, the context of death, and sexual passion.

l. 18   *Pardon*: I beg your pardon.

l. 20   *Pas de quoi, madame*: Don't mention it, madame.

ll. 37f.   *coming into social contact with Frau Chauchat*: what takes place is, of course, scarcely "social contact."

l. 40   *Certain inhibitions stood in the way*: Castorp's entire social background is opposed to his having any normal social contact with Chauchat. All the usual conventions of civilized discourse (using the formal form of address, even speaking French, p. 237, ll. 3f.) would be inappropriate in the context of his "relationship" with her ("not necessary, not desirable, not the right thing at all" [p. 237, l. 4]).

(237) ll. 5f.   *just as Pribislav Hippe had smiled...*: cf. p. 120, l. 31.

l. 12   *one bothersome person*: despite Hans Castorp's reassurance to Settembrini that the latter does not disturb him (cf. p. 191, ll. 16f.).

ll. 12f.   *Hans Castorp winced*: a typical guilty reaction of his when Settembrini disturbs his reveries.

ll. 14f.   *first greeted...*: cf. p. 55, ll. 6ff.

l. 19   *that smile not only shamed and sobered*: one of the rare occasions when Castorp is glad of Settembrini's sobering influence.

l. 24   *that little limping devil*: the devil is conventionally portrayed with a cloven hoof. This detail may have been copied from Goethe's *Faust* where the devil's servant (Mephistopheles) limps. Cf. note to p. 6, l. 16.

l. 26   *petersham*: cf. note to p. 54, l. 24. In the early twentieth century freethinkers were often portrayed in cartoons as wearing petersham. The coat is "ineluctable" (better: "inevitable") because it is the only one Settembrini possesses.

l. 30   *But what about your affairs?*: the ambiguity of the word "affairs" in the translation is absent from the original.

l. 37   *But one gets used to not getting used to it*: Castorp's fate at the Berghof is expressed in that leitmotivic phrase.

l. 41   *this isn't a Siberian salt mine*: Castorp has absorbed the phrase from Behrens (cf. p. 176, l. 9).

(238) l. 1   *you prefer Oriental metaphors*: the "East" (presently in the form of Chauchat) is Settembrini's enemy.

l. 2   *Asia is devouring us*: another little dig by Settembrini at Castorp's obsession.

l. 2   *Tartar faces*: the Tartars were a Mongolian people; the term is used disparagingly to mean "Asiatic."

l. 4ff.   *Genghis Khan ... lone wolves on dusky steppes, snow ... Schlüsselburg and Holy Orthodoxy*: all of these images symbolize

Settembrini's opposition to the "East" and what it represents for him: backwardness, oppression ("knouts"), mysticism, and the darker forces of nature. The Schlüsselburg (now: Shisselburg) is a castle on an island at the head of the River Neva, 25 miles east of St Petersburg. It got its name from its being a "key fortress" (the meaning of the name in German) for the protection of the city. During the time of the Russian Empire it became a notorious prison for political prisoners. There is a slight mistranslation here, too: in the original Settembrini speaks of "Steppenwolfslichter"—i.e. the eyes of the wolves from the steppes, and the phrase rhymes with the German for "Tartar faces" ("tartarische Gesichter").

ll. 6f.   *Pallas Athene ... as a kind of self-defense*: the goddess of civilization and wisdom. In Greek mythology she appeared as an armed warrior goddess who helped many heroes, including Heracles, Jason, and Odysseus (the latter having direct relevance to Castorp).

l. 7   *your Ivan Ivanovitches*: stereotypical name for Russians.

l. 11   *at least he knows his Latin*: a man who knows Latin earns Settembrini's respect, since he must be a cultivated and civilized person.

l. 12   *something Herr Settembrini never did*: he has a sense of humor and can be very witty—but he never laughs.

l. 18   *he reached for his inside breast pocket*: apart from the humor of Castorp's carrying his x-ray around with him, there is irony here in that his own x-ray image will soon be replaced in his pocket by Chauchat's.

ll. 19f.   *like a passport...*: now that Castorp "belongs" at the Berghof he has his "proof" ("a passport or a membership card" [l. 20]) with him at all times.

l. 23   *the funereal photograph*: the adjective associates the x-ray image with death.

ll. 25f.   *if there were other reasons for it*: i.e. he really doesn't want to see the evidence; the entire procedure is offensive to him.

l. 27   *Here you have your legitimation*: Settembrini would, of course prefer it if Castorp were healthy and did not have a legitimate reason for staying—or for allying himself with sickness. Settembrini's gesture as he hands the x-ray back ("turning his face away" [p. 238, l. 29f.]) reveals his distaste and disapproval.

ll. 32ff.   *you are aware ... what store I set*: Settembrini's view is that there is an element of charlatanry about the Berghof, and some patients who are not sick interpret their own x-rays to demonstrate that they are.

l. 34   *matters of physiology*: i.e. the normal state of the body. According to Settembrini, people see what they want to see.

(239) l. 19   *the way you are throwing the months around*: Castorp's new relationship to time (a result of the Berghof atmosphere) is viewed by

Settembrini as further evidence of Castorp's slide towards "Asia." His advice—"do not let them infect you with their ideas" [p. 239, l. 28])—the medical metaphor is very apt—is part of Settembrini's exhortation to resist the blandishments of the East by applying the principles of the West that are to be found in Castorp's *"higher* nature"—higher both in the physical sense (the reason as opposed to the lower body) and in the philosophical sense (more noble).

l. 26   *Mongolian Muscovites*: Settembrini's terms for the Russians at the Berghof are, not surprisingly, intended to be pejorative. This one refers to a historical period centuries before when the Mongols and the Muscovites (two separate races) interacted (by some estimates contemporary Muscovites have 50% Mongol genes).

ll. 31ff.   *Time, for instance...*: Settembrini joins in the discussion of time. For him time is precious and not to be "wasted." Doing nothing, behaving as if time were standing still, is "Asiatic," and signals the death of progress and the giving-over of the self to lassitude.

(240) l. 5   *Carpe diem*: seize the day; i.e. don't waste your time. (Latin, from an ode by Horace.)

l. 5   *an urbanite sang that song*: he means the Roman poet Horace (65 B.C.—8 B.C.), who in fact composed the words after he had retired to the country.

l. 7   *in the service of human progress*: Settembrini's perpetual theme: time and space are to be used rationally for the service of humankind and the goal of progress.

ll. 19f.   *with such pedagogic urgency*: Settembrini's sermons to Castorp are becoming more and more desperate—especially since he now has a clear opponent in the figure of Chauchat.

(241) l. 7   *International League for the Organization of Progress*: the idea for this League derives from the book Settembrini mentions below: see note to p. 242, l. 22.

l. 10   *Darwin's Theory of Evolution*: Charles Darwin (1809–82) demonstrated that all species of life have evolved over time from common ancestors through the process he called natural selection. The League to which Settembrini belongs is basing its program on the philosophy of "Social Darwinism"—the belief that society also evolves and, in fact, does so towards a perfect state. Such a belief has nothing to do with Darwin's theory of biological evolution.

ll. 19ff.   *The problem of the health of our race*: these views are suspiciously anti-humanistic. In essence, the League to which Settembrini belongs advocates a program of eugenics; that is, the "perfecting the human organism" (ll. 18f.) by a variety of measures, including "methods for combating its [the race's] degeneration" (ll. 20f). The elitist (and racist) nature of these proposals is indicated by the claim that such degeneration is "one lamentable side effect of increasing industrialization" (ll. 21f.)—in other words, the lower classes would be targeted for birth control, or other measures. Eugenics gained attention and favor in the early twentieth century and various jurisdictions (e.g. Sweden and the USA) passed eugenicist laws. It is also clear from Settembrini's remarks elsewhere that he means only the white race, since he repeatedly denigrates Asia (cf. "Asia is devouring us. Tartar faces in every direction you look" [p. 238, l. 2]).

l. 33   *progressive political parties*: a euphemism for those in favor of eugenics.

l. 36   *he felt like a man who had just lost his footing*: Settembrini's extreme and inflammatory ideas have deeply disturbed Castorp.

ll. 40f.   *these ... these efforts*: the hesitation indicates both Hans Castorp's surprise and his doubts about what he has just heard.

(242) l. 5   *Barcelona*: second largest city in Spain and center of the region of Catalonia (see next note).

ll. 5f.   *that city boasts of a special affinity...*: presumably as it is the center of Catalan society and culture. At the beginning of the twentieth century the Catalan nationalists called for more political and cultural independence. This might also be an anachronistic reference to the so-called "Tragic Week" of July 1909, in which there were protests against the drafting of reservists to go and fight in Morocco.

l. 9   *threatened me with death*: it is ironic that Settembrini was too ill to travel to the Congress. The "death threats" are meant, of course, in reverse: he would have risked his health if he had gone there.

ll. 11f.   *Nothing is more painful*: Settembrini's complaint relates directly to himself, but also has a transferred significance for Castorp.

l. 22   *The Sociology of Suffering*: the title of a book published in 1914 by Franz Carl Müller-Lyer (1857–1916) who wrote: "the goal of this movement is the well-organized state." Cf. Settembrini's statement that the "ultimate goal is the perfect state" (p. 242, l. 19f.).

l. 33   *all conceivable instances of human suffering*: just a moment's reflection will reveal what an ambitious, if not quixotic, undertaking this is. Cf. the narrator's later comment about its "boundlessness" being similar to the scope of Krokowski's lectures (p. 358, l. 26).

ll. 35ff.   *the chemical elements...*: we have now moved beyond the ambitious into the realm of ironic satire.

(243) l. 4   *belles-lettres*: i.e. literature.

ll. 7f. *all masterpieces of world literature*: Settembrini's assignment is to compile a volume that will offer summaries of all the works of world literature that speak of human suffering" (l. 5). Since almost *all* works of literature deal with suffering, the undertaking is an impossible task.

l. 14 *eradicating human suffering*: Hans Castorp's naïve categorization of Settembrini's task unwittingly reveals it as a sheer fantasy.

ll. 33f. *these atmospheric conditions*: Settembrini is fully aware of what the atmosphere of the Berghof can do to people.

ll. 35ff. *that isle of Circe*: Odysseus visited the island of Circe, where his men turned into pigs and began to grunt. (Cf. the game played on Walpurgis Night: a person with a blindfold must attempt to draw a pig, p. 325, ll. 12 ff.).

(244) l. 8 *I told you that on the very first evening*: cf. p. 84, l. 28f. (the evening of Castorp's first *full* day at the Berghof).

l. 9 *Yes, and at the time I was free to do so*: Castorp's analysis of his situation is, in Settembrini's eyes, an exercise in self-justification ("I know, and now you have your membership card in your pocket" [p. 244, l. 17]), although he cites Behrens's diagnosis as his justification for staying.

ll. 15f. *the whole pulmonary lobe...*: the phrase he had learned from Behrens's diagnosis of him, cf. p. 178, ll.33f.

l. 20 *an honest, classical device of rhetoric*: a phrase Castorp has absorbed from Settembrini; cf. p. 217, l. 34.

l. 28 *Hans Castorp's posture had stiffened*: this is a crucial scene, in which Castorp stands up to Settembrini and refuses to back down. The sentence: "Hans Castorp stood his ground" (p. 244, l. 30) reveals his determination. For the first time also he contradicts Settembrini head-on, instead of adopting his usual ploy responding in a jesting or non-committal manner (cf. p. 243, ll. 41f.: "It was impossible to reply with a quip ... as was Hans Castorp's usual method"). "The battle had been engaged," says the narrator (p. 244, ll. 29f.) and Castorp's responses to Settembrini reveal a new combative style. The battle-lines are also clearly drawn here: on the one side Settembrini, the "pedagogue" (p. 244, l. 31), and on the other side "a narrow-eyed woman" (p. 244, l. 32).

l. 40 *sophistry*: subtly deceptive argumentation.

(245) l. 5f. *spend the rest of my days in private lodgings*: which he will, in fact do, cf. p. 351, ll. 31ff.

ll. 10f. *you are not a man to sustain your better self here*: in Settembrini's eyes Castorp is a fine, young man, with all the correct values, but not strong enough to resist the temptations of the Berghof and the slide into decadence. Settembrini sees himself as fighting with all the power his reason can muster against the decay of the body, whereas he believes that Castorp has all too easily given in to the lures of the body.

ll. 17f. *whether it is not, rather, the* body *and its evil proclivities…*: Settembrini's views are clear: the body is not merely an insufficient vehicle for the propagation of Enlightenment, it is also the cause of the tendency to descend into a realm he despises: sex and quietism. Apollo (Settembrini) fights against the surge of Dionysus (Chauchat). Hans Castorp is, indeed, fascinated by the body (and one body in particular), and soon after this exchange with Settembrini he will study it in depth (cf. *Research*, pp. 270ff.).

l. 19 *What do you have against the body?*: the interruption is both an emotional reaction to Settembrini's words and also a declaration of war ("I've declared war on him" [l. 22]). Castorp's elaboration of this question: How can a humanist be opposed to the body? shows more reflective analysis.

ll. 22f. *But I've declared war on him*: Hans Castorp is fully aware of what he is doing and what his rebellion against his mentor represents: it is his full emancipation from the Italian's influence over him.

l. 38 classicismo *against* romanticismo: the battle in the novel, simply put, is between the "classical" view of life and the "romantic." Settembrini represents the former: reason, enlightenment, form, progress, democracy—the victory of life over death. For him, "romanticism" is the very opposite of classicism: the surrender to "nature" with all its conflicts and chaos, its mysticism and lack of clarity, its irrationality and unchecked emotionalism—and ultimately a fascination with death and a yearning for it.

(246) l. 6 *Prometheus*: see note to p. 155, l. 24.

ll. 8f. *charge of Christian obscurantism*: Hans Castorp's challenge to Settembrini ("What do you have against the body?"; p. 245, l. 19) is interpreted by Settembrini as an accusation that he is taking the position of those Christians who despised the body and revered the soul.

l. 14 *Plotinus*: 205–270, the most important philosopher of ancient Neo-Platonism (the belief that real things were but poor images of higher realities). Good listener that he is, Hans Castorp quotes Settembrini's words back at him during a later debate with Naphta, cf. p. 388, l. 24f. & and p. 445, ll. 31f.—much to the humanist's displeasure.

l. 18 *Porphyrius*: 233–309, Neo-Platonist philosopher, biographer of Plotinus and Pythagoras.

l. 22 *the Lisbon earthquake*: on 1 November 1755 a powerful earthquake destroyed a large part of the city and 30,000 people died. The event had a major effect on philosophical thinking in Europe, especially with reference to the relationship between God and evil in the world.

l. 23   *I've not been reading newspapers here*: for all his self-reflection and -analysis Hans Castorp is still extremely naïve, as this howler reveals.

ll. 24ff.   *I would note that it is regrettable…*: Settembrini castigates Hans Castorp's ignorance here and remembers it: cf. p. 373, l. 24.

ll. 29f.   *Goethe said something in his bedroom*: In 1823 Johann Wolfgang von Goethe (cf. note to p. 45, l. 9) had a sensation one night in his bedroom that an earthquake had taken placed in Messina (Italy). Several days later the news of the actual earthquake arrived.

ll. 33f.   *the earthquake in Messina*: 13 November 1823. The area had suffered many earthquakes, including a devastating earthquake (plus tsunami) in 1908.

l. 36   *Voltaire rose up against it*: among other comments, Voltaire (1694–1778) wrote a "Poem on the Lisbon Disaster, or an Examination of the Axiom 'All is Well'" (1756). As with Settembrini's earlier reference to Plotinus, his example of Voltaire is later also used against him by Castorp on p. 388, ll. 25ff.

(247) ll. 3f.   *those ancient Gauls*: in Roman times Gaul comprised the region of Western Europe comprising present day northern Italy, France, Belgium, western Switzerland and the parts of the Netherlands and Germany on the west bank of the River Rhine.

l. 7   *it is servile*: the word "servile" (in the German: "knechtisch") is an important leitmotif, and it belongs to the world of Naphta. It implies being bound in servitude. (The translation loses the precise verbal parallels: cf. p. 112, ll. 30f. where the word is translated as "slavish.")

l. 13   *What do you have against analysis?*: Settembrini's concept of analysis is quite different from that of psychoanalysis.

l. 31   *He is not a bad quibbler himself*: quite an admission from Settembrini, who for the first time has met his match in Hans Castorp. The word used in the German is "Räsonneur" and had been used earlier by Hans Castorp to categorize Settembrini (cf. p. 220, l. 29).

Humaniora

In the classical sense the "humaniora" comprised the study of the seven liberal arts of the medieval university: grammar, dialectics, rhetoric, arithmetic, geometry, music, and astronomy. But in the context of *The Magic Mountain* the term implies a new view of the human sciences: the study of humankind in an attempt to comprehend the totality of life. Thus in this sub-chapter Hans Castorp learns about medicine and the human body. The title of this sub-chapter is also ironic, since despite all the scientific discourse the real topic is Chauchat.

(248) l. 14   *Joachim was acting like a tyrant*: these are Hans Castorp's thoughts of course, and it is disingenuous of him to consider Joachim a tyrant, since it is he (Castorp) who mostly drags Joachim along to places (and people) where Joachim has little inclination to go.

ll. 24f.   *getting used to things ... getting used to not getting used*: the repeated theme of Castorp's getting used to "not getting used" to living at the Berghof is charted by his renewed enjoyment of his favorite cigar, Maria Mancini. The enjoyment of the latter makes him feel *physically* and therefore also *morally* at ease with his state ("Moral satisfaction reinforced physical pleasure" [p. 248, l. 31]).

ll. 39f.   *Director Behrens walking through the garden*: hint of a Biblical reference; cf. Genesis 3: 8: "And they heard the voice of God, walking in the garden" (German version). The biblical statement occurs after the Fall of Man through forbidden sex, and what follows in the novel is a highly sexualized discussion of cigars, and a further discussion of painting in which Chauchat (Eve) is the focal point.

(249) l. 13   *Behold, behold, Timotheus*: a quotation from the ballad "The Cranes of Ibycus" (1797) by Friedrich Schiller (1759–1805). The poet Ibycus is murdered in a wood on his way to a festival in Corinth. With his dying breath he beseeches a flock of cranes to bear witness to his murder. Later at the festival, the cranes fly overhead and one of the murderers utters the line: "Behold! Behold, Timotheus/The cranes of Ibycus!"—thus revealing their guilt. The line became an everyday saying in German to indicate that a secret had been revealed. In the biblical context it was Paul who performed the act of circumcision on Timothy (*Acts* 16: 1–3).

l. 21   *Let me have a look. I'm a connoisseur*: the German is more suggestively erotic: "I am a connoisseur and lover" ("Ich bin Kenner und Liebhaber"), thus lending a sexual undertone to the sentence. The rest of the dialogue is both highly sexual in connotation and ambiguous: both hetero- and homosexual undertones abound.

l. 22   *lovely brunette*: Behrens's characterization of the cigar connotes something feminine—and sexual. The conversations about cigars always have sexual connotations. Note also that the act of smoking separates the easily seduced smokers (Castorp, Behrens, Chauchat) from the bourgeois ascetic non-smokers (Settembrini, Joachim).

l. 23   *Maria Mancini*: see note to p. 11, l. 39.

l. 23 *Poste de Banquette*: a cigar to be smoked after dinner (supper). From the Spanish "postre de banquete" = dessert.

l. 24 *natural color*: no discoloration signified higher quality.

ll. 25f. *Sumatra-Havana wrapper*: hints at a connection with Peeperkorn. There are many allusive connections between this scene and the later arrival of Peeperkorn.

l. 28 *she has her little moods*: Castorp has assumed the metaphor initiated by Behrens and carries it further. His description of the cigar also sexualizes it.

l. 31 *let's exchange brands*: the phallic exchange continues the sexual innuendo. Cf. the connection to Hans Castorp's borrowing of a pen from both Hippe and Chauchat.

l. 32 *She has good breeding*: the entire conversation about cigars has the aura of masculine banter about women. However, there is also a strong element of sexual ambiguity in the scene: the two men exchange cigars and fondle each other's phallic symbols.

l. 33 *Saint Felix-Brazil*: location of famous cigar factories, founded by a German, Gerhard Dannemann.

ll. 35f. *A little caution is in order*: undoubtedly sexual in implication. The translation unfortunately loses the deliberate ambiguity of the original: the phrase "when dealing with her" is a rendition of the German word "Verkehr" which can literally mean both "dealing with it/her" and "during intercourse with it/her," with clearly sexual implications. Chauchat is definitely in the background of this conversation.

l. 39ff. *Each rolled his gift between his fingers*: this entire paragraph relates the cigars to a woman's body—cf. "slender body," "ribs," "pores," etc. [l. 41ff.], but is also unquestionably phallic.

l. 40ff. *there was an organic living quality*: the description continues the undercurrent of homoeroticism in the actions of the two men.

(250) l. 9 *The director loved imported cigars*: the translation adds a word ("cigars") that reduces the ambiguity of the original that says simply: "The director loved imports"—which is clearly also a reference to Chauchat (and perhaps to other women who have visited the sanatorium, such as the Egyptian princess, cf. p. 258, l. 12; and p. 538, ll. 22f.).

l. 11 *Henry Clay*: named after a U.S. senator (1777–1852).

l. 21 *kick the bucket*: the metaphor in the German is "abtanzen" (dance off, i.e. die), which connotes the sub-chapter "*Danse Macabre*" to come (cf. pp. 281ff.), as well as the First World War that is described as "the wicked dance" (cf. p. 706, l. 12).

l. 29 *my chest heaving away*: becomes a leitmotif; cf. p. 280, l. 38f. & p. 346, l. 30.

l. 30   *an injection of camphor*: camphor produces a feeling of cooling similar to that of menthol and acts as a mild local anesthetic. In cases of nervous excitement it has a soothing and quieting result.

ll. 34f.   *You paint sometimes…?*: this question comes out of the blue, but it reveals what has been going on in Castorp's mind while the talk has ostensibly been about cigars. He knows very well that Behrens paints, because Settembrini had told him (cf. p. 59, ll. 24f.).

l. 42   *Anch' io sono pittore…*: I, too, am a painter. "That Spaniard" was, in fact, an Italian: Correggio (1489–1534) is said to have called out these words when he saw Raphael's "Saint Cecilia" in Bologna.

(251) l. 1   *Landscapes?*: Hans Castorp can be cunning and devious when he chooses to be.

l. 6   *But no portraits?*: he already knows the answer to this question, cf. p. 205, ll. 22ff.

ll. 9f.   *But it would be very kind of you*: Castorp has finally maneuvered the conversation to where wanted it to go from the start.

ll. 13f.   *Behrens was so pleased and flattered…*: in the original his reaction is much more intense (and suggestive): "Behrens was delighted, flattered to the point of enthusiasm. He even went red with pleasure, and this time his eyes seemed about to shed tears."

l. 21   *I've tried something along that line…*: Hans Castorp has painted in watercolors (l. 24), but not yet in oils ("The real thing in oils?"; l. 23). In other words, he has not yet matured.

l. 34   *His hand definitely trembled…*: Behrens is nervous—about showing the cousins his paintings, or at inviting two young men into his apartment?

(252) l. 2   *"antique German"*: it means old furniture, recalling the 16th and 17th centuries.

ll. 3f.   *a fraternity cap and crossed swords*: dueling was common in German university fraternities; thus this image points forward to the duel between Settembrini and Naphta—and to the War.

ll. 4f.   *a small smoking alcove, done in "Turkish" style*: a fashion of furniture and decorative design based on Middle Eastern styles that flourished from the latter half of the 19th century until the late 1920s. It was favored especially for the men's smoking rooms once found in the homes of the wealthy, then for clubs, and finally, for cafés and restaurants.

l. 17   *Segantini*: Giovanni Segantini (1858–1899), very popular painter towards the end of the nineteenth century; reproductions of his paintings were commonly seen on the walls of middle-class houses.

l. 21   *dilettante style ... bad mistakes*: Behrens is clearly an amateur, as these initial comments indicate. This prepares the reader for the ensuing discussion of art (and the portrait of Chauchat).

l. 29   *The portrait of Clavdia Chauchat*: there are three things to be noted here: first, it is hanging in Behrens's living-room and has therefore a certain prominence; second; Hans Castorp sees it right away—which is not surprising because that is the reason why he is here; third, the portrait bears "only a very distant resemblance to her" (p. 252, l. ll. 31f.; also "a botched job," p. 253, l. 21), statements that ironically undermine much of the discussion that follows.

l. 32   *He intentionally avoided the spot*: all part of his plan.

l. 34   *Sergi Valley*: this is a mistake by Thomas Mann that has been perpetuated in the translation. The correct name of the valley (near Davos) is the Sertig Valley.

Sertig Valley

(253) l. 6   *he ought not to have recognized the lady at all*: i.e. if he hadn't known about the portrait beforehand and about Behrens's relationship with Chauchat, he would not have recognized her in the painting. The painting is definitely not a good likeness of Chauchat.

ll. 6f.   *any more than Joachim had recognized her*: without the help from Hans Castorp and Behrens Joachim would not have recognized the person in the portrait.

ll. 11f.   *recover damages*: for Joachim this is Castorp's "revenge" for Joachim's having prevented him from joining the group of patients on the veranda earlier (cf. p. 248, l. 11f.).

ll. 15ff.   *Frau Chauchat looked ten years older...*: this entire paragraph reveals what a poor piece of work the portrait is.

l. 21   *a rather botched job*: the narrator's characterization of the portrait is unambiguous.

l. 27   *As she lives and breathes!*: Castorp's dissembling continues.

l. 30   *twenty sessions at least*: this figure must have stuck a dagger in Castorp's heart.

l. 30f.   *How can one handle...*: although the surface meaning relates to the portrait, the metaphorical significance points both to the obsession with the person herself and to the world that she represents.

l. 32   *hyperborean cheekbones*: "hyperborean" originally referred to peoples who lived beyond (hyper) the "Boreas" (the North Winds): thus at the edge of the earth. In the nineteenth century the word came to describe the races of Northern Asia and Northwestern North America, whose physiognomy included narrow eyes and prominent cheekbones.

l. 37   *Yes—no—only superficially:* from a purely objective point of view Castorp's statement is accurate.

l. 38   *I know her more internally...*: although the Hofrat's description uses medical and physiological terminology, the words all have a secondary, implicitly sexual meaning.

ll. 39f.   *I pretty much know what's what with her...*: one can only speculate about what Hans Castorp thinks of this entire speech.

(254) l. 5   *the epicanthic fold*: a piece of skin on the upper eyelid that covers the inner corner of the eye.

l. 10   *an atavistic abnormality*: The term atavism denotes the tendency to revert to ancestral type. An atavism is an evolutionary throwback, such as traits reappearing that had disappeared generations ago.

l. 19   *terribly lifelike skin*: Castorp's enthusiasm and praise for the Hofrat's technique seems to be grossly exaggerated—but the following discussion of the painting makes it seem only slightly so.

ll. 21f.   *he brushed his hand ... the skin left exposed by her décolletage*: a substitute for the real thing.

ll. 24f.   *a rather crude effect*: the narrative technique often makes it difficult to distinguish between the narrator's views and those of Castorp. The following paragraph ("All the same Hans Castorp's praise was justified..." [p. 254, l. 26]) indicates that the discussion of the painting has reflected Castorp's views throughout ("We are simply describing Hans Castorp's impression" [p. 254, ll. 39f.]), and the conclusion ("the most remarkable piece of painting in the apartment," [p. 254, l. 42]) relativizes the previously critical comments—or vice versa.

(255) l. 5   *epidermis*: the outer layer of skin.

l. 9   *life's undergarments*: the sexual innuendoes continue.

l. 11   *a matter of science*: the Hofrat's praise of his own work as a precise rendition of the body's physiology is both an ironic exaggeration and is contradicted by the previous negative comments about the quality of the painting.

ll. 12f. *the horny and mucous layers...*: the outermost layer of the skin, the epidermis, is also called the "horny layer." The epidermis layer itself is made up of five sublayers, and the mucous layer is one of those, but it is not a layer of the outermost skin.

ll. 13f. *the imagined reticular layer...*: a lower layer of the skin. The word "imagined" means that the layer is not visible in the painting.

l. 14   *papillae*: the bases for the hair follicles. In the original Behrens uses a non-technical word ("Wärzchen") that connotes nipples.

ll. 29ff.   *Yes indeed, yes indeed*: the following scene is one of the funniest in the entire novel. The torrent of words that spills from Castorp's mouth—his excitement is revealed by their fragmentary nature—is accompanied by, and is a pretext for, his taking the portrait of Chauchat off the wall and placing it on the sofa ostensibly to give it more light ("it has absolutely no light here," ll. 40f.). The ideas could have issued from the mouth of Settembrini, since they advocate form as the basis of all human activity, including art. But Castorp's words are ironically relativized not only by their lack of form, but also by his ulterior motive (to get his hands on the portrait of Chauchat), and most of all by the fact that he is carrying in his hand the very denial of what he is saying.

(256) l. 8   *they are all humanistic professions*: in his stumbling way Hans Castorp is developing his own broader view of humanism—as a view of life that encompasses all human phenomena.

l. 11   *a realist*: he means that he graduated from a technical high-school ("Realgymnasium"), rather than a school that focused on the humanities (e.g. history, languages). Cf. note to p. 31, l. 6.

l. 21   *a kind of fifth faculty*: the traditional university had four faculties: Philosophy, Law, Medicine, and Theology.

l. 41   *forgetting to rehang the picture...*: it's not at all a question of his "forgetting." The image of Castorp carrying the portrait of Chauchat into the next room and placing it against his chair and then telling his companions that that is what he is doing ("it's fine there for the moment," [p. 257, ll. 10f.]), is without parallel in the novel.

(257) l. 2   *a Greek Venus*: The *Aphrodite of Milos*, better known as the *Venus de Milo,* one of the most famous works of ancient Greek sculpture. It was originally (mistakenly) thought to be the work of Praxiteles (see note to p. 257, ll. 6f.)

l. 6   *Phidias*: 490–430 B.C., regarded as the greatest of all Classical sculptors.

ll. 6f.   *that other fellow ... Hebrew-sounding way*: an obtuse reference to Praxiteles ("...es" is the "Hebrew" ending) whose most famous sculpture is of Hermes and Dionysus—a modern variation of which is facing the Hofrat: Castorp, with Chauchat's portrait.

Hermes and Dionysus

l. 18   *palmitin, stearin, oleïn*: palmitin is a fat that occurs in certain oils (e.g. palm, tallow and butter); stearin is a fat used in the manufacture of soap; oleïn is derivative of palm oil, often used in cooking.

l. 21   *Ambrosia*: in Greek mythology the food or drink of the gods.

l. 41   *everywhere you find a little something of interest*: Behrens's sexual allusions do not cease.

(258) l. 3   *Hans Castorp rolled the cylindrical coffee mill between his palms*: since the coffee-mill is decorated with obscene designs (cf. l. 7f.), this act has a sexual connotation.

l. 8   *he blushed*: Hans Castorp is still prudish in some ways: he turns red when he realizes that the images on the coffee mill are obscene.

l. 10   *my little kitchen fay*: his cook ("fay" = fairy).

l. 12   *an Egyptian princess*: see note to p. 250, l. 9. She arrives back at the Berghof at the same time as Peeperkorn (cf. p. 538, ll. 22f.).

ll. 15f.   *No, no, it doesn't bother me, of course*: he has recovered from his initial shock, but this disclaimer is only a half-truth.

ll. 17ff.   *The ancients are said to have decorated their coffins...*: a fact he learned from Settembrini, cf. p. 197, l. 22.

ll. 38f.   *if a man is interested in the body*: Castorp's reflections about the body and sickness have now brought him squarely into the anti-Settembrini camp.

l. 41   *I could have become a clergyman, too*: doctor, priest … what next?

(259) l. 4   *External circumstances*: his family and social milieu.

l. 7   *Ontogenetically speaking*: i.e. as far as the individual is concerned. The discussion of the function of the skin and its manifestations deals with the various possibilities of the skin's appurtenances to become erect. Since the real object of the discussion is Chauchat, the sexual connotations are manifold. Cigars, coffee-mill, the skin's erections (even in death: *rigor mortis*)—the sexual undertones are everywhere.

l. 18   *keratinized skin*: the process by which skin cells migrate upwards to the surface layer and are sloughed off.

ll. 21f. *Do you know how you blush or turn pale*: the physiological explanation relates directly to Hans Castorp's various reactions to life on the Berghof, but particularly to his "relationship" to Chauchat.

l. 25   *Blushing for shame*: relates to Krokowski's lectures (cf. p. 125, ll. 11ff.).

l. 27   *vasomotor nerves*: they control the dilation or contraction of blood vessels.

l. 31   *the cerebral cortex...*: a structure within the brain that plays a key role in memory, attention, perceptual awareness, thought, language, and consciousness.

l. 31   *vascular center*: blood vessels.

l. 31   *medulla*: The medulla oblongata is the lower portion of the brainstem. It deals with autonomic functions, such as breathing and blood pressure.

l. 33   *the vascular nerves*: small nerve filaments that supply the wall of a blood vessel

l. 37   *something perilously beautiful*: i.e. like Chauchat.

l. 42   *So that's what happens*: Castorp is, of course, reflecting about his experiences in the past few weeks. Behrens has accurately described how Castorp has been reacting physiologically to seeing Chauchat.

(260) l. 8   *the skin's sebaceous glands*: small glands which secrete an oily matter (sebum) in the hair follicles to lubricate the skin and hair.

l. 12   *without greasy cholesterol*: a waxy alcohol found in the cell membranes and transported in the blood plasma of all animals. It is an essential component of mammalian cell membranes.

ll. 14f. *the lad in the tale ... a pail of minnows*: reference to a fairy story by the Brothers Grimm: "The Lad Who Went Out To Learn To Be Afraid." He learns fear when his wife (the king's daughter) empties a bucket of fish over his bed as he sleeps.

ll. 24f. *the sound of especially beautiful music*: looking ahead to *Fullness of Harmony*, cf. pp. 626 ff.

ll. 25f. *when I first took communion...*: the effect of music and the religious experience are equated. Both have a similar effect on the sub-rational level.

l. 28   *a stimulus is a stimulus*: this entire conversation relates to Castorp's infatuation with Chauchat.

ll. 29f.   *Whether minnows or communion...*: Castorp had just referred to his communion (l. 25), using the word "Abendmahl," which means literally "evening meal." When Behrens employs the word here, clearly relates also to Castorp's reaction to seeing Chauchat at mealtimes. The German word connotes also the Last Supper and Peeperkorn's later feast (cf. p. 551, 34ff.).

(261) l. 9   *a histological fluid*: "histological" means "of the tissues" —so Behrens is speaking here of "tissue fluid."

l. 11   *turgor*: the pressure of the cell contents against the cell wall that maintains the form of the organism.

l. 14   *vasa lymphatica*: the vessels that convey the lymph, a fluid that acts as an intermediary for the distribution of nutrition from the blood and the reception of waste products.

l. 25   *dropsy*: an old term for the swelling of soft tissues because of the accumulation of excess water.

ll. 28ff.   *"Yes," he remarked softly after a pause...*: Hans Castorp's reaction indicates how deeply this explanation has affected him: he is relating Behrens's words to Chauchat. See also the following exchange between Castorp and Behrens.

ll. 30f.   *"The body!" he suddenly cried in a rapturous outburst...*: Hans Castorp's naiveté causes him to reveal his feelings. This "outburst" prepares for his rapturous praise of the human body in the sub-chapter *Walpurgis Night* (cf. p. 337).

(262) l. 5   *collagen*: the main protein of connective tissue in animals and the most abundant protein in mammals.

l. 8   *muscle plasma ... myosin*: an alkaline fluid in muscle that coagulates spontaneously, separating into myosin and muscle serum.

l. 9   *rigor mortis*: the ultimate act of the body's becoming erect. The only erection that has not been discussed is the most obvious one—the phallic—that is always in the background of this conversation.

ll. 11f.   *The anatomy of the grave*: a foretaste of the appearance of Naphta. In this speech Castorp is reproducing ideas he first heard from Settembrini (cf. p. 219, ll. 15 ff.), but now with their negative connotation.

l. 25   *une destruction organique*: an organic destruction. The use of the French brings Chauchat back into the conversation.

l. 26   *some Frenchman*: Claude Bernard (1813–78), French physio-
logist.

ll. 29f.   *if someone is interested in life…*: this is the central theme of
Hans Castorp's "education" at the Berghof, and thus of the novel, too.

l. 36   *Form is namby-pamby nonsense*: the statement reveals Castorp's fascination with dissolution and death.

ll. 37f.   *Literally kicking over the traces*: these words have accompanied Hans Castorp since his youth (cf. p. 34, l. 34) and were used earlier
by Behrens to describe him (cf. p. 359, ll. 29f.). In this context the phrase
has undertones of sexual penetration.

(263) ll.   18f.   *namby-pamby*: Joachim   uses   Castorp's   term—
ironically?

ll. 19f.   *kicking over the traces*: Behrens's expression, cf. p. 262, ll.
37f.

Research

This sub-chapter deals in considerable detail with Hans Castorp's study of
anatomy, physiology, and biology. It serves the important function of
extending and deepening his knowledge of life. Having been introduced to
the chemistry of the body (and of life) by Behrens, whereby Castorp's
fascination with life and death had been stimulated, he now undertakes his
own private course of study to expand his knowledge and further his
education. In this sub-chapter Castorp builds on that knowledge and
deepens it—and Chauchat is always in the background as he reads. In
responding to a critic who had complained that this sub-chapter was too
long, Thomas Mann stated that it was not mere caprice on his part, but
rather his deliberate intention to show that Hans Castorp develops his own
idea of what it means to be "human" through his research into the
processes of life, which leads him ultimately to his own ideal image of
organic life.

The scientific works that are summarized and discussed here are not
primarily intended to be understood as *scientific* texts, but rather as
literary reworkings that bear directly on the novel's themes: the sources
used by Thomas Mann are subtly manipulated in order to create a myriad
of leitmotivic relationships to many other parts of the novel. The
commentary that follows points out some of these relationships. In this
sub-chapter the reader can follow the process by which Hans Castorp
learns about the process of life and the chemical composition of the body.
His newly acquired knowledge leads him to all-important conclusions
about the unity of life and death—conclusions that will affect his behavior

henceforth and move him down the path to maturity. In all of Castorp's musings about the body and life, the image of Chauchat is ever-present: the "mystery of the body" includes both the actual bodily processes and his fascination with *her* body.

(264) l. 7   *Piz Michel, Tinzenhorn*: mountains near Davos.

l. 15   *All Souls'*: November 2, on which day the Roman Catholic Church commemorates the souls of the dead members of their faith.

l. 20   *Rhätikon chain*: near Davos. It stretches eastwards into Austria.

ll. 38f.   *between the resort and Davos-Dorf*: Davos consisted of two separate sections, Davos-Platz (the resort center) and Davos-Dorf.

(265) l. 16   *Schatzalp*: see note to p. 9, ll. 19f..

l. 18   *a warm foehn wind*: strong, warm dry wind, caused when a prevailing wind is forced over a mountain range.

l. 23   *skijoring*: sport in which the skier is towed by a horse or dogs.

l. 38   *the first day of Advent*: Advent starts on the fourth Sunday before December 25.

Tinzenhorn

(266) l. 9   *Mardi Gras*: literally, "Fat Tuesday." In the Christian calendar traditionally Shrove Tuesday before Ash Wednesday (a moveable religious feast). It is the final day of Carnival before Lent begins.

l. 20   *Sociology of Suffering*: see note to p. 242, l. 22.

l. 24   *the Muscovites*: archaic term for Russians; cf. note to p. 239, l. 26.

(267) l. 5   *the world turned magical and wondrous*: the evocation of magical wonder in connection with the blanket of snow is a metaphorical forecast of things to come in the sub-chapter *Snow*. See also next note.

ll. 12f. *the world seemed to be under a spell of icy purity...*: these lines evoke death. The narrator is preparing us (and Castorp) for the magical encounter with death in *Snow*.

l. 32   *the magic of the winter night*: see previous two notes.

l. 33   *music drifting up*: an essential element of Hans Castorp's experiences here.

(268) ll. 6ff.   *he tended here ... hasty ... chatter*: as we have seen on several occasions already (cf. p. 255, ll. 28ff.).

(269) l. 24   *Joachim poring over his Russian textbooks*: cf. note to p. 63, l.7.

l. 28   Ocean Steamships *no longer had anything to say to him*: not only his neglect of this work that he had brought with him, but also of the books on engineering sent to him by his family, shows his alienation from his intended profession.

ll. 35f.   *in various languages...*: Hans Castorp has been well educated—especially since reading scientific texts would be demanding.

(270) l. 7   *uncut pages*: at this time books were printed on large sheets of paper that were then folded and bound, but the edges of the pages were not cut. That was a job for the reader.

ll. 11f.   *the reddish light from his shaded lamp*: he doesn't actually need the lamp to read ("he could just as easily have read by the bright moonlight"; ll. 12f), but this detail introduces an erotic element into Hans Castorp's activity: after all, his study of life and the human body is closely connected with his fascination with Chauchat.

l. 18   *protoplasm*: believed to be the living contents of a cell, a belief now discredited.

l. 30   *cerebral cortex*: the structure within the brain that plays a key role in memory, attention, perceptual awareness, thought, language, and consciousness.

l. 35   *chloroform*: a chemical once used as a popular anesthetic.

l. 35   *chloral hydrate*: a sedative and hypnotic drug.

l. 35   *morphine*: a pain-killer derived from the sap of the opium poppy.

(271) ll. 6f. *an amoeba—a pseudopod*: an amoeba is a genus of protozoa (a micro-organism) that moves by means of pseudopods, temporary extensions of the organism.

ll. 19f.   *What jubilation had greeted...*: reference to the work of the biologists Ernst Haeckel (1834–1919) and Thomas Henry Huxley (1825–95). Haeckel had theorized that there were very lowly organisms consisting of "primitive slime" (*Urschleim*), and named them *Monera*. In 1868 Huxley described a specimen of such a phenomenon, supposedly dredged up from the North Atlantic in 1857 and he named it, in honor of Haeckel, *Bathybius haeckeli*. Haeckel then suggested that such a substance was constantly coming into being at the bottom of the sea. But it was later shown that the "slime" was produced by chemical reactions between the specimens and the alcohol used to preserve them.

Monera gypsum

l. 24   *archebiosis*: the origination of living matter from non-living.

l. 34   *dissolution*: repeating a key leitmotif of the novel that first occurred on Hans Castorp's arrival at the Berghof (cf. p. 12, ll. 24f.).

ll. 41ff.   *it was sensual to the point of lust...*: Note the sexual nature of the description in the rest of this paragraph (extending onto p. 272, l. 14).

(272) ll. 1ff. *It was a secret, sensate stirring...*: this entire paragraph is an excellent example of Thomas Mann's "creative" use of scientific texts. The language is frequently colloquial (cf. "ran riot"; l. 7), and the style is highly suggestive (cf. "awakened to lust"; l. 13) and connotative (Chauchat is in the background throughout).

l. 13   *decomposing*: dissolution again.

ll. 18ff.   *The image...*: this is, of course, Chauchat. This description of the human body is a good example of Thomas Mann's ironic style: the object of Hans Castorp's adoration is described in scientific terms that on the one hand demystify the idealization of the loved-one (cf. "its skin blemished with natural defects..."; ll. 19ff.), and yet on the other hand introduce a new kind of mystery about the body's composition and processes (cf. "The night of its pubic region..."; ll. 34ff.).

l. 22   *lanugo*: hairs that grow on the body to insulate it because of the lack of fat.

ll. 24f.   *its head crowned...*: an allusion to Chauchat's hair-style; cf. p. 74, ll. 40f. & p. 335, ll. 23f.

l. 24   *keratinous*: keratins are the major protein components of hair, wool, nails, horn, hoofs, and the quills of feathers.

ll. 25ff.   *its hands clasped behind the neck...*: Chauchat is conjured up. N.B. "a racial variation in the formation of the lid"—which repeats Behrens's description of Chauchat, p. 254, l. 5.

l. 35   *epithelial*: referring to the tissues composed of cells that line the cavities and surfaces of structures throughout the body.

l. 38   *the pleuroperitoneal cavity*: the body cavity containing both the lungs and the abdominal viscera; one of the two primitive partitions of the body of the embryo. The *pericardial cavity* contains the heart, and the *pleuroperitoneal cavity* contains the other internal organs.

l. 39   *mucous membranes*: membranes lining all body passages that communicate with the air, such as the respiratory and alimentary tracts, and having cells.

l. 40   *trachea*: the airway through which respiratory air passes.

l. 41   *hemoglobin*: a protein in red blood cells that carries oxygen.

(273) ll. 4ff.   *its scaffold of bones*: the description of the body's structure uses, in part, terms that belong to the world of technology that Castorp once embraced. The connection between his earlier activity and this new knowledge is thus established.

l. 11   *Serous cavities*: serous is the term used for various bodily fluids that are typically pale yellow and transparent, and of a benign nature.

l. 34   *algae*: photosynthetic organisms that occur in most habitats. They vary from small, single-celled forms to complex multicellular forms, such as the giant kelps that grow to 65 meters in length.

l. 34   *gelatin*: a translucent, colorless, brittle, nearly tasteless solid substance, extracted from the collagen inside animals' skin and bones. (Collagen is the main protein of connective tissue in animals and the most abundant protein in mammals, making up about 25% to 35% of the whole-body protein content.)

(274) l. 17 *embryology ... sternum*: Castorp holds a volume on the study of the development of the embryo on his sternum, a long flat bone in the center of the chest.

l. 21   *gelatin*: see note to p. 273, l. 34.

l. 22   *the mount of conception*: a concept that Mann found in one of his sources. It is not used in contemporary biology.

l. 23   *protoplasm*: the living contents of a cell. The term is not commonly used in modern science.

l. 26   *the male was a parasite...*: the green spoonworm (bonellia viridis)—which happens to be sexually dimorphic.

l. 27   *the male placed his arm down the gullet of the female*: this is Thomas Mann's metaphorical translation of the biological act. The tentacle of the organism is inserted into the mantle (a fold in the body) of the female. The male organism (probably a paper nautilus, a kind of octopus, is meant here) has a sperm-carrying arm, known as the hectocotylous arm, with which to impregnate the female. In the paper nautilus, this arm remains active and wriggling for some time, prompting the zoologists who discovered it to conclude it was some sort of worm-like parasite. It was duly given the name *Hectocotylus*, which held for some time until the mistake was discovered.

l. 30   *deserving a Greek and Latin name*: In 1829, the French naturalist George Cuvier (1769–1832) first identified and described a hectocotylus in the paper nautilus (an octopus of the genus *Argonauta* [Greek]) but at the time he thought that this detached arm was a parasitic worm. He named it *Hectocotylus octopodis* (Latin).

l. 31   *listened to the learned argument*: "argument" is a key motif of the novel. In fact, the German word used by the narrator is quite colloquial ("zanken"), that is, somewhat inappropriate as a description of an academic dispute. But the same verb recurs at other significant moments: for example, in describing the disputes between Settembrini and Naphta. Settembrini: "You should not be amazed that this gentleman and I argue frequently" [p. 373, ll. 8f.]), a fact that Hans Castorp remembers during his dangerous ski-trip ("...he's [Naphta] almost always right when you two argue" [p. 468, l. 35]). Although Settembrini and Naphta later find themselves in the shadow of Pieter Peeperkorn's huge personality, they can still attract the attention of the patients at the Berghof "with one of their elegant, passionate, academic arguments" (p. 576, ll. 36f.). The entire sub-chapter *The Great Petulance* (pp. 672ff.) deals with the argumentative atmosphere of the Berghof: "What was it then? What was in the air? A love of quarrels" ("Zanksucht"), p. 673, l. 11, concluding with the fatal duel between Settembrini and Naphta (pp. 693ff.). Ultimately, the novel ends with the fiercest argument of all: the First World War.

l. 31   *ovists and animalculists*: rival schools of scientific thought about the generation of life. During the 1700s, Dutch microscopist Anton van Leeuwenhoek (1632–1723) discovered "animalcules" in the sperm of humans and other animals. Some scientists speculated they saw a "little man" (homunculus) inside each sperm. An opposing school of thought, the ovists, believed that the future human was in the egg, and that sperm merely stimulated the growth of the egg. Ovists thought women carried eggs containing boy and girl children, and that the gender of the offspring was determined well before conception.

l. 40   *lamellae*: gill-like structures.

l. 40   *mucous membrane*: lining involved in absorption and secretion. The mucous membranes line various body cavities that are exposed to the external environment and internal organs.

l. 41   *blastula*: The blastula is an early stage of embryonic development in animals. It is also called blastosphere. It is produced by cleavage of a fertilized cell. The blastula precedes the gastrula in the developmental sequence.

(275)   l. 1   *gastrula*: a phase in the development of the embryo.

l. 2   *protozoon*: a single-celled, usually microscopic, organism, such as an amoeba.

l. 3   *epithelia*: gall bladder.

l. 3   *ectoderm*: The ectoderm is the start of a tissue that covers the body surfaces.

l. 4   *endoderm*: one of the germ layers formed during the development of the animal embryo.

l. 8   *glutens*: a composite of the two proteins found in some grass-related grains, notably wheat, rye, and barley.

l. 8   *mucin*: a group of proteins found in various human and animal secretions and tissues (as in saliva, the lining of the stomach, and the skin).

ll. 11ff.   *The human embryo lay there...*: there is a sharp contrast between the erotic fascination with the female body (i.e. Hans Castorp's obsession with Chauchat) and the harsh reality of life—the human embryo, when viewed objectively, is a pitiable bestial object.

ll. 13f.   *indistinguishable from an embryonic pig*: evoking the mythological association with the island of Circe (see note to p. 56, l. 1).

l. 26   *pineal gland*: a small gland near the center of the brain.

l. 30ff. *Anatomy presented...*: This entire section is another example of the narrator's creative fusion of science with Hans Castorp's search for meaning. Anatomy, we are asked to believe, reveals "the unity of all things human, the interconnectedness of all disciplines" (l. 37). Anatomy (in particular, the skeleton) reminds him of engineering ("his former ... profession"; l. 39). Thus the author has managed to find a scientific text about anatomy and adapt and incorporate it into the novel so that Hans Castorp's earlier engineering studies connect with his new research.

l. 34   *that adumbration of the human spirit*: Latin, the language of humanism, supplied the names of the parts of the body; thus medicine is linguistically a forerunner of humanism. But in the broader sense the study of body is a humanistic activity, since it embodies life and death, the two fundamental issues that confront Hans Castorp.

l. 36   *the skeleton ... new perspectives*: the skeleton is an important leitmotif in the novel, for the contrast is repeatedly drawn between form and formlessness, structure (e.g. a skeleton) and the lack of it. These opposites also reflect cultural-philosophical attitudes: several times the Russian language is described as "boneless" (cf. p. 113, l. 13, p. 225, ll. 7f., & p. 306, l. 22)—and this in its turn connotes the world of Chauchat and what she represents, as opposed to Settembrini. The skeleton, of course, also points to death—as it had done when Hans Castorp looked at Joachim's skeleton (cf. p. 214, l. 20).

l. 37   *the unity of all things human, the interconnection of all disciplines*: a significant insight that Hans Castorp achieves all by himself.

(276) l. 1   *In order to study something*: the study of technology and the human skeleton reveals parallels that reinforce Hans Castorp's belief in the unity of life.

ll. 16f.   *The bone of the upper thigh was a crane*: of course, it isn't, although it resembles a crane. It serves Thomas Mann's purpose to state it this way, in order to amalgamate Hans Castorp's previous studies with his current ones (cf. note to p. 275, ll. 30ff.).

ll. 20ff.   *He was delighted to see it...*: Hans Castorp's conclusions demonstrate both his independence of mind and his intellectual capacity for synthesizing knowledge: his broad comprehension of the unity of all living phenomena is a major step forward in his education.

l. 21f.   *his relationship to the femur ... lyric, medical, and technical*: Hans Castorp's reading has confirmed what Behrens had told him earlier: "It's a good thing ... when a man's relationship with nature is something different from the, let us say, purely lyrical" (p. 255, ll. 4ff.).

l. 24   *schools of humanist thought*: "humanism" for Hans Castorp means the unity of all knowledge in a mind that comprehends the interdependence of all things human. Cf. Castorp's comments to Behrens, p. 256, ll. 1ff.

l. 26   *protoplasm*: see note to p. 270, l. 18.

l. 33   *rigor mortis*: the chemical change in the muscles after death, causing the limbs of the corpse to become stiff (Latin *rigor*) and difficult to move or manipulate.

(277) l. 7   *medulla*: The *medulla oblongata* is the lower half of the brainstem.

l. 8   *optic thalamus*: older term for thalamus, a part of the brain that sends sensation, special sense and motor signals to the cerebral cortex, along with the regulation of consciousness, sleep and alertness.

l. 9   *pons*: a structure on the brain stem that regulates relaxation, and is associated with the sense of higher purpose.

l. 10   *cerebral cortex*: a structure within the brain that plays a key role in memory, attention, perceptual awareness, thought, language, and consciousness.

l. 22   *catabolism*: the set of metabolic pathways that break down molecules into smaller units and release energy.

ll. 26f.   *acquired characteristics to be inherited*: incorrect—but derived from Thomas Mann's source.

(278) l. 5   *bioblasts, the biophores*: a bioblast is a formative cell, and a biophore is one of the smaller vital units of a cell, the bearer of vitality and heredity.

l. 21   *ad infinitum*: to infinity.

l. 25   *archebiosis*: see note to p. 271. l. 24.

(279) ll. 8f.   *the microbes and protozoa of matter*: cf. note to p. 271, ll. 19f.

l. 9   *protozoa*: one-celled animals and the smallest of all animals. Most of them can only be seen under a microscope.

ll. 31ff.   *For a slightly tipsy young master…*: the word "tipsy" is Behrens's jocular epithet for "infected" (cf. p. 214, ll. 38f.).

l. 31   *the muffling art*: not in the original, which speaks literally of "a young adept somewhat tipsy at the core."

l. 33   *illicit matters*: i.e. his feelings towards Chauchat.

l. 41   *one researcher*: a precise source for this assertion has not been found. However, several writers known to Thomas Mann had written about the cosmos using metaphorical terminology. Older Greek mythology associates the Milky Way with a herd of dairy cows, where each cow is a star and whose milk causes the blue glow.

(280) l. 9   *out of humanistic and medical interest*: for Castorp, medicine is a branch of humanistic study (cf. note to p. 265, l. 34).

ll. 11ff.   *He learned pathological anatomy…*: the following paragraph is another example of Thomas Mann's technique in this sub-chapter. Although he is describing scientific processes, the language is anything but scientific: in fact, it is highly charged with Hans Castorp's emotional response to the text he is reading. The vocabulary bears a close relationship to the themes of the novel (cf. "dissolute" [l. 17], "contamination" [l. 26; the original speaks of "corruption"), "riotous living" [l. 31]).

l. 12   *the reddish glow of his table lamp*: see note to p. 270, ll. 11f. This small, but significant detail provides the atmosphere for a highly eroticized discussion of the genesis and nature of life, culminating in the open conjuration of Chauchat in the last eleven lines of the sub-chapter (p. 281, ll. 23ff.).

ll. 38f.   *with heaving bosom…*: the image had been used by Behrens earlier when speaking of his near-death experience (cf. p. 250, l. 29).

(281) l. 1   *disease was life's lascivious form*: the reflections in this paragraph revolve around the speculative view that the first stage in the process that led to the origin of life began when "spirit increased in density" (l. 6), leading to inorganic forms. The second stage of the origin of life occurred when the "spontaneous generation" (l. 10) of the organic out of the inorganic occurred. (The entire argument reflects the thinking both of Krokowski and Naphta.) At the time that the novel was written, there was no agreement about the origin of life, although the fundamental idea of biopoesis (i.e. the study of how life arises from inanimate matter through natural processes) was accepted. In the account given in the novel, however, the scientific process is retold in a highly metaphorical manner, anticipating Naphta's views.

ll. 23ff.   *He beheld the image of life…*: Castorp's anatomical studies culminate in the transfer of all his knowledge onto the figure of Chauchat: she is for him the embodiment of all he has learned. Despite all the knowledge he has gained about the true nature of the body he is still fascinated by *her* body and its mysteries. (The Will asserts its power yet again.) The kiss he receives from her is given in the context of sickness and death: thus when he embraces her, he is also embracing death. However, since Hans Castorp's research has led him to broader view of life that encompasses all of its phenomena (including sickness and death), when he embraces Chauchat, he is also embracing life in the wider sense.

Danse Macabre (German title: *Totentanz* = Dance of Death)

The word "Totentanz" was originally used to describe a series of pictures in which a dancing skeleton pulls a human being from life into death. In this sub-chapter Hans Castorp confronts cases of death in opposition to the prevailing attitude (supported officially by the Berghof administration) of avoiding the unpleasantness of dealing with human mortality.

l. 34   *the Austrian horseman*: cf. note to p. 12, l. 26 and l. 38.

(282) l. 17   *Hans Castorp avoided them…*: his alienation from the Flatland even extends to not wanting to meet people of his own age from "down there"—and especially not people from the North Germany or Hamburg.

ll. 20f. *these warbling, walking-stick-swinging wanderers*: at this time in Germany the activity of hiking in groups and singing folk songs was very popular with young people. The original speaks of "singers," not "warblers," and thus has no pejorative implication.

l. 29 *Cuxhaven*: a small town located at the mouth of the River Elbe (which runs through Hamburg). Cuxhaven became a town in 1907, but remained a part of the Hamburg urban area until 1937.

(283) l. 34 *their distant, low-lying homeland*: the phrase indicates the *psychological* distance between the Berghof and "down there."

(284) ll. 16f. *Tartar physiognomy ... "lone-wolf eyes"*: Settembrini associates Chauchat with everything he despises about the "East." In the German her eyes are "Steppenwolfslichter" = the eyes of a wolf from the steppes. Cf. note to p. 238, l. 4ff.

ll. 27f. *a carpenter's son...*: Jesus Christ. Settembrini is skeptical about the historical basis for the biblical story, but converts the Christian message into a universal secular principle.

l. 33 *amphibious*: Frau Stöhr's mangling of "ambiguous."

(285) l. 5 *Fafnir guarding his treasure*: In Norse mythology Fafnir was the dragon that guarded a treasure and was slain by Siegfried. The patients at the Berghof sanatorium and Thomas Mann's readers would understand this as a reference to Wagner's opera *The Ring of the Nibelung*, where Fafner [sic] begins life as a giant before turning into a dragon to guard the gold.

l. 8 *exactly like Pribislav Hippe's*: nowhere else does Hans Castorp mention Hippe's laugh.

l. 24 *lieder*: German art songs.

ll. 29f. *I bear my song of love/within my heart*: although the singer is mediocre, the song has a direct relevance to Castorp's emotional state. The fact that he studies the words as she sings ("reading the text," l. 35) indicates the importance of the words to him (a fact that will assume even greater significance later). It is also significant that he is relieved that both Settembrini and Chauchat leave the concert early so that he can devote himself to the music ("he was free to devote his full attention to the songs," ll. 40f.). In fact, in the original his emotion is stronger: we are told he is happy to be able to enjoy the songs "in freedom"—an unusual phrase to use to describe the feeling when two people leave a concert. This scene looks forward to his listening to music alone in the sub-chapter *Fullness of Harmony* (cf. pp. 626ff.). The song is a poem by Karl Henckell, set to music by Richard Strauss in 1896. Since Hans is reading the text, he will also be reading the rest of the verse: "Yes, the fact that I have found you, dear child/ Makes me happy for all the days that are granted to me."

l. 34   *with a peaceful heart*: i.e. not distracted by Chauchat's physical presence.

l. 37   *bel canto*: Italian for "beautiful singing"; in general, an operatic style of singing in a light and flexible manner, in contrast to a heavier "dramatic" style.

(286) l. 2f.   *probably even on polar expeditions*: in 1901–03 on a German Antarctic expedition under the leadership of Erich von Drygalski the S.S. Gauss became trapped in the ice for the duration of the winter; a member of the crew described regular music-making with "a band composed of a harmonica, flute, triangle and two pot-lids for a cymbal."

ll. 15f.   *the signs of life*: cf. p. 12, ll. 15ff. The statement is ironic, since they were really signs of the horseman's mortality.

l. 25   *demijohn*: a large container (usually 15 gallons).

ll. 36f.   *his cousin was talking almost like Settembrini*: the latter would have also criticized the mercenary interests of the sanatorium.

(287) ll. 30ff.   *they stepped across the room…*: the posture assumed when showing reverence, cf. p. 21, ll. 30ff., p. 296, l. 16, p. 304, l. 24, p. 315, ll. 24f., & p. 337, l. 8.

ll. 35f.   *with an expression … listening to music*: the similarity of the expressions on Hans Castorp's face points to the connection between music and death. Cf. also p. 36, ll. 34ff. & p. 216, ll. 7f.

(288) ll. 5f.   *more for the sake of the survivors*: since the dead do not care how they look, closing the eyes of a dead person is an action taken to spare the living from embarrassment.

l. 7   *myosin*: protein that governs mobility in tissues. In fact, it is not "too much" myosin that causes *rigor mortis*, but rather the lack of the agent that releases the myosin and allows movement.

l. 10   *in his element in more than one sense*: this sub-chapter cites several examples of Hans Castorp's innate affinity for dealing with death.

l. 17   *Kärnten*: Carinthia, at that time a province in the Austro-Hungarian Empire, bordering on Italy and Slovenia. It is now the southernmost province of Austria.

l. 22   *he was an orphan twice over…*: the preoccupation with death is an important stage in facing and overcoming it.

l. 24   *he "had been" an engineer*: Hans Castorp's use of the past perfect tense is an indication of his divorce from his previous life.

ll. 26f.   *a critical time in his life, perhaps even a turning-point*: he is putting into words a process that has already happened: the psychological truth has preceded the overt admission.

ll. 27f. *Joachim stared, scrutinizing him in horror*: Joachim is not prepared to accept that Hans has deserted the "Flatland" (and its values) and committed himself to the Berghof (and all that it implies).

ll. 38f. *Requisecat in pace ... Sit tibi terra levis. Requiem aeternam dona ei, Domine*: Let him rest in peace ... May the earth be light for you. Give him eternal peace, o Lord.

l. 40 *the official language*: Latin is not only appropriate because it is the religious language used to declare death, but also, on the metaphorical level, the indicator of frozen form (being a "dead" language).

(289) ll. 4f. *sacred Latin, the dialect of monks, a chant from the Middle Ages*: all this anticipates the arrival of Naphta and his philosophy of life. Hans Castorp reaches his own conclusions about death before Naphta even appears on the scene.

l. 8 *from the other one*: i.e. the view of life espoused by Naphta (whom Hans Castorp has not yet even met).

l. 10 *the religious and the freethinking*: the original speaks (literally) of "the pious and the free." The word "pious" is an important leitmotif (cf. p. 288, l. 11, where Hans Castorp "stood piously beside the bed") that symbolizes the recognition of the reality of death and darker side of life, whereas the "free" or "free-thinking" attitude is that of Settembrini who argues without pause for a positive view of life that emphasizes reason and progress and refuses to face the problem of death.

ll. 18ff. *Don Carlos*: Friedrich Schiller's play *Don Carlos* (1787) was used by Thomas Mann on more than one occasion to illustrate a view of life. Here he exploits the contrast between the formality of the King and his Spanish court (as an illustration of Settembrini's philosophy of life) versus that of the Spanish Queen who is conveniently French and who embodies all that Chauchat stands for.

l. 20 *his orders of the Garter and the Golden Fleece*: the Order of St. George and the Garter was founded by the English King Edward III in 1348, and Philip II of Spain was invested into the Order in 1554, on the occasion of his marriage to Mary, Queen of England. The Order of the Golden Fleece was founded by Philipp III of France in 1430. It is membership is confined to Catholics.

l. 20f. *slowly doffs his hat*: there is no such stage direction in the original.

l. 25 *And then the Queen says*: her speech comes, in fact, earlier than the King's entrance just mentioned.

ll. 25f. *'Twas otherwise in my own France*: connoting Chauchat and her view of life.

l. 28   *Everything is human*: one of the key lines of the novel. This is a major conclusion that Hans Castorp has drawn from his stay at the Berghof. Both the people around him and his own studies have led him to understand that to be truly "human" is to encompass all the phenomena of life. This includes both the conventional Humanism of Settembrini and the broader conception of the "humane" advocated by Chauchat.

l. 39   *stiff collars*: symbolizing the adherence to tradition and form.

l. 40   *bienséance*: decorum; correct, proper behavior.

(290) l. 1   *the Spanish spirit*: Spain is associated in the novel with formality.

ll. 14f.   *he gave me a nice lecture on the topic*: cf. p. 241, ll. 3ff.

l. 15   *wants to eradicate it systematically with an encyclopedia*: the naïve manner in which Castorp describes Settembrini's project reveals what a quixotic enterprise it is; cf. note to p. 242, l. 33.

l. 16   *downright immoral*: once again Hans Castorp shows his independence of mind.

l. 19   *Sir, give thoughts their freedom*: this is a famous line from Schiller's *Don Carlos*, the play that Castorp has just been discussing. The Marquis Posa entreats King Philipp of Spain to grant his subjects freedom of thought. (The more conventional translation is "Sire, give them freedom of thought." The phrase has gone into daily speech in German.) Hans Castorp's resistance to Settembrini's sermons implies here that the Italian wishes to inhibit Castorp's freedom of thought—perhaps somewhat of an overstatement, but a reflection of Castorp's fierce independence. The translation distorts the original somewhat.

l. 29   *Softly, softly, holy air*: "air" here means "tune." *Tannhäuser* plays a significant role as a leitmotif in the novel (see notes to pp. 23, l. 11; p. 64, l. 15; p. 83, l. 17; p. 546, l. 35; p. 632, l. 5; p. 702, l. 16). "Softly, softly..." is sung by Agathe in Carl Maria von Weber's opera *Der Freischütz*.

l. 35   *joined his ancestors long ago*: this is a repetition of a phrase used previously by Behrens ("ad penates") on p. 104, l. 36 and p. 178, ll. 20f.; cf. note to p. 104, l. 36. Castorp has absorbed the phrase and reproduces it here.

l. 36   *His eyes were simply huge even back then*: people suffering from tuberculosis often have red, swollen eyes.

(291) l. 13f.   *Yes, that would be another reason*: the real reason why Hans Castorp undertakes these visits is given in the following lines.

l. 16   *his own spiritual need...*: from the very start Castorp's leaning towards death has been an *inner* compulsion. His sympathy for the dying is an extension of his sympathy for death itself. However, his immediate motivation, as we are told, is to provide himself with some much-needed reinforcement (cf. "nourished and satisfied," l. 17) as a counterweight to the "numerous rebuffs such a need received daily, even hourly," l. 19), although we are not told what they are or by whom, and to the criticisms he has received from Settembrini. Thus for all his naïveté and apparently thick-skinned behavior he is still quite a sensitive soul.

l. 41   *prejudicial to the dignity of this place of suffering*: Castorp's disapproval of Frau Hessenfeld (who makes so many bets and is not really ill) indicates how seriously he takes the Berghof as a place for significant reflections about life.

(292) l. 5   *Max and Moritz*: see note to p. 229, l. 9.

l. 13   *Jüterbog*: town in north-eastern Germany about 65 km (40 miles) southwest of Berlin, with Slavic origins. The historical associations and the lawyer's "licentious" behavior connotes the world of Chauchat.

l. 23   *an offense to his own spiritual strivings*: ironic, of course, since his own behavior will soon mirror the lawyer's.

ll. 29f.   *the air at first was not just good...*: a leitmotivic phrase that originated with Behrens (p. 179, ll. 5ff.) and has already been repeated by Castorp (p. 192, ll. 27ff.).

l. 35   *Homeric laughter*: reference to the habit of the gods in Homeric epics to break out into uncontrollable laughter.

(293) l. 6   *the grim ripper*: Karoline Stöhr's mangling of "the grim reaper" (death).

l. 7   *impediment*: impertinent.

ll. 9f.   *agglomeration*: the precise meaning of "agglomeration" is a "confused mass."

ll. 12f.   Benedetto Cenelli*, in Schiller's translation*: a real howler from Karoline Stöhr. *Benvenuto Cellini*'s autobiography was translated by Goethe in 1803.

l. 29   *Posen*: a province of Prussia until 1918, with a large Polish population.

(294) l. 6   *feet first*: with the implication that she was going to die.

ll. 31f.   *love as a force conducive to illness*: cf. p. 123, ll. 35f.

l. 36   *orgasm of the brain*: a widely held view held that coitus was a minor epileptic fit. Freud wrote (1909): "The ancients said that coitus was a 'small epileptic fit'."

l. 39   *a certain modesty*: "modesty" in German is "Schamhaftigkeit" ("shamefulness"), and Krokowski's lectures about love and sex will exploit the ambiguity of the word "shame," which in German ("Scham") occurs in compounds (such as "Schamhaar" ["shame hair"] = pubic hair). His future observations are already hinted in this phrase.

(295) l. 17   *this incident, too, bolstered Hans Castorp's impression...*: the irony here resides in the fact that, for opposite reasons, Castorp now finds himself allied with Settembrini in his disapproval of the licentious aspects of Berghof life.

l. 37   *the odor of plants...*: Cf. the flowers round his grandfather's coffin earlier, p. 26, ll. 36ff. and the significance of flowers in Western funeral rites. (In Thomas Mann's first novel *Buddenbrooks* [1901], Thomas Buddenbrook comes into the flower-store of his "lover" Anna: "A damp odor of earth and flowers lay in the little store.")

ll. 40f.   *secretly ascribing symbolic importance*: it is not clear what the "symbolic" importance is. Perhaps Hans Castorp interprets his actions as symbolizing his recognition of the inevitability of death.

(296) l. 16   *the two cousins tiptoed...*: cf. note to p. 287, ll. 30f.

l. 32   *transudation*: the process whereby fluid passes through a membrane or pore. Here: she is sweating so profusely as to become dehydrated.

l. 38   *innocent of his daughter's susceptibilities and organic biases*: in the original the Major has an "organic innocence": as a soldier from the Flatland he is *organically* not susceptible to the perils (and spiritual adventures) of the Berghof.

l. 41   *dowry*: ironic—the "dowry" was her ill-health.

(297) l. 20   *her former life*: i.e. her previous bout of tuberculosis.

l. 33f.   *annoyed him no end*: cf. his similar feeling of superiority when he heard Chauchat speak German (cf. p. 209, l. 15).

ll. 35f.   *the prevailing egotism*: repetition of his thought from p. 291, ll. 14f.

ll. 39f.   *the earthy odor of the flower shop*: cf. note to 295, l. 37 above.

(298)   ll. 5f.   *silence and lowered gaze*: Joachim's reluctance is caused by his innate affirmation of life and duty and dislike of any phenomenon that detracts from his single-minded focus on health. That he permits himself—once again—to be taken in tow by Castorp is a sign of his polite and generous nature. For his part, Castorp acts with his accustomed ruthlessness when it is a matter of doing what *he* wants to do ("he would have to ignore Joachim's silent resistance" [ll. 10f.]).

l. 20   *the warm, earthy-scented air of the flower shop*: see notes above to p. 295, l. 37 & 297, l. 39f.

ll. 30f.   *the nurseries in Nice and Cannes*: both places were well-known for their flower markets.

l. 34   *Coburg*: city in Bavaria.

l. 40   *by the sweat of his brow*: biblical phrase from *Genesis* 3:19. The description in the original is even more ironic: "by the sweat of his brow he had sat in bed and tried to nourish himself."

(299) l. 11f.   *the doctor's self-interest was only too clear*: with the implication that Behrens's interest is to make money.

(300) l. 5   *with a shrug*: the typical gesture of the Berghof residents assumes a slightly greater significance here: the death of Leila is indicated.

ll. 6f.   *proper bit of courting ...*: Behrens's jocular way of treating the horror of death (in German he says: "just before the gate closed" which referred to the closing of the medieval city gates at dusk).

l. 8   *lung whistlers in their cages*: repeats Settembrini's reference to Mozart's *The Magic Flute*; cf. p. 59, ll. 1ff.

(301) l. 20   *from the nurseries of Nice or Cannes*: see note to p. 298, l. 30f.

l. 31   *Pneumothorax*: see note to p. 48, l. 38.

l. 37   *Zurich*: major city in Switzerland.

(302) ll. 23f.   *she died in the arms of her husband*: in fact, overfilling could easily be corrected by the release of some gas.

ll. 30f.   *Tous-les-deux*: see note to p. 39, l.11.

l. 32   *fumigated with H_2CO*: formaldehyde, a disinfecting agent.

l. 35   *Fridericianum*: the original "Fridericianum" was an art museum built by the Landgraf Friedrich II of Hessen in 1779. Since then many schools called themselves by the same name. There was one in Davos that had been founded in 1878 for tubercular students.

ll. 39f.   *Good Samaritans and Hospitallers*: the Knights Hospitaller is an organization that was founded in Jerusalem in 1080 to care for poor and sick pilgrims in the Holy Land.

(303) l. 2   *I've been hearing the most curious things about your behavior*: the narrator exploits the ambiguity of the German word "Wandel" that can mean both "behavior" and "change." Cf. note to p. 200, l. 29.

l. 3   *justification by good works*: a central doctrine of the Catholic faith.

ll. 10f.   *You are the more important personality—the one in greater danger*: Settembrini's concern throughout has been for Hans Castorp's spiritual well-being and for protecting him from influences and pre-occupations (e.g. death) that Settembrini considers to be pernicious.

l. 12   *one of life's problem children*: an important leitmotif in relation to Hans Castorp, even adopted by the narrator: cf. p. 706, l. 2..

l. 18   *"death's children"*: throughout this exchange Hans Castorp retains his independence of mind.

l. 23   *let the dead bury their dead*: cf. *Matthew* 8: 22, and *Luke* 9: 60.

l. 27   *a disruptive point of view*: "disruptive" is a little strong: "bothersome" would be more accurate, since the adjective ("störend") comes from the same verb that has applied to Settembrini throughout. Although Castorp is moved by Settembrini's comment, he still shows his skepticism by referring to the Italian as an "organ-grinder." Cf. note to p. 89, ll. 22f.

ll. 28ff.   *Yet even though Hans Castorp was prepared...*: a clear statement of Hans Castorp's independence of mind and action—especially significant is the fact that he listens to Settembrini "noncommittally" (l. 30). The sentence continues his practice of *"placet experiri."*

l. 32   *he should desist from his enterprise*: i.e. of educating himself about death and making up his own mind about the alternatives ("which still seemed ... to be beneficial in some vague way" [ll. 32f.]).

l. 38   *violets from Nice, heavy with the scent of earth*: cf. note to p. 295, l. 37.

(304) l. 4   *de son seul et dernier fils qui allait mourir aussi*: of her only and final son who was also going to die.

ll. 15f.   *Tous les dé, vous comprenez, messiés ...Premièrement l'un et maintenant l'autre*: both of them, sirs ... First the one and now the other. The pronunciation is, as in earlier encounters, heavily accented (dé = deux; messiés = messieurs).

l. 19   *comme héros, à l'espagnol*: as a hero, in the Spanish manner. The latter phrase connotes Don José in Bizet's opera *Carmen* with whom Castorp will later feel a personal association (cf. *Fullness of Harmony*, pp. 637 ff.). However, Lauro's behavior here is anything but humble in the face of death. Rather, his speeches are "unbearably high-flown."

ll. 19f.   *de même que son fier jeune frère Fernando*: just like his proud young brother Fernando.

l. 23   *rodomontade*: bombast.

l. 24   *on tiptoe*: cf. note to p. 287, ll. 30ff.

l. 28   *Saint Petersburg*: Russian city on the Baltic Sea, founded by Tsar Peter the Great in 1703.

l. 33   *pleural shock*: the body's possible reaction to an invasive procedure on the chest; it can lead to loss of consciousness, temporary paralysis, or other disturbances in the circulation.

ll. 33f.   *the fashionable operation*: the adjective ironically undermines the medical wisdom of the operation.

(305) l. 7   *the pleural lining*: the lining of the lung.

ll. 20f.   *the unbearable stench of hydrogen sulfide*: a colorless, toxic and flammable gas that is partially responsible for the foul odor of rotten eggs and flatulence.

(306) ll. 14f. *who thought it useful...*: "Russia"—and all that the term connotes—belongs to the complex of ideas surrounding Chauchat and (later) Naphta.

l. 15 *samovar*: a metal container traditionally used to boil water.

l. 16 *piroshki*: a savory filled pastry.

l. 17 *Cossacks*: a group of people living in the southern steppe regions of Eastern Europe and Russia.

l. 19 *all the more exotic*: the original speaks of "adventurous exoticism." Castorp's delight at hearing about Russia and its customs and hearing the Russian language spoken serves both to improve his knowledge and to stimulate his emotions. In so doing he is vicariously participating in Chauchat's world, which is manna to his soul. Through it all, he is conscious of the fact that this would appall Settembrini—as is indicated by his referring to these conversations with Ferge as "pedagogically forbidden territory" (l. 26).

l. 20 *Finno-Mongolian*: scholars had made attempts to connect Finnish and Mongolian peoples, in particular in respect of their languages.

ll. 22f. *the muddy, barbaric, boneless tongue ...*: the Russian language is repeatedly described in terms that associate it with the complex of ideas that comprise the "East": that is, the anti-rationalist attitude to life and the recognition of decay and dissolution as inherent elements in the process of life. The original describes the language literally as "hasty, washed out, totally unfamiliar, and boneless."

l. 26 *pedagogically forbidden territory*: i.e. Settembrini would not approve of his listening to Ferge with such pleasure.

l. 32 *his worm-eaten parts*: associates Ferge with Chauchat, whose interior Hans Castorp had described using the same adjective (cf. p. 141, ll. 35f.).

(307) l. 1 *a perfect Job, a Lazarus in a female body*: In the Old Testament Job is the biblical symbol of suffering; in the New Testament Lazarus is raised from the dead by Christ (see *John* 11: 41–44).

l. 6 *eczema*: an inflammation of the skin.

l. 8 *pleura*: the membrane that surrounds the lungs.

l. 9 *periosteum*: the membrane that lines the outer surface of bones.

l. 12 *esophagus*: the muscular tube through which food passes from the pharynx (back of the mouth) to the stomach.

l. 20 *the plagues of Job*: visited on him by Satan for seven years (cf. *Job* 5, 1—9).

l. 29 *a spouted cup:* a "feeding cup" with a spout that makes it easier for babies, and for sick and old people to drink liquids.

(308) ll. 13ff.   *he felt his whole being expand...*: the underlying motivation for Hans Castorp's actions is his desire to be become more closely acquainted with death (his innate "sympathy with death"), but on the surface his behavior appears to be so infused with pious Christian charity that no one can criticize him.

ll. 17f.   *from a military or humanistic-pedagogic standpoint*: i.e. neither Joachim nor Settembrini could reproach him for his actions.

l. 40   *He had not come here for that sort of thing...*: Joachim keeps his focus single-mindedly on his own cure so that he might return to his military duties as soon as possible.

(309) l. 14   *Hotel d'Angleterre*: literally: Hotel of England. This was the hotel in Davos that gave its name to the English Quarter.

l. 15   *Kurhaus*: originally the name of the building where the "cure" was administered, the word "Kur" was appropriated by hotels to boost their image.

l. 25   *tricot*: a knitted fabric.

l. 37   *Scotch*: should read "Scottish"; "scotch" is the whisky.

l. 37   *tam*: tam-o'-shanter, a cap of Scottish origin, usually made of wool, having a round, flat top that projects all around the head and has a pompon at its center.

(310) l. 1 *Dutchmen with traces of Malayan blood*: Peeperkorn's arrival is hinted at.

l. 3   *the Balkans*: a geopolitical and cultural region of southeastern Europe. The region takes its name from the Balkan Mountains, which run through the center of Bulgaria into eastern Serbia.

The Balkans

l. 3   *the Levant*: the Eastern Mediterranean.

l. 4   *for whom Hans Castorp had a certain weakness*: Castorp is attracted to the "adventurous world" (a more accurate translation than "a motley set of adventurers") that these people represent—a world that his cousin Joachim utterly rejects.

l. 19   *Schatzalp*: see note to p. 9, ll. 19f.

l. 33   *The bodies from the sanatorium*: recalling the information about the nocturnal transportation of corpses that he had heard from Joachim on his arrival (see p. 9, ll. 20f.).

l. 36   *the Bioscope Theater*: the "bioscope" was an early form of film-projector; the word came to be used for the cinema itself. "… the screen flickered" is a reflection of the bioscope's nickname: "the flickering screen."

(**311**) ll. 4ff.   *a rousing tale of love and murder…*: the silent film, *Sumurun* (1920) by Ernst Lubitsch (1892–1947). In Davos in 1908 there was no such film-theater, nor were such feature films or newsreels produced at that time.

ll. 11ff.   *Settembrini … would surely have renounced*: it is only to be expected that such trivial and superficial pleasures would be rejected by Settembrini. The fact that Hans Castorp is thinking this while watching the screen "and whispered as much to his cousin" (ll. 15f.), is evidence that he is engaging in intellectual analysis even when pursuing trivial pleasure.

l. 37   *reviewing a long cordon*: a mistranslation. A "cordon" is a decoration, an honor—so the President is simply sitting wearing a top-hat and his medals, listening to a welcoming speech.

l. 38   *landau*: coach with four seats.

l. 40   *Potsdam*: city close to Berlin. It was the residence of the Prussian kings until 1918.

l. 41   *New Mecklenburg*: an island in the Bismarck archipelago, Papua New Guinea, that from 1885 to 1914 was part of German New Guinea. It is now called New Ireland.

l. 41   *Borneo*: third largest island in the world, located in maritime south-east Asia between Malaysia, Indonesia and the Philippines. Since 1824 the island had been divided into British and Dutch controlled areas.

(**312**) ll. 1f.   *the Siamese royal court*: before 1939 the present Kingdom of Thailand was named Siam (the country reverted to that name between 1945 and 1949).

l. 3   *Samoyeds*: The Samoyed people are an Asiatic group of nomadic origin from North Russia and Siberia.

l. 5   *Hebron*: a city in the southern Judea. Throughout the Ottoman Empire (1517–1917), groups of Jews from other parts of the Land of

Israel, and exiles from Spain and other parts of the diaspora and settled there.

l. 5   *bastinadoed*: originally a Spanish word for the act of caning, in the literal sense of beating with a stick or similar implement. It is specifically used to refer to a form of torture or corporal punishment which consists of beating the soles of the offender's bare feet with a hard object, such as a cane or rod.

ll. 6ff.   *space was negated...*: the bioscope theater is portrayed as something mythical, a place where time and space are suspended—much like the Berghof itself is depicted.

l. 14   *this charming specter*: the original speaks of "shadow," and thus recalls the leitmotif of death.

ll. 37f.   *in dulci jubilo*: literally: in sweet joy.

l. 39   *dolce*: Italian for "sweet."

(313) ll. 18f.   *the relationship with poor Karen*: in the original the word "Verkehr" subtly connotes a sexual undertone to the relationship, which is only appropriate since Karen is in one sense a surrogate for Clavdia Chauchat. (Cf. also note to p. 249, ll. 35f.)

l. 21   *an end in themselves*: they have their roots in his "sympathy with death" (see next note).

ll. 26f.   *an intellectual tradition...*: cf. p. 289, ll. 7ff., where Hans Castorp distinguishes between the two traditions.

l. 28   *placet experiri*: cf. note to p. 96, l. 14.

l. 32   *promenade*: the word used is "Lustwandel" (cf. note to p. 45, ll. 23f.) which connotes a wider degree of pleasure. This is especially true as the original speaks ironically of their "promenade in the cause of duty."

ll. 33.   *Little Schiahorn*: mountain near Davos.

l. 35   *the Green Towers*: see note to p. 68, l. 18.

l. 36   *Dorfberg*: see note to p. 68, l. 18.

(314) l. 21   *Dorfberg*: see note to p. 68, l. 18.

l. 29   *necrosis*: death of living tissue.

(315) l. 17   *the genius of the place*: the word "genius" here signifies "spirit" or "muse." See note to p. 344, l. 10.

l. 20   *in no way ... devoid of substance*: i.e. connoting death.

ll. 24f.   *placing their weight on the balls of their feet*: the reverent posture, cf. note to p. 287, ll. 30f.

(316) l. 2   *youth rather than virtue*: an allusion to the German saying: "Youth has no virtue," which is equivalent to "Youth will have its fling."

l. 4   *the horizontal form of existence*: making it abundantly clear that earlier references to the "horizontal" were intended to connote death.

l. 11   *with open mouth and sleepy eyes*: the same attitude he had
assumed on the cousins' first visit to a dead person, cf. p. 287, ll. 34ff.

Walpurgis Night

This is one of the key chapters of the novel. Not only does Hans Castorp
finally engage in conversation with Clavdia Chauchat—which, in itself,
signifies a decision of momentous significance—but in so doing he also
fully emancipates himself from the pull of Settembrini whose urgent
warnings not to pursue her he ignores. Castorp's full participation in the
events of the Carnival signals his final commitment to the world represented by Chauchat, and this decision is cemented by his spending some
time with her in her room after the Walpurgis Night party. The Carnival
celebration is, however, not merely an act of pleasure and an opportunity
to indulge his emotions, it is also a deeply *pedagogical* experience (in a
sense of which Settembrini would not have approved). Through his
conversation with Chauchat (in French) Castorp learns yet more important
lessons about life and love and death—lessons that he takes to heart (and
remembers), since they come from the woman he loves and who
represents the world to which he is irresistibly attracted.

Walpurgis Night: according to Germanic mythology this was the night
(April 30) on which all the witches and demons gathered on the Brocken
Mountain (often called also the "Magic Mountain") in the Harz Mountain
range of Germany. The word has a double significance in German culture.
First, it is well-known in folk-lore; and second, it is known to cultured
people as the title of a central scene in Johann Wolfgang von Goethe's
play *Faust: Part I*, in which Faust participates in the celebrations on the
Brocken and sees the ghost of his dead lover Gretchen. The sub-chapter
subtly includes allusions to Goethe's *Faust*, almost all of which issue from
the mouth of Settembrini, who also conveys information about other
aspects of the associations aroused by Carnival and Walpurgis Night.
Carnival itself in Germany is not celebrated on April 30; it officially
occurs in the two weeks before Lent—however, in practice the celebrations may begin in early January.

The celebration in the novel takes place at Mardi Gras (cf. p. 317, l.
37), 29 February 1908.

ll. 17f.   *seven months*: see "Introduction", pp. 21f.
l. 23   *Mardi Gras*: see note to p. 266, l. 9.
l. 25   *Magnifique!*: magnificent.

ll. 26f. *As rollicking as in the Prater*: Settembrini quotes a line by Mephistopheles from Goethe's *Faust* (although in the German the narrator does not identify it as a quote, as the translation does). In the "Walpurgis Night" scene of *Faust*, Mephistopheles leads Faust up the Brocken Mountain to witness the antics of the assembled witches. The Prater is a large public park in Vienna, which from earliest times was the venue for various lively activities.

l. 28   *we play gallants most dashing*: another quotation from *Faust*, but not from the "Walpurgis Night" scene; rather, it is from the following scene ("Walpurgis Night Dream"). Settembrini's quotations from the play are not restricted to one character or scene, but are chosen to illustrate his view of the events unfolding on this evening at the Berghof. This quotation is by the spirits ("Irrlichter") who are present in this scene in Goethe's play.

l. 31   *maison de santé*: a mental hospital.

l. 33   *danses macabres*: dances of death; originally a late-medieval allegory. Settembrini's allusion here foreshadows the novel's ending in the First World War, which the narrator describes as a "the wicked dance" (p. 706, l. 12). The phrase alludes to the title of the preceding sub-chapter, the term used by Thomas Mann in both instances as "Totentanz"—the literal German equivalent of Dance of Death.

ll. 34f. *at half past nine*: the reference is to the dead patients: since ghosts and spirits appear after midnight, they will not be seen at a party that ends at 9.30 p.m.

(317) l. 4   *lusts of the flesh*: Hans Castorp, in fact, makes a significant pun on the word "carnival" here. He says that the dead patients have said "vale" (farewell) to the "flesh" ("carne"). The word "carnival" is supposed to have originated in saying farewell to meat before the Lenten fast period began. The irony here lies in the fact that Castorp—who will soon be spending some time with Chauchat in her room—is himself not about to "put aside 'all lusts of the flesh'."

l. 10   *Palm Sunday*: the Sunday before Easter, celebrating the entry of Jesus Christ into Jerusalem.

ll. 10f. *do they bake special pastries here?*: he means "Kringel," (also called "Christkringel"), which are traditionally baked for Palm Sunday and Holy Week), consisting of pastry filled with butter, cinnamon, and sugar (and often also some other filling, such as plums, or nuts and nougat), and formed into a half-circle before baking.

l. 11   *Holy Week*: the last week before Easter.

l. 11   *Easter*: Easter is a moveable that falls at some point between late March and late April each year following the cycle of the moon.

l. 11   *Pentecost*: the "fiftieth day"—forty-nine days after Easter Sunday.

l. 13   *Midsummer Night*: 24 June.

ll. 15f.   *I forbid you*...: once again Hans Castorp, to Settembrini's chagrin, has described the course of time with indecent haste. However, the phrase "to play so fast and loose" (ll. 6f.)—there is no mention of "time" in the original—also connotes Castorp's uncontrolled behavior to come on this evening.

l. 17   *Beg your pardon*: Hans Castorp's speech contains words and phrases that he has absorbed from others at the Berghof: "detoxify" (l. 18; Behrens), "one of life's problem children" (l. 21; Settembrini), "saddled me with" (l. 22; also Settembrini), plus the nickname "Rhadamanthus" for Behrens that he also learned from Settembrini (l. 21; and this time he gets it right [cf. his mistake on p.192, l. 15]).

l. 21   *one of life's problem children*: first coined by Settembrini, cf. p. 303, l. 12. Castorp has apparently accepted Settembrini's characterization of him.

l. 28   *finished*: Castorp's choice of word is unfortunate, as "finished" also indicates Joachim's eventual fate.

ll. 35f.   *toy trumpets*: traditional instrument used for making noise during the Carnival period.

(318) l. 9   *the moral scruples*...: for Hans Castorp to take the plunge and commit himself wholeheartedly to Chauchat and all that she represents involves his overcoming his upbringing and the deep-seated morality that he has acquired as the offspring of an upper middle-class bourgeois family.

l. 13   *Punchinellos and Harlequins*: Punchinello, often called Punch in English, is a classical character that originated in the Italian *commedia dell'arte* (literally: "comedy of art") of the 16/17th century and became a stock character in Neapolitan puppetry. His main characteristic, from which he acquired his name, is his extremely long nose, which resembles a beak. Harlequin (Arlechino) is probably the best-known character from the *commedia dell'arte*. He had his origins in street performers who wore masks to draw attention to themselves; eventually the story they acted became more complex and *commedia dell'arte* was born. It was full of bawdy comedy and slapstick and was the early forerunner of vaudeville and music hall. Harlequin was an agile, energetic, acrobatic prankster with an immense sexual appetite. Harlequin's love interest was Columbine.

ll. 28f.   *Behold bright flames illuminated*...: another of Settembrini's many references to Goethe's *Faust*. These lines are spoken by Mephistopheles to Faust in the "Walpurgis Night" scene, whereupon Faust declares that he wants to go where he can observe "evil." In the original the tables are "illuminated"—a word that will later be applied to Settembrini himself (cf. p. 455, l. 16).

(319) ll. 4ff. *But bear in mind...*: spoken by a spirit on the Brocken. The implication is that the scene that follows is not real (cf. Hans Castorp to Clavdia Chauchat, p. 330, ll. 41ff.). From this point on Settembrini's quotations from and references to *Faust* are designed to be warnings to Castorp to be on his guard: Settembrini fully understands the "dangers" that Carnival represents for Castorp's soul. Here the words warn Castorp against being led astray by deceptive "spells."

ll. 12f. *He searched his pockets for a pencil*: the parallel with the scene in the schoolyard with Hippe (cf. p. 120, ll. 5ff.) is prepared.

ll. 14f. *His bloodshot eyes wandered eastward for help...*: i.e. to Chauchat. The style reinforces the mythological dimensions of the events: in the original the poetic/archaic preposition "gen" is used for "towards."

l. 15 *the far left-hand corner*: left, because it symbolizes the "not-right," not-healthy, not-conventional.

ll. 16f. *a wider circle of associations*: Hans Castorp is fully aware of what Chauchat represents (sex, love, sickness, death).

l. 30 *My God*: the verbal parallel to Castorp's reaction to thinking about Chauchat figure (cf. p. 203, l. 27) and on seeing Joachim's skeleton during his x-ray examination (p. 215, l. 14) evokes the complex of motifs and images that are represented by the figure of Chauchat.

l. 32 *as custom allowed*: in the world Hans Castorp has left behind, social convention dictated and allowed certain fashions even more daring than Chauchat's dress on this evening, but none as "revealing" in their implications.

l. 34 *his earlier assumption...*: cf. p. 126, ll. 25 ff.

l. 37 *radiant illusion*: "that day" was the day of his fateful walk when he had remembered Hippe and returned to Krokowski's lecture, cf. p. 126, ll. 34.

ll. 39f. *an experience*: the fascination with and sexual attraction to a "sick, infected organism" is further evidence of his "sympathy with death" and his desire to experience and confront its ramifications. It is "against all good reason" (ll. 35f.), but there is nothing he can do about it: the motivation comes from sources deep in the psyche.

(320) ll. 4ff. *A party to your heart's desire...*: another quotation from the "Walpurgis Night Dream" in Goethe's *Faust*. The implication here is that young men and women hope to become couples this evening. In *Faust* the continuation of the text refers to the Underworld. Settembrini is fully aware of what the Carnival atmosphere may lead to.

l. 8   *mocha*: one third espresso coffee, two thirds steamed milk, and chocolate.

ll. 14ff.   *Settembrini ... made himself at home*: in fact, the verb used here is "hospitieren," a leitmotif that throughout has implied a *temporary* stay by someone who does not fully belong. The noun form ("Hospitant"—visitor) occurs several times (cf. p. 55, l. 41f.; p. 69, l. 24; p. 111, l. 2).

l. 17   *In the Harz Mountains...*: the Harz Mountains are located in North East Germany. The Brocken is the highest point. This is also a stage direction at the beginning of the relevant scene in Goethe's *Faust*.

ll. 18f.   *Now here's a holy mass*: another *Faust* quotation. The lines are spoken by Faust as he is pulled by the crowd up the mountain.

l. 24   *ladies in men's clothes*: this hints at Castorp's future listening to the *Tales of Hoffmann*, in which one of the leading male roles is sung by a woman. The motif of bisexuality (closely related to Castorp's infatuation with Hippe/Chauchat) is connoted by this detail.

l. 31   *Punchinello*: see note to p. 318, l. 13.

ll. 35f.   *Spanish grandee ... paper ruff*: connotes Castorp's family past and its values.

(321) l. 4   *And here alone comes Baubo now*: this quotation from *Faust* (spoken by "a voice") is a nasty dig by Settembrini at Frau Stöhr. In Greek mythology Baubo is an old woman who jested with Demeter when she was mourning the loss of her daughter Persephone. Baubo, as an old nurse, stands for the goddess as crone.

ll. 4f.   *added the next line, too*: the next line is: "She is riding on a pig." It is no wonder, therefore, that Frau Stöhr is outraged. However, there are further dimensions to this hidden reference: the pig will be playing a major role in the game that will shortly commence, and Castorp will find himself further embroiled in mythology when he courts Chauchat: Settembrini will liken Castorp's "fall" to the fate of Odysseus's men who are turned into pigs on the island of Circe (cf. note to p. 243, ll. 35f.).

l. 6   *an Italian turkey*: Frau Stöhr's response implies that Settembrini is a lascivious beast.

ll. 7f.   *used familiar pronouns*: it is customary at Carnival time to permit the use of personal pronouns among people who would otherwise speak to each other using the formal form. This mention here foreshadows Hans Castorp's exploitation of the convention both in talking to Settembrini and especially in his conversation with Chauchat.

l. 25   *"Silent Sister" and "Blue Henry"*: see notes to p. 85, l. 19 & p. 7, l. 39.

(322) l. 1   *a simple tricorn*: allusion to Hermes; cf. picture on p. 26.

l. 6   *Look closer now, my lad!*: Mephistopheles says this to Faust. What takes place here is a re-enactment in the novel (ll. 6–11) of the actual exchange between Mephistopheles and Faust in Goethe's play. In *Faust* when Mephistopheles says: "'Tis Lilith," Faust responds: "Who?"—which is Castorp's response in the novel. Thereupon Mephistopheles/Settembrini explains: "The first wife Adam had. You'd best beware." Settembrini's quote, however, is lost on Castorp who also thinks that Settembrini has slipped into the informal form of address that is permitted at Carnival time, so he, too, now addresses Settembrini in the informal manner.

l. 10   *The question delighted the man of literature*: naturally, because unbeknownst to Castorp and to the delight of Settembrini the two of them are re-enacting the scene from *Faust*.

l. 16   *Lilli*: another howler by Hans Castorp.

l. 18   *According to Hebrew tradition*: In the Book of Isaiah, Lilith is a kind of night-demon or animal, translated as *screech owl* in the King James Version of the Bible. Lilith also appears as a night demon in the Talmud and Midrash. Late medieval Jewish legend portrays her as the first wife and equal of Adam. Considering Adam inferior, Lilith left the Garden of Eden of her own free will. (Other stories claim Lilith refused to lie under Adam, as she considered that this was too submissive). Adam then bade three angels to find Lilith and bring her back. When Lilith refused, God punished her by commanding that she slay 100 of her children, called Lilin, each day. Lilith is also sometimes considered to be the paramour of Satan. All this, of course, is implied by Settembrini's use of the association: to him Chauchat is Lilith personified. Castorp's actions later that evening signify that he will "know" Lilith (in the Biblical sense).

ll. 22f.   *turn the lights back on*: as the representative of Enlightenment, Settembrini's self-appointed task is to awaken Hans Castorp from "unhealthy" dreaming (cf. p. 189, ll. 37f.).

l. 24   *isn't that what you're up to, Ludovico?*: Castorp's use of Settembrini's first name here is intended to communicate in the translation the former's use of the informal form of address throughout this speech.

l. 25   *He had drunk quite a bit of burgundy and champagne*: not separately, but as a mixture (cf. p. 318, l. 37: "Lawyer Einhuf set the tone by mixing champagne and burgundy"—the original makes it clear that he pours burgundy into the champagne). Thus Hans Castorp's behavior on this evening is at least partly because of his intoxication.

l. 26   *Now listen—that's enough of that*: Settembrini refuses to accede to the convention of using the second person familiar form at Carnival time. He insists on the formal form as the appropriate address for civilized people. The episode is an exemplary indicator of the basic conflict of this evening and of the philosophical battle waged in the novel.

(323) l. 2 *I have to overcome my own resistance*: Castorp's use of the second person singular form is a victory for the side of him that leans towards Chauchat. His conditioned behavior (the use of the formal form of address) has had to be conquered—with some effort ("give myself a poke" [l. 2f.]), but it is an effort that he gladly makes ("with all my heart" [l. 4]). Another element of his upbringing and socialization has been overcome. In the original he uses the same word ("Selbstüberwindung"—derived from Nietzsche) that will characterize his ultimate lesson about life.

l. 6 *With all my heart, yes*: Settembrini is both surprised and upset, but Castorp reaffirms his individuality.

l. 7 *seven months*: the symbolical time represents a caesura in Castorp's relationship with Settembrini. After seven months of "instruction" Castorp is now about to go his own way.

l. 14 *I paid strict attention*: Castorp's admission that he always listened earnestly to Settembrini's arguments. N.B. also: "everything you said was well worth listening to" (ll. 17–18; in the original he says: "Through you I have learned and come to understand so much.") Castorp's recognition of his teacher's contribution to his education is generous.

l. 15 *homo humanus*: cf. note to p. 57, l. 39.

l. 18 *Carducci*: cf. note to p. 56, l. 41.

ll. 19f. *world republic ... beautiful style*: cf. p. 154, ll. 31 & p. 156, ll. 27ff.

l. 27 *you're a representative of something*: a significant step in Hans Castorp's education is his recognition of the two camps that claim his allegiance—and he knows which camp Settembrini represents.

l. 33 *a young donkey*: the word in the original ("Mulus") is of Latin origin; it signifies a young student between leaving high-school and beginning university.

l. 36 *sine pecunia*: cf. note to p. 45, l. 17.

l. 37 *I have the clear feeling...*: whether he is fully aware of it or not, this speech by Hans Castorp represents his farewell to Settembrini.

(324) ll. 7f. *he downed his burgundy and champagne...*: in the original he takes "several large gulps."

ll. 10f. *Those sound like words of farewell*: indeed they are—although Castorp responds evasively (cf. "ducking the issue," ll. 12–13).

l. 24 *a Turkish fez*: a red felt hat in the shape of a sawn-off cone (see picture).

l. 29   *a man almost larger than life*: which associates him with the unearthly "powers" that stand behind him (cf. note to p. 129, ll. 17f.).

ll. 35f.   *a sugary arrack punch*: arrack is an oriental brandy; another foreshadowing of Peeperkorn's arrival.

l. 39   *Old Scratch himself atop them all*: yet another quote from *Faust*; this line is spoken by the "witches," who are acknowledging their ruler: Urian is a demon who rules witches and copulates with them. (This could thus also be seen as an oblique reference to Behrens's relationships with female patients.)

(325)   ll. 3f.   *cross-dressed masqueraders*: at Carnival time license is granted to act in many ways contrary to conventional standards; the theme of bisexuality is indicated.

ll. 5f.   *Handel's Largo ... a Grieg sonata*: the *Largo* is from the opera *Xerxes* (1738) by Georg Friedrich Handel (1685–1759). The sonata by Edvard Grieg (Norwegian composer, 1843–1907) might be his Piano Sonata in E minor (1865).

l. 16   *the profile of a pig*: clearly an allusion to Odysseus and the Island of Circe. See note to p. 243, ll. 35ff.

(326)   l. 11   *Hans Castorp joined the crowd*: Castorp's behavior is, as it so often has been, both impulsive and calculated: he orchestrates the scene so that he can approach Chauchat and ask her to lend him a pencil.

ll. 11ff.   *looking over Joachim's shoulder...*: an attitude that indicates intense involvement and one that he repeats in the presence of Naphta, cf. 392, ll. 23f.

l. 22   *He tossed the offending stump into the punch bowl*: scarcely the action of a cultured young man from Hamburg. He has thrown aside some of his good breeding—undoubtedly in part because of his intoxication.

l. 28   *as he well knew*: he has been aware all along of where Chauchat was located, and his behavior in this scene has been carefully planned.

ll. 32f.   *Eh! Ingegnere! Aspetti! Che cosa fa! Ingegnere! Un po di ragione, sa! Ma è matto questo ragazzo!*: Hey, engineer! Wait! What are you doing? Engineer! A little bit of reason, please! But he is crazy, this young man! This is Settembrini's final cry of warning and despair: the import of Castorp's actions is clear to the Italian. Castorp is merely approaching Chauchat, but Settembrini comprehends the full significance of the act: Castorp has once and for all left the Italian and made a decision for her. This is a major turning-point in the novel: from now on Chauchat dominates—and Settembrini's influence declines.

l. 37   *Ehh–!*: expression of frustration.

ll. 37f.   *he left the Mardi Gras festivities*: it is a sign of his admission of defeat—and he has no wish to witness the consequences. Reason has left—and Hans Castorp moves into the camp of unreason.

ll. 39ff.   *standing in the brick schoolyard...*: recalling the scene with Hippe, cf. p. 120, ll. 18ff.

l. 40   *epicanthic*: see note to p. 254, l. 5.

l. 41   *Do* you *have a pencil perhaps?*: the "you" is expressed using the familiar second-person form. The repetition of the scene in the schoolyard with Hippe begins (cf. p. 120, ll. 19f.).

(327) l. 1   *He was pale as death*: cf. p. 121, ll. 32f. The following scene parallels Castorp's memory of Hippe during his walk (cf. p. 120 ff.).

ll. 2ff.   *Nerves controlling the blood vessels...*: Hans Castorp had learned this from Behrens, cf. p. 259, ll. 24ff.

ll. 8f.   *the work of his body's sebaceous glands...*: the introduction of medical terminology to explain the physiological effects of profound human emotions is a frequent technique employed by Thomas Mann. It derives from a distrust and fear of emotion, and the ironic use of such a device is a means of restricting the power of the emotions over human behavior (cf. Hans Castorp's reaction to Joachim's death, p. 528, ll. 29ff.). Hans Castorp had learned of this aspect of physiology in his conversation with Behrens in the latter's apartment (cf. p. 260, ll. 8ff.).

l. 15   *schadenfreude*: pleasure in someone else's pain.

l. 24   *likewise using personal pronouns*: Chauchat at this point goes along with the Mardi Gras convention of informality.

l. 29   *a silver pencil-holder*: the original uses "Crayon," a French loan-word; cf. note to p. 120, ll. 24ff.

l. 32   *Voilà*: There!

l. 33   *waggling it back and forth*: the sexual allusion is obvious.

l. 37   *Clavdia's Tartar face*: cf. note to p. 238, l. 2.

l. 40   *Prenez garde, il est un peu fragile...C'est a visser, tu sais*: "Be careful, it is somewhat fragile ... You turn it, understand?" In their conversation Chauchat's mode of address oscillates between the formal and the informal forms: here she begins with a formal form and then continues with the informal form. Her instruction to Castorp is similar to the advice that Hippe had given him: "And don't break it" (cf. p. 120, l.

28), and it is Hippe's words that stick in Hans Castorp's memory as typical of the quality of Chauchat's voice (cf. p. 548, l. 7).

l. 41   *And as they both bent their heads...*: cf. p. 120, l. 27 where Castorp and Hippe enact a similar scenario.

(328) l.1f.   *the standard screw mechanism...*: sexually suggestive again.

ll. 3f.   *a formal stiff collar*: important for keeping his head from rolling uncontrollably. (Cf. his grandfather's posture, p. 23, ll. 34ff.)

l. 5   *A poor thing, but thine own*: Castorp uses an everyday rhyming phrase ("klein, aber dein"), but the rhyme is lost in translation.

ll. 6f.   *so that the two labials were left unsounded*: labials are words pronounced with the help of the lips. Thus in the English translation he would omit the "p" in "poor" and the "b" in "but." (In the German there is only one labial.)

ll. 8ff.   *you are witty, too*: in this initial exchange, Chauchat uses the informal "du"-form in German when addressing Hans Castorp.

ll. 11f.   *draw, draw well...*: the translation cannot convey the ambiguity of the final German verb that Chauchat uses ("draw yourself out"): she urges Castorp both to draw until he has had enough and to excel himself (which, of course, he is about to do).

ll. 30f.   *"Farewell!" he said*: another hidden quote from Goethe's *Faust*, but it is doubtful whether Castorp realizes it.

ll. 39ff.   *She, however, was forced to lie far back...*: her posture is almost "horizontal" and thus symbolical of what she represents. The "horizontal" position connotes the world of sloth, laxity, sex, and ultimately death (cf. note to p. 316, l. 4).

(329) l. 7   *You are conversant with my wardrobe*: Chauchat initially responds to Castorp using the familiar second-person pronoun.

l. 9   *by Lukaček*: the tailor's house will play an important role later as the residence of Naphta (and Settembrini). Thus in this manner Chauchat and Naphta are connected.

(329ff.) The conversation in French between Castorp and Chauchat (the French parts of the dialogue appear in English italics in the translation) represents a watershed in Castorp's development. Despite his disclaimer that he can barely speak French (p. 331, l. 25), his fluency in this conversation is remarkable. Apart from being a passionate declaration of his love for Chauchat, the conversation also signifies his definitive acceptance of the world-view that she embodies and symbolizes. The conversation also discusses some important concepts (e.g. the connection between love and death, the nature of freedom, the body) that are central to the novel and that Castorp will henceforth incorporate into his own view of life.

During the conversation Castorp consistently addresses Chauchat in the informal manner, whereas her mode of address to him alternates between the informal and the formal, depending on whether she feels comfortable with his comments. When he gets too personal, she reverts to the formal form (and insists that he do, too). For Castorp, French is the language of intimacy, and the informal form of address is the *only* form he can think of using towards her.

l. 29   *I have been giving freedom some thought of late*: the concept of "freedom"—especially in the realm of the personal—becomes a central concern for Castorp from this point onwards.

(330) l. 10   *Please, sir, speak German!*: This is a rather stilted way of conveying that Chauchat switches to the formal mode of address in saying: "Speak German, please!" Castorp's remarks have suddenly become too personal—when he speaks of her skin—and Chauchat wishes him to revert both to the formal form of address and the more "formal" language, German, so as to force him to "keep his distance." Despite her free-spiritedness and rejection of much of bourgeois convention, Frau Chauchat invokes that convention when it suits her—as here, when she attempts to have Castorp keep his distance.

l. 13   *a humanist pursuit*: in agreement with his comments to Behrens and Joachim, cf. p. 256, ll. 12ff.

l. 24   *his grandfather's blue, thoughtful eyes*: cf. p. 24, l. 23.

(331) l. 3   *it is a dream I know well*: i.e. Hippe.

l. 8   *life's problem children*: Castorp elevates his own case into the German dilemma.

ll. 10f.   *it would not have been too difficult...*: Chauchat is mildly chastising Castorp for not having approached her earlier.

l. 11   *It's a little late…*: Castorp does not yet know that Chauchat will be leaving the Berghof in the morning (cf. "I'm leaving," l. 40)—and that fact does not register with him here, although Chauchat hints at it.

l. 17   *Who just let fly with a few words in your direction*: Chauchat was obviously well aware of what was happening when Settembrini tried to stop Castorp's move towards her.

ll. 27f.   *With no responsibilities*: French, for Castorp, is the language of freedom—where he can forget the conventions and strictures that are associated with his mother tongue.

l. 32   *like drawing that piglet*: the pig evokes associations with Circe—and Settembrini's warning (cf. note to pp. 243, ll. 35f.).

l. 38   *I have used it with you all along…*: cf. p. 173, ll. 12 ff.

ll. 41ff.   *It took a while*...: Chauchat's announcement that she is leaving shocks Hans Castorp out of his dream-state and brings him back to earth—and to speaking German (p. 332, ll. 12ff.).

(332) l. 12   *What are you going to do?*: the shock of her news causes him to emerge from the dream-world of French and speak in the language of reason and reality.

l. 18   *Après dîner*: after lunch; see note to p. 74, l. 10. This is confirmed on p. 342, ll. 33f., where Chauchat leaves at 3 p.m.

l. 30   *I love freedom above all else*: the core of Chauchat's being.

l. 33   *Daghestan*: see note to p. 134, l. 42.

l. 34   *It is my illness that allows me liberty*: whereas others might find it frustrating that the physical deficiencies of the human body limit their ability to fulfil their goals (cf. Settembrini), Chauchat exploits her weakness to achieve complete spiritual freedom. She has overcome the physical limitations by accepting them and by leading her life the way she chooses. Her example is an important lesson for Hans Castorp.

(333) l. 4   *Within the humanist branch of letters called medicine*: another example of Castorp's all-encompassing view of what constitutes humanism. (Cf. his inclusion of painting in his view of humanism, l. 20).

l. 20   *an initiate in another humanistic discipline*: Castorp's somewhat obtuse way of indicating that he knows that Behrens has painted Chauchat's portrait—and perhaps has known her even more intimately than that.

ll. 40f.   *was there someone preventing your doing so?*: she means Settembrini—and his influence on Castorp.

l. 45   *The gentleman meant not a whit to me*...: the translation is a little extreme. Castorp actually says: "When my eyes see you, I hardly think of that man."

(334) l. 2   *It is quite possible that he will die*...: Castorp remembers these words and recalls them (in French) on p. 407, l. 39. Chauchat's prediction comes true, of course, and when Hans Castorp later reports it to her, she remembers her own words: cf. p. 549, ll. 7ff.

ll. 6ff.   *The idea of death doesn't frighten me*...: here, for the first time, Hans Castorp makes explicit the equation between love and death.

l. 17   *I always keep it in my wallet*: this is Castorp's identity card, to show that he "belongs" to the Berghof society of tubercular patients. But his own x-ray picture will soon be replaced by Chauchat's which he will receive from her in her room.

ll. 21f.   *I would much prefer to see the interior portrait*: this reveals a rather strange obsession with Chauchat's "worm-eaten" interior, but it reflects his fascination with dissolution and death.

l. 28   *papyrosy*: Russian word for cigarette.

ll. 37f.   *It seems to us that it is more moral...*: more words that Castorp takes to heart. He repeats them to Joachim in respect of Naphta (p. 379, ll. 30f), claiming he does not know why he says them in French (p. 379, l. 33) and then again to Chauchat when she returns to the Berghof (p. 548, ll. 33f.); she, however, does not seem to recognize her own words (p. 548, l. 35). In effect, these words are the sum of Chauchat's philosophy. Hans Castorp embraces it here, but later moves beyond it (cf. p. 548, ll. 33f.).

(335) l. 24   *You know the consequences, monsieur*: The removal of the Carnival hat and the return to the formal form of address signals the end of Carnival—and intimacy.

ll. 28f.   *That form of address...*: he had just heard this phrase from Settembrini's lips in German (cf. p. 322, ll. 27f.).

(336) l. 3   *And my fever?*: Castorp's fever is the physical manifestation both of his illness and of his heightened existence; but it is also his "fever" for Chauchat and all that she represents. For her part Chauchat tries to make light of Castorp's obvious infatuation with her: "it's an episode of no consequence that will pass quickly" (l. 5).

l. 23   *the lingering traces*: cf. p. 178, ll. 8 ff.

l. 31   *If your teachers could only see you*: Settembrini, certainly—and presumably earlier teachers in Hamburg: in other words, his present behavior is contrary to his entire North German, middle-class upbringing.

ll. 37f.   *My handsome bourgeois with the little moist spot*: Chauchat's description of Castorp is a perfect metaphorical summary of his state of being: he is the bourgeois with the eternal questions about life and death.

ll. 40ff.   *The body, love and death, are simply one and the same. Because the body is sickness and depravity, it is what produces death, yes, both of them, love and death, are carnal, and that is the source of their terror and great magic!*: this is a view of life typically called "Romantic." N.B. this is but a stage in Hans Castorp's progress: he will break out of this mode of thinking in the sub-chapter *Snow* (cf. pp. 466ff.). Many of the elements of this speech are taken from *I Sing The Body Electric* by Walt Whitman (1819–92).

(337) l. 1   *love and death*: a central leitmotif. The similar sounds of the two words in French ("l'amour et la mort") reinforce their close association. Certainly, there is an allusion here to the Romantic tradition that culminated in Wagner and the "Liebestod" of Tristan and Isolde. Since Whitman plays a role in this conversation, Thomas Mann could well have had in mind the following lines by Whitman that he cited in a 1923 essay in connection with the "sympathy with death": "Give me your tone therefore,/O Death, that I may accord with it,/Give me yourself for I see that you belong to me now above all, and/ are folded inseparably together you Love and Death are" ("Scented Herbage of My Breast").

ll. 3ff. *so impudent that it makes us blush with shame*: cf. Krokowski's lecture (p. 125, ll. 11ff.) and his remarks about the impudicus mushroom (cf. p. 358, ll. 38ff.). Castorp reproduces here in French what Krokowski had said earlier in German. N.B. how this speech by Hans Castorp mirrors all that has been said by Settembrini and Castorp's own critical reflections on the Italian's opinions.

l. 8   *remove your hat and walk on tiptoe*: the reverent posture; cf. note to p. 287, ll. 30ff.

l. 13   *an extremely humanistic affair*: cf. p. 256, ll. 1ff. & p. 486, ll. 11 ff.

ll. 16ff.   *Consider the marvelous symmetry...*: Hans Castorp celebrates the human body. And afterward, he wants to die (cf. ll. 34f.). There is also a comic element to all of this: in the midst of his hymn to the body, he intersperses anatomical terminology (e.g. "Let me touch in devotion your pulsing femoral artery" [ll. 30f.]), which is grotesquely incongruent with his hymnic effusions. In yearning to taste "the sweet inner surfaces of the elbow and the hollow of the knee," he has remembered what Behrens had told him about the lymph nodes, which are located "along the neck, in the armpits, at the crooks of the elbows, the backs of the knees, and similar intimate, sensitive spots on the body" (p. 261, ll. 19ff.).

l. 34   *the contours of the grave*: more correctly: the *anatomy* of the grave (a leitmotif); see note to p. 219, l. 20.

l. 34   *let me perish*: echo of Wagner's *Tristan and Isolde*, Act II, Scene 2: "Let me perish!" sings Tristan to Isolde (and later she to him).

(338) l. 2   *Adieu, my Carnival Prince*: Traditionally, the person chosen to be the "Prince of Fools" during Carnival time. N.B. Chauchat says "Adieu"—which implies that she will not see Castorp again.

ll. 6f.   *Don't forget to return my pencil*: This amounts to an invitation to come to her room. That Castorp does, in fact, go to her room is not explicitly stated here, but ample evidence is given later to leave little doubt: we are told that, although her never spoke to her the next day (p. 342, ll. 27f.), he gave her pencil back to her (cf. p. 342, ll. 9f. & p. 486, ll. 7f.), and that he heard directly from her lips that she would return (cf. p. 342, ll. 21ff.). We are also informed that he possesses—and carries with him—Chauchat's x-ray that she gave him after their late-night rendezvous (cf. p. 343, ll. 31ff.), and we are told of her flesh that "against all reason, Hans Castorp had tasted on Mardi Gras" (p. 382, ll. 41f.) "in one wicked, riotously sweet hour" (p. 344, ll. 1).

(339) Chapter Six

Changes

(339) ll. 1ff. The reflections about time are intended not as a contribution to a philosophical debate about the nature of time, but rather as the background to Hans Castorp's own dilemma. His time at the Berghof is increasingly without measurement (except for the daily routine), and since the environment of the sanatorium is, in any case, "hermetic," what it the meaning of time for him here?

(340) ll. 1f. *a naughty, but overwhelming desire...*: a somewhat obtuse reference to his desire for Chauchat, for which "he had now paid dearly" (l. 2): i.e. at the end of the previous sub-chapter he had gone to her room, spent "one wicked, riotously sweet hour" with her (p. 344, ll. 10f.), before she left the next day. See note to p. 342, ll. 9f.

ll. 3f. *buried under snow now since time out of mind*: underlining both the eternal nature of such questions and the mythological character of the location.

ll. 8f. *as Hans Castorp had himself noted one evening in French*: see p. 333, ll. 38f.

l. 14 *Gaffky scale*: a method of counting (on a slide under a microscope) the number of tuberculosis bacilli in a given area of sputum, developed by Georg Gaffky (1850–1918) in 1884. The scale ran from 1 (one to four bacilli) to 10 (enormous quantities).

l. 23 *just dropping by*: the leitmotif initially used by Behrens to describe his visit (cf. p. 104, l. 26).

l. 24 *a "life sentence"*: the sanatorium as prison. The ironic ambiguity of such a phrase lies in the fact that a "life sentence" could, in fact, be brief, if the patient died.

l. 27 *even his tablemates*: the fact that Joachim would talk about such a personal matter to his tablemates is an indication of his frustration.

l. 33 *Schatzalp*: see note to p. 9, l. 19f.

l. 34 *Arcadia*: a mountainous area of the Peloponnese in Greece. In mythology, Arcadia—and especially since Virgil's *Bucolica*—has signified an idyllic landscape where shepherds indulge in writing poetry and making love.

l. 39 *even if it kills me!*: prophetic words, unfortunately.

(341) ll. 1f. *certain things he had heard a third party say...*: cf. Chauchat's prediction of Joachim's death, p. 334, ll. 2f.

l. 7 *Cannstatt*: see note to p. 15, l. 3.

ll. 11f. *a certain incident*: i.e. Castorp's rendezvous with Chauchat. It is not completely clear how Joachim could be "undoubtedly aware" of this incident, although the word "undoubtedly" indicates that the narrator is speculating somewhat. Joachim would have observed his cousin's behavior on Walpurgis Night (as had other residents of the Berghof) and the matter was surely the subject of gossip (cf. note to p. 349, l. 16).

l. 12 *about which they never spoke*: because of their reticence in personal matters.

l. 13 *betrayal, desertion, and faithlessness*: Hans Castorp has acted on his erotic attraction to Chauchat, whereas Joachim has not acted on his attraction to Marusya. Joachim always acts out of a sense of "duty": his reason for being at the Berghof is to get better as soon as possible and to return to military service on the Flatland. Allowing himself to be "sidetracked" by his attraction to Marusya would thus be a dereliction of duty. This is the cause of Castorp's guilty conscience: he has, indeed, been guilty of an act of desertion—an act that symbolizes a rejection of the entire ethic of the Flatland.

l. 14 *a pair of round, brown eyes...*: Marusya.

ll. 39f. *all too hastily put into words...*: see p. 317, ll. 9ff., where Castorp "plays fast and loose with time," as Settembrini puts it (ll. 15f.).

(342) l. 2 *Pentecost*: see note to p. 317, l. 11.

l. 5 *Rhätikon chain*: mountain range on the south side of Davos that stretches into Austria.

ll. 9f. *and given it back to her...*: this is the first real clue we have that Castorp visited Chauchat in her room. The rest of this page contains a number of further clues that lead us to conclude that they spent some time together. At the end of Chapter Five Chauchat had said to Hans: "Don't forget to return my pencil" (p. 338, ll. 6f.). The final lines of the chapter follow: "And she left" (p. 338, l. 8). We are told that Hans Castorp did not "exchange a single word" with her on the day of her departure (p. 342, ll. 27f.), but he did return her pencil, as she had requested, and he had received in return her x-ray picture ("some little memento"—p. 342, l. 10). When did these events happen? They happened, "not during the conversation in a foreign language" (p. 342, l. 22), but rather "during an interval we have chosen to pass over in silence," the narrator coyly tells us (ll. 23f.). Furthermore, Chauchat assured Hans that she would return—an assurance he received "before returning to room 34 that night" (ll. 26f.), which was "considerably later than conscientious Joachim to his" (l. 15). All in all, it is quite clear that Hans went to her room, before returning some time later to his own. Cf. also the later reference to Chauchat "whom he had known and possessed for one wicked, riotously sweet hour" (p. 344, ll. 10f.).

l. 29   *dinner*: "lunch"; cf. note to p. 74, l. 10. Chauchat leaves the same day "at three that afternoon" (ll. 33f.). The translation remains consistent with Chauchat's statement to Castorp that she will be leaving "Après dîner"—also rendered as "After dinner" (p. 332, l. 18) instead of "After lunch."

(343) l. 18   *The great-aunt gave her some candies, "konfekti"*...: the original explains "konfekti" as "Russian jam," but the word could mean not just preserved fruit, but also anything sweet made of burnt sugar and fruit such as apricots. Since the great-aunt later distributes more "konfekti" in boxes (cf. p. 355, l. 3), the meaning here is some form of candy.

ll. 23f.   *on some other private occasion*: this is clearly Hans Castorp's own assumption (and fear).

l. 32   *not reddish-brown pencil shavings*: cf. p. 120. ll. 38f.

ll. 32f.   *a little plate of glass in a narrow frame*: in her room on the night of Mardi Gras Chauchat had given Castorp the x-ray picture of her chest, which he henceforth carries around with him in his inside pocket (see p. 342, l. 10), or places on a stand in his bedroom (see p. 429, ll. 9ff.).

ll. 38f.   *How often had he looked at it and pressed it to his lips*: for the full humor of this scene to emerge, one has to realize first what this is: namely, the x-ray image of someone's chest (and a tubercular chest, to boot), and then imagine Castorp's in his love-sick obsession gazing at it and kissing it.

(344) l. 10   *genius*: what is meant by this word here is something quite special. The word "genius" here is used in the sense of the Latin phrase: *genius loci* ("spirit of the place"). It implies the spirit that infuses a place and that is its essential nature and being. Thus, if Chauchat is the "genius loci" of the Berghof, then the sanatorium is, indeed, the place where everything that Chauchat represents is embodied: freedom, license, physical love, etc. The word has already occurred at p. 315, l. 17.

ll. 10f.   *known and possessed for one wicked, riotously sweet hour* ... i.e. his hour with Chauchat in her room.

l. 12   *delicate little song*...: cf. p. 137, ll. 31ff., where he rejects the sentiments expressed in trivial popular songs as being unworthy of what he feels for Chauchat.

ll. 15ff.   *During that hour*...: in Chauchat's room Castorp had continued his voluble ramblings. This paragraph—if we read it closely— tells us all we need to know about Castorp's secret hour with Chauchat.

l. 23   *his hour of adventure*: the translation flattens out the original somewhat; it should read "this hour of profound adventure." What was involved obviously in Hans Castorp's tryst with Chauchat was not merely a sexual encounter, but something deeper: the exploration of a way of life radically different from that of his bourgeois environment. This is made clear below when Hans asks which view will prevail, "the bourgeois or the other" (ll. 37f.).

l. 35 *joli bourgeois au petit endroit humide*: handsome bourgeois with a moist spot. This was Chauchat's description of Castorp on p. 336, ll. 37f.

ll. 35f. *a translation of Settembrini's phrase…*: it is not, of course, a direct translation—nor even a paraphrase. In fact, what is happening here is not a translation, but a *transmutation* of Settembrini's concept of Hans Castorp into Chauchat's view of him—a view that Hans has now accepted. His "moist spot," which he has always had, is his "fate"—the fascination with illness, the attraction to the darker side of life, the "sympathy with death"—in a word: Romanticism. In his book-length essay *Reflections of a Non-Political Man* (1918) Thomas Mann wrote: "'Sympathy with death' is not a phrase signifying virtue and progress. Is it not rather … the formula for and basic definition of Romanticism?"

(345) l. 3 One *mocking prophecy*: see p. 338, ll. 2f.

l. 9 *More toxic than we gave you credit for*: Behrens says literally "poisoned"—which widens the connotations to include his infatuation with Chauchat.

l. 18 *it could hurt like hell*: in the original "it hurts like the devil"—which is appropriate for Behrens (Rhadamanthus). He is doctor, artist, and devil.

l. 30 *that pleasant little chat…*: see pp. 251 ff. This yet another example of Hans Castorp's slyness: his conversation with Behrens on that occasion had been for him far more than a "pleasant little chat."

(346) l. 1 *the civilian*: here Behrens is repeating his description of Castorp from their first meeting (cf. p. 44, l. 36).

l. 11 *who was it that left just recently?*: once again, Castorp's feigned naïveté is a ruse—here to bring the topic of conversation around to Chauchat. In this speech he babbles away as if uttering unconnected thoughts, but the entire speech revolves around Chauchat.

l. 12 *Daghestan*: see note to p. 134, l. 42.

ll. 17f. *where the basic concepts are lacking*: Castorp is standing the world on its head: now he is suggesting that the routine and social order of the Berghof are the "basic concepts."

ll. 20 *so she happened to mention to me*: that was, of course, while he was in her room.

ll. 20f. *how did we get started talking about her?*: with his usual sly-ness, he has been contriving to bring the conversation around to Chauchat all along.

l. 30 *your chest started heaving*: cf. p. 250, l. 29 & p. 280, ll. 38f.

l. 32 *Bremen*: a port city in northwestern Germany, situated on the river Weser, about 37 miles south from the North Sea.

ll. 41f. *at the time I didn't know your model...*: but he was in love with her from a distance.

(347) ll. 2f. *I've had the chance to become personally acquainted with her*: Could there be a more oblique way of intimating that he slept with her?

ll. 4f. *if we may remind the reader*: see p. 171, l. 24. It would, however, seem that the words do have a little more meaning here.

l. 10 *we sort of fell into conversation*: omitting to add that they also sort of fell into bed together.

l. 10f. *Hans Castorp pulled air in ... the needle struck home*: at the precise moment that Castorp is telling Behrens that he got to know Chauchat just before her departure from the Berghof, the doctor jabs him with the needle. It is no wonder that the injections cause "an immediate, though momentary rise in temperature" (p. 345, ll. 22f.): in this case the cause is not merely medical.

ll. 11f. *That's a critical nerve you happened to hit there*: in more sense than one.

l. 13 *hurts like hell*: appropriate since it has been caused by the Devil (cf. note to p. 345, l. 18).

l. 13 *a little massage does help*: Behrens massages Castorp; the homoerotic overtones continue from the time of their exchange of cigars (cf. p. 249, ll. 31ff.).

ll. 21f. *we managed to communicate fairly well*: more slyness.

l. 23 *I can well believe it*: it should be clear from Behrens's reactions to Castorp's conversation that the former has guessed what Castorp is really getting at. "Rather nice, eh?" (l. 24) implies that he knows that Castorp has slept with Chauchat.

(348) ll. 1f. *No, we'll just have to console ourselves, my lad*: this comment makes it quite plain that Behrens knows what has been going on and how Castorp feels. Both Behrens and Castorp are ex-lovers of Chau-chat, so that now there is a bond between them.

l. 12 *their conversations*: i.e. such exchanges happened more than once.

ll. 12f. *cleverly steered by Hans Castorp*: he had wanted to find out whether or not Behrens was in communication with Chauchat, and if he had any idea when she might return. The results of these conversations were disappointing for Castorp.

l. 29   *her illness gave her that freedom*: i.e. not to conform to conventional bourgeois standards and to write polite letters.

ll. 30f.   *Signore Brunetto Latini*: see note to p. 156, l. 12.

ll. 32f.   *how to speak...*: Hans Castorp reproduces here Settembrini's words from p. 156, ll. 15f. However, since he is now firmly in Chauchat's camp, they do not represent anything meaningful to him now.

l. 36   *had unexpectedly entered his sickroom...*: see p. 189, ll. 37–41. He still has qualms of conscience when he thinks of Settembrini's opinion of his relationship with Chauchat. In some ways he is still under Settembrini's influence (cf. p. 349, ll. 31f: "he was very fond of Herr Settembrini, set great store by his presence").

(349)   ll. 11f.   *in the form of a mythological allusion...*: requiring one to have had a Western Classical education to understand it. (See next note.)

l. 16   *how did you like the pomegranate?*: an oblique reference to the myth of Persephone. Although a god, she was condemned to stay in the Underworld because she had eaten pomegranate seeds (cf. ll. 22ff.). The pomegranate also connotes the figure of Dionysus, since in one version of the myth the fruit was said to have sprung from his blood (an allusion that Thomas Mann had used earlier in *Death in Venice*). Dionysus is the god of wine and the exhilaration and ecstasy (often sexual) that wine produces. The image also connotes possibly Adam's eating of the apple in the Garden of Eden—and his consequent loss of innocence. Settembrini has drawn a conclusion from the events of Walpurgisnight: he assumes (correctly) that Hans Castorp has slept with Clavdia Chauchat. (N.B. also p. 149, l. 13: "...he kept up with the latest gossip"—more accurately: he was up-to-date with all the latest news.)

l. 31   *his trophy...*: Chauchat's x-ray.

l. 35   *the advantages of disgrace*: cf. note to p. 90, ll. 4ff.

(350)   l. 4   *tenente*: Lieutenant.

l. 16   *terra firma*: firm land.

l. 16   *the king's birthday*: the King of Italy, Victor Emmanuel III (1869–1947).

ll. 27f.   *I am the King of Babylon*: the quote is from the ballad "Belsazar" by Heinrich Heine (1797–1856): "Jehova, for you I have eternal scorn—/I am the King of Babylon." Belshazzar was, in fact, not the king, but a general. However, the biblical account (in the *Book of Daniel*) relates how Belshazzar, son of Nebuchadnezzar and the last king of Babylon, held a feast using the gold and silver goblets that had been stolen from the temple in Jerusalem. This act of "sacrilege" (Hans Castorp's term) resulted in the appearance of the words "Mene, mene tekel upharsin" ("You are weighed in the balance and found wanting") on the wall. That night Belshazzar was killed and Babylon was taken by the Persians.

ll. 29f.   *a great triumph of the human spirit*: Hans Castorp is deliberately using phrases of which Settembrini would approve. He is very cunningly trying to get back into the Italian's favor.

l. 35   *his ankles crossed*: cf. p. 54, l. 17.

(351) l. 4   *placet experiri*: see note to p. 96, l. 14.

l. 6   *sicuro*: of course.

l. 10   *per esempio*: for example.

l. 10   *such a luxury ark...*: the sinking of the *SS Titanic* (15 April 1912). Cf. p. 681, l. 5. (But this conversation takes place in the novel at Easter 1908.)

l. 11   *Prometheus's deed*: See note to p. 155. For Settembrini the Caucasus mountains were the "Scythian cliffs" (l. 12)—which gives Prometheus's deed even more importance in his eyes, as it was a blow against obscurantism. For Settembrini "Scythia" stands for barbarism (cf. his reference to "Parthians and Scythians," see note to p. 220, l. 17).

l. 13   *what about the other kind of hubris*: an oblique reference to Hans Castorp's straying from the path of reason at Mardi Gras.

l. 16   *Si o no!*: Yes or no!

ll. 17f.   *Hans Castorp stirred his spoon...*: he has fully understood Settembrini's point.

ll. 20ff.   *Are you not afraid of the second circle of hell...*: the Fifth Canto of Dante's *Inferno* (the first part of the *Divine Comedy*) leads into the second circle of Hell, the realm of the passions, of lust and carnal sin, the place for those who have surrendered their reason to the seductions of the flesh.

l. 23   *Gran dio*: Good God.

l. 29   *it was very like a goodbye*: Settembrini is aware that Castorp's evening with Chauchat signified his (Castorp's) decision to embrace her "philosophy" of life and, in effect, reject Settembrini's. While appreciating the noble qualities and positive aims of Settembrini's world-view, Castorp is drawn by his innate nature to "the other side." Settembrini's departure from the Berghof may therefore be seen as symbolical—although the debates will still continue.

ll. 33f.   *just as he had on another, similar occasion*: cf. p. 332, l. 15, when Chauchat had announced her imminent departure.

(352) l. 1   *I cannot get well...*: with metaphorical implications for his world-view.

ll. 17f.   *a Bohemian ladies' tailor*: it is, of course, ironic that Settembrini has found lodgings with someone whose origins (Bohemia) connote a world of values of which he would disapprove.

ll. 22f.   *not ... by sleigh, but on foot*: another sign of Settembrini's modest financial state.

(353) ll. 17f.   *on a totally wild and fraudulent basis*: i.e. without the blessing of the doctors.

ll. 25f.   *no prison ship, no Siberian salt mine*: these terms were originally used by Behrens (p. 176, l. 9) and then repeated by Hans Castorp (see p. 237, l. 41) to Settembrini. The denial that the Berghof is a kind of prison is ironically undermined when the metaphor is extended on l. 28 where the narrator speaks of Frau Salomon's being "sentenced to an additional five months." (Cf. also p. 461, ll. 15 ff. where the metaphors are repeated.)

(354) l. 23   *Midsummer Night*: June 21.

l. 23   *Pentecost*: celebrated 50 days after Easter; also known as Whitsunday.

l. 31   *whose face had turned blotchy*: as it had when Hans Castorp had talked about Marusya's bosom (cf. note to p. 70, ll. 36f.).

(355) l. 3   *konfekti*: see note to p. 343, l. 18.

l. 15ff. *without ever speaking to Joachim...*: This reticence between Hans Castorp and Joachim is typical of the polite reserve that both cousins maintain when such personal matters arise.

l. 17   *the name of someone else*: Chauchat. See previous note.

ll. 19f.   *Dutch guests whose appetites were so immense*: a harbinger of the arrival of another Dutch guest with a big appetite (Peeperkorn).

l. 31   *Samara*: region in southeast Russia.

l. 32   *Georgia*: small country on the eastern shore of the Black Sea, absorbed into the Russian Empire in the 19th century. It would not be difficult to guess which of the three men raised these topics of conversation.

l. 32   *through fog and slush*: preparing for the slogging of the First World War (cf. p. 704, l. 1).

(356) l. 15   *foehn*: see note to p. 265, l. 18.

l. 34   *Schwarzhorn*: mountain near Davos (cf. note to p. 8, ll. 29f.).

l. 35   *Scaletta Glacier*: near Davos (cf. note to p. 8, ll. 29f.).

(357) l. 10   *boutonnieres*: a boutonniere is a floral decoration worn by men, typically a single flower or bud.

l. 12   *lasted a long, long time, despite its diversions*: yet another repetition of the leitmotivic phrase "neither diverting, nor boring" ("langweilig—kurzweilig"). Cf. note to p. 83, l. 24.

l. 14   *soldanella*: commonly known in English as snowbell.

l. 39   *gentian*: conventionally identified as pretty, deep-blue flowers that are found in the Alps (although they grow in many other places, too, and can also be pink, red, or yellow in color).

(358) l. 1   *Ranunculaceae*: this plant occurs at several crucial moments of the novel (cf. note to p. 117, ll. 4–5).

l. 3   *androecium*: the male part of the flower in a flowering plant.

l. 3   *gynoecium*: the female part of the flower in a flowering plant.

l. 8   *But I don't think I'll wait for them*: A later reference to this statement reveals that it is spoken with a "quite ill-tempered" tone of voice (see p. 359, ll. 17f.). Joachim, of course, is impatient to leave and return to his military duties.

l. 17   *just as on that day...*: cf. pp. 121–22.

l. 22   *never have to stop*: the meaning is that he would never need to stop—because he would never exhaust his material.

ll. 23ff.   *Thousand and One Nights*: the Persian king marries a series of brides and has them all executed the next morning. However, when he marries Scheherezade, on the night of their marriage, she tells him a story—but does not finish it. The next night she finishes the tale and begins another. So it goes for 1001 nights.

l. 31   *love and* death: the topic is central to the novel.

l. 37   *glycogen*: glycogen is the storage form of glucose in animals and humans which is analogous to the starch in plants.

l. 40   *morel...*: edible fungus.

l. 40   *impudicus*: the scientific name of this morel is phallus impudicus. (So named by Linnaeus; see note to p, 363, l. 19.) "Impudicus" signifies "not chaste." (See image opposite.)

l. 41   *its form reminiscent of love*: i.e. phallic.

l. 41   *the stench given off*: these comments are reminiscent of Freud's claim in his "Three Essays on the Theory of Sexuality" that sexual arousal has a chemical basis. This idea had already been expressed on p. 185, ll. 18ff.

(359) l.1 *decaying corpse*: the connection between sex and death is established.

ll. 2f.   *viscous slime ... that dripped...*: the sexual innuendo is obvious.

l. 11   *obscure*: the malapropism is not so clear (neither in English nor in German), but she probably means "obscene."

Phallus impudicus

l. 13   *What Hans Castorp found amazing...*: Joachim would not normally want to talk about Chauchat, Marusya or Krokowski because those three figures represent a world that is antithetical to the values embodied in his devotion to military duty.

l. 19   *in an ill-tempered voice*: cf. p. 358, l. 8.

ll. 29f.   *who had kicked over the traces*: cf. p. 262, ll. 37f. where Behrens previously used the phrase to describe Castorp. It had first been said of Castorp by the narrator, cf. p. 34, l. 34 ("turn out to be a go-getter"), but the verbal parallel is lost in the translation.

l. 32   *an act of betrayal*: revealed at the end of the sub-chapter.

ll. 33f.   *on the evening of Mardi Gras*: i.e. with Chauchat.

ll. 34f.   *new treachery ... exacerbated*: the exaggerated language ironically undermines the seriousness of the matter.

(361) l. 6   *having educated himself to believe*: Hans Castorp has reached his conclusions about life by himself.

ll. 6ff.   *matter is the spirit's Original Sin...*: cf. p. 281, ll. 2ff.

l. 11   *impudency of matter*: the connection is established between Krokowski's lecture on the "impudicus" mushroom and the nature of life.

l. 11f.   *illness as life's lascivious form*: cf. p. 281, l. 1.

(362) ll. 1f.   *a diphthongized distortion of the vowel*: this is only possible in the case of the German word for "Enter" ("Herein") in which the second syllable is a diphthong.

l. 2   *saw his cousin vanish*: Hans Castorp's visits to Krokowski's office are viewed by Joachim as a "betrayal"—both because of his not being informed of these visits, and also because of what they imply: namely, that Hans Castorp has "joined the other camp."

Someone Else

The arrival of Naphta introduces an intellectual counterweight to Settembrini and provides further depth to the natural inclinations that Hans Castorp has been allowing to come to the surface at the Berghof. On the one hand, Naphta will provide him with much intellectual nourishment that reinforces his own philosophical leanings, but all the same Hans Castorp retains towards Naphta the same critical reserve that he has been showing all along vis-à-vis Settembrini. Thomas Mann himself commented that the exchanges between Naphtha and Settembrini serve the purpose of characterizing these two "extremists" who "propel everything to a point that is antithetical to life"—a conclusion that Castorp will also draw.

The verbal battles between Settembrini and Naphta address, among other things, the opposition between objective reality (Settembrini) and the subjectivity of all knowledge (Naphta). Settembrini is poor (cf. his clothing), but is a staunch advocate of the virtues of work and economic progress, as embodied in "Western" bourgeois culture. Naphta, on the other hand, is apparently well-off, but promotes idleness and contemplation—and this, together with his Eastern origins, associates him with the "Asiatic" principle in the novel.

Their endless disputes suggest that there is no one constellation of ideas that is valid in the modern world. Hans Castorp remains hovering between the two, recognizing that it is impossible to decide between the alternatives. The only valid stance is that of ironic detachment. In the end he progresses to his own more comprehensive view of humanity.

l. 6f.   *the vernal equinox* ...: the summer solstice: the equinox occurs when the sun, because the earth's axis is not tilted, is vertically above the equator: in the Spring around March 20. The summer solstice occurs when, because of the tilt in the earth's axis, the sun is at its extreme northern (or southern point), around June 20.

There is a symbolic element to the fact that Naphta appears on the scene at this date: the world is headed for darkness (cf. p. 365, l. 15: "it's all downhill from there"; and l. 18: "they are all headed back down into the dark").

l. 13f.   *the same ones*...: cf. p. 11, ll. 8ff.

l. 16   *the year was coming full circle*: the expression was first used by Virgil in his *Georgics*.

l. 18   *stars*: a plant that resembles a star.

l. 18   *chalices*: cup-like blossoms.

l. 18   *whimsies*: a kind of day-lily.

l. 19   *campion*: flowering plant, usually blooms in the Spring.

l. 23   *soldanella*: a small plant with rounded, leathery leaves and nodding blue, violet, or white flowers. Commonly known as alpenclock.

l. 23   *ciliated*: having minute hair-like organs that line the surfaces of certain cells and beat in rhythmic waves.

ll. 25f.   *for serious purposes*: all of Hans Castorp's efforts (since his conversation with Behrens) are aimed at understanding nature better.

l. 29   *a herbarium*: a container for storing preserved plant specimens; here presumably some kind of album.

(363) l. 7   *his ordinary blue eyes*: the adjective relates to Hans Castorp's being called "an ordinary young man" (cf. p. 4, l 1), but the meaning here is "simple."

l. 7   *corolla*: the inner envelope of floral leaves of a flower, usually of delicate texture and of some color other than green; the petals considered collectively.

l. 10   *anthers*: the pollen-bearing part of the stamen.

l. 11   *pistil*: The pistil is the term for the central female reproductive organ around which the other flower parts are arranged.

l. 15   *sepals*: the outermost group of floral parts.

l. 19   *his Linnaeus*: Karl von Linné (Swedish botanist; 1707–78) wrote an authoritative and compendious book that classified and named plants—and his system is still widely used today. Linnaeus is the Latin version of his name. Cf. Hans Castorp's comment on p. 358, ll. 4f.: "I really think that I shall add some botanical tomes to my collection."

l. 20   *comparative morphology*: comparing form and structure (as opposed to function) of living things.

l. 23   *humanistic science*: it is consonant with Hans Castorp's newly-gained understanding of life that his study of botany is also integrated into his overall view: namely, that all living phenomena are connected and that to study such phenomena is profoundly "humanistic."

ll. 28ff.   *We automatically used...*: cf. p. 362, l. 6f.

ll. 34ff.   *The sun will very soon enter Cancer...*: in astrology the Sun enters Cancer at the summer solstice. Around 22 July the Sun enters Leo; and around 23 August the Sun enters Virgo.

(364) ll. 1ff.   *the ancient heavenly signs...*: the twelve signs of the zodiac.

ll. 6ff.   *the ceiling of an Egyptian temple...*: the temple of Hathor in Dendera (north of Thebes), on whose roof the first depiction of the zodiac in Egypt was found. Hathor was the Egyptian goddess of love—and Hans Castorp equates her with Aphrodite, the Greek goddess of love.

l. 7   *Thebes*: a city in Greece that played an important role in Greek myth, as the site of the stories of (among others) Oedipus and Dionysus.

l. 7   *the Chaldeans*: inhabitants of Mesopotamia (the area between the Tigris and the Euphrates) whose last great ruler was Nebuchadnezzar. There is no indication how Hans Castorp has acquired this knowledge. These remarks by Hans Castorp about the Chaldeans ("that ancient tribe of Semitic or Arabic magicians, highly trained astrologers and diviners"; ll. 8f.) prepare us for the meeting with Naphta. Castorp refers again to the Chaldeans as "Semites, and so practically Jews" (p. 365, ll. 38f.) at the precise moment that he and Joachim notice Settembrini and Naphta in front of them.

l. 11   *dodecatemoria*: the division of the sun's apparent orbital circle into twelve equal parts, each part corresponding to a sign of the zodiac.

l. 14   *not quite like him either*: Hans Castorp has developed a view of "humanity" that is much broader and more all-encompassing than that of Settembrini.

ll. 18f.   *Uranus was only recently discovered*: in 1781 by William Herschel (1738–1822).

l. 20   *Recently?*: Hans Castorp's understanding of the word changes during the course of the novel. He had objected to Joachim's use of the word soon after his arrival (cf. p. 51, l. 21) in relation to eight weeks previous, but here he himself employs it in respect of an event 120 years ago. He then proceeds to describe 3,000 years ago as "recent" (l. 23).

(365) ll. 11ff.   *Midsummer Night!...*: Hans Castorp is referring to traditional celebrations that accompany the summer solstice, or that take place on the 24th of June and the preceding evening.

l. 18   *headed back down into the dark*: immediately after Castorp makes this comment, Naphta appears.

l. 34   *You're talking like a civilian*: Joachim's description of Hans Castorp (first used by Behrens, cf. p. 44, l. 36) is accepted by him and he repeats it to Naphta on p. 371, ll. 38ff.

ll. 34f.   *Without war...*: Hans Castorp only half agrees with this, because in his (broader, more profound) view, that is the nature of life anyway (cf. l. 36: "Yes, it has that tendency").

l. 35   *Moltke*: Helmut von Moltke (1848–1916) had asserted that war would bring renewal to the German nation—an assertion widely reported in the press 1914/15.

l. 36   *it has that tendency*: Hans Castorp's meaning is quite different from Joachim's. The latter implies that society stagnates without war, whereas Castorp takes the broader and more profound view (as a result of his researches) that the whole of life is involved in a process of decay and dissolution.

ll. 37ff. *intending to return to the Chaldeans...*: Castorp's speculation that the Chaldeans were "practically Jews" (l. 38f.) prepares him mentally for the appearance of Naphta.

l. 38   *Semites*: since the end of the eighteenth century the term was used to denote people who are descended from Sem, the oldest son of Noah, and who speak a Semitic language.

(366) ll. 1f.   *Hotel Belvedere*: prominent Davos hotel, built in 1875.

l. 11   *on the right flank*: in general, the right-hand side in the novel symbolizes the "right" (i.e. good) position.

l. 12   *Sapristi!*: a mild expletive, cf. "Good heavens!"

l. 27   *Naphta*: cf. Genesis 49:21: "Naphtali is a hind let loose: he giveth goodly words." Naphtha is also the Russian for petroleum, and in Galicia (where Naphta was born) the oil-fields were known as "Naphtha-springs." In both German and English the word "naphtha" signifies volatile and flammable hydrocarbons that are used as solvents. Naphta lives up to the associations that his name evokes.

l. 28   *caustically*: obviously a key word in relation to Naphta, as it occurs four times in the space of ten lines.

l. 39   *petersham*: see note to p. 54, l. 24.

l. 42   *at first glance...*: repeats the motifs of p. 54, ll. 22ff. Settembrini's ideas, like his clothing, are old and threadbare, but may still be taken "at first glance" to be new.

(367) ll. 7f.   *tanned or sunburnt...*: the two intellectuals are pale—a reflection of their preoccupations and an ironic comment on their distance from real life.

ll. 19f.   *He had a cold...*: Naphta's views, too, are ironically undermined by his fragile health. The fact that his cold is ignored by the others is consonant with the general attitude of Berghof patients that colds are not "reçus" (i.e. recognized; cf. note to p. 162, l. 24).

l. 24   *princeps scholasticorum*: a prince of teachers. "Scholasticism" was a philosophy of the Late Middle Ages that was based on Aristotelian dialectics and closely tied to religion. It could also be used pejoratively to mean pedantic scholarship and empty knowledge.

l. 25   *Aretino*: Pietro Aretino (1492–1556), Italian poet, (in)famous for his lewd verse

ll. 25f.   *held brilliant court...*: quote from Aretino.

(368) l. 1   *our Voltairean*: i.e. man of reason. See note to p. 246, l. 36.

l. 4   *Humor*: the Latin word gave rise to the medieval belief that a person's health was governed by four "humors": blood, phlegm, yellow bile, and black bile.

l. 6   *Saint Catherine of Siena*: 1347–1380, Dominican nun, author of Dialogues.

l. 14   *monism*: belief that everything has one essence, that there is only one kind of ultimate substance.

ll. 14ff. Note that in the debates between Naphta and Settembrini the dialogue often occurs (as in the thirteen exchanges in these next lines) without actually identifying the speaker—thus tending to cause confusion even in the reader's mind. This is also the case on p. 371, p. 374, & p. 377.

l. 23   *dualism*: the view that the world is based on two principles, such as God and the world, body and soul, good and evil.

ll. 25f.   *Solet Aristoteles quaerere pugnam*: Aristotle seeks to start an argument (in his books).

ll. 27f.   *Aristotle shifted the reality...*: according to Plato, ideas exist independent of individuals. Aristotle, on the other hand, affirmed that ideas existed inside individuals.

l. 28   *pantheism*: the belief that the whole of nature embodies God.

l. 31   *Thomas*: Saint Thomas Aquinas (1225–1274), Italian philosopher and theologian; author of *Summa Theologiae* (one of the most important works of Catholic theology) and founder of Thomism, which integrated Christian theology and Aristotelian philosophy.

l. 31   *Bonaventura*: Saint Bonaventura (1221–1274). The most important Franciscan theologian.

(369) ll. 8f.   *a larger definition of freedom*: Hans Castorp has quickly perceived that Naphta's world-view is broader than that of Settembrini. The latter is an advocate of reason, enlightenment, and progress—and the exclusion or suppression of all things that endanger and inhibit such positive elements; whereas Naphta's world-view encompasses all the negative phenomena as well.

l. 19   *Fridericianum*: cf. note to p. 302, l. 35.

l. 23   *with Lukaček*: his lodging with the Bohemian tailor ironically undermines his world-view.

l. 37   *the same impatience*: wishful thinking on Settembrini's part.

l. 41   *inimicus humanae naturae*: an enemy of human nature.

(370) l. 2   *Bernard of Clairvaux*: Bernhard von Clairvaux (1091–1153) was the most influential churchman of his age who elucidated the relationship between the church and God as a mirror of that between bride and bridegroom.

ll. 13f. *I've seen you wink at the girls*: apparently a frequent habit of Settembrini (cf. p. 60, ll. 7ff.).

l. 18 *Andate, andate!*: Stop, stop!

ll. 20f. *The East despises action*: an idea he had espoused to Hans Castorp earlier, cf. p. 154, ll. 24f.

l. 21 *Lao-tzu*: Chinese philosopher (sixth century BC), father of Taoism. The ideas expressed on ll. 20ff. are derived from an essay by Maxim Gorky (1868–1936).

l. 25 *quietism*: cf. note to p. 111, ll. 19f.

l. 26 *Fénelon*: François de Salignac de la Mothe-Fénelon (1651–1715), archbishop, and leading advocate of quietism: that is, a complete indifference to worldly things, embracing poverty, the dissolution of the personality and a total submersion in the contemplation of God.

l. 28 *Molinos*: Miguel de Molinos (c. 1628–1697), the chief apostle of quietism (see note to p. 111, ll. 19f.). For Molinos the way to God was through the "soft and savory sleep of nothingness"; where the soul is content to do nothing but wait in dreamy musing till the message comes.

ll. 33ff. *Contemplation, retreat…*: Hans Castorp's thoughts reveal how he now views his stay at the Berghof: it is a place of retreat (cf. "hermetic pedagogy"; p. 565, l. 24), where in ideal contemplation he can reflect about life.

ll. 40f. *all my years down in the flatlands*: Hans Castorp's actual words are, in fact, more telling: he speaks of "the mill" (i.e. "the tread-mill") down on the flatlands.

(371) l. 13 *Ebbé*: Well then.

ll. 25f. *you are once again dividing the world in two*: cf. p. 368, l. 16, where Settembrini had first uttered this accusation. Hans Castorp repeats the phrase (in an ironic manner) at the end of the chapter, p. 380, l. 12.

l. 28 *homo Dei*: literally: man of (= made by) God. In *Genesis* (1.26) Man had been created "in the image of God." This became a fundamental belief in the Middle Ages. Mann's explanation for his use of the term in the novel was as follows: "The hero of [the] novel was only seemingly the nice young man, Hans Castorp, … in reality it [the hero] was the *homo dei*, Man himself with his religious question about himself, about his whence and whither, his essence and his goal, his place in the universe, the secret of his existence, the eternal enigmatic task of humanistic thinking."

ll. 30f. *the English invented economic social theory*: a little lesson that Hans Castorp remembers and inserts into his private conversation with Naphta later, cf. p. 386, ll. 31ff.

l. 39 *my cousin often reproaches me…*: cf. p. 365, l. 34.

ll. 41f.   *as I've mentioned on several occasions*: see p. 108, l. 3 & p. 182, ll. 37f.

(372) l. 8   *bienséance*: correct, proper behavior (cf. p. 289, l. 40).

l. 9   *Spanish sense of honor*: the implication is of a strict code of honor, a commitment to duty, and an emphasis on social status.

l. 11   *starched ruff*: alludes back to the portrait of Hans Castorp's grandfather; see p. 24, l. 30 ff.

l. 18   *church and king*: the phrase had been used by Prussian conservatives since 1817 as a positive view of the ideal state—and attacked by liberals.

l. 29   *it is a life of pure form…*: picked up by Castorp and repeated back to Joachim later, cf. p. 380, ll. 1f.

ll. 31f.   *Spanish Counter-Reformation*: movement within the Catholic Church in the sixteenth and seventeenth centuries in an attempt to respond to Protestantism.

l. 32   *Napoleon*: Napoleon Bonaparte (1769–1821), French Emperor (1804–1814).

l. 32   *Garibaldi*: Giuseppe Garibaldi (1807–1882), instrumental in the unification of Italy 1860.

(373) ll. 8f.   *this gentleman and I argue frequently*: the verb used is "zanken," (quarrel, squabble) a leitmotif that not only occurs when Settembrini and Naphta argue, but also indicates other conflicts, note to p. 273, l. 31.

l. 24   *As on a previous occasion*: see p. 246, ll. 24 ff.

l. 29   *the Young Turks*: reform movement in the Ottoman Empire that attempted to liberalize society and expand the Empire. It originated 1889 among military students and then expanded to other groups, leading to the revolution of Kemal Atatürk and the Turkish War of Independence and culminating in the founding of the Turkish Republic in 1923.

l. 34   *Abdul Hamid*: the Turkish Sultan Abdul Hamid II (1842–1918; Sultan 1876–1909), the last absolutist Ottoman emperor; he sought a close alliance with Germany. Since Naphta says "If Abdul Hamid falls…," the time of this conversation is clearly early 1909, when the Sultan was under considerable pressure. In the summer of 1908 the Young Turks in Salonika revolted and marched on Istanbul. Abdul Hamid capitulated and agreed to several democratic reforms. An attempt to stage a counter-revolution in April 1909, however, was suppressed and the Sultan, suspected of supporting it, was deposed.

ll. 39f.   *English Balkan Committee*: a private committee, consisting of leading figures of English society, business, and politics. The British Foreign Office attempted to influence it to favor British investments in the

Balkans. The reference to "good ties" (l. 39) refers to the fact that the Chairman of the Committee was Noel Burton, a Freemason.

l. 40   *Reval program*: in 1907 King Edward VII of England visited Reval (Russia), as a public demonstration of England's friendship with Russia.

(374) l. 1   the *Dardenelles*: a treaty of 1842 decreed that only Turkish ships may pass through the narrow strait that connects the Mediterranean Sea with the Black Sea. In this manner, the Russian fleet's freedom of movement was curtailed.

ll. 1f.   *if Austria manages...*: in 1908 Austria-Hungary had formally annexed Bosnia and Herzegovina (which had been under Austrian administration since 1878). The resentment caused by this annexation led to the assassination of Archduke Franz Ferdinand of Austria (the heir to the throne), and this was the proximate cause of the First World War.

ll. 4f.   *Nicholas loves peace*: Tsar Nicholas II of Russia (1894–1917).

l. 5   *the Hague Conventions*: in August 1898 Nicholas II had invited the European powers to attend a Peace Conference at The Hague in an attempt to persuade them to agree to arms limitations. The delegates met from 18 May 1899 to 27 July 1899, but were able to agree only on the establishment of a tribunal to handle disputes. At a second Conference in 1907 this tribunal was transformed into the International Court of Justice.

ll. 7f.   *that little mishap in the Far East*: in 1904/05 Russia unsuccessfully went to war against Japan in an attempt to gain Manchuria and Korea.

l. 14   *Pan-Germanism*: the belief that all German-speaking people should be united in one country.

ll. 24f.   *Take British policy, England's need to secure buffer states around India...*: to protect both the fragile occupation of India (from Russia) and the valuable trade.

l. 26   *the potentates in Saint Petersburg*: the capital of the Russian Empire until 1917. This is another reference to the ill-fated invasion of Manchuria in 1905.

ll. 29f.   *reawakening sleeping rivalries...*: reflecting historical political tensions between Russia (of which St. Petersburg was the capital at this time) and the Austro-Hungarian Empire (of which Vienna was the capital).

l. 33   *Holy Roman Empire*: The Holy Roman Empire existed from 800 A.D. until 1806 A.D. Its full title was the Holy Roman Empire of the German Nation. Its creators took the view that it was a) replacing the Roman Empire, b) it was Christian (hence Holy), and c) it was German. The first Emperor was Charlemagne, crowned by the Pope on Christmas Day 800 A.D. For most of its history the Emperor came from the Hapsburg family, until in 1806 Napoleon conquered Prussia and Austria and abolished the Empire. After the fall of Napoleon, the Hapsburgs assumed the seat of the Emperor in the Austro-Hungarian Empire until 1918.

l. 35   *caesaropapism*: unification of secular and spiritual powers in one ruler.

l. 36   *Kremlin*: the palace in Moscow that was the home of the Russian emperor.

l. 37   *Hofburg*: the palace in Vienna that was the seat of the Austrian Emperor.

l. 37   *Luther*: Martin Luther (1483–1546), defiant German reformer who attacked the abuses of the Catholic Church.

l. 38   *Gutenberg*: Johannes Gutenberg (c. 1395–1468), credited with inventing moving-type printing (about 1439).

(375) l. 10   *The Brenner Pass*: One of the major routes over the Alps. Italy had been demanding since the middle of the nineteenth century that the Brenner Pass, which constituted a natural, geographical boundary, form the border between Italy and Austria; but since the area south of the Brenner Pass (South Tyrol) was traditionally German-speaking, the Brenner Pass as the border was not acceptable to Austria. (It became the border after the First World War.) Settembrini's pacifism has its limits: he despises Austria ("the principle of obduracy"; cf. p. 154, l. 32 & p. 700, l. 27) and wants South Tyrol for Italy. His pacifism is thus mere rhetoric, and the narrator enjoys revealing the ambivalence of Settembrini's position (as Thomas Mann himself commented). The underlying message here is that nationalism goes deeper than pacifism. It is in the nature of human beings and nations to be in conflict with each other. Life is a battle with teeth and nails. Civilization is merely a thin veneer; war reveals the true nature of humanity. This is an essentially Schopenhauerian view of life—and it is also reflected in Naphta's views.

l. 10   *The liquidation of Austria*: Settembrini's humanistic pronouncements are undermined by his belligerence towards Austria.

l. 18   *My cousin and I*: In the conversations with Settembrini, it is, of course, Hans Castorp whom Settembrini is chiefly addressing—and Castorp makes almost all of the responses.

ll. 21f.   *Herr Settembrini has more than once...*: cf. p. 154, ll. 9ff. where Settembrini laid out these views to Hans Castorp and Joachim. Despite the fact that Castorp says: "I can quote him verbatim" (ll. 28f.), note here his critical recounting of Settembrini's views: e.g. "... hardly a principle of peace, I don't suppose" (l. 23) and "...as a seasoned civilian I was somewhat appalled by it" (ll. 29f.) Naphta is quick to pick up on this: "Now you have been convicted by you own pupil of harboring warlike tendencies" (ll. 38f.). (N.B. the slight mistranslation in l. 23: "I don't suppose" should read "I suppose."

ll. 30f. *feet of doves*: the phrase probably derived from Nietzsche: "Thoughts that come on the feet of doves, control the world" (*Thus Spoke Zarathustra* III, 192).

l. 31   *pinions of eagles*...: Hans Castorp is quoting Settembrini's own words back at him, cf. p. 154, ll. 35f.

ll. 39f.   *Assument pennas et aquilae*...: biblical quotation, from Isaiah 40. 31.: "But they that wait upon the Lord shall renew their strength; they shall mount up with wings as eagles; they shall run, and not be weary; and they shall walk, and not faint." (The German version of the Bible uses the word "wandeln" for "walk" [see note to p. 200, l. 29]).

l. 41   *Voltaire*: (see note to p. 246, l. 36) had urged Frederick the Great to form an alliance with Emperor Joseph II of Austria and Empress Catherine the Great of Russia to wage war against the Ottoman Empire in order to liberate the Greeks. Frederick refused.

(376) l. 7 *All motion, however, is circular*: repeating his thoughts from p. 365, ll. 4ff.

l. 9   *My cousin and I were speaking*: of course, it was Hans Castorp who, as usual, was doing all the talking: cf. p. 365, ll. 2ff.

l. 17   *infusoria*: collective term for tiny aquatic animals with a primit- ive structure. This is essentially the process that Hans Castorp had gleaned from his studies in the sub-chapter "Research"—although his thoughts were more focused on Chauchat and what she represented than on Settem- brini's idea of progress.

ll. 25f. *the Rousseauian idyll*: Settembrini's summary of the eight- eenth century's belief in the original goodness of man, which has been "perverted and ruined" (l. 23) by "social errors" (ll. 22f.) is derived from Rousseau's "Discourse on the Sciences and the Arts" (1751), in which the author argued that progress in art, science, and technology tend to make human beings less virtuous and less happy.

ll. 38f. *the Crusades*: a series of religion-driven military campaigns waged by much of Christian Europe against external and internal oppo- nents, stretching from 1095 to 1272.

(377) l. 15   *a positive interpretation of law*: what is meant here is law that is made by the state, in contrast to natural law.

l. 20   *ius divinum*: divine law. According to Catholic doctrine, divine law results from the Holy Scriptures and tradition, and it is unchangeable.

(378) ll. 17 *Master of the Lodge*: implies that Settembrini is a Freemason (although the use of the appellation "Master" here is anachron- istic, since it was not used for members of a lodge until after 1925).

l. 34   *Princeps Scholasticorum*: cf. note to p. 367, l. 24.

l. 34   *scholastics*: "schoolmen"—in other words, those academics who espoused a strict system of learning that emphasized dialectical reasoning. Cf. also note to p. 367, l. 24.

ll. 38f.   *Adriatica von Mylendonk*: cf. p. 59, ll. 13ff.

(379) l. 4   *And that nose is Jewish*...: Joachim's anti-Semitic slur is indicative of the mood of the age: even people whom we would regard as decent and upright citizens (such as Joachim) were tainted by the social milieu in which they grew up. The novel itself contains other examples of the narrator's subconscious prejudices: "A Jewish woman from Romania with the very plain name of Frau Landauer" (p. 538, ll. 29f.); "Fräulein Levi with the ivory complexion" (p. 67, l. 4); "plump, freckled Frau Iltis" (p. 67, 5); "fat Frau Salomon from Amsterdam" (p. 73, l. 22); and "frizzy-haired Tamara" (p. 321, l. 35). Yet another subtle prejudice is revealed by the reference to a "Moor with woolly hair"—especially since in German the text states that the woolly-headed Moor was *"nevertheless* very elegant" (cf. p. 437, l. 24; emphasis added).

l. 5   *Semites*: cf. note to p. 365, l. 38.

l. 7   *But of course we'll visit him*: Castorp is once again speaking for both of them.

l. 8   *the Chaldeans*: see note to p. 364, l. 7.

ll. 16f.   *And you started in on 'time' on your first day here*: cf. p. 63, ll. 37ff.

l. 20   *Freedom dwells within the mountains*: first line of a Bavarian song, written to commemorate the death of King Ludwig II (1845–86). It also points forward to Hans Castorp's preoccupation with the opera *Carmen*, where the hero, Don José, deserts his post and follows Carmen to the mountains (see p. 637 ff.).

l. 24   *the Carbonaro*: see note to p. 150, l. 4.

ll. 29f.   *namby-pamby concepts*: Castorp is quoting himself, cf. note to p. 262, l. 36.

ll. 30f.   *to lose himself and let himself be ruined*: Castorp speaks these words in French, as Joachim remarks one line later. He is quoting, of course, Chauchat's words on Mardi Gras (see p. 334, ll. 37f.), and he will quote them again in German to Chauchat on p. 548, ll. 33f.

(380) ll. 1f. *someone whose life is pure form*: these were Settembrini's words, see p. 372, ll. 27ff.

l. 5   *Brenner Pass*: see note to p. 375, l. 10.

l. 12   *dividing the world in two*...: repeating the charge that Settembrini leveled against Naphta; cf. p. 368, ll. 15f.

The City of God and Evil Deliverance

ll. 15f.   *the astronomical summer*: i.e. after June 22.

l. 17   *Aquilegia … Ranunculaceae*: it grows in abundance in the place where Hans Castorp had the nose-bleed and recalled the schoolyard episode with Hippe (see pp. 117 ff.). Here he reflects on all the "many and varied impressions and adventures" (p. 381, ll. 2f.) during the past "adventurous year" (l. 13). Botanically speaking, the blue aquilegia does not occur around Davos, but it is necessary within the context of the novel to connote the associations relating to Hans Castorp and his story.

Since this is the place where Hans first had his Hippe-vision, it connotes the entire realm of the erotic, the bisexual, and the attraction to freedom, sickness and death—which were later embodied in the figure of Chauchat and which he came to realize form a significant part of his own innate being. The intellectual arguments of Settembrini have been absorbed and critically evaluated—and their virtues have been recognized—but those virtues are fighting a perpetual (and losing) battle against "life" in all its variety and chaos (Apollo will always be defeated by Dionysus). The fact that he no longer suffers nose-bleeds in his favorite place is taken to be a sign that he is finally acclimatized—not merely in the physical sense of having got used to the altitude, but also in the philosophical and spiritual sense that he has accepted his "fate" as a figure in whom the struggle between life and death will be fought. His enjoyment of his Maria Mancini cigar shows that he has achieved equilibrium—but the vistas that have been opened up to him in the past year have changed him forever. However, he is by no means free of discomforts, but he has come to terms with their physical manifestations.

ll. 22f.   *his premature, freewheeling walk*: cf. p. 117, ll. 11ff.

l. 29   *omitting detours, arias…*: cf. his first walk, p. 115, ll. 33ff.

(381) ll. 10f.   *here in the same spot…*:cf. p. 117, ll. 4f. & ll. 28ff.

(382) ll. 16f.   *Some people never get used to it…*: cf. p. 12, ll. 11f.

l. 21   *blue-blossoming meadow*: see note above to p. 117, l. 4 re the significance of the "blue flower."

l. 23   *a habit for his grandson*: Hans Castorp has thus close connections with his grandfather—not simply through his line of descent, but more important, by way of his natural predilection: the drooping head that can he held up only by artificial means. Castorp's other reflections about "similar, secret private associations" (ll. 26f.) lead him to the contemplation of the relationship between life and death.

l. 40   *scapulae and humeri*: shoulder-blades and arm-bones. The humor of the scene consists in Hans Castorp's lying on an alpine meadow (in his favorite place) and holding the x-ray of Clavdia Chauchat's tubercular chest up to the sky so that he can gaze at it—and when he does this, "his skittish heart" stops and does a somersault (p. 383, ll. 1f.).

ll. 41ff.   *the flesh ... of which, against all reason...*: see note to p. 342. ll. 9f.

(383) l. 6   *That sublime image of organic life*: cf. p. 272, ll. 15 ff. and p. 281, ll. 16 ff. The phrase "sublime image" (in German: "Hochgebild") is a key term in understanding Hans Castorp's developing concept of humanity (and it occurs four times in the brief span of a page and a half). For Settembrini, as Castorp recognizes, the "sublime image" is that of the *homo humanus* (see note to p. 57, l. 39) who conceives "politics, rebellion, and eloquence" (p. 383, l. 210) as the be-all and end-all of existence. But Castorp's concept of the "sublime image of *organic* life (emphasis added) includes as well the worlds of Chauchat and Naphta, plus what he has learned from his own scientific studies. His concept derives from the term "homo Dei" first used by Naphta (cf. p. 371, ll. 28), but he has expanded its meaning to give it a wider significance.

l. 7   *that frosty starlit night*: cf. p. 272, l. 16.

ll. 20ff.   *Greece...*: the original uses the word "Hellas" which implies Ancient Greece. Thus the "sublime image" that Settembrini imagines is quite different from Castorp's: the Italian's image derives from the central ideals of ancient classical culture and includes "politics, rebellion, and eloquence," whereas Hans Castorp has developed a much broader view that recognizes and encompasses all of life's phenomena.

ll. 24ff.   *the two sides of analysis...*: from being initially skeptical about psychoanalysis, Hans Castorp has come to understand it as "beneficial to action and progress" (l. 25), but also, since it delves into irrational, subconscious areas of the human psyche, as leading to those "darker" areas of life that are associated with sex, dissolution, and death.

ll. 26ff.   *images of the two grandfathers*: cf. p. 151, ll. 33ff.

ll. 34f.   *"playing king"*: this phrase is the translator's rendering of the German verb "regieren" (literally: rule, reign, or govern). Thomas Mann explained what he meant by the word when he wrote to his English translator, Helen Tracy Lowe-Porter: "... it is the playful and childish word that the young Hans Castorp uses privately for his politico-philosophical speculations, and in this case a quite precise and literal translation would be appropriate." She attempted to convey the meaning of the word with the phrase "taking stock." Perhaps the two translations and Thomas Mann's own explanation will help the reader understand the process that takes place in Hans Castorp's mind during these sessions of "playing king." From time to time (as on p. 383, ll. 6ff.) he reviews with a

critical eye all the experiences he has had, trying to decide which elements
are useful for his personal growth.

(384) l. 1 *Homo Dei*: see note to p. 371, l. 28.

ll. 36f.   *"How do," the tailor said...*: the greeting is a Swiss dialect
word, but pronounced with "heavy Bohemian accent" (l. 36)—both
indicators of Lukaček's being out of place.

l. 41 *Something elegant...*: Since Chauchat had told Castorp on
Mardi Gras that her dress had been made by Lukaček (cf. p. 329, l. 9), it is
a reasonable assumption that he is making a subjective connection here.

(385) l. 3 *Will it have sleeves?*: Hans Castorp relates the dress
directly to Chauchat (cf. his fascination with her arms in a gossamer
sleeve, p. 203, l. 18)—but his assumption is ironically undermined by
Lukaček's explanation: "it's for an ol' lady" (l. 4).

l. 31 *a naïve pietà*: a representation of the Virgin Mary cradling the
dead body of Christ; first seen around 1300 in Germany.

Pietà

(386) ll. 13f. *Presumably from the Rhineland*: the "Rhineland" is an
imprecise term referring to areas on both sides of the River Rhine.

ll. 27f.   *some notions of the Middle Ages...*: if Castorp has been
"working on them," then it can only be since he met Naphta. The latter's
words have obviously given Castorp a lot to think about.

ll. 31f.   *no economic and social theory*: Naphta himself had intim-
ated this in his debate with Settembrini the first time Hans and Joachim
had met him; see p. 371, ll. 30f.

ll. 36f.   *it is an anonymous, communal work of art*: Castorp is
clearly impressed by these ideas (cf. p. 387, ll. 6f.: "every word of
everything you have said interests me") and he quotes these epithets later
(p. 397, l. 11), much to the displeasure of Settembrini.

l. 38   *signum mortificationis*: warning sign of death.

ll. 39f.   *the Romanesque period*: 11th and 12th centuries, characterized chiefly by monumental church architecture.

(387) l. 3   *De miseria humanae conditionis…*: *On the Misery of the
Human Condition*. Innocent the Third (1161–1216) wrote this work early
in the thirteenth century. Despite its morbid content it was enormously
popular and survives in almost 700 manuscripts.

ll. 6f.   *every word of everything you've said interests me*: because
Naphta embodies the darker side of life to which Castorp is attracted.

ll. 18f.   *You can regard the pietà from the sofa*: in a repetition of the
scene in Behrens's sitting-room, when Castorp placed Chauchat's portrait
where he could see it better (see pp. 255–56), Naphta encourages him to
sit where he can see the pietà to good advantage—which is appropriate
since both pictures are concerned with aspects of existence that belong in
the same realm.

l. 23   *Accidenti!*: My goodness!

(388) l. 24   *Plotinus*: Hans Castorp here quotes Settembrini's words
back to him, and the latter is not amused (cf. note to p. 246, ll. 14f.)

l. 25   *Voltaire*: this also comes from Settembrini (cf. note to re p. 246,
ll. 36 ff.).

ll. 28f.   *one could…call an absurdity an intellectually honorable
position*: an idea that he had acquired from Settembrini (cf. p. 246, ll.
18ff.) who was citing Porphyrius. These three references by Castorp reveal
that he has remembered Settembrini's words—uttered long ago—and has
thought about them. His comments here concerning the relationship
between the rejection of nature's chaos by Plotinus and Voltaire and the
rebellion against nature implicit in Gothic art show his ability to process
the ideas he hears and to form his own opinions on the basis of them. In
this case he merges earlier Settembrini's comments with Naphta's recent
ones to develop his own synthesis—one that is, unfortunately, not what
Settembrini wants to hear, as it places Castorp in Naphta's camp. In so
doing he waggishly uses Settembrini's own words against him: "absurd"
and "honorable" were Settembrini's terms (see p. 246, ll. 18f.); here
Castorp employs them in categorizing the pietà.

l. 34   *like a porcelain plate*: cf. p. 367, l. 40f., where Naphta's voice is described as sounding like a piece of cracked porcelain.

l. 39   *making good use of gifts received*: Settembrini is fully aware that Castorp has cited him, and he rebukes him here with sarcasm.

(389) l. 9   *Konrad of Marburg*: first papal inquisitor in Germany (1180?–1233). Known for his ruthlessness and cruelty, he was assassinated in 1233.

l. 16   *Jacobins*: extremist republicans who during the French Revolution instituted the Reign of Terror (1793/94).

ll. 33f.   *Copernicus will be routed by Ptolemy*: Nicolas Copernicus (1473–1543) advocated the heliocentric system (the sun as the center of our planetary system) in opposition to the centuries-old view that the earth was the center of the universe (the geocentric system), which had been refined by Ptolemy (85?–165?), the Greek astronomer (thought to have been born in Alexandria, Egypt).

l. 39   *voluntarism*: the belief that the will is superior to the intellect and emotion.

(390) l. 12   *Saint Augustine*: (354–430), pre-eminent early Christian theologian and still a central figure in ecclesiastical thought.

l. 17   *quod erat demonstrandum*: what was to be proved. Widely used as the final statement in a mathematical or philosophical proof.

ll. 18f.   *The great scholastics…*: cf. note to p. 367, l. 24.

ll. 23f.   *The argumentation of the Holy Office…*: the Holy Office (Sanctum Officium) in Rome was the highest authority responsible for the protection of the Catholic faith.

l. 24   *Galileo*: Galileo Galilei (1564–1642) had advocated the heliocentric system. He was called before the Inquisition and recanted his belief.

l. 26   *Eh, eh!*: exclamation.

l. 27   *professore*: professor.

ll. 28f.   *Do you believe in truth…*: here Settembrini parodies the Catholic catechism: "Do you believe in God…"

(391) l. 3   *Lactantius*: Lucius Caelius Firmianus Lactantius (240?–320?), early Christian author, known as the "Christian Cicero" because of his classical style.

l. 4   *Constantine the Great*: (272–337); the first Christian Emperor. By an edict in 313 he legalized Christianity in the Roman Empire.

l. 7   *Platonic philosophy*: i.e. the view that the ultimate truths can be known by reason working from innate ideas.

l. 21   *pragmatism*: a philosophical stance that claims that an ideology or proposition is true if it works satisfactorily, and that the meaning of a proposition is to be found in the practical consequences of accepting it.

l. 35   *your Renaissance astronomers*: Tycho Brahe (1546–1601); Nicolas Copernicus (1473–1543); Galileo Galilei (1564–1642); Johannes Kepler (1571–1630), all of whom contributed to the proof that the sun was the center of our planetary stem.

(392) ll. 6f. *Prussianism or Gothic reaction*: "Prussianism" here is meant in the sense derived from Oswald Spengler (see "Introduction," pp. 18f.): the willingness of the individual to submit to the collective will for the good of the state, which in its turn is governed by an elite hierarchy with dictatorial powers. "Gothic reaction" means a return to medieval circumstances.

l. 24   *much as he had when drawing his pig*: see p. 325, ll. 12ff.. Although the parallel is not quite precise, more important is the implication: Castorp is as fascinated by the world of Naphta as he was by the symbolism of the pig.

(393) l. 39   *Benissimo!*: really, really good.

l. 39   *Social contract...*: reference to the *Social Contract* (1762) by Jean-Jacques Rousseau (1712–78), in which the author argued that individuals should voluntarily subject themselves to the general will, and that correspondingly, government receives its legitimacy from free citizens, not by virtue of the accident of birth.

(394) ll. 16f.   *Above all else...*: quote from Virgil's *Aeneid*, 6, 283.

l. 39   *Gregory the Great*: he means Gregory VII (1020–85) who asserted papal supremacy and exerted considerable political influence during a period of turmoil in Italy.

l. 39   *City of God*: book by St. Augustine in the early fifth century; in it Augustine advocated a preoccupation with the mystical, heavenly City of Jerusalem, rather than with earthly matters.

(395) l. 6   *Cursed be the man...*: this is actually a quote from *Jeremiah*, 48,10.

l. 13   *your Manchester eyes...*: Naphta is referring to the extreme laissez-faire economic policy of the British Industrial Revolution. Manchester, center of the cotton-weaving industry, stood as a symbol of unrestrained industrialization and trade.

ll. 29f.   *another form of exploitation...*: in the medieval view, Time was a divine gift. Thus making a profit out of Time, was exploiting one of God's gifts for material ends—and that amounted to blasphemy, a crime against God.

l. 34   *Benissimo!*: Wonderful! Hans Castorp uses Settembrini's word (cf. p. 393, l. 39) to praise Naphta's argument.

l. 41   *Thomas Aquinas*: see note to p. 368, l. 31.

(396) l. 16   *City of God*: cf. note to p. 394, l. 39.

l. 22   *Gregory the Great*: see note to p. 394, l. 39.

l. 31   *Roma locuta*: Rome has spoken. The complete quote reads: "Rome has spoken—the matter is settled"—which is what Settembrini is implying by his use of the curtailed quotation. The phrase derives from the authoritative pronouncements of the Pope.

(397) l. 11   *both anonymous and communal*: Castorp repeats Naphta's words from earlier, see p. 386, ll. 36f. Settembrini is not amused.

ll. 13f.   *You may learn, but please do not perform*: Settembrini still views Hans Castorp as a student, not an independent thinker. He repeats this admonition on p. 445, l. 34 & p. 505, ll. 35f.

(398) l. 11   *Addio, padre*: Farewell, father. In calling Naphta "father," Settembrini is playing on Naphta's connections with the Jesuits (cf. note to p. 401, l. 26), although the latter is not officially a Jesuit priest. (Cf. Settembrini's exaggerated titles for Hans Castorp and Joachim.)

ll. 18f.   *De miseria humanae conditionis*: see note to p. 387, l. 3.

(399) l. 6   *private and cozy*: Castorp uses Settembrini's own words (cf. p. 398, l. 28).

l. 12   *Carbonaro*: see note to p. 150, l. 4.

(400) l. 20   *to the point of drawing blood*: Settembrini means it merely metaphorically here, but it is an ironic prediction of things to come.

l. 31   *that old motto of Petrarch's*: i.e. "placet experiri"; cf. note to p. 96, l. 14. This was not, in fact, an "old motto" of Petrarch, but rather a remark he made about his experiments with vines that was transformed by a late-19th century German scholar into the myth that it was his motto.

(401) l. 26   *the Jesuits*: members of the Society of Jesus, founded by Saint Ignatius of Loyola (1491–1556) in 1534. In earlier times they were known as the "Soldiers of Christ," because of their militancy.

l. 29   *so the man's a Jesuit*: historically inaccurate, as Jews were prohibited from entering the Jesuit order from 1594 to 1946.

l. 32   *padre*: See note to p. 401, l. 26.

ll. 36ff.   *He then spent a few years....*: in fact, a Jesuit who had completed the novitiate (l. 35) would not have been permitted to teach.

l. 40   *Fridericianum*: cf. note to p. 302, l. 35.

(402) l. 4   *takes care of its own*: a widespread belief, but also a reflection of prejudiced ignorance.

l. 10 *private, and especially cozy*: Castorp again (cf. p. 399, l. 6) uses Settembrini's own description of his lodgings (see p. 398, l. 28), albeit modifying the description slightly.

l. 27 *broadens one's horizons*: it must be clear to Hans Castorp that Settembrini would not approve of his making "many a visit" (l. 26) to Naphta, to further his "education," but Castorp can be very determined.

l. 38 *your grandfather...*: cf. p. 153, ll. 37f.

(403) l. 19 *he has a moist spot*: Castorp takes the image that Chauchat applied to him (cf. p. 336, ll. 37f.) and applies it to Naphta. The implication is that Naphta, too, has a constitutional weakness that determines his view of life. We are to learn later that Naphta, indeed, has "incipient lung disease" (p. 434, l. 9; cf. also p. 437, ll. 6f.).

ll. 22f. *one of life's problem children...*: those who gravitate towards the Romantic view of life—all of them have "a little moist spot."

l. 23 *a handsome Jesuit with a little moist spot*: Chauchat had called Hans Castorp: "My handsome bourgeois with the little moist spot" (p. 336, l. 37f.). Castorp applies her description of him to Naphta (using French)—thus establishing a parallel between the two of them. He quotes the same phrase back to himself when thinking about Naphta during a later conversation (cf. p. 457, l. 10). The fact that Hans Castorp takes two phrases that have been used to describe him and applies them to Naphta reveals how attracted he is to the latter's views and to the medieval fascination with death. (Hans Castorp uses the alliterative phrase: "joli jesuite..." Thus the translation "handsome" is somewhat ironic—especially when applied to the ugly Naphta.)

l. 33 *the Society*: the Society of Jesus. See note to p. 401, l. 26.

ll. 39f. *I visited you in your room one day*: see p. 189, ll. 36 ff.

(404) ll. 11ff. *imprint this on your minds...*: Settembrini's speech that follows is his most earnest warning about the dangers of the fascination with death. For him, such a fascination leads to a divorce from reason and progress, and a descent into a realm where self-control and discipline are abandoned and lust (in all its forms) rules supreme. In his dualistic world-view, death is simply the principle opposed to life. It will be Hans Castorp's challenge to move beyond this simple dichotomy and to reach a more all-encompassing view of life.

l. 14 *actu*: action, deed (Latin).

l. 24 *just as I told you that day*: cf. p. 197, ll. 16ff.

l. 28 *mephitic*: polluted air that cannot be breathed.

ll. 37f. *homo Dei*: man made by God (see note to p. 371, l. 28.). Now, however, this image—originally expounded by Naphta—has taken on a different form following Hans Castorp's reflections in his "blue-blossoming meadow" (l. 39) where he surveys all the influences to which he has been subjected. His reflections result in his giving it his own meaning.

An Outburst of Temper/Something Very Embarrassing

(405) l. 26   *affectation*: she probably means "infection."

l. 28   *ring of Polycrates*: in Greek mythology the tyrant Polycrates threw a valuable ring into the sea, where it was swallowed by a fish. A fisherman caught the fish and presented it to Polycrates. When the latter came to eat the fish, he found the ring inside it. Frau Stöhr has got her classical allusions mixed up: she probably means her "Achilles heel" (i.e. weak point).

(406) l. 7   *humbug*: this unflattering characterization of Naphta would be better rendered by hair-splitter, pedant, or sophist ("Rabulist").

(407) l. 13   *teleology*: belief that there is a design in nature and a final cause.

ll. 22f.   *there is really no time...*: renders time mythical: the new is the same as the old.

l. 39   *It is quite possible that he will die*: Castorp quotes to himself (in French) Chauchat's words at Mardi Gras (see p. 334, l. 2).

(408) l. 8   *I'll never, ever find my way back...*: this thought is closely connected to "being lost to the world" (cf. p. 584, l. 27) and the desire to find one's way back to peace (cf. p. 642, l. 20).

l. 32   *Piraeus*: the harbor of Athens.

(409) ll. 2f.   *auscultation*: see note to p. 130, l. 31.

l. 6   *vesicular*: see note to p. 175, ll. 14f.

l. 8   *phthisis*: see note to p. 61, l. 8.

ll. 8f.   *concupiscence*: strong sexual desire, lust.

l. 10   *you're running a cathouse*: an admission that Behrens denies a few minutes later (cf. p. 411, l. 20f.).

l. 12   *rhonchial*: describing the wheezing sound heard when the doctor listens the chest (using a stethoscope), caused by an accumulation of mucus or other material.

ll. 12f.   *The more the rhonchial pack...*: Behrens's comment here reflects a commonly held belief at the time.

l. 30   *Gaffky*: cf. note to p. 340, l. 14.

ll. 39f.   *as blotchy as the first time*: cf. p. 70, l. 35f., where Joachim reacts to Hans Castorp's comment about Marusya's ample bosom.

(410) l. 2   *You can take Constantinople...*: the city had been the scene of many battles between Christian forces and Ottoman Turks. The latter captured it in 1453.

ll. 2f. *you'll be robust enough...*: the translation here bears little resemblance to the original. Behrens says, in fact: "You'll be strong enough to take over the supreme command in the Marches." The original contains an untranslatable pun, but the reference to the "Marches" (the term used for the buffer provinces to the east of Germany) connotes the border territories between Germany and Slavic-Wendish lands—and thus connects to Hippe and Chauchat.

ll. 8f. *I wish to report...*: Joachim speaks to Behrens using military style, as if Behrens were his superior officer.

l. 13 *toss in the towel*: the German idiom (correctly translated here) speaks of throwing down your musket.

l. 14 *desertion of duty*: it belongs to the confusion of values at the Berghof that Behrens can describe Joachim's decision to return to the Flatland to perform his military duties as a "desertion of duty"—desertion, namely, of his medical obligations. Joachim's action will become a "wild departure" (p. 413, ll. 11f.).

l. 32 *No matter what the risk?*: the question is ambiguous—implying both the military risk and the risk to Joachim's health.

l. 34 *Yes, sir, Director Behrens, sir*: the translation attempts to show that Joachim maintains the military form of response.

(411) l. 5 *one year before*: cf. p. 177, l. 18.

l. 29 *Signor Amoroso*: Mr. Lover. In Italian comedy, "amoroso" was the traditional name for the young man in love, Here, however, Behrens means it in the sense of "pimp" (cf. his previous references to "running a cathouse" [p. 409, l. 10], and being taken for "the owner of a cathouse" [p. 411, l. 21]).

ll. 29f. *the Toledo...*: street in Naples, famous for its prostitutes.

l. 32 *Bon voyage!*: Have a good trip!

l. 41 *the Polypraxios-Nölting affair*: cf. p. 408, ll. 21ff.

(412) ll. 19f. *first heard Herr Albin's voice*: cf. p. 77, ll. 3ff.

ll. 29f. *via Landquart and Romanshorn*: see commentary, p. 3, l. 10.

l. 30 *the wide, unfathomable lake*: Lake Constance. However, at the beginning of the novel the lake was described as "once thought unfathomable" (cf. p. 3, l. 8).

l. 31 *whose frozen surface...*: a well-known ballad by Gustav Schwab (1792–1850) tells of a man on horseback in the middle of winter on the German side of Lake Constance, looking for the Lake, but darkness falls and he gets lost. When he comes to a village and asks the way to the Lake, he learns that he has ridden across the frozen lake in the darkness and is now in Switzerland. The shock kills him.

ll. 36f.   *all the things...*: that is, all those matters that are excluded from the bourgeois ethic.

(413) ll. 6f. *as Joachim had done...*: cf. p. 112, ll. 9ff.

ll. 15f. *But Herr Settembrini was only a representative...*: "of things and forces worth hearing about, but not without qualification"—note Hans Castorp's skeptical-critical attitude.

ll. 30ff.   *real desertion of duty*: if Hans Castorp were to exploit Joachim's decision to leave as an excuse for his own departure, this would constitute a far more serious "desertion" because he would be abandoning the process of his education and enlightenment before it was complete.

l. 32   *homo Dei*: see note to p. 371, l. 28. Castorp's "higher" duty is to pursue the development of his "sublime image" of the "man of God" wherever it leads him; and to leave the Berghof now would signify his own desertion of that higher duty.

(414) l. 4   *temp*: cf. note to p. 169, ll. 14f.

l. 11   *the quietists*: see note to p. 370, l. 28.

l. 25   *Bon*: Good.

l. 28   *trace-kicking*: cf. note to p. 262, ll. 37f.

(415) l. 39   *Poveretto*: Poor man.

(416) l. 18   *He was wearing a hat...*: Joachim signals that he is rejoining the bourgeois world (cf. note to p. 5, l. 32).

ll. 21f.   *Schiahorn*: Mountain north of Davos. It forms a background for the Schatzalp Sanatorium.

Schiahorn

l. 22   *Green Towers*: Mountain near Davos.

l. 22   *Dorfberg*: Mountain near Davos.

(417) l. 16   *"Hans!" he said...*: the cousins have not addressed each other with their first names until now. Joachim's natural reserve breaks down at this emotional moment—as will Settembrini's when he takes his leave of Hans Castorp (cf. p. 702, l. 36).

An Attack Repulsed

(417) l. 23 *Orchis and columbine*: the latter is the aqulegia (of the ranunculus family)—see p. 380, ll. 17ff.

l. 27   *All Souls*: cf. note to p. 264, l. 15.

l. 29   *Advent*: begins on the fourth Sunday before December 25.

ll. 30f. *days like the one on which...*: cf. p. 247, ll. 36ff.

(418) l. 4 *in the same spot...*: he may be sitting in Settembrini's seat, but this does not symbolically mean that he accepts uncritically all that the Italian says.

l. 16   *niello-silver*: a technique of ornamenting silver, developed in Tula (Russia) and in India.

ll. 22   *his own hopelessly elegant Latinity*: a nice ironic touch. Settembrini's "Latinity" as a symbol of his commitment to reason and form is firmly opposed to the "boneless" (i.e. formless) nature of the Russian language and thus by extension Slavic names. His "attempt," therefore, to pronounce a Czech name is nothing more than an attempt to impose his philosophy on a world that has a different view of life.

l. 29   *Halle*: city in Saxony (Germany).

ll. 34f. *the union of sickness and stupidity...*: see note to p. 95, ll. 16ff.

ll. 35f. *Settembrini had rebuked him*: cf. p. 96, ll. 2ff.

ll. 39f. *the nationalist aspirations of the Bohemian*: the Bohemians (present-day Czech Republic) wished to be autonomous within the Austro-Hungarian Empire.

(419) l. 9 *Saint Petersburg*: see note to p. 304, l. 18.

ll. 11f. *North Cape*: cape on the island of Magerøya in northern Norway, often referred to as the northernmost point of Europe.

(420) l. 19 *upper world*: since the Berghof is the Underworld.

ll. 25f. *regions whose barometric pressures...*: as Hans Castorp's uncle, Consul Tienappel, had stated long ago, cf. p. 35, ll. 20ff.

ll. 27f. *the missing family member*: the word used in the original ("dem Abhandengekommenen") has wider implications, as it implies being "lost to the world" (cf. note to p. 584, l. 27).

l. 30   *an attack was due*: the exaggerated vocabulary indicates the nature of the visit: Hans Castorp and his new view of life are under siege.

l. 40   *calm*: to emphasize Hans Castorp's demeanor, the word occurs seven times in the space of the next three pages. His calmness is also allied with resoluteness, cf. p. 423, l. 33 & p. 424, l. 1.

(421) l. 3 *hard-riding*: i.e. uncomfortable (it has a hard ride); cf. p. 416, l. 31.

l. 6 *wearing neither hat nor overcoat*: Hans Castorp signals the world to which he now belongs.

l. 8 *directed him to get off now*: repeats the scene when Hans Castorp himself arrived (cf. p. 5, ll. 30ff.). In fact, James Tienappel reprises many aspects of Hans Castorp's own arrival and experiences—including meeting Krokowski and Behrens, and being attracted to a woman (and therefore death).

l. 39 *We're never cold*: contrasts with his comment to Joachim on his arrival: "Don't they heat the rooms?" (cf. p. 12, l. 1). The dead do not feel the cold.

(422) l. 11 *its first effect...*: Castorp is repeating what he had learned from Behrens shortly after his arrival (cf. note to p. 179, ll. 5f.).

l. 27 *Behrens had recently saddled him...*: Hans Castorp uses the word that Settembrini had originally used, cf. p. 55, ll. 29f.

l. 39 *they used the bobsled...*: cf. p. 9, ll. 20f.

(423) l. 1 *The room had been fumigated...*: with formalin (H_2CO) as Hans's room had been, cf. p. 11, ll. 22f.

ll. 3f. *not an exodus, but an exitus*: a play on words. Since Joachim left alive, his departure was an "exodus" (leaving), whereas a dead patient would have made a permanent "exitus" (exit).

l. 13 *pneumothorax*: cf. note to p. 48, l. 38.

l. 15 *pleural shock*: cf. note to p. 304, l. 33.

(424) l. 15 *caseation*: necrosis (death) of living tissue, whose degeneration results in a soft, cheesy substance.

l. 20 *pneumectomy*: surgical removal of all or part of a lung.

ll. 23f. *gangraena pulmonum*: pulmonary gangrene, that is: death of lung-tissue, usually a complication following pneumonia.

l. 41 *chansonette*: female singer (of popular songs).

(425) l. 2 *Sankt Pauli*: entertainment district of Hamburg.

l. 28 *Harvestehuder Weg*: boulevard in Hamburg. Cf. note to p. 28, l. 12.

(426) l. 23 *his guest*: the term used is "Hospitant," which has been applied to Castorp throughout the novel. But now Hans Castorp is the "permanent resident."

l. 31 *pulled one of James's eyelids down...*: just as he had done to Hans Castorp, cf. p. 45, l. 12.

ll. 35f. *a light case of* tuberculosis pulmonum: just as he had diagnosed in Castorp, cf. p. 45, l. 20. Behrens also recommends that James

Tienappel take the rest-cure for a while (cf. l. 38), as he had also recommended to Hans Castorp (cf. p. 45, ll. 19f.; & p. 426, ll. 32f.).

l. 40   *they promenaded*: using the term ("Lustwandel") that had been applied to the walks of Hans and Joachim.

(427) l. 31   *promenade*: cf. previous note.

(429) l. 9   *a little plate of dark glass*: Chauchat's chest x-ray. Hans Castorp's placing of the photograph on a wooden stand imitates Behrens's placing of the canvas of Chauchat's portrait on an easel.

(431) l. 14   *Judas Iscariot...*: In the *Acts of the Apostles* (1: 18) it is related how Judas used the thirty pieces of silver he had received for betraying Jesus Christ to buy a field, but he fell down and burst "asunder in the midst, and all his bowels gushed out."

ll. 18f.   *the citizens of Palermo...*: from the end of the seventeenth century until 1881 affluent citizens of Palermo were buried in the catacombs of the Capuchin monastery, where there were eventually 8,000 skeletons, some of which sat on chairs. The way to the monastery from the town goes past the Porta Nuova.

l. 39   *bon voyage*: farewell.

(432) l. 2   *Lake Constance*: the postcard cannot have come from "Lake Constance," because there is no such place. Like Hans Castorp, James Tienappel would have taken the boat across Lake Constance, so that the postcard would have been mailed from (presumably) where boarded the ferry on the way back—i.e. Rorschach (cf. note to p. 3, l. 10).

l. 12   *a short constitutional*: cf. note to p. 426, l. 40.

ll. 19f.   *a final shrug*: the "flight" of James Tienappel brings Hans Castorp to the realization that he will now never return to the life that his family had mapped out for him. The act of shrugging is a symbolical gesture that indicates a lack of concern, a dismissal of the Flatland ethic, and ultimately the full acceptance of the Berghof world.

Operationes Spirituales

The title of this sub-chapter means "Spiritual Exercises," and it refers to the daily obligations of Jesuits (see note to p. 437, l. 40).

l. 22   *Galicia*: province in the Austro-Hungarian Empire (see map).

l. 23   *Volhynia*: Russian province.

l. 25   *shohet*: kosher butcher.

l. 29   *Law of Moses*: the Torah, the central document of Judaism.

l. 30   *the Talmud*: a record of rabbinic discussions pertaining to Jewish law, ethics, customs, and history. It is the authoritative body of

Jewish tradition, comprising the two books *Mishnah* and *Gemara*, second only to the Hebrew Bible in importance.

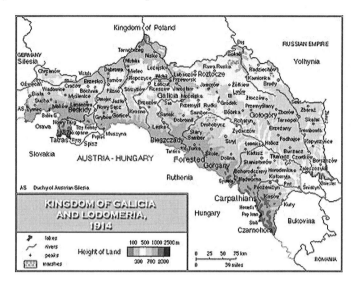

Galicia

l. 34   *Leib*: (Yiddish) "lion." However, the name also connotes the body (a central leitmotif of the novel), the site of so many bloody acts.

(**433**) l. 13   *proceeded according to the Law*: i.e. the prescribed forms of ritual slaughter. Thomas Mann's description of Elia Naphta's slaughtering practices is not strictly accurate (e.g. the animal was supposed to be immobilized by binding it and laying it on the ground—so that it could not have "buckled and [fallen] dead" [ll. 15f.]), but it serves the purpose of depicting the slaughter as demonstrating "pitilessness" (l. 17) and "cruelty" (l. 18), which are both allied with piety—a combination that influences the boy Leo's outlook on life. Cf. ll. 18ff: "the idea of piety became bound up with cruelty, just as the sight and smell of spurting blood was bound up in his mind with the idea of what is holy and spiritual." A trail of blood will follow Naphta throughout the novel.

Also inaccurate is the mention of the assistant's catching "the spurting, steaming blood in basins" (ll. 4f.; that was not the practice)—an action that owes more to traditional prejudice (about Jewish ritual murder) than to reality. In these descriptions Thomas Mann was unable to free himself from the subconscious prejudices of the day.

l. 16   *goyim*: non-Jew.

l. 26   *Torah*: the central document of Judaism; also called the "Law of Moses," comprising the first of three sections of the Hebrew Bible.

l. 32   *baalshem*: rabbi who, by calling on God, can work miracles.

l. 33   *zaddik*: a righteous and saintly person; spiritual leader; term used to designate a Hasidic rabbi.

ll. 33f.   *using only blood and spoken charms*: in fact, this was prohibited by Jewish law; nevertheless, the belief that this happened was common in anti-Semitic propaganda.

ll. 37ff.   *During a pogrom...*: having inaccurately depicted the act of ritual slaughter, the narrator now describes the cruel death of Elia as stemming from the prejudices that the text itself has embodied. No doubt Thomas Mann is condemning the pogrom, but the text shows that he was still trapped in the mentality of his age.

(434) l. 4   *Vorarlberg*: province in the Austro-Hungarian Empire, adjacent to Switzerland; now the easternmost province of Austria.

l. 8f.   *From his mother he had acquired incipient lung disease*: Naphta is sick from birth.

l. 30   *Reichsrat*: from 1867 to 1918 the Reichsrat was the Parliament of the Austrian part of the Austro-Hungarian Empire.

l. 33   *Talmudic*: see note to p. 432, l. 30.

(435) l. 1   *Ill River*: tributary of the Rhine that runs through Vorarlberg.

l. 4   *the Morning Star*: the actual name of the college in Feldkirch, Vorarlberg, known by its Latin name Stella Matutina.

l. 4   *Society of Jesus*: see note to p. 401, l. 26.

l. 15   *Marx*: Karl Marx (1818–1883). *Das Kapital* (Capital, 1867–).

l. 16   *Hegel*: Georg Wilhelm Friedrich Hegel (1770–1831), influential German philosopher.

l. 33   *Goethe*: cf. note to p. 45, l. 9.

l. 33   *pietism*: movement within Lutheranism that emphasized individual piety.

(436) ll. 3f.   *Stella Matutina*: see note to p. 435, l. 4.

ll. 9ff.   *Naphta was by instinct both a revolutionary and an aristocrat...*: he is full of paradoxes.

(437) l. 24   *a ... Moor with woolly hair...*: another indication that the narrator is not free of the subtle prejudice common at that time, especially as the German adds that the Moor was "*nevertheless* very elegant" (emphasis added).

ll. 29f.   *a Silesian count*: at this time Silesia was a part of the German Empire. After 1945 the region was awarded to Poland (with some small areas going to the Czech Republic).

l. 31   *Modena*: ancient city in Italy.

l. 33   *Tisis*: suburb of Feldkirch (Austria), with a Jesuit novitiate where novices underwent their training before being admitted to the order.

l. 40   *operationes spirituales*: spiritual exercises. Jesuits were obliged to spend an hour a day examining their conscience, and another hour of introspection.

(438) ll. 4f.   *Ad haec quid tu?*: What do you say about that?

ll. 7f.   *ut in aliquem gradum quietis in anima perveniat*: so that in his soul he might achieve a measure of peace.

ll. 8ff.   *Except that, once achieved, such "peace."*…: the strict routine was suspected of driving some novices to madness.

l. 10   *his peace that of the graveyard*: cf. the Romantic notion that only in the grave could one find peace.

ll. 12f.   *except by way of physical ruin*: this will eventually be Naphta's fate, of course.

l. 15   *The father provincial*: was responsible for a "province" of the Order. Here the "province" of Germany is meant.

l. 18   *The four minor orders*: the lowest ranks in the Christian clergy, namely: doorkeeper, lector, exorcist, and acolyte (the text lists them in the wrong order). These were stages that the seminarian went through before becoming a subdeacon and progressing to the major orders.

l. 19   *his "simple" vows*: poverty, chastity, and obedience. These vows were taken originally by religious orders, such as the Franciscans and Dominicans in the 12th and 13th centuries, and the members of many other orders and religious congregations, including the Jesuits, subsequently also adopted them. (Cf. Hans Castorp to Joachim, p. 489, ll. 11f.)

l. 20   *Falkenburg in Holland*: a Jesuit College located in Valkenburg, south of Maastricht.

l. 29   *philosophy and humanities*: not the modern subjects, but rather the Jesuit curriculum. Philosophy included logic, natural and moral philosophy, metaphysics and mathematics. The "humanities" comprised grammar, history, poetry and rhetoric.

(439) l. 22   *three fingers of his right hand raised*: one for the Father, one for the Son, and one for the Holy Ghost.

l. 23   *Naphta, too, had sworn an oath to a flag*…: the Jesuit flag is black, with a dagger and red cross above a skull and crossbones. On the flag is written the words: "Iustum Necar Reges Impios" (It is just to exterminate impious or heretical kings, governments, or rulers.)

l. 34   *rules of spiritual exercise*: the German uses the term for military exercise, underscoring the military analogy even more. Ignatius of Loyola wanted the Jesuits to be soldiers of Christ.

l. 35   *Frederick the Great*: a mistranslation. This "Prussian Frederick," of whom the original speaks, was Frederick William I (1688–1740) who introduced exercise rules for the Prussian army in 1726/27.

ll. 37ff.   *He would speak of...*: the rest of this paragraph is taken directly from the Exercises of Ignatius of Loyola (see note to p. 440, l. 13).

l. 37   *dos banderas*: two flags.

(440) l. 1   *capitán general*: commander-in-chief, the highest military rank in Spain.

l. 2   *Lucifer*: fallen angel, associated with Satan.

l. 2   *caudillo*: army commander.

l. 5   *bienséance*: see note to p. 289, l. 40.

l. 5   *a combination...*: one that he had already established twice before: cf. p. 290, ll. 4f. & p. 372, ll. 8ff.

l. 5   *stiff collar and Spanish ruff*: cf. Hans Castorp's description of his grandfather, p. 24, ll. 4ff. The association of Naphta, the Jesuit, with Spain (the origin of the order), and thus with Hans's grandfather (Spanish ruff) is intended to connote conservative tradition, rigid form, and self-discipline.

l. 11   *insignes esse*: literally, be significant.

l. 13   *Loyola*: Ignatius of Loyola (1491–1556), founded the Jesuit Order, drew up the rules, and became its first General in 1541.

ll. 15f.   *ex supererogatione*: above and beyond the call of duty.

ll. 16f.   *rebellioni carnis*: insurrections (plural) of the flesh. Cf. p. 496, l. 38, where Hans Castorp applies the term to Joachim.

l. 20   *agere contra*: to take action against.

l. 21   *resistere*: to resist.

l. 24   *capitán general*: see note to p. 440, l. 1.

l. 24   *the Prussian Frederick*: see note to p. 439, l. 35.

l. 26   *Attaquez donc toujours!*: Always attack!

l. 35   *Knights Templar*: created after the First Crusade (1096) to protect the safety of pilgrims on their way to Jerusalem, the Templars were both monks and soldiers. The order was disbanded in 1307.

l. 41   *patriotic war against Vienna*: Settembrini wants Italy to gain the territory south of the Brenner Pass from Austria (cf. note to p. 375, l. 10).

(441) l. 4 *Nickel*: Goschwin Nickel (1582–1664), a German Jesuit priest, elected the 10th Superior-General of the Society of Jesus.

l. 12   *belligerently*: the adverb used is from the leitmotif "to quarrel" ("zänkisch"), cf. note to p. 373, ll. 8f.

l. 13   *amor carnalis*: the love of the flesh.

l. 14   *commodorum corporis*: the love of physical comfort.

l. 36   *Requiem aeternam*: eternal rest: the opening words of the Christian Requiem Mass (Mass for the dead). "Eternal rest grant unto them, o Lord, and let perpetual light shine upon them."

(442) ll. 6f.   *Christian reverence for human misery*: Hans Castorp has absorbed (and reproduces here) the words uttered on Walpurgis Night by Clavdia Chauchat: "The great moralists have never been especially virtuous, but rather adventurers in evil, in vice, great sinners who teach us as Christians how to stoop to misery" (p. 334, ll. 38ff.).

(443) ll. 39f.   *If one of his companions...*: Settembrini suggests that anyone (including Hans Castorp) who "sees" a dead person must be mentally ill—thus condemning in advance Hans's experiences at the séance later (see the sub-chapter *Highly Questionable*, pp. 644 ff.).

(444) l. 18   *pazzi*: madmen, fools.

ll. 32f.   *Hans Castorp stated he believed every word...*: If so, he certainly changes his mind later.

ll. 36f.   *a disturbance*: the same word that Hans Castorp uses to describe Settembrini's frequent effect on him (cf. note to p. 89, ll. 22f.).

(445) l. 1   *Dante*: cf. note to p. 155, l. 32. The scenes referred to here are in Dante's *Divine Comedy*, where the sufferings of the damned are described. Dante's Purgatory is a mountain that rises in seven stages to an earthly Paradise at the summit.

l. 11   *Most Worthy Knight of the Sun*: Grade of Freemasonry.

l. 11   *Vicar of the Solomon*: in the Swedish system of Freemasonry the eleventh and highest grade. The "vicar" was in charge of the national order. Solomon is also seen as a symbol for Christ, and is thus Christ's representative on earth. (The number seven played an important role in the rituals of this lodge.) This reference by Naphta is, of course, ironic: Settembrini, the rationalist, would not wish to be connected with Christianity.

l. 24   *in statu degradationis*: in a state of humiliation. Hans Castorp has studied the organic decay of the body (cf. *Researches*), and now he receives the religious (Catholic) view of the body's corruption.

l. 29   *pudoris et confusionis sensum*: a feeling of shame and confusion. Naphta's views on the body relate closely to Hans Castorp's own researches, cf. *Research*, pp. 280f.

l. 30   *Saint Ignatius*: cf. note to p. 440, l.13.

l. 31   *the humanist Plotinus...*: Hans   Castorp   is   quoting   to Settembrini's own words from p. 266, l. 14, but since he does so in order to agree with Naphta's views, Settembrini tells him to be quiet and listen (l. 34). Cf. also p. 388, l. 30, where Castorp previously quoted Settembrini on Plotinus.

(446) ll. 1f. *Quis me liberabit de corpore mortis huis?*: Who will deliver me from the body of this death? (*Romans* 7, 24).

(447) l. 2 *bastinado*: method of torture in which the soles of the feet are beaten. Cf. note to p. 312, l. 5.

l. 10   *Saint Elizabeth...*: Saint Elizabeth of Hungary (1207–1231), married to Landgrave Hermann I of Thuringia (hence she is also known as "Saint Elizabeth of Thuringia"), famous for her charitable work. The episode related by Naphta is a stock element of her legend.

l. 11   *Konrad von Marburg*: see note to p. 389, l. 9.

ll. 12f.   *the third choir of angels*: in the hierarchy of angels the First Choir (the highest) is the Seraphim (the Lofty Ones, the spirits of love), the second the Cherubs (the spirits of harmony), and the third the Thrones (the spirits of Justice).

(448) l. 3 *Wehsal*: the word does mean "pain" or "agony" and it is a somewhat archaic word today, but the word "obscure" is the translator's addition. Thomas Mann occasionally liked to make such puns in his texts (cf. note to p. 574, l. 29).

ll. 6f.   *very shabby leather gloves*: another symbolic indicator of the "holes" in Settembrini's views.

l. 20   *like watching someone flog...*: the translation loses the association connoted in the original which plays on the Jesuit order's requirement that its members obey God's authority blindly—as if they were corpses.

l. 28   *international congress on cremation*: it is appropriate that the freethinker, Settembrini, would be involved in such a movement. Until the middle of the twentieth century the Catholic Church forbade cremation because of the belief in the resurrection of the flesh.

(449) l. 41 *He deserts to the colors*: cf. p. 423, ll. 5f. (Cf. later p. 586, l. 36.)

(450) l. 4 *obscene symbols...*: see p. 197, ll. 22f, & p. 258, l.8.

l. 18   *Nuremberg and Regensburg*: both cities had torture chambers dating from the late Middle Ages.

l. 24   *Porcheria!*: Piggishness!

(451) l. 1 *the Inquisition*: there were, in fact, several Inquisitions, but the most infamous ones were the Spanish Inquisition (established 1478;

abolished 1834) and the Roman Inquisition (established 1542). The chief function of the Inquisition was to eradicate heresy.

l. 32   *Ma che!*: Oh, come on!

ll. 39f.   *The French system of deportation*...: in the nineteenth century the French government deported criminals to various Pacific islands.

(452) l. 18   *youth in search of light*: perhaps a reference to those waiting to be accepted into a Freemason lodge; they were described as "searching for light."

ll. 27f.   *Vengeance is mine*: cf. *Deuteronomy* 32: 35 & *Romans* 12:19.

l. 29   *should not repay evil with evil*: cf. *Romans* 12: 17 & 1 *Thessalonians* 5: 15.

l. 31   *scientific determinism*: the belief that every state of affairs, including every human event, act, and decision is the inevitable consequence of previous states of affairs.

ll. 35f.   *the most banal rubbers-and-umbrellas bourgeois periods*...: i.e. the middle class citizen carries an umbrella out of excessive caution (there are no rubbers in the original). Thomas Mann had used the same words in his *Reflections of a Non-Political* Man (1918) in claiming that everyone had wanted the First World War (otherwise it would not have happened), because bourgeois society at the time was at a dead end. This has led some commentators to interpreting Naphta's words here as a prediction of the First World War.

(453) ll. 24ff.   *You feel a desire to kill*...: preparing for the duel that is to come.

(454) l. 31   *O Satana! O ribellione!*: Oh Satan, oh rebellion! Cf. note to p. 57, l. 22.

ll. 34f.   *a Devil on the right*...: Thomas Mann is quoting here an episode from the life of Johann Wolfgang von Goethe (cf. note to p. 45, l. 9). The latter sat between two disputants, Lavater and Basedow, and he felt as if he were between two prophets. (Cf. also *Luke* 24. 13–35, where Jesus, after the resurrection, walks between two apostles unrecognized.)

(455) ll. 3f.   *che guazzabuglio proprio stomachevole!*: What a disgusting mishmash!

l. 16   *illuminatus*: although there were many groups of "illuminati," the one most commonly referred to is the Bavarian Illuminati, which was a secret society founded during the Enlightenment. The word is often used, however, to indicate anyone who belongs to a secret order that wishes to control world affairs.

l. 17   *monist*: one who believes that that there is unity in reality (cf. p. 368, l. 14).

l. 37   *death wearing a Spanish ruff*: cf. p. 290, ll. 4ff.

(456) l. 27   *to be human was to be ill*: cf. Krokowski's remark to Hans Castorp that he "never met a perfectly healthy person before" (p. 16, ll. 27f.). Also cf. Hans Castorp's own conclusions about the nature of life and disease, pp. 280f.

l. 29   *back to nature*: a simplification of Rousseau's ideas.

ll. 30f.   *Rousseauian prophets*: i.e. all those who preach "back to nature."

ll. 41ff.   *As if progress...was not due solely to illness*: Naphta represents Nietzsche's views.

(457) l. 10   *a handsome Jesuit...*: Castorp repeats to himself in French the phrase he had used earlier to characterize Naphta (cf. p. 403, l. 23). It is a variant of how Chauchat had described Castorp himself on Walpurgis Night: "My handsome bourgeois with the little moist spot" (cf. p. 336, ll. 37f.).

l. 11   *Well, lion, roar*: Variation of "Well roared, lion" from Shakespeare's *Midsummer Night's Dream*, V, 1, 249. See note to p. 219, l. 23. Hans Castorp is clearly enjoying the dispute.

l. 19   *Davvero, è criminoso!*: In all seriousness, it is a crime!

(458) l. 15   *anonymous and communal*: cf. p. 386, ll. 36f.

l. 17   *Hegel...*: see note to p. 435, l. 16.

ll. 22f.   *a tiresome bother*: one of the leitmotifs that accompany Settembrini. (On Settembrini as "bothersome," see notes to p. 89, ll. 22f, p. 191, ll. 16f., p. 237, l. 12, & p. 303, l. 27.)

ll. 27ff.   *a drill book...*: cf. p. 439, ll. 32ff.

ll. 30ff.   *he did not believe in pure knowledge...*: cf. p. 390, ll. 28ff., where Settembrini espoused these ideas.

l. 35   *whatever profited man...*: cf. Naphta's earlier assertion, p. 390, l. 38.

(459) l. 18   *bombast*: Hans Castorp uses a noun ("Windbeutelei") based on the word that he had used to describe Settembrini on their first meeting: "What a windbag!" (cf. p. 60, l. 14) and later p. 220, l. 29: "windbag."

(460) l. 1   *two armies...*: cf. p. 439, ll. 39ff.

l. 2   *dos banderas*: two flags (of heaven and hell). Cf. p. 439, ll. 38 ff.

Snow

A key sub-chapter, in which Hans Castorp arrives at his most important conclusion about life and death. His ski-excursion in the snow is not merely a physical adventure, but also—and primarily—a spiritual one. His journey into the frozen wilderness is a journey into himself, in an attempt to face deathly danger and to see if he can withstand and overcome it (cf. p. 467, l. 35ff.). He willingly seeks out death and confronts it. Having risen from the Flatland to the challenging heights of the Berghof sanatorium, he now leaves the latter behind (in the valley) and climbs towards the dangerous peaks that he had viewed on his initial trip by train up the mountain. This sub-chapter contains many leitmotivic allusions to what has gone before in the novel, and in particular, to the debates between Settembrini and Naphta. Hans's adventure enables him to put their arguments and opinions into perspective and to develop his own position, which takes both of their world-views into account and at the same time moves beyond them. His dream in the snow-storm results in his reaching conclusions about the appropriate stance to take in life and he resolves to remember what he has learned. However, the "message" is ironized by the fact that by the same evening he is already no longer sure what it was.

l. 22   *horizontal lifestyle*: since they spend many hours a day lying on their balconies. The tan belies their true state of health.

l. 29   *pneumothorax*: see note to p. 48, l. 38.

ll. 29f.   *Aviateur diplomé...*: certified pilot and lieutenant in the German Navy.

l. 31   *at dinner*: lunch; cf. note to p. 74, l. 10.

(461) ll. 16f.   *prison ship or Siberian salt mine*: Behrens frequently denies that life at the Berghof is like being in prison. But his denial here is undermined by the statement on l. 24 that Frau Salomon has been given a "life sentence." Cf. also p. 176, ll. 8f. and p. 353, ll. 25 ff.

l. 20   *wild departures*: the leitmotif that recurs whenever someone (e.g. Joachim) thinks of leaving the sanatorium without the doctors' approval is intensified by the identification of the sanatorium as a monastery and a prison.

l. 23   *Amsterdam*: major city in the Netherlands.

l. 24   *life sentence*: the term is jocularly used (as part of Behrens's vocabulary) to refer to a long stay at the Berghof, but it also has the ironic undertone of meaning "death sentence."

l. 29   *bizarre and outlandish*: in the original these regions are described literally as "adventurous and eccentric."

(463) ll. 6f. *Gazing into cottony nothing...*: predicting what will happen to Hans Castorp during his skiing adventure.

ll. 8ff.   *And yet there could be no purer sleep...*: the snowy landscape evokes associations with the icy stillness of death. This image will recur many times throughout this sub-chapter.

ll. 14ff.   *This soft, ghostly pantomime...*: the metaphors that describe
the snowy landscape recall the confusion that Hans Castorp had experienced when listening to the debates between Settembrini and Naphta (cf.
p. 381, ll. 5ff.: "palpable reality was often no longer distinguishable from
what had merely been thought"). This had all been foretold during his
initial train-journey, cf. p. 5, ll. 8ff.

ll. 26f.   *it was a chaos of white darkness, a beast*: the vivid image
makes it clear what Hans Castorp will later be facing.

l. 30ff.   *And yet Hans Castorp loved life in the snow*: the snow
around Davos bears for Hans Castorp the same figurative meaning as the
sea-shore did when he was younger. This is a repeated theme in the novel,
cf. p. 466, ll. 22ff., p. 467, ll. 25ff., & p. 471, ll. 18ff.

(464) ll. 15ff.   *to be alone with his thoughts*: it is important to
remember that Hans Castorp indulges in his practice of "playing king" all
the time; he is constantly reflecting about what he has experienced.

ll. 18f.   *a freer, more active, more intense experience...*: the snow
and the mountains attract his interest—not just because "they are there,"
but also because they symbolize his intellectual and spiritual aspirations.

l. 38   *"getting used to not getting used"*: cf. note to p. 248, ll. 24f.

l. 40   *moist spot*: cf. p. 178, l. 32, where Behrens first diagnoses it.

(465) ll. 5ff.   *his more recent, broadening perspective...*: Hans Castorp's personal progress distinguishes him from the other patients who do
not share his desire for enlightenment.

l. 18f.   *like Mercury himself*: Mercury is the Latin name for the
Greek Hermes and the wings on his feet are his attributes as messenger of
the gods. Cf. note to p. 232, l. 7 and picture p. 26.

l. 23   *guardian angel*: it seems as if Settembrini feels that Hans
Castorp's new venture will be beneficial to his "education."

ll. 26f.   *Prince of Shades*: Hades; thus this is a reference to death.
Settembrini is unwittingly predicting what, indeed, will happen to Hans
Castorp "up there." Cf. also p. 55, ll. 29f. & p. 56, l. 1.

(466) ll. 1f.   *his ankles charmingly crossed*: as they had been when
Hans Castorp had first seen him (cf. p. 54, l. 17).

l. 17   *telemark turn*: method of turning on skis, invented in Norway in
the 19th century, that does not, however, "put on the brakes" (l. 16).

ll. 19f.   *cupping his hands...*: recalling Settembrini's warning to
Hans Castorp on Walpurgis Night, cf. p. 326, ll. 32f.) The leitmotif is
repeated on p. 468, ll. 24ff. and p. 471, l. 30.

ll. 24f.   *a deathly silence*: one of the key leitmotifs of this sub-
chapter, cf. e.g., p. 467, l. 5 & l. 21 ("primal silence"), p. 467, l. 9

("fathomless silence"), and p. 468, l. 13 ("deadly silence"). Castorp's ski-trip is a journey into Hades, accompanied by many metaphors for death.

l. 26   *Clavadel*: village near Davos.

l. 27   *Frauenkirch and Glaris*: villages near Davos.

l. 27   *Amselfluh massif*: near Davos.

Amselfluh

(467) l. 7   *his head tilted to the side*...: the position he assumes when listening to music (cf. p. 37, ll. 2f.)—and contemplating death.

ll. 28f.   *valley of the Dischma*: valley near Davos.

l. 30   *Seehorn*: mountain at the entrance to the Dischma valley.

l. 31   *Drusatscha woods*: near Davos.

l. 32   *Rhätikon*: see note to p. 342, l.5.

l. 33   *Schatzalp*: see note to p. 9, ll. 19f.

ll. 37ff.   *He reveled in the skill*...: the act of learning to ski enables Hans Castorp not just to go further afield geographically, but—as the metaphor makes clear—to explore spiritual realms where he has never been before. The wild, snowy landscape will be the location of the next dangerous adventures he will undertake.

ll. 40ff.   *On one side might be*...: this description of the landscape recalls his train journey from Landquart to Davos (cf. p. 5, ll. 3ff.).

l. 42   *cyclopean*: suggestive of a Cyclops (a race of one-eyed giants), thus very big; huge.

ll. 9ff. *this world...*: this entire paragraph portrays the snowy environment as a mythological world, full of mystery and danger. It is a world, however, that is not hostile, merely "indifferent and deadly" (l. 13).

l. 25   *secret, holy fear*: he is aware of the potential dangers represented by the snow—and he knows that he is going to challenge those dangers.

l. 25   *Sylt*: an island in Northern Germany.

l. 29   *blow on his little horn*: which is what, in effect, Settembrini does when he thinks that Hans is "in danger."

ll. 32   *As a young man...*: the beginning of a key passage that continues to p. 468, l. 23. In Hans Castorp's previous experience the sea had represented danger—but only up to a certain point: there was always a lifeguard on duty and Castorp never went beyond a certain limit. He had at that time no "taste for extending the contact with deadly nature until it threatened with its full embrace" (ll. 35f.; i.e. death). But at the Berghof he has learned about his "sympathy with death" and has acquired the courage to face death, to venture to master the fear of death because of his sympathy with it (p. 468, ll. 1f.).

Thomas Mann commented on this sub-chapter as follows: "The sea is not a landscape, it is the experience of eternity, of nothingness, of death, a metaphysical dream; and it is the same with the regions of thin air and eternal snow. ... Look at Hans Castorp in his civilian breeches and his luxury skis as he glides into the primeval stillness, the highly threatening and the non-familiar, the not even antagonistic, but superior and indifferent. He confronts it, as he also confronts the intellectual problems which his fate drives him to face, but what is in his heart? Not "a feeling for nature," which would imply some attachment. No, it is fear, a respectful fear, if you will, religious awe, physical-metaphysical horror—and something more: disdain, genuine irony in the face of the overpoweringly stupid, a mocking shoulder-shrug in the face of gigantic forces which in their blindness can destroy you, to be sure, but towards which even in death he would demonstrate human defiance."

(468) ll. 12ff. *And if there was something uncanny...*: the debates between Settembrini and Naphta had introduced him to realms that were "uncanny," but the "deadly silence" (l. 13) of the snow is of a different order of magnitude.

l. 18   *Hans Castorp's sympathy...*: similar to his "sympathy with death," since the "vast winter wilderness" is a place of potential death.

ll. 20ff. *a suitable arena...*: the snowy wilderness, with its threat of imminent death, seems to him the appropriate place to take stock of all that has happened and all that he has learned and to come to conclusions about life and the state of humankind.

l. 23   *homo Dei*: see note to p. 371, l. 28.

ll. 24f.   *tooting danger on his little horn*: see note to p. 467, l. 29.

ll. 25f.   *called out through his cupped hands*: cf. p. 466, l. 19f.

ll. 29f.   *Eh, ingegnere...*: Hey, engineer, A little bit of reason, please! Cf. p. 326, ll. 34f.

l. 31   *ragione*: reason.

l. 31   *ribellione*: rebellion.

l. 32   *a wind-bag and organ-grinder*: the original words Hans Castorp had used to categorize Settembrini (cf. p. 60, l. 14 & p. 54, l. 35).

l. 40   *leading he knew not where...*: he has embarked on a journey without a clear path or goal—one that might even lead him into nothingness. The intended meaning is both real and metaphorical.

(469) l. 8   *Praeterit figura huius mundi*: "the form of this world will perish." Hans Castorp may have heard it from Naphta, but it is to be found in 1 *Corinthians* 7: 31: "for the fashion of this world passeth away."

ll. 8ff.   *a Latin that was not humanist in spirit*: i.e. negative and nihilistic, and therefore contrary to Settembrini's use of the language.

l. 16   *wickedly spied upon perhaps*: when he looked at Joachim's heart in the x-ray (cf. p. 215, ll. 5ff.).

l. 24   *greenish-blue light*: cf. p. 118, ll. 17f., where Castorp describes the color of Hippe's eyes. This is also the color of Chauchat's eyes (cf. p. 143, ll. 31ff.).

l. 28   *Tartar slits...*: cf. p. 238, l. 2, where Settembrini spoke of "Tartar faces" and then continued "lone wolves on dusky steppes"—by which he had meant the eyes of the wolves (cf. note to p. 238, l. 2 ff.).

l. 31   *Il est à visser, tu sais*: You turn it, you understand? Cf. p. 327, l. 40.

l. 32   *melodious words coming from behind*: from Settembrini, cf. p. 326, ll. 31ff.

(470) ll. 12ff.   *His soul was still weighed down...*: what is involved here is clearly more than the average skiing excursion.

ll. 16f.   *He had set out shortly after dinner*: "after lunch"; cf. note to p. 74, l. 10.

(471) ll. 7ff.   *Snowflakes were too regular*: the snowflake, as an example of "inorganic substance" (p. 470, l. 41), represents frozen form, i.e. death (cf. p. 471, ll. 9ff.).

l. 12   *deviations from symmetry*: as in Greek temples.

ll. 19ff. *Hans Castorp nodded his head*...: the snowy landscape reminds him of the dunes by the sea—but here there is an added dimension: the raw danger of death.

l. 23 *sleep-inducing*: like other things in his life (e.g. music, beer) this effect clouds his reason and renders him susceptible to the irrational.

l. 25 *his own winged independence*: Hermes.

ll. 25ff. *No path ahead demanded he follow it*...: this is not merely a geographical description, but rather a metaphorical indication of his determination to explore new spiritual territory.

ll. 27ff. *At first he had left tracks in the snow*...: his decision is to lose himself totally in the new environment and not to rely on rational aids (cf. "the man blowing his little horn," l. 30). At this point he has abandoned Settembrini and all that he represents, in order to follow "his own innermost feelings" (l. 31).

l. 30 *man blowing his little horn*: cf. note to p. 466, ll. 19f.

l. 39 *the wild silence, this uncanny world that boded no good*: he is fully aware that he is courting the most extreme danger.

ll. 42ff. *Fear had made him realize*...: this sentence makes it quite clear that Hans Castorp set out with the purpose in mind to lose his way deliberately and to subject himself to the ultimate test.

(472) ll. 6ff. *Although if he waited*...: an extremely important leitmotif occurs here, that of finding "his way home" (l. 7f.). The key to Hans Castorp's "education" is his overcoming of his "sympathy with death" and his realization that, while death (peace and nothingness) has its attractions and is an essential part of existence, it must be overcome in the interest of acquiring a healthy view of life. Towards the end of the novel the symbolic significance of the "Lindenbaum" song (cf. p. 640, ll. 31ff.) will become apparent: its message of "coming home" and finding peace is (for him) nothing more than a message of death (cf. p. 642, l. 20)—a message that he acknowledges and overcomes (cf. p. 643, ll. 19f.). "Finding your way" home comes to mean finding a healthy solution to the dilemma of life.

(473) l. 5 *seven fur coats*: reinforcing the fairy-tale like quality of the events.

(474) ll. 1f. *he was staring into nothing*...: the encounter with death begins.

l. 2 *ghostly shadows of the external world*: the German is, significantly, more ambiguous, when it speaks of the "world of appearances." This mythical world of death is the true reality.

ll. 36f. *the day Rhadamanthus first discovered*...: cf. p. 178, l. 32.

(475) l. 6 *covered beneath hexagonal symmetry*: i.e. dead.

l. 7   *with his little horn*: cf. p. 466, ll. 19f, p. 467, l. 29, & p. 468, l. 24.

l. 8   *a snowy cap cocked to one side*: a reference to Clavdia Chauchat's hat on Walpurgis Night: "a simple tricorn of white paper set rakishly to one side" (cf. p. 322, ll. 1f.).

l. 10   *sotto voce*: "under voice" (Italian), to speak softly. The language is appropriate since he does not want the Italian to hear him.

l. 12   *spoke without the consonants*: as on Mardi Gras to Chauchat, cf. p. 328, ll. 6f.

l. 13   *reminded him of a previous occasion*: i.e. his conversation with Clavdia Chauchat on Walpurgis Night, cf. pp. 328, ll. 6f.

l. 19   *an alien, impartial ... person*: Settembrini. Hans Castorp has a rational moment here.

ll. 22ff.   *This is the typical mode of experience...*: he is fully aware that his present situation places him in mortal danger and that to die now would mean that he would be like one "who never finds his way home" (ll. 23f.)—i.e. never solves the metaphysical dilemma he faces.

ll. 27f.   *illness ... batters its victim*: these were Settembrini's words, cf. p. 443, ll. 5 ff.

ll. 30ff.   *And yet you have to fight...*: despite the extreme conditions Hans Castorp has a clear mind about what he needs to do: fight against the natural urge to yield to the attractions of death. He is also perceives the two sides of the coin: on the one hand, death has its attractions (as he has learned in the course of his stay at the Berghof), but on the other hand, "they mean you great harm" (l. 34), and he has no intention of giving into those attractions here and now and dying (cf. "lie down and be covered by stupid, precise crystallometry," l. 38). The metaphor of getting home occurs twice here (ll. 34 & 35), once in a negative sense (dying), and once in the positive sense (surviving).

(476) l. 8   *The familiar blend...*: on the one hand, his natural inclination to lethargy; on the other hand, his intellectual curiosity.

ll. 12f.   *he quivered with exhilaration...*: a clear indication of the effect that the discussions between Settembrini and Naphta have had on Hans Castorp.

l. 16   *attacks of self-narcosis*: a repetition of the word from p. 475, l. 29.

l. 18   *hexagonal symmetry*: repetition of the phrase from p. 475, l. 6.

l. 19   *this feeling of duty*: towards life.

l. 20   *it was mere ethics...*: Hans Castorp is recounting Naphta's earlier remarks (cf. p. 454, ll. 11ff.), but in his own words—proof that he has absorbed and thought about them.

l. 24   *burnous*: a long cloak of coarse woolen fabric with a hood.

ll. 38ff.   *But that in no way lessened the present dynamic tempt-ation…*: the influence of Naphta and his nihilistic views.

(477) ll. 2ff.   *the promptings of a creature in Spanish black…*: all these images derive from Naphta's arguments. Cf. also p. 290, ll. 4ff. & p. 455, l. 37.

l. 6   *ragione*: reason.

ll. 30ff.   *it was the familiar hut…*: he has been skiing around in a circle, getting nowhere. The image is also meant metaphorically: he has not yet made any real progress.

l. 34   *the labial sounds omitted*: cf. p. 328, ll. 6f. Cf. also p. 475, l. 12, where this had already happened.

ll. 37ff.   *You ran around in a circle…*: the futility of his immediate exercise leads Hans Castorp to fear that he will never find his "way home" (i.e. to a place where death has been overcome).

l. 41   *never found your way home*: a key motif that is intended metaphorically and relates closely to the discussion of the "Linden-baumlied" (cf. p. 641, ll. 37ff.).

(478) l. 23   *pass on*: this is an attempt to convey in English the ambiguous meaning of the German verb ("umkommen") which means both "come around" (i.e. in a circle) and "die."

(479) l. 6   *this amateurish drink*: a slight mistranslation. It should say "this pleasant drink."

ll. 14f.   *Kulmbach beer his first evening…*: cf. p. 67, ll. 26ff.

ll. 15ff.   *talk about fish sauces…*: Hans Castorp's mind is confused here: he mixes together several impressions from earlier occasions.

l. 18   *melodious little horn*: cf. p. 467, l. 29, p. 468, l. 24, p. 471, l. 29, & p. 475, l. 6f.

ll. 26f.   *he knew nothing about what was going on*: not merely does Settembrini know where Hans Castorp is and what he is doing, he also does not know of the spiritual adventures that he is undertaking.

l. 30   *Mardi Gras*: see note to p. 266, l. 9.

l. 32   *son crayon*: his or her pencil. See p. 480, ll. 10ff.

ll. 33ff.   *But what was that about "position"?*: What follows here is a reflection with multiple meanings. The horizontal position is the location of the patient during the rest-cure. But it also connotes sex (Hans Castorp's visit to Chauchat's room) and death.

(480) l. 1   *Kulmbach beer*: see note to p. 66, l. 9.

l. 10   *son crayon*: Hans Castorp's thoughts play on the dual meaning of the phrase—and connote the realm of the bisexual.

ll. 36ff.   *It was a park that lay before him…*: the next 5 pages lead Hans Castorp to his most significant insight and to the ultimate message of the novel. Hans Castorp's dream is both Arcadian and horrifying. It has been generally accepted that the Arcadian scenes in the dream were based on 5 pictures by the German painter Ludwig von Hofmann (1861–1945). However, in 1954 Thomas Mann (who owned Hofmann's "The Spring") admitted only to a possible influence: "In the case of Hans Castorp's dream in the "Snow" chapter, I certainly was not thinking of a specific painting by Ludwig von Hofmann. But it is possible that a general memory of the particular beauty that this painter realized in his work played a role. I cannot be more specific."

Ludwig von Hofmann: "The Spring"

(481) l. 14   *a world-famous singer…*: presumably the Italian tenor Enrico Caruso (1873–1921).

l. 37   *And yet he remembered it*: the obvious question arises: How could Hans Castorp remember something he has never seen? The implication here is that there is a collective unconscious. Cf. note to p. 485, l. 37.

(482) ll. 14ff. *people, children of the sea and sun…*: this is the metaphor for the happy, harmonious society.

l. 37   *the recoiling bow*: in fact, bows do not recoil.

(484) l. 16   *without so much as a frown*: the repetition of an important leitmotif is lost in translation. In the original the word "verfinstert" is used, which is the leitmotif that has followed Hans Castorp since p. 27, l. 14 & p. 37, l. 40f. ("the shadow of respectability"). Here the implication is that the boy is *not* evading the harsh truth of reality.

l. 25   *propylaea*: hall of pillars through which one reaches the sacred part of a temple.

l. 37   *two stony female figures*: Demeter and her daughter, Persephone. The latter had been abducted by Hades and taken to the Underworld. Demeter searched for her all over the earth and finally, with the help of Zeus she was able to see Persephone for a part of each year. The two women were at the center of the ancient Eleusian Mysteries (initiation ceremonies held every year at Eleusis in ancient Greece). Hans Castorp's entrance to the temple is thus analogous to the ancient mysteries. Those who were initiated into the mysteries were promised a better fate after death. Hans Castorp's reward is his vision of the people of the sun.

(485) ll. 8ff.   *Two half-naked old women...*: this scene is a reference to the myth of Dionysus and his followers, the maenads. In Greek mythology, maenads were the female followers of Dionysus. Their name literally translates as "raving ones." Often the maenads were portrayed as inspired by him into a state of ecstatic frenzy, through a combination of dancing and drunken intoxication. In this state, they would lose all self-control, begin shouting excitedly, engage in uncontrolled sexual behavior, and ritualistically hunt down and tear animals (and sometimes men and children) to pieces, devouring the raw flesh. Thus the Dionysian excesses of this scene stand in stark contrast to the apollonian description that has just preceded it. In evoking Dionysus the text is also evoking Asia (since Dionysus was born in India), and Hans Castorp's fascination with death. The horrifying dream is based ideas formulated in Freud's essay "The Infantile Recurrence of Totemism" in *Totem and Tabu* (1913).

l. 37   *We dream anonymously and communally...*: cf. p. 386, l. 36f. Castorp has absorbed Naphta's words (and adapted them). This idea also connects with the "collective unconscious" (cf. note to p. 481, l. 37), hence the following lines: "The great soul ... dreams through us, so to speak..." (ll. 38ff.).

(486) ll. 1ff. These next two pages are a summary of what Hans Castorp has learned, culminating in his conclusion on p. 487, ll. 26f.

l. 5   *about kicking over the traces*: first used by Behrens, cf. p. 262, ll. 37f. (and by the narrator even earlier, cf. p. 34, l. 34 [translated as "go-getter"]).

l. 5   *I have passed on...*: see note to p. 478, l. 23.

l. 7   *I have known flesh and blood*: i.e. in two senses: first, through his studies on his balcony, but also through his night with Clavdia Chauchat (cf. *Genesis* 4:1 and *Matthew* 1: 25).

l. 11   *our interest in death and illness...*: cf. Castorp's words on p. 262, ll. 29f. when talking to Behrens: "And so if someone is interested in life ... it's death he's particularly interested in. Isn't that so?" This later formulation is a *reversal* of the earlier statement: the reversal indicates the progress in Castorp's thought. It represents a crucial moment in Hans Castorp's development. As Thomas Mann wrote in 1926: "This phrase is the turning-point, when the inclination to illness reveals itself as the beginning of a higher stage of health."

l. 13   *his true state and condition*: cf. p. 468, l. 21f., where Hans Castorp describes himself as being "burdened with the duties of 'playing king' in regard to the state and condition of the homo Dei."

ll. 24ff.   *I shall hold to their side...*: Hans Castorp's dream had showed him the "people of the sun" (p. 482, ll. 14f.) who lived life conscious of the terrible acts taking place in the background. Neither Settembrini nor Naphta, each of whom is too one-dimensional, allow for this scenario. Hans Castorp has now embraced a wider view of life.

l. 26f.   *forever tooting his little horn of reason*: see note to p. 467, l. 29. The image has recurred several times in this chapter (see note to p. 475, l. 7).

ll. 28ff.   *It's mere ethics...*: cf. Naphta on p. 454, ll. 8ff.

l. 30   *guazzabuglio*: cf. note to l. 20. It is ironic that Castorp dismisses Naphta's arguments by using one of Settembrini's words.

ll. 35ff.   *With their question...*: cf. p. 455, l. 33.

ll. 41ff.   *homo Dei*: cf. note to p. 371, l. 28. Hans Castorp here develops the middle ground between the extremes. He situates himself between Naphta and Settembrini, that is: between death and life. On the one hand, he recognizes the reality of the body, of disease and death; but on the other hand, he resolves to overcome their fascination and strive towards health and life. (N.B. following this conclusion by Hans Castorp, the debates between Settembrini and Naphta take up far less space.)

l. 41   *kicking over the traces*: cf. note to 267, ll. 37f.

(487) ll. 1f.   *somewhere between...*: the "mystical community" is Naphta's vision of society, and the "windy individualism" is Settembrini's.

l. 9   *I will remember it*: he says it three times on this page—and still forgets it.

ll. 11f.   *You take off your hat...*: cf. p. 337, l. 8, where Hans Castorp had said this to Chauchat. Hans and Joachim had assumed this respectful attitude when visiting the dead Austrian horseman (cf. p. 287, ll. 31f.) and the cemetery (cf. p. 315, ll. 25f.).

l. 13   *the ceremonial ruff of what has been*: the image derives from Hans's grandfather (cf. p. 24, l. 30) and has been used by Hans many times already in his contemplation of death.

l. 13   *you put on austere black*: which he had earlier suggested would be appropriate, cf. p. 290, ll. 4f.

l. 15   *kicking over the traces*: see note to p. 262, ll. 37f.

l. 16   *Death and love—there is no rhyming them…*: as he had done to Clavdia Chauchat on Walpurgis Night, cf. p. 336, ll. 40 ff. He has moved beyond that position now: he has superseded the Romantic equation of the body, love and death and has attained a higher plane that recognizes the supremacy of the humanistic vision.

ll. 19f.   *form … comes only from love and goodness*: another indication of Hans Castorp's development. In his conversation with Behrens (p. 262, ll. 33ff) Castorp has declared form to be "namby-pamby nonsense" (l. 36)—which revealed his inclination towards dissolution and death. Now he has reversed himself and advocates form (i.e. life).

ll. 26f.   *For the sake of goodness and love…*: Thomas Mann himself described this sentence as both the most important sentence of the novel and its ultimate message. "*The Magic Mountain*," he wrote, "is largely still a Romantic book, a book about sympathy with death. But it shows the way out of a personal world of suffering into a world of new social and human morality."

ll. 28ff.   *I've long been searching for that truth…*: Hans Castorp presents his coming to the Berghof sanatorium as a compulsion: he was driven there by his search for an answer (cf. p. 31, ll. 26f.).

l. 32   *I will always remember*: but he does not—and he has to rediscover this truth later.

(488) l. 23   *the hexagonal monster*: the snowstorm that could have brought death.

l. 36   *Brämenbühl*: mountain near Davos (see note to p.166, l. 8).

l. 40   *He flung one hand high above his head*: a gesture typical of him, cf. p. 156, ll. 40f. & p. 369, l. 5.

(489) ll. 5f.   *by bedtime he was no longer exactly sure…*: Hans Castorp's dream had consisted of striking images and a rational message. But the power of his reason (Apollo) is always dominated by his innate inclinations (Dionysus). Or to put it another way: The Will (in the Schopenhauerian sense) will always be victorious. The fading of his most important insight is a reflection of the narrator's ironic skepticism.

A Good Soldier

A Good Soldier: the German title of this sub-chapter ("Als Soldat und brav") arouses direct associations with Goethe's *Faust*. Faust stabs Valentin, the brother of his lover Gretchen, and as Valentin is dying, he says to his sister: "Now through the slumber of the grave/I go to God, a soldier brave" ("als Soldat und brav"). "Valentin's Prayer" from Gounod's opera *Faust* will later become one of Hans Castorp's favorite recordings (cf. pp. 639 ff.).

This subchapter also abounds in descriptions of the history and practices of Freemasonry that serve as a metaphor for Hans Castorp's experience at the Berghof. The parallel is drawn between Hans Castorp's "education" at the Berghof and the process of initiation followed by free-masons: the masonic temple is a metaphor for the Berghof sanatorium, a place for research into the secret of life.

While Settembrini naturally praises the noble ideals of Freemasonry and its desire to promote a new world order based on the ideals of enlightened democracy, Naphta belittles Settembrini's Freemasonry as a colorless, bourgeois shadow of what was once a carrier of deep mystery: the introduction of the element of the irrational into the movement was a welcome antidote to the dominance of utilitarian rationality.

l. 12 *poverty, chastity, and obedience*: see note to p. 438, l. 19. Hans Castorp sees a close connection between the military and spiritual professions (cf. p. 289, ll. 38ff. & p. 373, ll. 3ff.). He draws parallels between Joachim's military life, Settembrini's Freemasonry, Naphta's Jesuits and Behrens's student corps—all of which emphasise hierarchy and obedience, and all of which suppress sensuality and the temptations of the flesh.

(490) l. 1 *regimental love feasts*: in the nineteenth century heavy drinking was common in the German army. The "love feasts" (German: "Liebesmahle") were sybaritic banquets. Joachim's passion for the military life assumes a homosexual connotation through his use of this word when reporting on them to Castorp: "He often wrote me about them" (p. 503, l. 8).

l. 22 *between clenched teeth...*: he is imitating Settembrini, cf. p. 56, l. 14 & p. 415, l. 39 (where the sibilant pronunciation is lost in translation).

l. 27 *any sense of kinship ... having dwindled*: all signs of his alien-ation from the Flatland and his previous life.

l. 33 *the body must obey the soul*: this may be a veiled Biblical reference to either *Genesis* 3:16 ("Your desire will be for your husband,

and he will rule over you," or to *Ephesians* 5.22 ("Wives, submit to your husbands as to the Lord").

l. 35   *Sapienti sat*: abbreviation for: "verbum sapienti sat est": a word is enough to the wise.

(491) l. 14   *my 'd'gods' comrade*: from Krokowski, cf. p. 360, ll. 22f.

l. 24   *pneumotomist*: "pneumotomy" is the incision of the lung, so this (rare) word describes Behrens as a practitioner of that art.

l. 25   *Utrecht*: city in the Netherlands.

l. 26   *Gaffky*: cf. note to p. 340, l. 14.

ll. 27f.   *spitting on the walkways*: strictly forbidden; cf. note to p. 7, l. 39.

l. 38   *Barcelona*: city in Spain, center of the area known as Catalonia.

(492) l. 1   *blepharospasmosis*: a blepharospasm is an uncontrolled muscle contraction, such as an abnormal tic or twitch of the eyelid.

l. 23   *ready to kill a fatted calf...*: the image derives from the parable of the prodigal son in the New Testament (cf. *Luke* 15:23). In biblical times, people would often keep at least one piece of livestock that was fed a special diet to fatten it up, thus making it more flavorful when prepared as a meal. Slaughtering this livestock was to be done on rare and special occasions. Thus in the Bible when the prodigal son returns, the father "kills the fatted calf" to show that the celebration is out of the ordinary.

l. 40   *Cannstatt*: see note to p. 15, l. 3.

(493) l. 15   *the lake that was like a sea*: see note to p. 3, l. 7. Joachim returns to the Berghof via the same route that Hans Castorp took.

l. 34   *I see, thanks for letting me know*: the translation loses the jocular mock-military tone of the original: Hans Castorp says: "Thank you, sir," as if he were talking to a superior officer. Hence the next sentence: "Joachim was ... unaware of any possible insult" (ll. 35f.).

(494) l. 14   *his sense of having returned home*: an ironically ambiguous phrase, since it also implies having found peace in the grave.

(495) l. 10   *Allgäu*: a region in the southwest of Germany, extending to the Alps.

l. 15   *Caucasus*: The Caucasus is a geopolitical region located between Europe, Asia, and the Middle East. "From behind the Caucasus" means that Chauchat has come from Asia back into Europe.

l. 17   *Pyrenees*: a range of mountains in southwest Europe that form a natural border between France and Spain and extend for about 267 miles from the Bay of Biscay to the Mediterranean Sea.

ll. 22ff. *That comes from the Asiatic East and her illness...*: The thoughts that follow help us understand the nature and configuration of the philosophical camps according to Hans Castorp, as a result of his reflections on what his two "tutors" have told him. The "humanistic middle" lies between two extremes: one the one hand, the rigidity of form found in ultraconservative attitudes (cf. "the Inquisition, starched ruffs, Loyola, the Escorial"); and the other hand, the laxity of "Asia" with it total lack of form (cf. "slamming doors").

Caucasus Mountains

l. 29   *the Inquisition*: cf. note to p. 451, l. 1.
l. 29   *Loyola*: cf. note to p. 440, l. 13.
l. 29   *the Escorial*: cf. note to p. 550, l. 8.
(496) l. 23   *all his fraternity phrases*: throughout the novel Behrens's speech is characterized by the jovial and colorful jargon that he learned in his student days.
l. 30   *Some people go to Spain…*: i.e. Chauchat (cf. p. 495, l. 10).
l. 30   *bandera*: flag; or company; i.e. his military unit. However, the use of the Spanish word implies an association with the opera *Carmen*, where the hero, Don José, does not return to his "bandera" but deserts.
l. 37 *rebellio carnis*: rebellion of the flesh. He has absorbed this phrase from Naphta (cf. p. 440, ll. 16f.).

l. 38   *Saint Anthony*: St. Anthony (251–356) is regarded, somewhat misleadingly, as the founder of Christian monasticism. In the conventional recounting of his life, while he was living as a hermit, he was subjected to manifold torments and temptations (from beautiful women), but he not only survived them; he emerged serene and spiritually rejuvenated.

(497) l. 21   *H₂CO*: chemical formula for formaldehyde.

ll. 26f.   *refused to obey humanistic norms*: i.e. the body does not listen to reason.

l. 33   *constant duels*: verbal, of course; but a harbinger of their actual duel.

l. 38   *Freemason*: Freemasonry is a fraternal organisation that arose from obscure origins in the late 16th to early 17th century. It now exists in various forms all over the world, and these forms all share moral and metaphysical ideals, which include, in most cases, a declaration of belief in a Supreme Being.

(498) l. 1   *its two-hundredth anniversary*: according to one of Thomas Mann's sources freemasonry had been founded in 1717.

ll. 9ff.   *What do you expect?...*: Naphta gives a scathing indictment of the futility of Settembrini's philosophy of life ("the whole moth-eaten classicistic-bourgeois ideology of virtue" [ll. 11f.]). For him Settembrini's views are like rocks—the current frozen form of an earlier reality. For Naphta "the living Spirit" (l. 29) is the only true reality.

l. 9f.   *Carbonaro*: cf. note to p. 150, l. 4.

ll. 10f.   *his charcoal-burner's faith...*: the phrase implies a simple-minded acceptance of things.

ll. 40f.   *places his feet...*: if a Freemason wants to approach another mason, he places his feet in a right angle, and no other Freemason refuses the approach.

l. 41   *special grip...*: a means of recognizing each other among Freemasons.

(499) ll. 1ff.   *Our good Third-Degree Master...*: a mistranslation. The original speaks of "our three-points brother." Freemasons recognize each other by setting three points before a Freemason's name. Thus they were called (satirically) "three-point brothers" by opponents.

ll. 8ff.   *whether they led him...*: The candidate who is being accepted into the order, is led through dark passageways, and is made to wait in dark rooms, before being admitted to the brightly-lit hall. Naphta's description of Freemasonry is quite different from Settembrini's categorization of the movement.

l. 11   *catechized him*: questioned him about the firmness of his religious beliefs.

ll. 11f.   *holding up a skull...*: part of the ceremony in a masonic lodge included the lighting of three lights, turning the face to the East, symbolizing the fact of human rebirth through the lodge. In the ceremony in which the initiate is accepted into the lodge, the oath is administered before the lights, a skull, and swords—the newcomer is threatened by placing the point of the sword on the initiate's breast.

ll. 21f.   *such blatantly Spanish requirements*: the strict formality places it in the realm of Spain and rigidity (cf. "downright military, Jesuitical," l. 22).

l. 33   *Illuminati*: See note to l. 36 below.

l. 34   *Society of Jesus*: see note to p. 401, l. 26.

l. 36   *Adam Weishaupt*: (1748–1830), founded the Order of Illuminati in 1776. It was a secret organization opposed the mystical and irrational tendencies of certain lodges and whose members strove to attain leading positions in government, church, and society, and whose mission was to establish a New World Order, based on Enlightenment ideals, which meant the abolition of all monarchical governments and religions. The order collapsed in 1784/85 as a result both of internal conflicts and state prohibitions. Since the order was organized along military lines, similar to the Jesuits, it is fitting that Joachim be associated with it.

ll. 42ff.   *a life of which it was later purged...*: The opposing positions of Settembrini and Naphta are reflected in the enmity that existed between the Illuminati and the Jesuits in the 18th century.

(500) ll. 2f.   *Jesuitical obscurantism*: i.e. opposed to Enlightenment. Settembrini had used a similar phrase when talking to Hans Castorp previously (cf. p. 246, ll. 8f.).

l. 8   *Clermont*: city in the Auvergne region in Central France (now called Clermont-Ferrand). There were constant rumors about connections between the Jesuit College and the Masonic Chapter in Clermont.

l. 9   *Rosicrucianism*: The term Rosicrucian (symbol: the Rose Cross) describes a secret society of mystics, allegedly formed in late mediaeval Germany, holding a doctrine "built on esoteric truths of the ancient past," which, "concealed from the average man, provide insight into nature, the physical universe and the spiritual realm." The "Gold und Rosenkreuzer" (Golden and Rosy Cross) was founded by the alchemist Samuel Richter in Prague in the early 18th century as a hierarchical secret society composed of internal circles, recognition signs and alchemy treatises. Under the leadership of Hermann Fictuld the group reformed itself extensively in 1767 and again in 1777 because of political pressure. Its members claimed that the leaders of the Rosicrucian Order had invented Freemasonry and only they knew the secret meaning of Masonic symbols. Its members were strongly opposed to the Illuminati.

l. 14   'strict charges': a better translation would be "strict observance." This was a variation of Freemasonry that developed a complicated system of secret rituals and grades that gained acceptance for a while in eighteenth-century Germany.

l. 16   *Scottish Rite*: one of several Rites of Freemasonry. A Rite is a series of progressive degrees that are conferred by various Masonic organizations or bodies, each of which operates under the control of its own central authority. (Thomas Mann's information here is not quite accurate: it was the Scottish Rite that introduced a multiplicity of degrees.)

ll. 19f.   *religious orders of knights*: belief that the Freemasons could be traced back to the medieval Knights Templar—a belief that was embraced in particular by the strict observance.

l. 20   *the Knights Templar*: see note to p. 440, l. 35.

l. 21   *poverty, chastity, and obedience*: see note to p. 438, l. 19.

l. 22   *the patriarch of Jerusalem*: In 1099 Jerusalem was captured by Crusaders, inaugurating the Kingdom of Jerusalem, which endured almost 200 years. A Roman Catholic hierarchy was established in the Kingdom under a Roman Catholic Patriarch (i.e. Archbishop).

l. 27   *Doctor Angelicus*: "angelic doctor"; the name given to Thomas Aquinas (1224–74), who is held in the Catholic Church to be the model teacher for those studying for the priesthood. He is considered by many Catholics to be the Catholic Church's greatest theologian and philosopher.

l. 29   *the Grand and Templar lodges*: the Grand Lodge was the governing body of all the lodges; a Templar lodge adhered to principles derived from the medieval Knights Templar (cf. p. 500, ll. 29ff.).

l. 30   *a Perfect Master*: in the Scottish Rite, a Perfect Master is the title of the 5th rank of the 33rd degree.

l. 30   *a King of the East*: Freemasonry reveres the East as the highest station in the Lodge.

l. 30   *a Grand High Priest*: leader of a Masonic Chapter.

l. 31   *Exalted Prince of the Royal Mysteries*: "Prince of the Royal Secret" was the 32nd of 33 degrees (ranks).

l. 38   *their century's sophistries*: i.e. people who doubted the philosophy of the Enlightenment.

(501) l. 12   *physica mystica*: title of a work published by J.G. Jugel in 1779.

ll. 15f.   *the philosopher's stone*: The philosopher's stone is a legendary substance, supposedly capable of turning inexpensive metals into gold; it was also sometimes believed to be an elixir of life, a chemical preparation with the unlimited potential to transform, useful for rejuvenation and possibly for achieving immortality. For a long time, it was the most sought-after goal in Western alchemy. In the view of spiritual alchemy, making the philosopher's stone would bring enlightenment upon the maker and conclude the Great Work. It could transform gravel into precious stones, make sick people healthy, make iron into gold, rejuvenate, uplift spiritually. There is a strong sexual component: *prima materia* is conceived as bisexual and portrayed as *res bina*—a human being with both a male and a female head, or Mercury, carrying the staff with two opposing snakes.

l. 16   *aurum potabile*: "drinkable gold"; just as gold is considered the finest metal, the hermetics also thought of it as the finest medication. Alchemy strove to understand the laws of the material world, including the transmutation of base metals into noble ones that would cure diseases, rejuvenate human beings and increase potency.

l. 18   *purification ... of matter*: the Romantics believed that magic was the transformation of material.

l. 19   *lapis philosophorum*: see note to p. 501, ll. 15f.

l. 20   *mercury*: the alchemists called all volatile substances "mercury," but especially quicksilver (*mercurius communis*).

l. 20   *res bina*: "twofold matter" (i.e. both male and female).

l. 21   *prima materia*: "primary matter"; according to alchemists, the alleged primitive formless base of all matter.

l. 23   *magical pedagogy*: Naphta's description of magic-alchemistic pedagogy implies that Hans Castorp's "education" is similar to an alchemistic transmutation. Thomas Mann himself commented (1925) that the Berghof Sanatorium is "the hermetic retort in which simple material is forced and purified into an inconceivably noble form." Naphta describes the principle of this ennobling process as "masculine-feminine" ("männlich-weiblich") and "bisexual"—thus connecting it to the central theme of androgyny (cf. Hippe/Chauchat).

ll. 24f.   *glanced upward...*: Naphta has, in fact, just described what is happening to Hans Castorp at the Berghof.

l. 29   *the epitome of all hermetism*: secret science or knowledge, deriving from the Greek god Hermes Trismegistos who was reputed to have sealed glass jars with a magic seal.

l. 34   *our old canning jars*: Hans Castorp's memory of his youth permits him to reflect on the nature of the hermetic and its significance: just as the preserves in the canning jars are "withdrawn from time" (p. 502, l. 2), so is he at the Berghof.

(502) ll. 7ff. *The apprentice must be fearless...*: The apprentice is sent into the grave as a test of bravery—and is then mysteriously saved.

ll. 14ff. *the maze of corridors...*: the initiate is led into the darkest arcades, the most confusing passages, the depths of the mountain, the depths of the soul.

l. 16 *the cult of the coffin*: relates to Hans Castorp's later fascination with the gramophone (cf. p. 627, ll. 24f.). Just as the neophyte freemason undergoes this passage of initiation, so does Castorp. The tests to which the apprentice mason must subject himself are the metaphorical equivalent of Hans Castorp's own rite of passage.

ll. 20ff. *the neophyte...*: the apprentice, thirsty for knowledge, begs for acceptance, for enlightenment about the secrets of life.

l. 27 *a guide to final things*: for Naphta the "final things" go far beyond the enlightened ideals of freemasonry. In his interpretation the rituals of freemasonry conceal another goal which is religious in nature, but also leads back to the ultimate mysteries of life (cf. p. 503).

l. 31 *Scottish Rite*: see note to p. 500, l. 16.

l. 33 *Master Mason*: the highest degree in Freemasonry.

l. 33 *the mystery of transubstantiation*: In Roman Catholic theology, transubstantiation is the change of the substance of bread and wine into the body and blood of Christ.

(503) l. 4 *feast of love*: The early Christians ate an evening meal together and called it "agape." The Greek word "agape" points to the pagan origins of the Christian feast, which was later transformed into the Holy Communion. The word used is the same ("Liebesmahl") as used for the regimental banquets described by Joachim (cf. note to p. 490, l. 1).

l. 7 *regimental love feasts*: see note to p. 490, l. 1,

l. 10 *cadet taverns*: notorious for excessive drinking.

l. 16 *cult of Isis*: Isis was a goddess in Ancient Egypt whose worship spread throughout the Greco-Roman world. She was worshipped as the ideal mother and wife, patron of nature and magic; friend of slaves, sinners, artisans, the downtrodden, as well as listening to the prayers of the wealthy, maidens, aristocrats and rulers. The celebration of the Mysteries of Isis (particularly in the Roman Empire) symbolized the overcoming of death and rebirth.

l. 16 *the Eleusinian mysteries*: see note to p. 484, l. 37.

l. 21 *secrets of Aphrodite*: Aphrodite (Roman: Venus) was the goddess of love and beauty. In Homer's *The Iliad* Zeus advises Aphrodite: "No, my child, not for you are the works of warfare. Rather concern yourself only with the lovely secrets of marriage..." (Book 5, line 428).

l. 22   *the Feast of Roses*: Freemasons celebrated the festival of John the Baptist on June 24, in which roses played a significant role. There are hints that the festival veered towards the Bacchic (i.e. drunken excess).

l. 24   *bacchanalian excess*: drunken revelry; the term derives from the cult of the Roman god Bacchus in whose honor wild and orgiastic festivals were held.

ll. 30ff.   *The lodges were modernized...*: i.e. they were purged of all the unwelcome elements that reflected the darker side of life (which Naphta call "a higher life" [l. 30]) and reformed to embody Enlightenment ideals.

l. 39   *Knight of the T-square*: Together with the hammer and sickle, the square (not the T-square—see illustration) and compass was one of the most important symbols of Freemasonry. The Square and Compass or sometimes known as "The Light" is representative of the 33rd degree in a Freemason's level of achievement. Once a mason has reached the 33rd degree, he becomes a Master Mason. This symbol has, over the years, come to be recognized as the standard emblem of Freemasonry.

Masonic symbols

l. 42f.   *they not only demand higher education...*: these were conditions of acceptance—high fees limited those who could be considered.

(504) l. 9   *be on your guard*: cf. p. 399, ll. 17ff., where Settembrini warns Hans and Joachim to be on their guard with Naphta.

l. 16   *standing behind him are powers*: Settembrini had said the same about Naphta, cf. p. 402, ll. 19ff. (The same was said about Behrens, cf. p. 129, ll. 17f.)

l. 18   *proselytizer...*: a person who energetically strives to convert someone else to the person's faith.

l. 19   *And what sort of emissary are you?*: just as Hans Castorp had from the start listened to Settembrini with a healthy skepticism, so Naphta, too, is subjected to critical scrutiny.

l. 30   *Rivista della Massonera Italiana*: the official periodical of the Italian Freemasons, founded in 1879 in Milan.

l. 32   *"royal craft"*: another term for Freemasonry.

l. 40   *20,000 lodges...*: Thomas Mann found this figure in one of his sources.

l. 41   *Haiti and Liberia*: by the time of Haitian Independence (1804), there were already several Masonic lodges catering to French colonists. The idea of mystical fraternities also appealed to Haitians whose ancestors had developed their own secret societies in Africa. After Independence, they joined Masonic lodges in great numbers and freely used fraternal imagery in other sacred contexts.

The Masonic Order of Liberia was formed in 1867 based on principles of Freemasonry, which had been gleaned by former slaves from their masters in the United States prior to their being "returned" to Africa.

(505) ll. 2ff.   *Voltaire, Lafayette, and Napoleon...*:

Voltaire: see note to p. 246, l. 36.

Lafayette: Joseph Marquis de Lafayette (1757–1854) played a major role both in the American War of Independence and the French Revolution.

Napoleon: Napoleon Bonaparte, (1769–1821) later known as Napoleon I, was a general during the French Revolution, the ruler of France as First Consul of the First French Republic and Emperor of the First French Empire.

Franklin: Benjamin Franklin (1706–1790) was one of the Founding Fathers of the United States of America. He was a leading author and printer, satirist, political theorist, politician, scientist, inventor, civic activist, statesman, and diplomat.

Washington: George Washington (1732–1799) served as the first President of the United States of America (1789–1797).

Giuseppe Mazzini: (1805–1872) was an Italian patriot, philosopher and politician. His efforts helped bring about the modern Italian state.

Garibaldi: Giuseppe Garibaldi (1807–1882) was an Italian military and political figure, and a member of the Carbonari (see note to p. 150, l. 4).

King of England: Edward VII (1841–1910; King from 1901 until his death).

l. 7ff.   *university fraternities*: Hans Castorp explains the effect that joining a German university fraternity had on a person's life and career.

You were a member for ever, and members were assisted in their careers by former members, especially in the civil service.

l. 17   *Massoneria*: see note to p. 504, l. 30.

l. 22   *most of them residing in your native land*: the term "anti-politics" ("Antipolitik") had been coined in Germany in 1907 by people disenchanted with the current political situation.

l. 31   *the Spanish lodges*: the history of Spanish freemasonry has been described as "turbulent," and freemasonry in Spain was prohibited by law from the mid-nineteenth century.

(506) l. 3   *the perfection of humanity*: according to some sources the ultimate goal of Freemasonry is the perfection of humankind.

l. 3   *the new Jerusalem*: the concept of a "new Jerusalem" tradition-ally comprises the belief in a new Holy City for the saints, but by extens-ion also means a better world. In the writings of Emanuel Swedenborg (1688–1772), the New Jerusalem described in the Bible is a symbol for a new dispensation that was to replace or restore Christianity. This stems from the belief that Jerusalem itself is a symbol of the Church, and so the New Jerusalem in the Bible (cf. *Revelations* 21: 1–4) is a prophetic description of a New Church, which began to be established around 1757.

ll. 7f.   *he who withdraws from that sacred task...*: Settembrini makes a hidden reference here to Mozart's opera *The Magic Flute* (1791). Cf. Sarostro's aria "Within these hallowed halls..." ("In diesen heiligen Hallen..."; II, 12): Whomever these lessons do not please,/Does not deserve to be a human being ("Wen solche Lehren nicht erfreuen,/Verdient nicht, ein Mensch zu sein"). Settembrini quotes same aria on p. 510, l. 14.

ll. 9f.   *the art of governance*: this is, in effect, what Hans Castorp does when he "plays king." Cf. p. 383, ll. 33ff., where we are first told of this activity: in both contexts the same word is used in the German ("regieren"; "Regierung"). Note that Castorp immediately repeats the word (l. 11), aware of its significance.

l. 11   *Governance*: Hans Castorp might well be surprised by Settem-brini's use of this word (in German: "Regierungskunst"), because it is the word he uses for taking stock of his experiences.

ll. 12f.   *those Illuminati who were Masons*: in 1790 Adam Weishaupt (see note to p. 499, l. 36) published his major work: *Pythagoras or Reflections about the Secret World and the Art of Governance*. The word in the title (governance) is the same word used by Settembrini.

l. 13   *a regent degree*: the highest degree outside the inner circle.

l. 17   *Perchè?*: Why?

ll. 21ff.   *But there is a Biblical story...*: cf. *Matthew* 22, 15–22; 15–22; *Mark* 12, 13–17; *Luke* 20: 20–26.

l. 33f.   *Écrasez l'infâme*: "Crush the infamy." Famous line by Voltaire (see note to p. 246, l. 36). The phrase refers to abuses of the people by royalty and the clergy that Voltaire saw around him, and the superstition and intolerance that the clergy bred within the people.

l. 41   *the temple of society*: in accordance with the concept of the New Jerusalem (cf. l. 1ff. above).

(507) l. 1   *the Grand Orient of France*: The Grand Orient de France was established in 1733 and was, until the end of the 19th century, the only Masonic Order in France. "Grand Orient" is another name for "Grand Lodge"—the highest organizational entity of masonic lodges. The translation mistakenly assumes that the term refers to a person, instead of an institution; thus the following two pronouns ("his") should read "its."

l. 6   *I find it terribly Catholic...*: a conclusion he can draw only because of his recent conversation with Naphta (cf. p. 499, ll. 31ff.).

ll. 18f.   *the invention of the printing press*: by Johann Gutenberg (c. 1395–1468) around 1439.

l. 19   *the Reformation*: The Protestant Reformation, an attempt to reform the Catholic Church, was a Christian reform movement in Europe. It is thought to have begun in 1517 with Martin Luther's Ninety-Five Theses.

l. 24   *the Great Reformer*: Martin Luther (cf. note to p. 374, l. 37).

l. 30   *Wendic-Slavic-Sarmatian*: the combination of racial adjectives is intended to associate Luther with Eastern and primitive (that is, non-European) origins. On Wendic-Slavic see note to p. 118, l. 16. The Sarmatians were a people of Iranic origin who migrated from Central Asia to the Ural Mountains around fifth century B.C. and eventually settled in most of southern European Russia, Ukraine, and the eastern Balkans. They were closely identified with the Scythians (cf. note to p. 220, l. 17). It is, of course, a gross distortion and exaggeration by Settembrini to attempt to categorize Luther in this way. See also note to p. 624, l. 25.

l. 32   *a fatal weight*: see note to p. 508, l. 1.

l. 39   *Caro! ... Caro amico!*: My dear … My dear friend.

(508) l. 1   *Positioned between East and West...*: reflects Thomas Mann's view that Germany sits in the middle between the East (communism) and the West (humanism), and that Germany's task is to find its own path—in fact, to "save" Europe from chaos.

l. 11   *a certain obstinacy...*: he is still not convinced by Settembrini's arguments.

ll. 23f. *And two he has slain…*: a (mis)quotation from Friedrich Schiller's poem, *Die Bürgschaft* (*The Pledge*), l. 76f.: The original speaks of the hero's killing of three men. Schiller's ballad demonstrates the moral that there is nothing more noble than to lay down one's life for a friend. The context of this reference implies that Settembrini believes that Germany will have to conduct itself in a similar manner—that is, break free through violent acts.

l. 29   *Laughter is the sparkle of the soul*: a quote from the Italian poet Firenzuola (1494–1543).

l. 34   *union … born in Hungary*: information from Thomas Mann's source.

ll. 38f.   *Brother Quartier la Tente…*: Edouard Quartier-la-Tente (1855–1924). From 1900 to 1905 he was Grand Master of the Swiss Grand Lodge Alpina, and after 1902 Director of the International Office of Free-masonic Relations.

l. 40   *Esperanto*: see note to p. 623, l. 13. According to one source the World Federation of Freemasonry was founded at the World Esperanto Congress in Bern, Switzerland on 30 August 1913.

(509) ll. 5f.   *events unfolded rapidly*: reference to historical events in Portugal. On 5 October 1910 the Portuguese monarchy was deposed and a republic declared. The head of the Portuguese Grand Lodge was rumored to have played a major role.

l. 33   *as if it were a matter of life and death*: another foreboding of the eventual mortal duel between Naphta and Settembrini.

(510) l. 12   *Your Beatrice is returning*: In Dante's *Vita Nuova* (1293) Beatrice is adored as the angelic and unreachable goal of all yearning. When she dies at age 25, that serves to emphasize her unreachability. In the *Divine Comedy* she accompanies Dante though Paradise, where Virgil (who had guided Dante through Inferno and Purgatory) cannot go because he is not a Christian). In *The Magic Mountain* Virgil/Settembrini and Beatrice/Chauchat fulfil these roles—although the world of the novel is not divided into three.

ll. 12f.   *all nine rotating spheres of paradise*: since Virgil was not a Christian, he is replaced by Beatrice as Dante's guide to the heavenly spheres.

l. 14   *the friendly guiding hand*: reference to *The Magic Flute*. In Act 2, Scene 12 Sarastro sings: "In these hallowed halls revenge is unknown,/If someone falls,/ love guides him to duty./Then he wanders led by the hand of a friend/Happily and gladly into a better land." ("In diesen heiligen Hallen/Kennt man die Rache nicht,/Und ist ein Mensch gefallen,/Führt Liebe ihn zur Pflicht./ Dann wandelt er an Freundes Hand/ Vergnügt und froh ins bessere Land.")

l. 14   *your Virgil*: cf. note to p. 60, l. 4.

l. 15   *medio evo*: Middle Ages.

ll. 15f.   *Franciscan mysticism*: St. Francis of Assisi (1181–1226) founded of the Franciscan Order that advocated a mystical philosophical approach, in opposition to the advocates of St. Thomas Aquinas (see note to p. 368, l. 31) whose more rational approach is favored by Settembrini. Dante/Beatrice/Chauchat/mysticism stands opposed by Settembrini/Thomism.

l. 24   *ranked above Homer*: Virgil (cf. note to p. 60, l. 4).

ll. 24f.   *on more than one occasion*: perhaps, but not in the text. Naphta's only reference to Virgil had occurred on p. 394, ll. 18f.—without critical intent.

l. 28   *Dante*: see note to p. 155, l. 32.

ll. 31f.   *that fawning poet laureate ... Julians*: "the Julians" refers to the imperial house founded by Julius Caesar and his nephew Augustus. Following Julius Caesar's death in 44 BC, his great nephew Octavius ruled as part of a triumvirate until he assumed complete control in 31 BC (and became the first emperor). The four emperors who followed Augustus (Tiberius, Caligula, Claudius, and Nero) are usually referred to as the "Julian Emperors," because each had some relationship to Julius Caesar. Since Virgil died in 19 BC, and Augustus ruled from 31 BC to 14 AD, the charge that Virgil was the "poet laureate and flunky of the Julians" is an exaggeration.

l. 35   *a full Augustan wig*: reference to the huge wigs worn at the court of Louis XIV. The association with the Augustan period aimed to bring the French "classical" culture of the seventeenth century in close contact with the Roman period and thus underscore its importance. In Naphta's eyes, however, it was an age of foppery.

l. 40   *his favorite era*: the Middle Ages, when Virgil had been venerated both for his poetry and his magical powers.

l. 40   *Virgil*: see note to p. 60, l. 4.

(511) l. 2   *those victorious morning years...*: the Middle Ages again.

ll. 7ff.   *once again one age was heading for the grave...*: Naphta's view here reflects that of Oswald Spengler (see "Introduction," pp. 18f.) that history is cyclical and that the Western world is in decline.

l. 12   *reservatio mentalis*: mental reservation.

ll. 18f.   *the stones of their ancient edifices...*: the stones from Roman ruins were often used to build new structures, as for example the Basilica of Santa Maria Maggiore in Assisi.

ll. 35ff. *whether the classical tradition…*: raises the question of whether Western humanism will be a permanent phenomenon or merely a historically limited one that will inevitably decline.

(512) l. 17 *periwig*: the full term for "wig."

ll. 29f. *the Gorgon's head*: the look of the Gorgon Medusa turned you to stone. Perseus chopped off the Gorgon's head and gave it to Athene. However, the separated head could still turn the viewer to stone.

l. 31f. *the humanist fear…*: reflects Tolstoy's view that the ability to read and write does not necessarily bring wisdom and true knowledge of life. Many people who cannot read or write have more wisdom than those who can.

ll. 33f. *a Gongorist, a Marinist*: terms used to describe Baroque poets. "Gongorism" was affected elegance of style, for which the Spanish poet Gongora y Argote (1561–1627), among others of his time, was noted. The original speaks of "Secentist" which comes from Italian "seicento" = 17th century. The word "Marinist" derives from Giambattista Marino (1569–1625) whose complex style had a great influence on Italian poetry in the 17th century. He is considered the founder of the school of Marinism, later called Secentismo, characterized by its use of extravagant and excessive conceits. Marino's conception of poetry, which exaggerated the artificiality of Mannerism, was based on an extensive use of antithesis and a whole range of wordplay, on lavish descriptions and a sensuous musicality of the verse, and enjoyed immense success in his time, comparable to that of Petrarch before him.

l. 34 *estilo culto*: Spanish: elevated style. In the 17th century Spanish poetry was similar in style to Italian and heavily influenced by Marino. This style became known as culteranismo; it is characterized by a very ornamental, ostentatious vocabulary and a message that is complicated by a sea of metaphors and complex syntactical order. The name blends culto ("cultivated") and luteranismo ("Lutheranism") and was coined by its opponents to present it as a heresy of "true" poetry.

ll. 37f. *Wolfram von Eschenbach*: (c. 1170–c. 1220); a German knight and poet, regarded as one of the greatest epic poets of his time.

(513) l. 4 *a Latin windbag*: although Naphta calls "the literary man" in general a windbag, the barb is aimed at Settembrini. The word has already been used several times by Hans Castorp (cf. p. 60, l. 14; p. 146, ll. 18f.; p. 220, l. 29).

l. 14 *generosità*: generosity, magnanimity.

l. 17 *uomini letterati*: men of letters, educated people.

l. 21 *high-minded youth*: i.e. Hans Castorp, cf. ll. 28f.

l. 25   *the presence of a warrior*: Joachim, whose noble qualities Hans Castorp can see more clearly when contrasted with the two adversaries. However, Joachim's eventual fate is also forecast by Hans's observation of "the new look" in Joachim's eyes (ll. 27f.).

ll. 29f.   *the day Settembrini had solemnly tried...*: cf. p. 507, ll. 39ff.

l. 31   *obstinacy*: the attitude he had assumed earlier, cf. p. 508, l. 11.

l. 32   *They carried everything to extremes...*: a true categorization of Settembrini and Naphta—culminating in their duel.

ll. 34ff.   *whereas it seemed to him...*: Hans Castorp reaches the conclusion that the truth, as far as it exists at all, lies somewhere in the middle. This is his position, where the author wished him to be located: in the middle, between the extremes. Thomas Mann said of the two intellectual rivals: "They are both extremists and pursue everything to an extreme that is contrary to life."

l. 38   *wrapped in reservations*: he preserves his skepticism which has been present from the very start.

(514)   l. 1   *He rose up to defend literary genius*: a slight mistranslation: the original speaks of "the genius [i.e. spirit] of literature."

l. 4   *the Egyptian god Thoth*: originally a moon god; later, because connected with the orbit of the moon, also responsible for time; usually portrayed with the head of an ibis or in the form of a baboon. The association with "the Hellenistic god Hermes the Thrice Great...." and all of his responsibilities is consonant with Settembrini's championing of the cause of human progress and reason. Naphta, on the other hand, emphasizes the god's mystical associations.

l. 5   *the inventor of writing*: in Plato's *Phaedros* Socrates ascribes to Thoth the invention of writing, mathematics, astronomy, and dice-playing.

l. 8   *palaestra*: here "school" is meant. In the palaestra in Ancient Greece boys learned only boxing and wrestling; in Ancient Rome they learned all physical activities there.

Palaestra at Olympia

l. 9   *agonistic rhetoric*: combative argument (such as Settembrini and Naphta engage in).

l. 11   *Signor Brunetto Latini*: see note to p. 156, l. 12. Castorp has remembered what Settembrini said about Latini some time ago.

l. 13   *To which Naphta responded...*: Naphta points out the other attributes ascribed to Hermes. These contrasting features are typical of the sometimes conflicting characteristics attributed to ancient gods.

l. 17f.   *a grabber and guider of souls*: Hermes as the guider of souls into the Underworld (*hermes psychompompos*) is a common motif in Thomas Mann's works after 1911.

l. 19   *cabalistic*: usually associated with certain forms of esoteric Jewish mysticism, but here probably meant to imply any kind of secret knowledge.

ll. 22f.   *death ... clad in a blue coat*: Hans Castorp is here associating death with the Nordic god Odin, who was depicted in a blue coat and who represented death, the god of poets, and the inventor of runes.

l. 30f. *Alexander*: Alexander the Great (356 BC–323 BC), also known as Alexander III of Macedon, an ancient Greek King and one of the most successful military commanders in history: he is presumed undefeated in battle. By the time of his death, he had conquered most of the world known to the ancient Greeks.

l. 30   *Caesar*: Gaius Julius Caesar, 100 BC–44 BC, a Roman military and political leader. He played a critical role in the transformation of the Roman Republic into the Roman Empire.

l. 30 *Napoleon*: see note to p. 505, ll. 2ff.

ll. 30f.   *Frederick the Prussian*: Frederick II, also known as Frederick the Great 1712–1786), was King of Prussia (1740–1786) and made Prussia into the most powerful state in Germany.

l. 31   *Lasalle*: Ferdinand Lassalle (1825–1864), a German jurist and socialist political activist.

l. 31   *Moltke*: Helmuth Karl Bernhard Graf von Moltke (1800–1891) was a German Field Marshal. The chief of staff of the Prussian Army for thirty years, he is widely regarded as one of the great strategists of the latter half of the nineteenth century, and the creator of a new, more modern method of directing armies in the field.

l. 35   *forty thousand characters*: in fact, a large number of these are unused historical variants.

l. 36   *Eh, eh*: Italian expression of objection.

l. 41   *improvement of humankind*: one of the aims of Freemasonry.

(515) ll. 3ff.   *The purifying ... effect of literature*: the debate concerning literature between Settembrini and Naphta that follows reflects

Thomas Mann's own life-long debate with himself (that he had first broached in public in his novella *Tonio Kröger* [1905]). Settembrini reflects the conventional view of literature as a civilizing force, while Naphta's views contain the essence of Thomas Mann's own self-doubts: that literature is a sham, and that the transmutation of real life into literary form kills it (life), and that the artist is, in essence, a charlatan (see "Introduction," pp. 10f.).

l. 29   *the Inquisition*: The Inquisition was a Roman Catholic tribunal for discovery and punishment of heresy, which was marked by the severity of questioning and punishment and lack of rights afforded to the accused. Cf. also note to p. 451, l.1.

l. 30   *the Fehme*: medieval secret tribunal that dealt with crimes that deserved death (and carried out the sentence in secret).

l. 41   *reçus*: recognized. Joachim had used it earlier in reference to Hans Castorp's cold, cf. p. 162, l. 24.

l. 41   *the two duelers*: an ironic hint of their fate to come (see pp. 688ff.).

ll. 41ff.   *the two duelers passed over the remark*: Settembrini and Naphta are ironically portrayed as being so wrapped up in their debate, they are blind to Joachim's indisposition.

(516) ll. 15f.   *hers were the ones that wandered off*: the medical practitioner knows the truth.

ll. 30f.   *the word "cold" was taboo*: cf. Hans Castorp's experience, p. 163, ll. 23f.

l. 31   *laryngoscope*: a medical instrument used to obtain a view of the vocal folds and the glottis, which is the space between the cords. The first laryngoscope was invented in 1854 by Manuel Patricio Rodríguez García.

l. 33   *Formamint*: see note to p. 164, l. 9.

l. 33   *gutta-percha*: an inelastic natural latex produced from the sap of the gutta percha tree. Here the product is probably in the form of a bandage.

(517)   passim: The fact that the two cousins fail to look each other in the eye is a sign of how serious the issue is; their natural reticence towards one another where emotional issues are concerned reaches its culmination in the latter stages of Joachim's illness.

ll. 15f.   *a new light ... in Joachim's eyes*: changes to the constitution of the eyes were a symptom of tuberculosis of the throat.

l. 23f.   *to cough himself out*: a rare example of a Teutonism in the translation: "to cough oneself out" is a German phrase equivalent to coughing until it stops.

l. 32   *out of turn*: i.e. out of the normal schedule of visits.

(518) l. 18   *cauterant*: a substance used to sear or burn living tissue in order to stop bleeding.

(519) l. 22   *a scarecrow divinity*: in roman gardens statues were often placed depicting Hermes with an erect penis. Their intention was to scare off thieves.

ll. 34f.   *you think that will ingratiate you…*: a hidden quote from Gotthold Ephraim Lessing's drama *Nathan the Wise* (1779).

l. 36   *if your cousin calls you a civilian*: it was, in fact, Behrens himself who had first called Castorp that (cf. p. 44, l. 36).

(520) l. 23   *I can hold my own*: there is a little pun here in the original, where the narrator says that he can "be a man" (i.e. Mann).

l. 35   *laryngeal tuberculosis*: tuberculosis of the throat

l. 36   *tracheal membranes*: the tissue constituting what is more commonly known as the windpipe.

l. 37   *locus minoris resistenciae*: location of small resistance.

ll. 39f.   *we'll do everything possible and feasible*: the literal meaning of the original is much more ironically ambiguous: "We'll do everything that is good and expensive."

(521) ll. 1f.   *Later, later…*: tuberculosis of the throat would not have been kept a secret.

ll. 3f.   *it must be awkward…*: a leitmotif that applies also to Castorp and Chauchat talking about Peeperkorn (cf. p. 588, l. 37), and Castorp and Peeperkorn talking about Chauchat (cf. p. 600, ll. 5f.).

l. 22f.   *Hans Castorp walked on his cousin's left*: right and left have a symbolical function throughout the novel. The explicit mention here that Hans Castorp now "kept consistently to the left" indicates symbolically the adverse course of the next weeks.

l. 36   *bienséance*: cf. note to p. 289, l. 40.

(522) ll. 3ff.   *as a wise man once cleverly put it*: Epicurus (341–270 BC), Greek philosopher.

l. 18   *bienséance*: cf. note to p. 289, l. 40.

(523) ll. 14f.   *in conversation with Marusya…*: a sign that Joachim has abandoned his military goals and has succumbed to his fate.

l. 38   *a permanent horizontal position*: a prelude to death (cf. p. 316, l. 4).

(524) l. 31 *moribundus*: see note to p. 104, l. 34.

(526) l. 8   *the temptation to wander in circles…*: reference to Hans Castorp's adventure in the subchapter *Snow* (cf. pp. 471ff.).

l. 27   *this serene course*: in German the word used is "kordial" ("cordial"). Thomas Mann probably intended to indicate that Joachim's heart would give out before the worst manifestations of tuberculosis could manifest themselves (cf. p. 527, l. 24: "his weak heart"). Thus, as medical authorities later pointed out, he should have written "cardial" ("kardial," i.e. of the heart), not cordial (serene). When this was later pointed out to Thomas Mann, however, he would admit only that it was "half an error."

l. 28   *edema of the glottis*: an abnormal accumulation of fluid in the vocal chords.

l. 31   *camphor injections*: a cough suppressant and topical analgesic. See also note to p. 250, l. 30. (N.B. the mention of "side effects" (l. 31) points to the fact that camphor can be toxic.)

(527) ll. 12ff.   *His body felt nothing...*: a reflection of Settembrini's views on illness and suffering, cf. p. 443, ll. 5ff., and recalled by Castorp during his snow adventure, cf. p. 475, ll. 29f.

ll. 16f.   *he had a heavy beard...*: cf. Joachim's appearance at the séance, p. 671, ll. 27f.

(528) l. 2   *Geneva bands*: two strips of cloth that hang from the front of the collar of some clerical and academic robes. They may be made of black material.

ll. 5ff.   *He repeatedly stretched out his right arm...*: this motion, also known as floccillation (picking at the bedclothes), is often seen in delirious, feverish, or dying people. Cf. the gesture made by Elly Brand during the séance (p. 668, l. 34ff.).

ll. 25f.   *the English naval officer*: cf. p. 11, ll. 15f.

l. 27   *earth's vale*: the Latin Bible in *Psalms* 84: 7 speaks of the earth as a "vale of tears."

ll. 28ff.   *an alkaline, salty liquid...*: at this moment of extreme emotion the narrator breaks the emotional tension by giving us a scientific explanation of tears. This ironic device is employed as a defense mechanism against the pain of the moment.

l. 30   *mucin*: cf. note to p. 275, l. 8.

l. 32   *an injection of camphor*: see note to p. 526, l. 31.

(529) l. 1   *kicked over the traces*: the phrase originally used by Behrens of Castorp, cf. p. 262, ll. 37f.

l. 12   *pure, silent form*: death is frozen form.

ll. 15f.   *An antique helmet...*: points forward to the appearance of Joachim during the séance, wearing a helmet from World War I (cf. p. 672, ll. 5ff.).

l. 20   *Beethoven's Erotica*: she means Beethoven's Eroica Symphony (Symphony no. 3).

l. 24   *Un giovanetto tanto sympatico, tanto stimabile!*: a very likable, honorable young man.

l. 31   *Naphta was temporarily in a superior position*: death is contrary to everything that Settembrini stands for.

l. 38   *a Delphic remark*: ambiguous—the pronouncements of the oracle at Delphi were notorious for their ambiguity.

Chapter Seven

Stroll by the Shore

l. 10   *a few casual comments of the late Joachim*: cf. p. 112, ll. 1ff.

ll. 16ff.   *the story which also can only present itself in successive events...*: the fundamental distinction between creative writing and the visual arts had been stated in Germany in the eighteenth century by Gotthold Ephraim Lessing (1729–81) in his essay *Laocoön* (1776). In this essay Lessing had formulated the view that creative writing presents actions that follow one another in time, whereas the visual arts represent figures in space, but only at one precise moment. Neither of the media can do precisely what the other one does. The comments by the narrator here reflect Lessing's views.

ll. 24ff. *Narrative ... has two kinds of time*: the narrator draws a distinction here between the time it takes to narrate a story, and the time that is covered by the story.

(532) l. 4f.   *"Five Minute Waltz"*: the reference may be to Chopin's well-known "Minute Waltz." Joachim had earlier referred to a piece of music lasting seven minutes (cf. p. 112, ll. 12f.).

l. 8f.   *short on boredom ... long in the telling*: the translator's attempt to convey a frequent leitmotif that depends on an untranslatable play on words ("kurzweilig"—"langweilig"); cf. note to p. xii, l. 7 & p. 83, l. 24. See also p. 534, ll. 22f.

l. 13   *an illusory, or, to be quite explicit, diseased element*: as well as the narrator's explanation of this phenomenon as a temporary suspension by the reader of the appreciation of the actual passage of time, we should also note the connotation of "diseased" to imply the suspect nature of the enterprise of narration—a lifelong concern of Thomas Mann. From his earliest stories he always held the writer in suspicion of being an outsider or even a charlatan (see note to p. 515, ll. 3ff.).

l. 15   *hermetic magic*: "hermetic" is one of the central leitmotifs of the novel. "Hermetic" implies a special opportunity for growth and development. The "hermetic" location of the Berghof sanatorium—which constitutes a separate world away from "normality," a location where space is self-contained and time is suspended—permits things to happen (both trivial and profound) that could only happen in a special place. Thus Hans Castorp's "education" is enabled by the closed ("hermetic") atmosphere of the Berghof, where the assembled figures act upon his character as if he (and they) were in a chemical retort.

Thomas Mann's remarks about "time and the novel" revolve around the fundamental idea that, on the one hand, an author can describe large periods of time in a short narrative space, or, on the other hand, the text may narrate the events of only a few minutes, but in so doing require much longer to do so. The reader unconsciously suspends disbelief in accepting that the events of a few minutes may take up a much longer time to narrate, while the opposite can also be true: large periods of time can pass in a short narrative space. The analogy that the narrator draws with drug-taking is yet another indication of Thomas Mann's innate feelings of guilt about the entire narrative enterprise.

ll. 17ff.   *The diaries of opium-eaters...*: It has been pointed out that the analogy with the drug-taker's experience is faulty: the drug-taker's experience of a long period of time within a short actual time-span is not precisely the same as a succession of events compressed by a narrator into a shorter *narrative* period.

l. 31   *"time novel"*: an attempt to translate the untranslatable German term "Zeitroman." The meaning of the latter is ambiguous: it can mean "a novel about the age" (in this case the period 1907–14), or it can also be (as Thomas Mann's wants it to be, in order to exploit the ambiguity) literally translated as "time novel," i.e. a novel about time.

l. 37   *Joachim wove those comments*: cf. p. 112, ll. 1ff. That was at the beginning of August 1907; it is now December 1909, so it was two years and four months earlier.

l. 38f.   *certain alchemistic enhancement of his own character*: this comment reinforces the proposition that the Berghof offers an "hermetic" environment—like an alchemist's retort that makes lead into gold—that heightens the character and knowledge, even of people, such as Joachim Ziemssen, whose life under "normal" circumstances would not encompass such thoughts as he encounters—and enunciates—at the Berghof.

(533) l. 5   *"time novel"*: see note to p. 532, l. 31.

l. 7   *his wild departure*: Joachim had left the Berghof "without permission"—in effect, he had "checked himself out of hospital," with fateful consequences. Joachim left the sanatorium in September 1908, after Hans Castorp had been there for thirteen months. Joachim served with his army unit for nine months, was hospitalized in May 1909, and returned to the Berghof in August 1909, two years after Castorp's arrival. He died at the end of November 1909.

ll. 10f.   *How long ... had Frau Chauchat not been present?*: Clavdia
Chauchat had left in March 1908 (cf. p. 342, ll. 36ff.) and she returns in
mid-December 1909. On her return Castorp has been at the Berghof for
two years and four and a half months.

ll. 18f.   *a phenomenon no less disquieting*: the "hermetic" nature of
Hans Castorp's stay at the Berghof has caused him to lose his appreciation
of the passage of time. There is a fairy-tale quality to the suspension of
Castorp's loss of his sense of time, and this, too, fits in with the novel's
repeated references to fairy-tales and myth—indeed, with its implicit claim
to be a modern myth.

l. 20   *his first evening here*: cf. p.83, l. 33. It was, in fact, the first
evening of Hans Castorp's first full day at the Berghof.

(534) ll. 5f.   *it was patently most unconscionable to pay no attention
to time*: once again, Hans Castorp's guilty conscience emerges. In
"normal" life, time is very important, and the conscientious citizen pays
scrupulous attention to it. But at the Berghof time has little meaning, apart
from the daily requirements of the rest-cure and mealtimes. The "patient"
at the sanatorium lives in a cocoon (an "hermetic" world) where time
becomes unimportant. All well and good—except that the engineer-in-
training cannot overcome the innate conviction that this attitude to time is
unethical, even sinful.

ll. 22f.   *making it diverting in a boring sort of way...*: Castorp's play
on words here goes back to his earlier play with the same words, note to p.
532, ll. 8f.

l. 23   *out of pure disgust early on*: cf. p. 14, ll. 18f.

ll. 28ff.   *from his first day...*: cf. p. 72, ll. 27ff.

ll. 30f.   *his first slight, and relatively innocent, dizzy spell*: cf. p. 67,
ll. 26f.

l. 39   *a hibernating dormouse*: the translator has translated accurately,
but the word in German "Siebenschläfer" (literally: "seven sleepers") is
also a reference to the mediaeval legend that tells of seven youths in
Ephesus who in the face of the persecution of Christians flee into a cave
that is then walled up. 372 years later the mouth of the cave is uncovered
by chance, and the seven youths are discovered asleep. When they wake
up, they believe they have been asleep for only a year. The reference in the
novel plays both on the number seven and on the overall relation of the
novel to myth and legend: Hans Castorp's experience at the Berghof is
similarly a period when time stands still. Castorp will be awakened from
his long "sleep" at the end of the novel when the First World War breaks
out—and the same word is used (cf. p. 699, l. 27).

(535) l. 5 *the slang idiom that Joachim once used*: The reference is to p. 69, l. 35ff. where Hans Castorp (not Joachim) says, about the body after death: "The hair and nails keep on growing, and for that matter, in terms of the chemistry and physics, or so I've heard, it's a regular hustle and bustle in there." The expression ("hustle and bustle") offended Joachim's sensitivities (cf. p. 69, l. 38: "What sort of an expression is that?"). The error lies in Thomas Mann's text, a fact that he admitted when it was drawn to his attention by a correspondent in 1954.

ll. 6ff. *His hair and nails were growing too...*: The rest of this paragraph underscores Castorp's distorted perception of time since he has been at the Berghof. This is, again, merely a feature of the total disruption that his being has suffered.

ll. 22ff. *the reprehensible pleasure*: his playing with and "wasting" of time in this manner gives him pleasure in the context of the Berghof, but he also cannot escape the inevitable guilt feelings that derive from his "flatland" mentality. "Down there," in the world of commerce and the ethical imperative to engage in productive activity, wasting time, as Castorp is doing, would certainly be considered "reprehensible."

(536) l.1 *principled flatlanders*: those average, normal members of bourgeois society who would agree with the sentiments of the previous paragraph.

l. 14 *the nimble, mincing steps*: an image repeated on p. 565, ll. 7f.

ll. 25f. *the disgraceful habit ... worthy of our gravest concern*: the narrator is now having a little fun at Castorp's expense. Having permitted Castorp the luxury of adopting a new standard from which to view the passage of time—albeit with concomitant vestiges of guilt—the narrator now ironically adopts the typical standpoint of a person from the Flatland and both passes judgment ("disgraceful") and expresses "gravest concern"—both phrases intended to elicit a smile from the perceptive reader.

ll. 29ff. *There are situations in life on earth...*: the following thoughts are an expansion of what Hans Castorp had contemplated in the sub-chapter *Snow* (cf. p. 463, ll. 36ff.).

l. 34ff. *a state of being for which Hans Castorp always felt a great partiality*: cf. note to p. 463, ll. 30ff.

ll. 39f. *because you are lost to time..*: a foretaste of Hans Castorp's later assertion that he is lost to the world (cf. p. 584, l. 27).

(537) l. 29 *the professor who was first struck by this notion*: Arthur Schopenhauer.

ll. 37ff. *We can only be grateful...*: the remainder of the sub-chapter takes a firm position in the center, between the extremes. This is where

Thomas Mann places Hans Castorp and subjects him to the various influences of the extremists in the novel: Settembrini, Naphta, and even Joachim, whose excessive devotion to his soldierly duty leads to his death (ironically, from disease, not in battle). Settembrini's critical stance, while it had been ironically undermined, is still the narrator's preference, as long as it results in service to the idea of humanity. Thus Hans Castorp's attitude to the passage of time is also excused because it is in direct opposition to the "extremist" view of conventional bourgeois society: the demand that human beings should always be "productive" is excessive, and thus the rebellion of Hans Castorp against this is an integral element of his taking the middle position. Joachim's adherence to the bourgeois principle of duty at all costs—and his resulting fate—imply to Hans Castorp that this is also not the ideal. Thus his "disgraceful" and "wicked" behavior (the words are meant ironically again) is only so if judged from the bourgeois standpoint.

(538) ll. 7f. *a melancholic show-off*: Behrens. Cf. p. 45, l. 2, where he calls Joachim a "zealot" (using the same word).

Mynheer Peeperkorn

With the introduction of this major character at such a late stage of the novel, we encounter the final significant influence on Hans Castorp. Peeperkorn acts as an ironic counterpart to all the figures that have so far heavily influenced Hans Castorp's outlook on life. For Peeperkorn is the opposite of intellect or ethics: he is a simply an overpowering "raw" personality—and as such, he ironically places all of the other major figures in the shade and attracts Castorp to his side. The name "Peeperkorn" has clear allusions both to spice and corn—the latter further connoting the alcohol made from corn (see below, notes to pp. 542–43). Various commentators have pointed out connections to i) a character, Peerenbom, in Theodor Fontane's novel *Der Stechlin*, a Dutch-Javanese coffee-dealer from Batavia; ii) the colloquial German verb "peepern" (to like to drink alcohol); iii) pepper, hinting at the profession of spice-trader from Java, and iv) corn, whose ambiguous meaning points to both bread and wine. It is part of the deliberate allusiveness of the novel that such (relevant) connotations may be brought to mind.

The portrayal of Peeperkorn is also ironic: like all the other patients at the Berghof, he, too, is sick, a victim of his own frequent acts of over-indulgence and intemperance. The "classic gifts of life," to which he frequently refers, consist almost exclusively of eating and drinking. (See p. 594, ll. 1ff. for the narrator's irony: "… He drank.") There is also an implicit criticism that the cult of the personality is likewise questionable: to grant Peeperkorn mystical qualities is to suspend judgement.

Peeperkorn's first name is Pieter. He is the biblical Peter of the New Testament, and he remembers so vividly the story of the Garden of Gethsemane—because it is his story, a story of insufficiency (cf. his impotence). Apart from the ubiquitous references to the number seven, the Peeperkorn sub-chapters also contain many allusions to the number 3: for example, he orders 3 bottles of wine, then three of champagne, he drinks wine in three gulps, organizes the game of 21, and takes the trip to waterfall on third day after his attack at 3 p.m., plus many more. These allusions reinforce the parallel with Peeperkorn as a quasi-divine figure. The notes will give more information about this aspect.

But Peeperkorn is both a "holy" and a "pagan" figure: the name Peeperkorn literally means spicy grain. Spice points to India—and thus to Dionysus who conquered India and taught its inhabitants the art of wine-growing.

l. 15   *Java*: nowadays the largest island of Indonesia. At the time of the novel the island was a part of the Dutch East Indies.

ll. 21f.   *that polyglot of the idiomatic phrase*: i.e. Behrens can say something idiomatic in several languages.

l. 24   *his remarkable coffee service*: cf. p. 258, ll. 3ff.

l. 24   *those sphinx cigarettes*: cf. p. 258, ll. 26f.

l. 29   *a Jewish woman from Romania with the very plain name...*: another sign that Thomas Mann was not free of the subtle prejudices of his age (cf. note to p. 379. l. 4).

(539) ll. 7f. *spread great confusion over our hero*: not because of any intellectual or philosophical confusion that might emanate from Peeperkorn, but simply by the fact that he arrives at the Berghof with Clavdia Chauchat.

l. 16   *his wild and dubious performances*: cf. p. 294, ll. 11ff.

ll. 24f.   *more or less took him to task*: Castorp is upset that Behrens had not warned him that Chauchat would be arriving with Peeperkorn—as if Castorp and Behrens were somehow in collusion. (Cf. Castorp's comment on l. 40, that he and Behrens are "companions in misery.") Chauchat had left the Berghof on 1 March 1908 and now returns in the middle of December 1909; thus Castorp has been "waiting" for her for over 21 months.

l. 27   *Pyrenees*: see note to p. 495, l. 17. It is not clear how Behrens knows about this trip—unless he was in regular communication with Chauchat (a fact that he had earlier denied; cf. p. 347, ll. 37ff.).

l. 28   *my languishing Céladon*: Céladon is the name of the shepherd-hero in the novel *L'Astrée* by Honoré d'Urfé (1607–27). The novel was hugely successful all over Europe and the name of the hero became synonymous with a suffering lover.

l. 34   *a malign tropical fever..*: Peeperkorn's majestic personality is, inevitably, ironically undermined by his state of health: like everybody else at the Berghof sanatorium, he is chronically ill.

ll. 41ff.   *"Odd duck, definitely eccentric..."*: The detailed description of Peeperkorn that Castorp gives shows how closely he has been observing the newcomer—a fact not overlooked by Behrens: "I see you've given him the once-over" (p. 540, l. 19).

(**540**) l. 19   *I see you've given him the once-over*: The translation is unable to cope with a very clever word-play by Thomas Mann: Behrens uses the phrase "aufs Korn nehmen," which, indeed, means "to take into one's sights." But the German word "Korn" awakens an immediate association with Peeperkorn's name and with his favorite beverage—gin—which he calls "Korn," with many verbal associations (cf. note to p. 542, ll. 41ff.).

ll. 20   *you'll have to come to terms with his being here*: Behrens is certainly fully aware of Castorp's feelings towards Chauchat.

ll. 22ff.   *It has been left to him ... we could not have done all that much better ourselves*: Thomas Mann's little joke—since Hans Castorp's description of Peeperkorn came from Mann's own pen. Note also that we have a very detailed account of what transpires at Peeperkorn's table, thanks to Hans Castorp's "eavesdropping" (p. 542, l.1).

The physical description of Peeperkorn ostensibly derives from the figure of the German dramatist Gerhard Hauptmann (1862–1946), whom Mann knew and with whom he had spent some time in Italy just before composing the Peeperkorn sections of the novel. Although Mann later denied the connection once Hauptmann had discovered it (the latter commented: "This idiotic pig is supposed to bear a resemblance to my insignificant person?"), he had, in fact, admitted it previously in several letters (and also later apologized to Hauptmann in a personal letter). Nevertheless, Peeperkorn is a fictional figure, and the connection to Hauptmann, which is supported by many other details in the novel (e.g. Peeperkorn's pants pockets), does not need to be belabored.

l. 27   *pained lips*: the word "pained" and variations of it occur many times in relation to Peeperkorn's mouth, lips, or speech. Other features that are repeatedly described are the wrinkles in his forehead, his broad hands and their nails, his head of white hair, and his typical gesture with finger and thumb making a circle.

(542) l. 11   *très bien*: very good.

l. 28   *Emerentia*: St. Emerentia is appealed to by people suffering
from stomach and digestive ailments.

ll. 41ff.   *bread...*: a wealth of connotations is released by Peeperkorn's ambiguous use of the word and his eventual clarification of his
meaning. He uses the German word "Korn" which is more ambiguous than
its English translation. The combination of bread and wine evokes both
Christ and Dionysus, pain and pleasure.

(543) l. 10   *A gin, a Schiedam gin*: Peeperkorn actually asks for a
"genever," which is a type of gin made in Holland and Belgium, from
barley, rye and wheat (whereby we have another connection to bread), and
flavored with juniper. The town of Schiedam in southern Holland was
famous for its gin distilleries.

l. 16   *The little glass was so full...*: the connection with bread is
maintained throughout this paragraph—c.f. "bread" runs down the side of
the glass, and Peeperkorn "chews" the liquid before swallowing it.

l. 28   *The Hague*: city in the Netherlands; seat of the government.

l. 28   *Scheveningen*: seaside resort near The Hague.

l. 29   *a "money magnet"*: she means, of course, a "magnate."

l. 32   *Transcaucasian*: i.e. from her husband who lives beyond the
Caucasus Mountains.

(544) l. 21 *His intentions had been of the most delicate, prudent
sort...*: even in the old-fashioned world of the Berghof (where, however,
there is plenty of sexual activity, albeit discreet), Hans Castorp's thoughts
before Chauchat arrives back are so singularly naïve and chivalrous, as to
be quite humorous. This entire paragraph gives expression to his thoughts,
so that when the narrator declares: "He had not given a thought to fetching
Clavdia from the station" (ll. 22f.)—the opposite is meant: of course, he
had thought of that (and, of course, he had rejected it). The remainder of
the paragraph portrays Castorp's acute discomfort at not knowing how to
approach Chauchat on her return and resume contact with her. His
awkwardness leads to farcical assumptions on his part: Would she perhaps
prefer that he remind her "immediately" (l. 27) of what had happened on
Carnival Night? (What on earth does he think of her, or at least of her
memory?) Oh no, that would be too coarse—and it would only be proper
for him to keep his actions now within the limits of decency, since going
to bed with her had clearly "by its very nature exceeded the bounds of
Western reason and behavior" (ll. 29f.). He will simply greet her from a
distance in the dining-room (a wish that, in any case, does not come true
[see p. 545, ll. 31ff.]). This chivalric attitude, he assumes, will bring him
his just rewards "at the appropriate time" (l. 35). The narrator is clearly

having a lot of fun at Hans Castorp's expense. There is, of course, a bitter (and delicious) irony in the fact that all of these considerations are proven to be futile when she arrives in the company of Peeperkorn.

l. 25 *one whose illness granted her such freedom*: these are Chauchat's own words, spoken in French on Walpurgis Night (cf. p. 332, l. 34) that Castorp has absorbed and that are now reported to us as part of his thoughts.

(545) ll. 4f. *Hans Castorp had not slept much that night*: Chauchat's arrival with Peeperkorn has obviously disturbed Castorp deeply.

l. 17 *her "lone-wolf eyes"*: the description comes from Settembrini, cf. notes to p. 238, l. 4, p. 284, l. 17 & p. 469, l. 28.

ll. 23f. *whose current rights of possession...*: Castorp is implying that he has some prior rights of "possession" to Chauchat because of the one hour that they spent together.

l. 26 *amateur portraits*: the reference is to Behrens's portrait of Chauchat which had clearly disturbed Castorp by what it implied about the doctor's relationship to her.

(546) l. 12 *Quartan fever*: the typical effect of malaria. The sanatoria in Davos, apart from treating tuberculosis, advertised themselves as also specializing in malaria and tropical diseases. The deeper dimension of this affliction lies in its implications: for three days Peeperkorn is healthy (i.e. holy) and for four days he is sick (i.e. earthly).

Vingt et un

The title of this sub-chapter refers to the card-game ("Blackjack") that is played in the novel, but also takes its place in the novel's number symbolism (three and seven). The ensuing scene is both a bacchanalian feast and a Passion Play—the last supper of Christ surrounded by his disciples, with John (Hans is the shortened form of Johannes = John) sitting to his right. The manifold references to Dionysus and to Christ (plus various other cultural references) lend the scene the aura of a modern myth: the recreation at this time and place of archetypical cultural patterns.

(546) l. 16 *weeks, three or four probably*: throughout this sub-chapter the narrator plays with the number symbolism of three and four in order to associate Peeperkorn with both the holy and the pagan.

ll. 23f. *bothersome indeed and in a much cruder fashion than Herr Settembrini*: it is significant that the effect of Peeperkorn, the man of pure personality and no intellect, on Castorp is far greater than the character of Settembrini had been. On Settembrini as "bothersome," see notes to p. 89, ll. 22f, p. 191, ll. 16f., p. 237, l. 12, & p. 303, l. 27.

ll. 28f.   *who had not the least notion what an odd light past events cast upon him*: this, of course, is Hans Castorp's perspective once again. What "light" should Hans Castorp's rendezvous with Chauchat cast upon Peeperkorn? Since Chauchat was, in any case, a married woman, in what way would her so brief association with Castorp affect Peeperkorn's public image? It is unlikely here that Castorp is also thinking about a possible past relationship between Chauchat and Behrens, as he (Castorp) tends to see such matters always through his own ego.

l. 35   *Pilgrims' Chorus*: from Wagner's opera *Tannhäuser*.

(547) l. 6   *optical gadgets*: cf. notes to p. 82, ll. 5ff.

ll. 23f.   *important disclosures concerning the organization of human progress*: cf. p. 240, ll. 34ff. One is vague about "the degree of pastness" because that conversation took place two years and three months earlier.

l. 26   *double lecterns*: see image below.

l. 30   *portieres*: heavy curtains in front of a doorway.

l. 31   *a plush-covered Renaissance chair*: cf. p. 328. l. 34ff., where he drags the chair (or an identical one) for Chauchat to sit in.

(548) l. 2   *Maria Mancini*: cf. note to p. 11, l. 39.

l. 5   *huskiness*: a somewhat too concrete translation of the leitmotif that has accompanied Chauchat's voice throughout the novel, cf. p. 211, l. 20 (where the word is translated as "opaque"). The German word ("verschleiert") is intended to connote mystery and the realm of intuitive knowledge.

l. 7   *Glad to. And don't break it*: cf. p.120, ll. 23ff. where Castorp borrows the pencil from Hippe, and p. 327, ll. 29ff. where he borrows one from Chauchat. The words here, however, are Hippe's, but the voice ("a voice of destiny") is both Hippe's and Chauchat's.

ll. 19f.   *"dead" was the first word of any importance...*: i.e. for Hans Castorp their previous conversation is being continued.

l. 30   *zealot*: cf. Behrens's use of the word on p. 45, l. 2 & p. 538, l. 7.

l. 30   *rebellio carnis*: the rebellion of the flesh. Castorp acquired the phrase from Naphta (cf. p. 440, ll. 6f.).

ll. 33f.   *it is more moral to lose oneself or let oneself be ruined than to save oneself*: these are Chauchat's words that she spoke in French on Walpurgis Night (cf. p. 334, ll. 38f.). When Castorp repeats them to her here (albeit in German), she does not recognize them. However, in the context in which Hans Castorp uses these words here (i.e. in relation to Joachim's life and death), the meaning is changed. Whereas Chauchat had uttered the words as a justification for her own life-style, Hans Castorp invokes Joachim to invest the words with the *opposite* meaning: his cousin sacrificed himself to something higher (his duty). Joachim had a noble aim, that went beyond the mere selfish, but his body betrayed him. Castorp has once again made ethical progress and learned from his experience. It is significant that he has moved beyond Chauchat's philosophy of life.

l. 35   *I see monsieur is still a philosophical ne'er-do-well*: "still" refers to their conversation on Walpurgis Night. "Ne'er-do-well" is an oblique reference to *The Life of a Ne'er-do-well* (1826) by Joseph von Eichendorff (1788–1857), a book that Thomas Mann esteemed highly and whose naïve and unassuming protagonist he described as "a ... moving and elevating symbol of pure humanity, of humane-romantic humanity, that is to say: of the German man."

l. 39   *He was not a humane person*: there was always a conflict between Settembrini's enshrining of critical reason—the faculty that never loses control nor permits the emotions nor the erotic to govern one's life—and Chauchat who embodies the physical, the erotic, the life force as principles that override all other considerations. Also involved here is Thomas Mann's belief that there was a specifically "Russian" humanity that was very closely allied to the German form. The long-suffering Russian people demonstrated the same devotion to hope and humanity that long-suffering Christians had also shown.

(549) ll. 7ff.   *But did I not say your that your cousin would die...?*: cf. p. 334, ll. 2f.. Clavdia does remember saying this to Castorp.

l. 10   *Yes, you did, Clavdia*: the translation cannot convey the fact that Castorp says this to her in French, using the familiar "tu"-form—although the addition of "Clavdia" (not in the German text) is an attempt to indicate Castorp's glide into informality. Hence her intemperate response (in German, using the formal form): "Let us have none of that, monsieur!" (l. 11).

ll. 19f.   *You can't believe how cold his brow was, Clavdia*: once again, the addition of her name is the translator's attempt to indicate Castorp's use of the familiar form of address.

l. 21   *Again! Is that any way to talk to a lady...*: Again, her response makes sense only if one knows that Castorp has used the informal form of address. Chauchat is attempting to maintain the fiction that they know each other only formally and that therefore they should be using the formal form of address.

l. 22   *Should my words be humanistic rather than humane*: the distinction is important. Settembrini represents the more rationalistic view of humanity, whereas Chauchat embodies a more spiritual, empathetic ("Russian") attitude. Both of them have had an effect on Castorp, and he has found a position that combines the two views.

l. 25   *Quelle blague!*: What nonsense!

l. 28   *For you*: Castorp uses the familiar "du"-form in German. Chauchat does not protest this time.

l. 30   *They just wouldn't let you out of here, that's all*: Chauchat addresses Castorp in French and she uses the familiar "tu"-form.

ll. 36f.   *But it's not an intermittent fever*: Castorp is alluding here, of course, to Peeperkorn. The German term ("Wechselfieber") implies change—which is appropriate as Peeperkorn's figure alternates between being suggestive of Christ and Dionysus.

l. 38   *Des allusions?*: Allusions? That is to say: "Now you are making allusions?" Chauchat understands perfectly Castorp's reference to Peeperkorn.

l. 40   *And where were you, Clavdia?*: Castorp uses the familiar form again.

(550) l. 1   *Mais c'est un sauvage*: Literally: "But he is a savage." In the original French Chauchat uses the third person as a means of both protesting Castorp's use of the familiar form when addressing her and of distancing herself from him.

l. 1   *Moscow*: major city in Russia, but not the capital at this time.

l. 3   *Baku*: city and port in Azerbaijan (annexed by Russia in 1813), adjacent to Daghestan.

l. 6   *The Kremlin*: a historic fortified complex at the heart of Moscow (cf. note to p. 374, l. 35).

l. 8   *The Escorial*: built by Philip of Spain (1527–98) between 1563 and 1584 outside Madrid, it is at the same time a monastery, palace, and his burial place. For Thomas Mann, who visited it in 1923, it had close relevance to the figure of Naphta and the concept of "obedience and Spanish honor."

ll. 9f.   *in Catalonia*: district in northeastern Spain, fiercely independent (thus appropriate for Chauchat to visit).

l. 10   *sardana*: Catalan dance.

l. 12   *C'est charmant*: It is charming.

l. 13   *almost a fez*: cf. Behrens' headgear on Walpurgis Night, p. 324, l. 24.

l. 13   *boina*: a beret worn by the Basques.

ll. 24f.   *ami bavard de la Méditerranée, son maître et grand parleur*: his loquacious friend from the Mediterranean, his master and orator.

l. 30   *I carry yours here*: by day Castorp carries Chauchat's "portrait" (her chest x-ray) around with him in his inside jacket pocket, and at night he places it in a photograph frame on his bedside-table.

l. 41   *the demands of Western civilization*: the ironic phrase underscores Chauchat's consciousness of (and adherence to) the polite forms of social intercourse, despite her claims to freedom from convention.

(551) ll. 6f.   *a sea-captain's hand*: a jocular allusion to Thomas Mann's model for the figure of Peeperkorn, Gerhart Hauptmann: "Hauptmann" in German means "captain." The description recurs on p. 554, l. 23; p. 559, l. 38; 567, l. 40; p. 582, ll. 4f. & l. 36, p. 596, l. 14, p. 598, l. 21, and p. 603, l. 9.

ll. 38f.   *Invite whomever you find*: an allusion to *Matthew* 22.9: "Go ye therefore into the highways, and as many as ye shall find, bid to the marriage." The scene that follows contains many allusions to Jesus and his disciples and takes on the appearance of a Last Supper.

(552) ll. 11f.   *They were twelve in all when they sat down*: the Biblical allusion is obvious. This supper, however, also carries clear allusions to Dionysus (Bacchus), including the description in the original of the wine-goblets (l. 22) as "Roman."

l. 13   *Vingt et un*: twenty-one, known in North America as Blackjack, and in Britain as Pontoon.

l. 15   *Chablis*: Chablis refers to a wine region of Burgundy (France) that produces a dry white wine.

l. 15   *three bottles to start with*: the "divine" nature of the occasion is underscored by the number three. Note that Peeperkorn soon orders three more (l. 39f.).

l. 23   *Malaga grapes*: from Malaga (Spain); the grapes are dried in the sun before being pressed to produce a sweet wine.

l. 24   *"divine"*: the deliberate ambiguity in the use of the word here underscores Peeperkorn's role as a Christ-figure.

l. 26   *he took charge of the bank first*: in Blackjack one person deals the cards and acts as "banker," and all the players play in turn against the banker.

ll. 37ff.   *Squeal, madame, squeal*...: Frau Stöhr's naïve reactions to the card-game are interpreted by Peeperkorn as coming from animalistic depths ("from deepest..."; l. 39). He is Dionysus, partaking of the Dionysian mysteries.

(553) l. 11   *a Monte Carlo casino*: town in Monaco, renowned for its casinos and gambling.

l. 14   *tours*: card game.

l. 14   *chemin de fer*: French version of Baccarat.

l. 15   *ma tante, ta tante*: card game.

l. 15   *différence*: Swiss card game.

(554) l. 29   *omelette aux fines herbes*: plain omelet, seasoned with herbs.

l. 37   *these gifts of God*: note the ambiguity: Peeperkorn himself has supplied these gifts.

l. 38   *Dutch gin*: juniper-flavored gin, first sold in the seventeenth century as a medicine (cf. note to p. 543, l. 10).

l. 39   *with eager devotion*: underlines the quasi-religious nature of the occasion.

(555) ll. 1f.   *a speeding troika*: a sled drawn by three horses side-by-side.

l. 7   *emotional vigor*: a key concept for the understanding of Peeperkorn. The ageing Peeperkorn is conscious of his declining physical powers—which means primarily his declining sexual power. His lack of sexual potency leads him to commit suicide.

l. 20   *The unforgivable sin lies in–*: The sentence is not completed, but the following paragraph makes it clear that Peeperkorn's own internal fear is also contained in this unfinished statement. We will discover later what that fear is.

l. 39   *a token of our inadequacies*: the word "inadequacies" conveys the fact that Castorp uses a word that implies "impotence"—unaware, of course, that that is precisely Peeperkorn's fear.

(556) l. 10   *the brotherhood of informal pronouns*: the German custom of agreeing to use the informal form of address ("du") between two people who have decided to become friends. The agreement is conventionally sealed with a drink.

l. 16   *Inadequacies*: although Castorp had used this word a few minutes ago, it has obviously registered in Peeperkorn's brain—as is indicated by his following words: "Fine and horrifying." It is horrifying for him because impotence is his greatest fear. He will use the word "inadequacy" again in a few moments (cf. l. 37).

ll. 17f.   *Life's holy, feminine demands upon our manly vigor and honor–*: Peeperkorn's fear of impotence is expressed in this statement.

l. 23   *Even drunken Bacchus*: see image below (by Peter Paul Rubens).

ll. 32ff.   *Life is a woman...*: this speech is a clear exposition of Peeperkorn's view of life: once a man's sexual potency has gone, he can no longer do justice to life.

ll. 36f.   *the proof or collapse of our resilient manly desire...*: the litmus-test for a man, according to Peeperkorn.

ll. 38ff.   *The defeat of feeling in the face of life ... doomsday*: Peeperkorn's judgment of his own state is merciless. The use of the word "inadequacy" again, while consistent, also hides the theme of impotence.

(557) l. 12   *caustic chatter*: this critical comment shows that Castorp is clear in his own mind about the nature of Naphta.

ll. 24ff.   *Your remarks, Mynheer Peeperkorn...*: it is deliciously ironic that the following speech by Hans Castorp consists of effusive babblings that make almost no sense at all—as if he has not only been impressed by Peeperkorn's "majestic" personality, but has also adopted his manner of speaking.

l. 34   *inadequacy*: occurs twice in Hans Castorp's speech (l. 34 & p. 558, l. 3), but it is not at all clear that he realizes its full implications.

(558) ll. 7ff. *Had he found the courage...*: the narrator is suggesting that Castorp's hour with Chauchat makes him feel that he has a certain right to be so bold. Castorp still seems to think naïvely that he has some prior right of possession over Chauchat.

ll. 35ff. *Wine—... the philanthropic invention of a god who is in fact associated with civilization*: Dionysus, the god of wine.

l. 41   *Cimmerians*: for Homer, the inhabitants of a land at the Western edge of the ocean, who never saw the sun (cf. *Odyssey*, Book 11, 13–19).

(559) ll. 2f. *with enthusiasm, with intoxication*: Castorp has absorbed the Dionysian view. His comments here run directly counter to what Settembrini would have said.

(560) l. 1   *The flesh...*: "The spirit is strong, but the flesh is weak" (cf. *Matthew* 26, 41; and *Mark* 14, 38).

ll. 9ff. *Gethsemane*: a garden at the foot of the Mount of Olives in Jerusalem believed to be the place where Jesus and his disciples prayed the night before Jesus's crucifixion. (cf. *Matthew* 26, 37–45; and *Mark* 14, 33–41).

ll. 19f. *His head tilted to one side*: the traditional portrayal of Jesus on the cross.

ll. 20f. *the throes of lonely death*: more associations with Christ on the cross.

ll. 33f. *Gothic agony ... sybaritic dimple*: combines the images of Christ and Dionysus. The "Gothic agony" is a reference to medieval depictions of Christ where his agony (in the German text "Schmerz") relates to the "Man of Sorrows" ("Schmerzensmann")—a term reserved in German for Christ. And his face and attitude take on the appearance of Christ on the Cross. "Sybaritic" derives from the town of Sybaris (a Greek town in Southern Italy) renowned for the luxuriant lifestyle of its inhabitants.

ll. 34f. *Behold the hour is at hand*: *Matthew* 26, 45. The biblical quotations reveal that Peeperkorn sees himself in the role of Jesus.

ll. 37f   *three bottles of Mumm & Co. ... and petits fours*: the numbers three and four. Since 1875 the firm of Mumm's produced a brand of champagne with a red ribbon.

l. 37   *Cordon rouge, très sec*: red ribbon, very dry.

l. 38   *petit fours*: literally: "little ovens." They are described in the following sentence.

(561) ll. 15ff. *Frau Magnus's eyes had turned red...*: even in a subsidiary character the Dionysian life-principle takes charge: "she admitted that she felt as if life were coursing through her" (l. 17f.)

l. 19   *bacchanalia*: originally the name for wild and mystic festivals of the Roman god Bacchus; here is the general modern sense of drunken revelry. The narrator has repeatedly drawn a parallel between pagan and Christian models: Peeperkorn is both Dionysus and Christ (cf. Peeperkorn's statement: "Holy in every sense of the word, both Christian and heathen"; p. 562, ll. 16f.): the God of Wine and the God of the Eucharist are united.

l. 22   *chartreuse*: a French liqueur composed of distilled alcohol flavored with 130 herbal extracts. The liqueur is named after the Grande Chartreuse monastery where it was formerly produced.

l. 23   *crème de vanille*: generic for liqueur with vanilla flavoring.

l. 23   *maraschino*: a bittersweet, clear liqueur flavored with Marasca cherries, which are grown in Dalmatia, Croatia.

l. 32   *the deterrent example offered by St. Peter and friends*: none of those who are present wants to abandon this modern Christ, as St. Peter and the other disciples did in the garden of Gethsemane (cf. note to p. 560, l. 9ff.).

(562) l. 4   *pleural shock*: cf. note to p. 304, l. 33.

l. 17   *both Christian and heathen*: apart from the allusions to Peeperkorn as a Christ-like figure, there have also been parallels to a heathen god: cf. p. 556, ll. 23f. & p. 560, ll. 21f.

(563) l. 7   *Gethsemane*: see note to p. 560, l. 9ff.

l. 39   *a manifest personality*: Hans Castorp's recognition of Peeperkorn's significance.

(564) ll. 19f.   *Because I cannot exchange kisses on the brow with your traveling companion*: a kiss on the brow would mean that Castorp and Chauchat knew each other only formally—whereas Castorp insists that their relationship from the start (and especially since their one intimate encounter) has been on a level that demands a kiss on the lips, or none at all. (Cf. Castorp's assertion on Walpurgis Night referring to the his use of the informal mode of address: "I've used it with you all along, and will for all eternity"; p. 331, l. 38.)

Mynheer Peeperkorn (continued)

The Peeperkorn experience helps Hans Castorp bring the two figures, Settembrini and Naphta, further into perspective. The strong influence that Peeperkorn's personality has on him is illustrated by his adoption of Peeperkorn's judgment that they are both "little chatterboxes" (p. 565, l. 23). The enclosed world of the Berghof has subjected him to a process of "hermetic pedagogy" (p. 565, l. 24) that has caused him to be exposed to various intellectual and philosophical currents. The encounter with Peeperkorn, however, serves the invaluable purpose of placing those influences in contrast to a man whose personality exudes a life-force independent of ideology—and this life-force drowns out all the intellectual games that have preceded it. (It is ironic, of course, and inevitable, that Peeperkorn's life-force is undermined by his own weakening state: life, even in its most powerful manifestation, is always diseased and fated to perish.)

(564) l. 30 *Flüela Valley*: valley near Davos. The waterfall is fictional.

l. 34 *the dance of death*: associating not only with the sub-chapter *Danse macabre*, but also with the First World War.

(565) ll. 7f. *A little hand ... mincing along*: cf. p. 536, ll. 14f.

l. 11 *an addict's dream...*: cf. p. 532, ll. 18f.

ll. 18ff. *just as it was resolved in Hans Castorp's own mind*: the intellectual contortions of Settembrini and Naphta are overshadowed by Peeperkorn's sheer personality. It is equally important to note that Castorp reflects here about the people around him and what they mean for his personal growth.

l. 20 *tugging at both sides of his soul*: cf. p. 454, ll. 34f., where Castorp was described as being in the middle between two devils.

l. 23 *little chatterboxes*: one manner of gauging the influences on Hans Castorp is to take note of the vocabulary he absorbs from his various "mentors."

l. 27 *a tremendous disruption*: the same word as has been used to describe Settembrini (cf. note to p. 303, l. 27). "Disruption" is a little strong; "disturbance" would be better. Settembrini has been described throughout as "bothersome."

l. 31 *a lady from whom Hans Castorp had borrowed a pencil...*: Chauchat, of course; cf. p. 327, ll. 27ff.

ll. 40f. *a tourist thirsty for knowledge*: the translation glosses over the fact that the original implies that Hans Castorp is a traveler who is gaining education ("Bildungsreisender")—in the tradition of the "Bildungsroman" (cf. "Introduction," pp. 24f.).

(566) l. 9 *the experiences he needed for growth*: a clear indication that Hans Castorp (as well as the narrator) is aware of the process in which he is involved. This is a process of education, and the protagonist is at all times aware of that process and of his need to bring his critical faculty to bear on all the phenomena that confront him.

ll. 10f.   *Frau Chauchat was instinctively annoyed*: it is a delightfully ironic twist that Castorp's increasing intimacy with Peeperkorn should annoy Chauchat. See also p. 567, l. 29: "[She]…joined briefly in their conversation, or—to record Hans Castorp's general impression—monitored it a bit." (See also p. 567, ll. 31ff.; p. 570, ll. 12ff.; p. 571, ll. 8ff.)

l. 30   *baldachin*: a canopy over an altar or throne.

l. 32   *Telegraaf*: Dutch daily newspaper.

(567) l. 29   *monitored*: cf. note to p. 566, ll. 10f.

l. 35   *experienced the inner glow of joy*: Castorp has failed to resume an intimate relationship with Chauchat, but the fact that his closeness to Peeperkorn upsets her, results in his taking, nevertheless, a certain pleasure in her reaction.

(568) l. 4   *antipyretic*: a medicine that reduces fever.

l. 4   *quinine*: a natural white crystalline alkaloid having antipyretic (fever-reducing), antimalarial, analgesic (painkilling), and anti-inflammatory properties and a bitter taste.

l. 14   *a dancing heathen priest*: cf. note to p. 562, l. 17.

l. 15   *Yes, a splendid substance…*: this paragraph is based on one of the repeated themes of the novel: the closeness of life and death, of health and disease, of medicine and harm.

l. 33   *protein and poison*: the intermingling of such themes is a fundamental structural principle of the novel. The proximity of life and death, the presence of death in life, is a theme that finds expression in a multitude of ways. Here, the mention of protein repeats a linguistic leitmotif that occurs throughout the book. For example, protein, as a constituent of tears, had been on Hans Castorp's mind as he stood at the death-bed of Joachim and cried (see p. 528, l. 30). The fundamental closeness of life and death is clearly expressed in the sentence: "…the world of substances was such that they all concealed both life and death simultaneously, all were both therapeutic and poisonous" (ll. 36ff.).

(569) l. 1   *with unusual coherence*: Peeperkorn is an expert in exotic plants and trees from which medicines and poisons are extracted. More important, Peeperkorn is quite clear about the relationship of life and death, and his remarks are a further indication that a "personality," a non-intellectual, can divine the nature of existence better than people such as Settembrini and Naphta.

l. 7   *quinine*: see note to p. 568, l. 4.

l. 9   *atropine*: a highly poisonous substance, derived from the root of the deadly nightshade plant (atropa belladonna); used in minute doses as a pain-killer.

l. 12   *cinchona*: plant native to South America, used earlier to treat malaria, but dangerous if taken in large amounts.

l. 12   *Cordillera*: the Andes Mountains in South America.

l. 14   *Jesuits' powder*: common name in the 17th century for cinchona (a South American shrub) which was brought to Spain by a Jesuit in 1643.

l. 16   *Java*: see note to p. 538, l. 15.

ll. 19f.   *the epidermis and the cambium*: the outer-most layer and the layer beneath the surface of plants that gives rise to secondary growth.

l. 20   *ligneous plants*: plant with hard, woody parts.

l. 23   *New Guinea*: the second largest island on the planet, located north of Australia. From 1884 to 1914 the Western half of the island was under Dutch administration.

l. 25   *Antiaris toxicaria*: also known as upas; an evergreen tree of the Breadfruit family, common in the forests of Java whose secretions are poisonous.

l. 25   *manzanilla tree*: one of the most poisonous trees in the world. Its name means "little apple"—from its superficial resemblance to an apple tree.

l. 32   *Strychnos tieuté*: a climbing shrub (also found in Java) that gives a juice known as upas tieuté, used by the natives as a virulent arrow poison.

l. 33   *upas-rajah*: "upas" is derived from the Javanese word for poison. (It is also found in Malay.) The literal meaning of the word is "king's poison"—which is appropriate for Peeperkorn.

l. 37   *strychnine*: a toxic, colorless crystalline alkaloid that causes muscular convulsions and eventually death through asphyxia or sheer exhaustion. The most common source is from the seeds of the *Strychnos nux vomica* tree. Strychnine is one of the most bitter substances known.

l. 37   *in close dynamic relationship*: Peeperkorn is describing here the effect that the poisons will have on him later, cf. p. 615, ll. 12ff.

l. 40   *crow's-eye tree*: the seeds of this tree contain (among other things) strychnine—hence the Latin name of the tree *strychnos nus vómica*.

ll. 40f. *Coromandel coast*: on the Eastern side of the Indian sub-continent, around Chennai.

(570) l. 12   *quartan attacks*: see note to p. 546, l. 12.

l. 32   *getting used to not getting used*: the leitmotif that accompanies Hans Castorp (cf. p. 476, ll. 9f) is now applied to the difficult social relations among his "motley circle of friends" (ll. 31f.).

l. 36   *shrewdly life-affirming*: Hans Castorp has been described as "shrewd" throughout the novel; now his new attitude to life ("life-affirming") is emphasized—and the words are repeated in the next paragraph (cf. p. 571, ll. 2f.).

(571) l. 15f.   *those words (spoken in his Mediterranean tongue…)*: on Walpurgis Night, as Hans Castorp ignored Settembrini's blandishments and called out for a pencil in order to draw a pig. Settembrini, fully under-standing what Castorp was doing (i.e. moving over into Chauchat's realm) had shouted after him not to lose his reason (cf. p. 326, ll. 32f.).

ll. 19f.   *this pretty little bourgeois lad…*: Chauchat's characterization of Hans Castorp on Walpurgis Night, cf. p. 336, ll. 37f. (The French word "joli" from that night has been rendered into German here as "hübsch" = handsome, as it was also earlier, cf. p. 336, ll. 37f. & p. 403, l. 23.)

ll. 23f.   *calm little songs from the flatlands…*: throughout the novel Hans Castorp has tried to distinguish his love for Chauchat from the "simple" kind of love expressed in "songs from the flatlands" (cf. p. 137, ll. 30f.), although on that previous occasion he himself hummed such a song. Cf. also p. 226, ll. 21f. & p. 227, ll. 27f.

l. 27   *Tartar slits*: cf. p. 238, l. 2, p. 284, l. 16, & p. 469, l. 28.

(572) l. 1   *his Spanish terrorism…*: although Chauchat and Naphta have a certain commonality in their rejection of reason as a sufficient means to comprehend life, Naphta's extreme views do not accord with Chauchat's more "humane" nature.

l. 8   *disruptive*: the word that Hans has applied to Settembrini throughout is now applied to Chauchat as she is perceived by Settembrini and Naphta.

l. 14   *two viziers*: The vizier was the highest official in Ancient Egypt to serve the king, or pharaoh. Castorp's playful description of his two mentors demonstrates once again his critical emancipation from them.

l. 30   *impaired … the sly observer*: Castorp is the "sly observer" who sees the impairment of Settembrini and Naphta.

ll. 36   *an honest device of classical rhetoric*: Settembrini's phrase, cf. p. 217, l. 34.

(573) l. 2   *cerebrum*: brain.

ll. 19f. *There are so many different kinds…*: Hans Castorp puts Settembrini in his place by implying that Settembrini's cleverness is the worst kind of stupidity. The Italian is not amused.

l. 21   *bon mot*: a clever saying or witticism.

ll. 24f.   *the misanthropic nature of paradoxes*: cf. p. 219, ll. 1ff.

l. 31   *guazzabuglio*: mishmash. Settembrini's word, cf. p. 455, ll. 3f.

ll. 33f.   *to concern oneself with mysteries…*: this is not only an aspect of Hans Castorp's strong spirit of inquiry (cf. *placet experiri*), but also a pre-emptive justification for his later involvement in the séance (cf. p. 650, ll. 26ff.).

l. 36   *he has us all in his pocket*: Castorp's comments on Peeperkorn reveal once again that he is able, while fascinated by the "mystery" of Peeperkorn's personality and its hold over people, to retain critical distance and view the man as a phenomenon worthy of consideration. The word "mystery" ("Mysterium") connotes both Christ and Dionysus.

(574) ll. 8ff.   *the physical dimension … suitable for our earnest consideration*: Castorp's summary of Peeperkorn's effect on people is remarkable for its insight—as it is for its boldness. His avowed reason for insisting so strongly on his fascination with and study of Peeperkorn is the need "to edify ourselves" (l. 21). He justifies himself, therefore, by claiming (correctly) that a consideration of the mystery of a personality such as Peeperkorn's is part of the educational process.

l. 11   *things always get mystical*: Chauchat is in the background again.

l. 27   *Hans Castorp no longer got tangled up…*: a sign of his maturity and clear thinking.

l. 29   *like a man*: the author indulges in a little joke here. In the German he writes "wie ein Mann"—which means both "like a man" and "like a Mann" (i.e. Thomas Mann). Cf. also note to p. 448, l. 3. Note that the narrator is praising Hans Castorp for his courage and his perceptions.

(575) ll. 6f.   *Gregory the Great and the City of God*: two of Naphta's themes (see p. 394, ll. 39ff.).

l. 16   *mundus vult decipi*: the world wants to be deceived.

ll. 19f.   *Go ahead and despise distinctions…*: perhaps a reference to Goethe's *Faust*: "Reason and Science you despise,/Man's highest powers: now the lies/Of the deceiving spirit must bind you/With those magic arts that blind you…" (ll. 1851–55).

l. 30   *your weakness at things Asian is well known*: nasty little dig at Castorp's infatuation with Chauchat.

l. 39   *Beatrice*: she was Dante's love. See note to p. 155, l. 36 & p. 510, l. 12. Settembrini means that Peeperkorn has stolen Chauchat away from Castorp.

(576) l. 3   *have me play cock of the walk*: a sexual connotation is certainly implied here.

l. 15   *point d'honneur*: point of honor.

ll. 26f.   *a conversation about jealousy...*: because he wants to reserve his "student" Hans Castorp for himself.

l. 29   *cock-of-the walk nature*: Here the narrator seems to be implying that Settembrini's interest in Hans Castorp is both pedagogic and homosexual. Thomas Mann several times suggested that the conventional view of a virile, aggressive man might be better amended in order to facilitate more companionship between the sexes. The fictional approximation of Hippe and Chauchat was formalized in a 1925 essay on marriage in which he predicted such a development.

(577) ll. 34f.   *an ideal, communistic City of God*: cf. p. 396, ll. 10ff., where Naphta first espoused this idea.

ll. 37f.   *true Luciferian revolutionary thought*: a reference to Carducci's *Hymns to Satan*, cf. p. 56, l. 41.

ll. 39f.   *Inquisitions*: see note to p. 451, l. 1.

(578) l. 3   *Eh, eh*: Italian expression of objection.

ll. 9f.   *the world's proletariat...*: cf. Naphta's earlier espousal of this view, p. 396, ll. 10ff.

ll. 22f.   *wine, women and song in a downright Luther-like fashion*: Luther is supposed to have said: "He who does not love wine, women and song, Remains a fool his whole life long." The provenance of the saying is doubtful.

l. 29   *Rosengarten*: a medieval German epic from the early 13th century. The monk Ilsan defeats 52 knights in battle and gains the right to kiss the lovely Kriemhild 52 times. All in all, the figure is most unmonklike.

l. 38   *canon law*: the law of the Catholic church, independent of state law.

(579) l. 4   *canonical share*: that portion of a dead person's estate that went to the prelate or bishop.

l. 7   *the denizens of the underworld*: "If I cannot move the gods, I will make the Underworld shake" (Virgil, *Aeneid* 7, 132). The line was used by Freud as motto on the title-page of *The Interpretation of Dreams* (1899).

l. 30   *the refined priestly concept of indulgence*: the forgiving of sins following the payment of money. The practice began in the Middle Ages, at the time of the Crusades. At first, crusaders were forgiven for their future sins (e.g. killing) before they left. Later, relatives were permitted to purchase forgiveness for them. After death, people go to purgatory, in order to do penance for all their sins on earth. Believers could purchase their release from time in purgatory by making a donation to the church. It was the gross abuse of this mechanism (the church increasingly used it simply to raise money) that caused Martin Luther's protest.

(580) l. 14   *peripatetic*: wandering. Appropriate, since the tradition of a wandering dispute goes back to Aristotle, whose school was called peripataeia.

l. 28   *Cerebrum, cerebral...*: Peeperkorn repeats his comments from p. 573, ll. 2f.

(581) l. 14   *a tourist thirsty for knowledge*: cf. note to p. 565, ll. 40f.

ll. 17ff.   *He tilted his head towards his shoulder...*: another description evoking Peeperkorn as a suffering Christ-like figure (cf. p. 560, ll. 19f.).

l. 23   *the sybaritic dimple*: "sybaritic" implies a seeking for pleasure and comfort (cf. note to p. 560, ll. 33f.).

l. 24   *the dancing heathen priest*: cf. p. 568, l. 14.

l. 30   *arguing*: the leitmotif "zanken" is used; cf. note to p. 274, l. 31.

l. 39   *logomachy*: a dispute (in words).

(582) ll. 1ff.   *fear*: the categories become somewhat confused. Peeperkorn's "fear" is caused by his loss of masculinity. Castorp associates Peeperkorn's desire to maintain his masculinity with "honor," and "the zeal for duty"—which are military characteristics.

l. 10   *foehn*: see note to p. 265, l. 18.

l. 31   *Jupiter's bird*: in Greek mythology the eagle was Jupiter's bird and in antiquity it was associated with military victory. In this scene there are hints of Tolstoy and events from his life.

l. 36   *Good fellow*: Peeperkorn addresses the eagle by using the word "Gevatter," which is also associated in German with death: "Gevatter Tod" = Grim Reaper. The connotation renders Peeperkorn's words ironic: he is invoking his own death.

(583) l. 1   *antinomies*: a term used in logic to describe literally means the mutual incompatibility, real or apparent, of two principles.

l. 7   *Platz or Dorf, at an inn in Glaris or Klosters*: Platz and Dorf are the two main sections of Davos (see note to p. 3, l. 2). Glaris and Klosters are places near Davos.

l. 11   *Veltliner*: a variety of white wine grape.

l. 16   *Russian galoshes*: a type of rubber boot that is slipped over shoes to keep them from getting muddy or wet.

l. 21   *North Cape*: see note to p. 419, l. 11f.

(584) l. 6   *Marusya when Joachim...*: cf. p. 523, ll. 14f.

l. 12   *Do give me a timbre-poste*: Chauchat asks him for a postage stamp using the formal form ("Sie").

l. 13   *a gown with a rounded neckline...*: the style of Chauchat's dress is not dissimilar to what Peeperkorn was wearing in bed when Castorp visited him, cf. p. 566, ll. 36ff.

l. 17   *Kirghiz eyes*: cf. notes, to p. 140, l. 4 & p. 143, l. 15.

l. 17   *timbre*: stamp (French).

l. 18   *Tant pis pour vous*: Too bad for you. (She uses the formal form again.)

l. 27   *The world is lost to me now*: This line is from a poem by Friedrich Rückert (1788–1866) that was set to music by Gustav Mahler in 1901.

l. 28   *papyrosa*: cigarette.

l. 39   *With the critical eye of a lover...*: Castorp contemplates what Chauchat has said critically, but in the manner of a lover, i.e. indulgently. However, significant here is the fact that even the woman he loves is subject to his critical eye (as she has been all along).

(585) l. 8   *C'est ça*: That's all.

ll. 22f.   *one time before*: on Walpurgis Night; cf. p. 328, ll. 37ff.

ll. 34f.   *I would ask you to speak in a less fragmentary fashion*: Castorp's sentences are taking on the structure of Peeperkorn's (with which Chauchat is, of course, quite familiar). In this sentence, Chauchat in fact uses the impersonal "one" (not even the formal "you")—thus attempting to render more distance between them.

ll. 36f.   *your practice of guessing at fragments*: he assumes she must be quite good at understanding fragments from living with Peeperkorn.

(586) l. 5   *Voyons, mon ami*: Well then, my friend.

l. 5   *foolish stubbornness*: Chauchat uses an adjective that connects Hans Castorp's manner of speaking to her with the foolishness conventionally permitted at Mardi Gras.

l. 9   *Illness gives you your freedom*: repeating what Chauchat had said to him on Walpurgis Night, cf. p. 332. l. 33.

ll. 26f.   *sur le chantier*: on the docks. Chauchat's characterization of Castorp's profession is rather pejorative.

ll. 29f.   *You can't mean that the way Settembrini does*: for Settembrini, Castorp's planned career as an engineer was a noble calling, exemplifying the Western goal of human progress, aided by the achievements of technology. Chauchat finds such a career—and such a goal—irrelevant; hence her belittling of Castorp's once-planned future.

l. 32 *a wild departure*: a common description of a patient's departure against medical advice; cf. Joachim's departure, p. 413, ll. 11f.

l. 36 *For me it would be deserting the colors*: Castorp's use of the metaphor demonstrates the manner in which the usual ideas about life and duty are thrown into question in the hermetically-sealed world of the Berghof. Whereas his cousin Joachim had "deserted" the rest-cure in order to do his duty as soldier (which he considered more important), Castorp is now clear in his own mind about his own personal choices. For him to leave the sanatorium, as Settembrini seriously and Chauchat flippantly recommend, would be deserting his duty to himself, which he believes lies in exploiting his illness to achieve a better understanding of existence—and thus a higher plane.

(587) l. 8 *Quelle génerosité! Oh là, là, vraiment*: What generosity! Well, well, truly.

l. 9 *homme de génie*: man of genius.

l. 14 *alchemistic, hermetic pedagogy*: although Castorp has his basic knowledge of alchemy from Naphta (cf. p. 501, ll. 17ff.), he has applied it to the nature of the Berghof world and the process he has experienced there. The image suggests that, as if an alchemist's chemical retort, he has been transmuted from base into noble metal (cf. the words that follow: "an enhancement, a transubstantiation to something higher"). While the word does mean the changing of one material into another, in modern usage it signifies the transformation of bread and wine into the body and blood of Christ during the Catholic mass. Castorp's view of his own enlightenment is certainly not modest.

ll. 16f. *Naturally, the substance that is forced upward...*: Castorp is not at all modest about his potential when he arrived at the Berghof.

ll. 18f. *I have been an intimate with sickness and death*: sickness as a potentially ennobling quality is a central idea of the novel (but note that it is not always the case that sickness ennobles: cf. Frau Stöhr and Castorp's remarks about her, p. 95, ll. 11ff.). An acquaintance—even a confrontation—with death (cf. the sub-chapter *Snow*) can lead to (is necessary for) profounder reflections about life—which is the ultimate message of the novel.

ll. 19f. *even as a boy I borrowed a pencil from you*: the episode with Hippe (cf. p. 120, ll. 19ff.) was repeated by the episode on Walpurgis Night (cf. p. 326–27). Chauchat cannot possibly know to what he is referring.

l. 22 *res bina*: the binary principle. Cf. p. 501, ll. 15f.

l. 22 *lapis philosophorum*: the philosopher's stone. Cf. p. 501, ll. 15f.

ll. 23f.   *For the love of death leads to the love of life and humanity*: the Romantic yearning for universality includes an affinity for death (what Thomas Mann called a "sympathy with death"); but the person who overcomes this affinity, this sympathy, can progress to a higher plane on which the love of life and humanity is stronger and more genuine, precisely because death has been faced and overcome. This is, in essence, a reformulation of what Hans Castorp has concluded following his dream in the sub-chapter *Snow*.

l. 24   *it came to me upon my balcony*: now we know what Hans Castorp has been doing all those hours during the rest-cure.

l. 26   *the one is the regular, direct, and good way*: the "conventional," bourgeois view affirms life by duty, achievement, technological progress. Castorp implies that this "good" way, while it does implicitly affirm life, is, in fact, an artificial construct because it suppresses the reality of death: it is a bastion against the inevitability of death and avoids confronting it. As such, it is philosophically and ethically the inferior position. Thomas Mann himself confirmed this on several occasions, most clearly when he wrote a speech on his fiftieth birthday (1925): "There are two ways to embrace life: one that knows nothing about death; this one is rather simple and robust, and another that does know about it, and only this one, I believe, has the full spiritual value. This is the way of artists, poets and writers."

l. 28   *You are a silly philosopher, Hans Castorp*: Chauchat uses the informal form ("du") here. The translation attempts to indicate this by the addition of Hans's name. She also uses the same adjective as before (cf. note to p. 586, l. 5).

l. 31   *en philosophe*: as a philosopher.

ll. 33ff.   Chauchat continues to use the familiar form for her next speech ("That's enough impertinence…"; l. 33), but reverts to the formal form for her following speech ("And with whom you are on such friendly terms…"; p. 588. ll. 5f.).

l. 38   *you knew from Behrens that I was still here*: we are not told how Castorp could possibly know this. Is it merely an assumption on his part? Cf. note to p. 538, ll. 24f.

(588) ll. 5f.   *for your own enrichment*: Chauchat is well aware of the pedagogical nature of Castorp's stay at the Berghof. She reverts here to the formal form of address.

l. 12   *All due deference to your philosophizing*: the familiar form again.

ll. 17ff.   *Do you love him passionately ... He loves me*: the words sink into Hans's consciousness; he will repeat them to Peeperkorn later (see p. 593, ll. 13f.).

ll. 27f.   *the fear of the feeling being left behind in Gethsemane*: Castorp makes the connection between Peeperkorn and Christ. The betrayal of Christ in the garden of Gethsemane is paralleled by Peeperkorn's being "betrayed" by his loss of masculinity. Cf. p. 560, ll. 9ff. & p. 561, l. 32f.

l. 29   *That's not a stupid way to put it, Hans*: the familiar form again.

l. 30   *You understand. Fear of the feeling...*: Naturally, Chauchat must be intimately aware of Peeperkorn's dilemma. She is clearly very impressed with Castorp's reading of the situation.

l. 34   *C'est exact*: Exactly.

l. 34   *There are a lot of worries—you know, difficulties*: her words (and the way in which she is playing with Hans's fingers at this moment) reveal her awareness of Peeperkorn's dilemma and suffering.

l. 37   *Isn't it rather shabby of us...*: Later, when Hans is talking to Peeperkorn about Chauchat, the former will ask the same question of Hans (see p. 600, l. 5f.).

(589) l. 2   *guazzabuglio*: mishmash. Settembrini's word (see p. 455, ll. 3f.).

l. 7   *his fear that his feelings will fail him*: the very tasteful circumlocution raises Peeperkorn's problem to the level of a question about the meaning of life itself.

l. 20   *timbres-poste*: postage stamps.

l. 26f.   *your own egoistic experience*: Chauchat's view of Castorp's stay at the Berghof is still that he is being rather self-indulgent—that he sees all of his experiences (including with her) as elements of his program of personal growth. She has a point.

l. 31   *That was very kind of you*: she uses the familiar form of address.

l. 36   *establish an alliance*: their relationship now enters a new phase; from the erotic it now moves to the platonic. Cf. also p. 590. l. 31, where the narrator speaks of *caritas*. (However, Castorp's erotic love for her never fully disappears, as the sub-chapter *Fullness of Harmony* shows.) Chauchat proposes a "pact" to Castorp (and he accepts): a bond through Chauchat to Peeperkorn. The kiss they exchange is a sealing of love, but it is no longer *eros* (sexual, use of the informal pronoun), but rather *caritas* (non-sexual, use of the formal pronoun, Hans Castorp's pledge to serve someone else, and service to life).

l. 39   *tu sais*: you know (informal).

l. 39f.   *I'm afraid sometimes that something may happen to him*: Chauchat senses already that Peeperkorn may be suicidal.

l. 41   *Enfin*: Well then.

(590) ll. 14f.   *Krokowski's elaborate ... way of speaking*: cf. p. 123, ll. 35ff.

l. 31   *caritas*: love in the non-sexual sense. In the Christian sense "caritas" is love of one's fellow human beings.

(591) l. 6   *Telegraaf*: see note to p. 566, l. 32.

l. 20   *the quartan fever*: see note to p. 546, l. 12.

(592) ll. 4f.   *He has consecrated his citizen's pike...*: originally said by Settembrini of his grandfather (cf. p. 153, ll. 37f.) and restated by Castorp later (cf. p. 383, ll. 21f.).

ll. 5f.   *so that salami will have to pass through customs...*: Hans Castorp's jocular-pejorative reference to Settembrini's ultra-nationalistic stance vis-à-vis Austria (cf. p. 154, ll. 34ff. & p. 440, ll. 40f.).

l. 6   *Brenner Pass*: cf. note to p. 375, l. 10.

ll. 9f.   *he does not enjoy the privilege...*: as already noted (cf. note to p. 54, ll. 22ff.), Settembrini's clothing constitutes an ironic comment on his ideas: they are neat and tidy, but rather threadbare. Peeperkorn is perceptive. Note Hans Castorp's response below (ll. 17f.).

l. 13   *a problem child of life*: Settembrini's term for Hans Castorp, cf. p. 303, l. 12.

ll. 21f.   *he gets his funds from dubious sources*: an elliptical reference to the Jesuits. Cf. Settembrini's comment, p. 402, ll. 19ff.

(593) ll. 13f.   *Do you love him then?*: Castorp takes his specific question to Chauchat (see p. 588, ll. 17ff.) and turns it into a general statement about women and love.

l. 27   *our duty to feel*: Peeperkorn's way of indicating the male obligation to be potent.

l. 28   *the terrible disgrace when the feeling is lacking*: i.e. his feeling of impotence. Note how lucidly he speaks here.

ll. 28f.   *when there is an inability...*: clear statement of Peeperkorn's impotence.

l. 30   *I thirst*: said by Jesus Christ on the cross (cf. *John* 19: 28).

l. 40   *He spilled a little wine...*: the symbolism is obvious (wine = blood).

(594) l. 3   *our manly vigor*: Peeperkorn's meaning could not be clearer. By raising male potency to the religious level, Peeperkorn is endowing it as the highest value in life. That is, life depends on fertility for its continuance, and if the male is not potent, life will cease.

ll. 9ff. *it is an eruption of divine disgrace ... a horror that never leaves the mind*: Peeperkorn's impotence is a "horror" because he sees it as God's judgment on him. Once again, Peeperkorn is quite lucid when talking about the topic that preoccupies him all the time ("...never leaves the mind"; ll. 10f.). Cf. also p. 596, ll. 10f.: "Mynheer spoke in an unusually precise and compact style this afternoon."

l. 11 *He drank*: this final act following this speech is an ironic comment on Peeperkorn's character and opinions.

(596) l. 28 *philopena*: the word derives from a party game in which two people eat the same nut (especially a double nut). Peeperkorn believes that Castorp and Chauchat have made an agreement to speak to each other a certain way (cf. p. 589, l. 36).

l. 41 *bloodstains, red wine stains*: the symbolism is a little less subtle than Thomas Mann's usual style.

(597) ll. 15f. *you found it nonsensical...*: cf. p. 564, ll. 19f.

(598) l. 12 *when I cast aside certain pedagogic fetters*: that is, escaped from the control of Settembrini on Walpurgis Night (cf. p. 326, ll. 31ff.).

l. 14 *a past experience*: Hippe.

ll. 16f. *the use of informal pronouns achieved its full meaning*: a very tasteful way of answering Peeperkorn's indirect question: "You were Clavdia's lover during her previous stay here" (p. 597, ll. 41f.). Cf. also p. 598, ll. 7ff.

ll. 28ff. *whether or not you count...*: Hans Castorp has admitted that he and Clavdia were lovers, but excuses the event by describing it as merely an episode at Carnival time, when the normal rules of behavior are suspended. As such, it didn't really happen ("And so it would have been only half a lie had I denied your observation"; ll. 32f.)

l. 37 *a grievous loss*: a better translation would be: a painful loss.

(599) ll. 7ff. *And there was one more reason, Herr Peeperkorn...*: the entire following paragraph is a jumble of ideas that tumble from Hans Castorp's mind and mouth. One can imagine the speed with which he tries to justify himself and extract himself from a difficult and embarrassing situation. In his attempt to explain away his rendezvous with Chauchat as something innocuous, he expresses his own suspicion that she earlier had an affair with Behrens (for how could Behrens have painted that picture of her without their having become intimate?). The speech is very humorous.

l. 17 *precedents ... predecessors*: the translator's clever attempt to render Mann's play on words here. Castorp speaks of "Vorgänge" (events) and "Vorgänger" (predecessors).

l. 34 *a while ago*: cf. pp. 592, ll. 41 ff.

l. 39 *to call myself 'the man'*: the original is more drastic, as Castorp says: "I would feel boastful and tasteless if I referred to myself as a "man," whereas Clavdia is certainly a woman." The implication is that Castorp is not a very masculine person—just as Chauchat with her lack of children, her androgynous figure, and her similarity to Hippe, is by no means a typical woman.

(600) ll. 5f. *Isn't it rather shabby of us to speak about her in this way?*: Chauchat had asked Castorp the same question when they were talking about Peeperkorn (cf. p. 588, l. 37).

ll. 8f. *humane*: Castorp uses Chauchat's word.

l. 9 *freedom and genius*: more words borrowed from his recent conversation with Chauchat, cf. p. 587, ll. 10ff.

l. 10 *But only recently I had occasion...*: in his conversation with Chauchat (cf. pp. 587f.).

l. 16 *beyond the Caucasus*: cf. notes to p. 134, l. 42 & p. 495, l. 15.

ll. 18f. *it is her illness that confers such freedom upon her*: a recasting of what Chauchat had asserted on Walpurgisnight, cf. p. 332, l. 34.

(601) ll. 8f. *women do not particularly enjoy seeing their lovers getting along*: this is the first time in this long conversation that Castorp had actually admitted (without circumlocution) being her lover.

ll. 22ff. *I've been up here a long time...*: he has been at the Berghof for two and a half years—but more significant is his loss of a sense of time.

l. 30 *it may bring nations closer together*: Settembrini's phrase from p. 153, l. 1.

l. 32 *they lie in darkness...*: Castorp ascribes his abandoning of the engineering profession to his innate (initially unconscious) opposition to the bourgeois ethic. His being attracted to Chauchat is a manifestation of his true nature: his "sympathy with death" and the attraction of the "darker" side of existence.

l. 38 *her eyes met mine and fascinated me*: because they reminded him of Hippe.

(602) l. 6 *the flatland is entirely lost to me now*: this is the third allusion to the song by Friedrich Rückert (cf. p. 195, l. 37 & p. 584, l. 27).

ll. 9ff. *I once read a story...*: it is the opera *Carmen* by Georges Bizet (1875). The story has great significance for Hans Castorp, although it should be noted that he interprets it so as to mirror his perceptions of his own situation. He has obviously been familiar with the opera, at least superficially, for some time: earlier he had heard extracts from it on his balcony (cf. p. 161, l. 26), and he had once suggested to Joachim that they go down to the Kurhaus in the hope of hearing a concert, during which

Castorp hoped to hear "…that aria from Carmen: 'Through every long and lonely hour, in prison there I kept your flower'" (cf. p. 232, ll. 28f.). In the later sub-chapter *Fullness of Harmony* the opera will gain its full significance for him as a reflection of his relationship with Chauchat (see p. 637–39). His recalling of the opera here—"A pointless story really … But then, why did it occur to me?" (ll. 20f.)—indicates the effect that the opera has had on his subconscious mind.

l. 20   *A rather pointless story…*: it is, of course, anything but pointless. For Castorp it has direct relevance to himself and his relationship to Chauchat (cf. also his recounting of the plot of the opera in the sub-chapter *Fullness of Harmony*, p. 637, ll. 18ff.).

(603) ll. 4ff.   *a bond of brotherhood…*: this forms a precise parallel to the alliance that Castorp had recently entered with Chauchat.

l. 11   *Link arms with me*: drinking to friendship (brotherhood) involves linking the arms while taking a drink. Thereafter, the two people use the familiar form of address to each other. See note to p. 556, l. 10.

l. 13   *Are you satisfied, Hans Castorp*: this is the translator's way of letting us know that Peeperkorn addresses Hans with the familiar second-person pronoun for the first time.

l. 14   *Mynheer Peeperkorn*: Hans still avoids using the familiar pronoun and, in fact, utters it only near the end of the sub-chapter (cf. l. 29).

l. 23   *being but a woman, may not be quite so pleased…*: Hans Castorp is being sly yet again. He can imagine Clavdia's reaction when she hears Castorp and Peeperkorn using the familiar form to each other—he might well say that she "may not be quite so pleased."

l. 27   *Our beloved*: Peeperkorn admits to their joint status.

l. 29   *Fare thee well*: Hans uses the familiar form for the first time—but he reverts to the formal form in the very next sentence. From here to the end of the sub-chapter he is still uncertain about which form to use.

l. 31   *this rash form of address*: a form, however, that he had no problem using when talking to Settembrini (on Mardi Gras) or Chauchat (in three conversations).

l. 32   *Herr Settembrini bursting in…*: as he had done when Castorp was day-dreaming about Chauchat (see p. 189, ll. 37 ff.).

l. 35   *You'll have at least three days…*: familiar form, followed by the formal form ("[you] will be able to meet each day's demands").

l. 36   *will be able to meet each day's demands*: i.e. he wishes Peeperkorn might recover his potency (and implies thereby that he himself has no more sexual claim to Chauchat).

l. 37   *as if I were you*: familiar form.

(604) *Mynheer Peeperkorn (Conclusion)*

l. 4   *he had a special fondness for falling water*: the reference is to his walk in the Hippe sub-chapter (cf. p. 117, l. 12: "falling water").

ll. 14f.   *His little circle of seven friends*: the number symbolism is maintained.

l. 29   *quartan fever*: see note to p. 546, l. 12.

(605) ll. 4f.   *In his public conversations with Peeperkorn ...*: Castorp finds himself now trying to avoid revealing his familiarity with both Peeperkorn and Chauchat.

l. 7   *philopena*: the word that Peeperkorn had used (p. 596, l. 28) to describe Castorp's behavior towards Chauchat. For his part Peeperkorn similarly avoids the second person (cf. p. 605, l. 37: "How are you doing, my son") which in the original reads: "How goes it, my son?"

l. 16   *quartan attack*: see note to p. 546, l. 12.

l. 24   *two landaus*: an open carriage capable of seating four people.

l. 31   *ulster*: see note to p. 5, l. 32.

(606) l. 26   *Summer Night's Dream*: the translation is a little too literal. The German "Sommernachtstraum" is Shakespeare's *A Midsummer Night's Dream*.

(607) ll. 1ff.   Wehsal's outburst is a more extreme version of what Castorp suffers in silence.

l. 21   *and tears roll down his cheeks*: cf. note to p. 169, ll. 28f.

(608) l. 20   *metempsychosis*: transmigration of souls.

ll. 20f.   *hydrostatics*: laws of the movement of fluids.

ll. 36ff.   *But there was a story...*: a story by Charles Perrault (French fairy-tale writer, 1628–1703) tells of a bad-tempered girl who refuses to give an old woman a drink of water and whom the latter curses by causing her to produce snakes and toads every time she opens her mouth. "She made herself so hateful that her own mother drove her out of the house. No one would take in the miserable girl, so at last she went into a corner of the woods and died."

(610) l. 7   *bareheaded*: the fact that all the men are bareheaded signifies their tacit allegiance to the Berghof environment. See also note to p. 5, l. 32.

ll. 25ff.   *waterfall*: the waterfall is fictitious, although several commentators have surmised that it is based on Thomas Mann's memory of certain locations.

ll. 38f.   *menacing, threatening trumpet calls and brutal male voices*: the master of the Dionysian revels, Peeperkorn, has led them to a place in nature where those revels may be imagined. However, there is a further metaphorical dimension here: the vocabulary also connotes associations with the First World War (also an expression of Dionysian excesses).

(611) ll. 28ff. *Herr Settembrini...*: the democrat is powerless against the might of Nature.

l. 30 *flung one hand above his head..*: a typical gesture—as he had done on Walpurgis Night when Hans Castorp had moved towards Chauchat (cf. p. 326, ll. 24f.). Cf. also note to p. 488, l. 40.

ll.41ff. *And suddenly he began to speak....*: Peeperkorn's "speech" is drowned out by the sound of the waterfall: even his majestic personality must bow before the force of Nature.

(612) l. 23 *the image of the Man of Sorrows*: the parallel with Christ is evoked once again (cf. note to p. 560, ll. 33f.).

ll. 24f. *sybaritic roguishness...*: see note to p. 560, ll. 33f. This is the third time that Peeperkorn has been portrayed as both Christ and Dionysus (cf. p. 560, ll. 33ff.; p. 581, ll. 17ff.). The heathen priest, with whom Peeperkorn had also earlier been identified (cf. note to p. 562, l, 17) is also evoked here (l. 25).

ll. 40f. *Almost nothing was said on the ride home*: Peeperkorn is really coming "home": the next night he is dead.

(614) l. 24 *the notions department*: i.e. the department of a large store where items for sewing, etc. may be purchased.

(615) l. 12 *The dose cannot have been all that large...*: these remarks by Behrens recall Peeperkorn's edification of Hans Castorp earlier (cf. p. 568–70), during which he stressed both the small doses needed and the interaction of the vegetable and the mineral.

l. 14 *Dynamics*: Peeperkorn's emphasis on the "dynamic" nature of the interaction (p. 569, l. 21 & l. 37) is recalled here by Castorp as he completes Behrens's sentence.

l. 30 *adopting formal pronouns himself*: the occasion demands formality; the formal pronouns are a defense-mechanism against the overpowering feeling of loss. In addition, the use of the formal pronoun confirms the change in the relationship between Castorp and Chauchat: it has now retreated inside the bounds of Western civilized society—and that is why he can now kiss her on the brow (cf. p. 616, l. 6).

ll. 36f. *for him the failure of feeling in the face of life ... a divine disgrace*: Castorp quotes Peeperkorn's own words (see p. 594, l. 10).

ll. 38f. *he regarded himself as God's instrument of marriage*: with a sexual implication. Dionysus and Christ are joined in an act of consummation, both sexual and spiritual—the sum of three and four.

l. 39 *That was a bit of royal foolishness*: even in the face of Peeperkorn's "majestic" personality, Castorp retains his critical faculty.

(616) l. 1   *C'est une abdication*: It was the easy way out. The French word ("abdication") is suitably ambiguous: it means taking the easy way out, but also implies (fittingly) a royal abdication. (Thomas Mann himself used the word in a letter to describe Peeperkorn's suicide.)

The Great Stupor

l. 23   *the poison of imperial tedium*: Behrens is referring to the dissatisfaction expressed in some quarters with the unification of Germany in 1871. He uses the reference to warn Castorp not to complain.

(617) ll. 2f.   *Your symptoms of toxification have not squared with the undeniable improvement in your localized condition*: this is a medical diagnosis, but it also has a metaphorical meaning. Hans Castorp's "localized condition" is much better since he has achieved more clarity about the meaning of his life.

ll. 5f.   *even the worst grouser and crepehanger...*: His Imperial Majesty, Kaiser William II (1888–1918) was renowned for saying: "I will not tolerate pessimists" ("crepehangers").

ll. 18f.   *from the first your symptoms should not have been traced exclusively to tuberculosis*: Behrens now realizes that Castorp's "illness" is not caused by tuberculosis—but he still gives the wrong diagnosis.

l. 22   *coccus*: cf. note to p. 193, l. 30.

l. 25   *a strep infection*: a streptococcal (strep) infection is caused by streptococcus, a bacterium responsible for a variety of health problems.

(618) l. 1   *these poor things but thine own*: probably untranslatable reference to a well-known line from Goethe's Faust, when Mephistopheles says: "Das sind die Kleinen/Von den Meinen" ("These are the small ones of mine"). It is appropriate that Behrens should refer to a line by Mephistopheles, as Settembrini had earlier called him "the imp of Satan" (cf. note to p. 94, l. 31). The colloquial saying "small, but yours" ("klein, aber dein") had occurred earlier (cf. p. 328, l. 5).

l. 4   *strepto-vaccine therapy*: the tubercular patient with other symptoms was given inoculations to combat the secondary infection. These inoculations were developed from blood samples taken from the patient. It was a disputed and questionable procedure—and one that Thomas Mann's wife, Katia, had been subjected to (with negative results).

l. 13   *cocci*: see note to p. 193, l. 30.

l. 33   *"brother"*: because Peeperkorn and Castorp had drunk to "brotherhood"—i.e. agreed to use the familiar form of address to each other (cf. p. 603, ll. 4ff.).

(619) ll. 9f. *life without time*...: in the course of the novel his subjective experience of time has resulted in a loss of the awareness of the passing of time. The sameness of every day (first experienced when he was confined to his bed; cf. p. 180, ll. 21ff.) has led not just to a sense that time stands still, but also a loss of temporal orientation. The latter is closely related to the embracing of "Asiatic" values.

l. 27 *à la Lumière*: August and Louis Lumière were most famous for their contributions to the invention of moving pictures, but in 1907 they also developed the "autochrome" which was the first viable color photograph process—from which Hans Castorp has benefited insofar as he has Chauchat's x-ray picture. This chapter of the novel takes place in 1910.

l. 28 *the flash of magnesium*: the early form of flash photography.

(620) l. 8 *Milka nougats*: a creation of the Suchard chocolate factory in Switzerland. Milk was first added to chocolate in 1901 and the name "Milka" from "Milch" (milk) and "Kakao" (cocoa) was registered as a trade-mark.

l. 8 *chocolat à la crème d'amandes*: chocolate with almond cream.

l. 8 *Marquis napolitains*: Neapolitans, waffles with a hazelnut filling.

l. 9 *cat's tongues*: long, oval, thin chocolate wafers.

ll. 10f. *Sketching pigs*...: see p. 325, ll. 11 ff., where Behrens ("a high-placed personage"; p. 620, l. 11) organized the pig-drawing game on Walpurgis Night—with fateful consequences for Hans Castorp.

ll. 22f. *know it from the Director himself*: as he had advocated earlier, cf. p. 409, l. 13.

l. 36 *the arrival of his Egyptian Fatima*: cf. p. 538, ll. 22ff.

l. 39f. *the clear-eyed goddess*: i.e. mathematics. Athena, the goddess of wisdom, was so named in Homer's *Odyssey*.

(621) l. 4 *the squaring of the circle*: an insoluble problem.

l. 16 *Zacharias Dase*: (1824–61) possessed the ability of doing arithmetic very rapidly in his head—and demonstrated this talent in public performances. The value of pi, calculated to 200 places, was the subject of an article that Dase published in a mathematical journal in 1844.

l. 26 *Archimedes*: 287–212 BC; Greek mathematician, physicist, engineer, inventor, and astronomer.

(623) l. 13 *Esperanto*: a constructed (i.e. not natural) language. Its name derives from Doktoro Esperanto, the pseudonym under which the inventor of the language, L. L. Zamenhof, published the first book describing it, the *Unua Libro*, in 1887.

l. 22 *solitaire*: Solitaire, also called Patience (the word used in German), is any of a family of single-player card games.

l. 27   *elevens*: card game explained in the text (ll. 27ff.).

(624) ll. 4f.   *to "bother" him...*: a recurring leitmotif, cf. note to p. 546, ll. 23f.

l. 6   *Accidente!*: an Italian cry of surprise.

l. 12   *thirty-two*: i.e. he has just started his thirty-third game, after playing the game successfully three times; note the number symbolism.

l. 19   *the Freemason*: cf. note to p. 497, l. 37.

ll. 19f.   *The Balkan League*: an alliance of Serbia, Montenegro, Greece and Bulgaria against the Ottoman Empire during the Balkan Wars (1912–13). In Settembrini's eyes the League is aimed at Austria-Hungary.

l. 25   *Sarmatian despotism*: cf. note to p. 507, l. 30. Settembrini's argument is that, as much as he hates the Austro-Hungarian Empire, he is loath to give his support to the members of the Balkan League, because this would further the aims of the Russians, whom he disparagingly calls "Sarmatians"—i.e. primitive and uncivilized.

l. 39   *placet experiri*: see note to p. 96, l. 14.

(625) l. 10   *a thunderstorm*: Hans Castorp is unwittingly foreseeing the First World War, cf. the final chapter of the novel, *The Thunderbolt* (pp. 696ff.).

l. 12   *Last Judgement*: in Christian belief, the Last Judgment is the judgment by God of all nations. It will take place after the resurrection of the dead and the Second Coming (cf. *Revelation* 20: 12–15).

l. 17   *In its fraternity jargon and cadence...*: Behrens always speaks in a very colorful manner, and his speeches are filled with the jargon of German university fraternity life.

l. 25   *a Sister of Mercy*: this not the religious order founded in Ireland in 1831, but rather the German organization of Roman-Catholic nursing sisters, founded in Alsace in 1734.

ll. 32f.   *seated nowadays at the upper end of the Good Russian table*: Castorp has taken the seat formerly occupied by Peeperkorn.

l. 37   *tubercle bacillus*: the full name for TB and the primary cause of tuberculosis.

l. 41   *cocci*: see note to p. 617, l. 22.

(626) l.1   *tubercles*: in anatomy, a tubercle is a round nodule, small eminence, or warty outgrowth found on bones, skin, or within the lungs in tuberculosis. Here, however, the reference is to the tubercle bacillus which was at this time carried by almost everyone.

l. 11   *strepto-vaccine therapy*: see note to p. 618, l. 4.

Fullness of Harmony

This sub-chapter is of central importance. We have already seen the increasingly significant role that music has played in the novel. From the first word (*Vorsatz* in the German; see the note to p. xi for a discussion of its multiple meanings), music has been present and has been employed to express the novel's themes. We had been told that "Hans Castorp loved music with all his heart, its effect being much like that of the porter he drank with his morning snack—profoundly calming, numbing, and 'doze'-inducing" (p. 36, ll. 24ff.). Music's soporific effect had caused Settembrini to question its ethical content and to condemn it as "politically suspect" (see p. 112, l. 33). At other times throughout the novel, too, music had played a significant role. But in this sub-chapter music—and its ultimate significance for Hans Castorp—receives full treatment. It is no longer the merely soporific effect that holds sway (although he does still dream a little as he listens), but rather the profound personal significance that certain pieces of music have for him. The five selections discussed in detail in this chapter—they are his favorites in the Berghof's collection of recordings—are related by Castorp directly to his own experiences and fate at the sanatorium. It is important to recognize that these interpretations are highly personal—even eccentric—because Castorp reinterprets the selections to accord with his own world-view and in the light of what has happened to him. In essence, the description and discussion of the musical selections that fascinate and enthrall him constitute a reprise of the major themes of the novel. Castorp's intensified fascination with music also demonstrates his growth: as idiosyncratic as his interpretations of his favorite selections are, they nevertheless lead him to important conclusions, especially with regard to the final selection, Schubert's "Lindenbaum." It should be noted that *every* musical selection that is mentioned in this sub-chapter has relevance to the central issues of the novel. Even though the pieces of music that are mentioned before Hans Castorp takes charge of the gramophone are ostensibly played for the mere entertainment of all the guests, these selections nevertheless have direct relevance to the world of the Berghof and even to Castorp himself. This sub-chapter is rich in metaphorical allusions and leitmotifs: the text repeatedly refers back to earlier motifs and events, and the allusiveness of this sub-chapter surpasses perhaps any other in the novel.

(627) ll. 5f. *the stereoscopic viewer*...: on these three items cf. notes to p. 85, ll. 5–10.

ll. 20f.   *no wretched crank-box*...: the gramophone was invented in 1887 by Emil Berliner (1851–1929), and the earliest models had to be operated mechanically and had a large trumpet-like attachment to magnify the sound.

ll. 24f.   *stained a dull black*: the choice of color is deliberate (connoting death), as we will discover a few pages later when Hans Castorp settles down to listen to his favorite pieces (cf. p. 633, ll. 13ff.). It is entirely appropriate that the gramophone (symbolizing death) should be introduced by Behrens (cf. ll. 38ff.) who as Rhadamanthus rules over the dead. The gramophone becomes the focal point of Hans Castorp's latest reflections on love and loss, life and death.

l. 31   *ebonite*: a very hard rubber (the name comes from a brand name). However, although the first recording disks were, indeed, made of ebonite, after 1896 disks of shellac were used, as the sound quality was superior. Thus the reference to "ebonite disks" is anachronistic, as the events in this sub-chapter take place in 1912 or 1913.

l. 34   *sinuous tube ... pliant, movable joints*: the playing arm of the gramophone connotes Chauchat's arm.

l. 40   *warehouse*: a mistranslation. In the original Behrens asserts that there is nothing better in the "genre" (i.e. of its type)—but he pronounces the French word in an eccentric way.

(628) l. 3   *Stradivarius*: A Stradivarius is a stringed instrument built by members of the Stradivari family, especially by Antonio Stradivari (1644–1737).

l. 3   *Guarneri*: Guarneri is the family name of a group of highly acclaimed violin-makers from Cremona in Italy in the 17th and 18th centuries.

l. 4   *raffinemang*: Behrens's attempt to reproduce the pronunciation the French pronoun "raffinement" (refinement).

l. 4   *Polyhymnia*: a fictional brand name, but appropriate, since Polyhymnia was the Greek muse of song.

l. 7   *There's the library*: Behrens actually says "literature"—which is more appropriate because the texts that accompany many of the musical selections are of great significance.

l. 12   *books laden with hidden magic*: this phrase ("Zauberbücher") establishes the close connection between music and the novel's themes. The word "magic" recurs many times throughout this sub-chapter, especially later in relation to the "Lindenbaum" song.

ll. 20f.   *a toe-tapping Offenbach overture*: the first selection made by Behrens is a perfect example of Thomas Mann's subtle technique. All the pieces of music—even those whose name is not given, but whose provenance we can detect (there are seven of them)—invite us to connote a wealth of associations, most of which relate to Chauchat and what she represents. In this case, Jacques Offenbach's overture to his opera *Orpheus and Eurydice* (1858) conjures up the Underworld (where the action of the opera takes place), which is the designation that Settembrini had given the Berghof soon after Hans Castorp's arrival (cf. p. 56, ll. 1ff.; the association of the Berghof with the Underworld has been noted repeatedly throughout the novel). Death is, of course, also evoked by the reference: music and death are closely allied in this sub-chapter. Furthermore, the specific mention of the aria: "Ach, ich habe sie verloren" ("Oh, I have lost her"; l. 26) invites us to make the connection with Castorp's loss of Chauchat. Note that the recording is instrumental only, but the narrator deliberately gives us the title of the aria, so that we might draw the connection to Castorp. Offenbach's aria is, in fact, a parody of the famous aria in Gluck's *Orpheus and Eurydice* (1762): "Che faro sensa Eurydice" ("What will I do without Eurydice?")—which in the German version reads: "What will I do without you, whom I love so ardently?"

There is a delicious irony in the fact that Behrens would choose this piece of music as the first one to be played—since he is both Director of this particular Underworld (i.e. the Berghof) and also fully aware of Castorp's loss of Chauchat (a loss that perhaps he himself is feeling, too).

l. 29   *tutti*: musical term meaning "all together."

l. 37   *shameless cancan*: most appropriate for the Berghof, where licentious behavior has been the norm. In the opera the cancan is performed by a chorus-line of gods and goddesses as part of a revel in Hades. On Walpurgis Night Castorp and Chauchat did not perform the cancan, but he did ask her to dance (cf. p. 329, l. 12).

(629) ll. 1f.   *a celebrated Italian baritone*: perhaps Tito Ruffo (1877–1953).

ll. 7ff.   *a showpiece aria*: Figaro's opening aria from Rossini's *The Barber of Seville* (1816). The description that follows is clearly intended to connote satirically the figure of Settembrini and his manner of "performing" (cf. "the art of his phrasing," "a master of the irresistible effect," "a virtuoso," etc.)—especially since the performance ends—"or so it seemed" (this is a *sound* recording)—with "one hand thrust in the air" (l. 14) which is a gesture typical of Settembrini (cf. p. 156, ll. 40f.; p. 369, l. 5; p. 488, l. 40; p. 611, l. 30). The fact that the listeners at the Berghof also "almost died laughing" (l. 9) at his performance adds to the aura of satire.

ll. 8f.   *eh, il barbiere. Di qualità, di qualità! Figaro qua, Figaro là, Figaro, Figaro, Figaro*: hey, the barber. The best, the best! Figaro come here, Figaro, go there, Figaro, Figaro!

l. 9   *parlando falsetto*: parlando singing is a style where the rhythm—and often the pitch—of the tune are usually observed, but the "singing" sounds more like the speaking voice than the singing voice. Falsetto describes a male singing in a high register (actually, sung in the female range) in a voice that cannot blend with the (normal) chest voice.

l. 13   *aria da capo*: from the beginning again. The phrase "native aria da capo" is actually a reference to the custom in Italian opera houses of calling out "da capo" to a performer after a particularly bravura performance, as an invitation to sing an encore.

ll. 17f.   *A French horn ... folk song*: one can only speculate what piece this might be (one scholar suggested it might be some variations on an Austrian folksong). The instrument invites, however, wider connotations to other elements of the novel. First, horns have appeared throughout the novel as an important leitmotif. During his *Snow* experience Hans Castorp had recalled the lifeguard blowing his horn on the beach at Sylt to warn those who had dared to brave the dangerous surf (cf. p. 467, l. 29). The warning horn is transferred in his mind to Settembrini, whose cupped hands and cry of warning remind him of his childhood experience (cf. p. 468, l. 25), and who henceforth is identified with the warning voice of reason. Thus the seemingly innocuous piece of music on the "French horn" reminds us of Hans Castorp's *Snow* experience, particularly as we are told that the horn's variations are "discreet" (p. 629, l. 17), a phrase that recurs in the discussion of the "Lindenbaum" (p. 643, ll. 2f., translated as "with some caution") in connection with Hans Castorp's memory of Settembrini's warning against relapsing into Romanticism. But it suggests other associations, too: this horn evokes the French horns of *Carmen*. Indeed, there is a direct verbal connection to the later discussion of this opera (cf. p. 637, ll. 18ff.) where the bugles that sound retreat are first called "trumpets ... a bugle call" (p. 637, ll. 28f.), then "French bugles—or Spanish horns" (p. 638, l. 22). Thus even as brief an item as this French horn playing "lovely, discreet variations on a folk song" connotes a wealth of wider associations.

l. 19   *La Traviata*: by Giuseppe Verdi (1853). The story of this opera is relevant to Hans Castorp's fate: the tubercular Violetta, a courtesan, has an affair with a young middle-class man, Alfredo. She gives him a flower that she asks him to return (cf. Chauchat and her pencil). After a visit from Alfredo's father, she abandons Alfredo, and by the time she and Alfredo are reunited, she is confined to her bed and dying of tuberculosis.

The aria is most probably "Ah, fors a lui…" from Scene Five of Act One, in particular, the third part of this aria: "Sempre libera." In the first part of the aria ("E strano"), the consumptive Violetta asks herself if she could truly be in love, for, if so, it would be the first time a man had set her heart on fire. In the following section she wonders whether Alfredo might be the man she has always dreamed about: "He, who in quiet vigil stood before my door and infected me with a new fever..." However, her lyrical mood is interrupted by new doubts about herself and she asks: "What can I hope for? What can I do?" She answers: "Find pleasure, perish in the vortex of the senses!"—at which point the music reaches a climax of lyrical and dramatic intensity. The final section of the aria ("Sempre libera...") is an assertion that freedom and pleasure are the twin poles of her existence. The relation of this aria to Chauchat—at least in Castorp's mind—is obvious. The words of the final aria ("Sempre libera...") echo Chauchat's declaration that "it is more moral to lose oneself and let oneself be ruined than to save oneself" (p. 334). This musical selection also relates to *La Bohème* (where the heroine also dies of something akin to consumption) and to *Carmen*. The singer is perhaps Luisa Tetrazzini (1871–1940).

    ll. 19f.   *the ghost of a world-famous violinist*: the violinist Joseph Szigeti (1892–1973) identified himself as the performer.

    l. 21   *romance by Rubenstein*: from *Soirées de St. Petersburg* (*Evenings in St. Petersburg*) by Artur Rubenstein (1829–1894). Originally a piece for piano, it had been adapted for piano and violin. (Scholars disagree about which work it is: either Romance in F-sharp, no. 11, opus 75, or Romance in E-flat major, opus 44, No. 1.) The oblique reference to St. Petersburg arouses, of course, associations with Chauchat. Furthermore, the piece sounds as if it is being played "as if behind veils"—which connotes Hans Castorp's fascination with Chauchat's arm behind its sleeve of gauze (cf. p. 126, ll. 25ff.), but even more to the references to the voices of Hippe and Chauchat as being "veiled" (cf. p. 118, l. 33 & p. 327, ll. 26f.), as well as the characterization of Hippe's and Chauchat's eyes as having a "veiled, dusky look" (cf. p. 119, ll. 38f. & p. 143, ll. 12f.). Note: it is still Behrens who is choosing the records.

    l. 24   *the latest imports*: the tango had been developed at the end of the 19th century in Buenos Aires and Montevideo, and had been imported to Europe around 1910.

    (630) ll. 17f. *Barcarole*: from Offenbach's opera *The Tales of Hoffmann* (1881). (A barcarole is a folk song sung by Venetian gondoliers, or a piece of music composed in that style.) It is not clear who requested or selected this work, but its ironical relevance to Hans Castorp is significant. First, the opera deals with tuberculosis—and it does so in a critical, satirical manner. Second, this particular piece of music, we are told, "sounded sweet enough to their ears" (i.e. the patients listening). Well it might have, since it is acts as yet another commentary on Castorp's personal situation. In the opera Hoffmann, a bachelor, has a male companion, Niklausse, whose caring attitude towards him becomes somewhat ambiguous as the plot unfolds. In the famous "Barcarole" Hoffmann joins with Giulana, a courtesan who wishes to destroy him:

Le temps fuit et sans retour emporte nos tendresses
Zéphirs embrasés, versez-vous nos caresses,
Zéphirs embrasés, donnez-nous vos baisers,
Belle nuit, ô nuit d'amour, souris à nos ivresses,
Nuit plus douce, que le jour, o belle nuit d'amour!

Time flies and carries off our acts of tenderness, never to return
Glowing winds, bathe us with our caresses,
Glowing winds, give us your kisses,
Beautiful night, o night of love, smile on our passion,
Night sweeter than day, o beautiful night of love!

Whoever requested that particular record was clearly fully aware of Hans Castorp's amorous night at the Berghof! There is also a further dimension to this reference: in the opera the figure of Hoffmann's companion Niklausse is played by a mezzo-soprano in a so-called "trouser-role" (i.e. a woman playing a man). This fact connotes Hans Castorp's interest in sexual ambiguity, his identification of Chauchat with Hippe, his attraction to "his" flower, the blue ranunculus, which he himself describes as "bisexual" (cf.p. 358, ll. 1ff.), his musings on the ambiguity of "son crayon" (cf. note to p. 480, l. 10), and his discussions of "res bina" and "prima materia" (p. 501, ll. 21). His relationship to his cousin Joachim may well be latently homoerotic—which would also relate to this seemingly innocuous recording.

l. 21   *How like them*: Hans Castorp disapproves of the other patients' untidiness in respect of the records, but his criticism is ironically undermined by the fact that his own slipshod conduct leads to the recording of Valentine's Prayer being found in the séance room (cf. p. 670, ll. 33ff.).

l. 39   *ebonite disks*: cf. note to p. 627, l. 31.

(631) l. 11   *artistic folk songs*: there is a body of musical works in German music that consists of folk songs adapted by classical composers into a new "artistic" form ("Kunstlied").

ll. 13f.   *There was one in particular…*: this is Schubert's "Lindenbaum" that will become one of Hans Castorp's favorite recordings and whose significance for him will be discussed later (see pp. 640–43). It is, of course, important that he has known it "since childhood," as this reconfirms his innate affinity to the Romantic world-view.

ll. 37f.   *vibrato and portamento*: vibrato is a musical effect, produced by a regular pulsating change of pitch. Portamento primarily denotes a vocal slide between two pitches.

(632) ll. 5f. *Blick' ich umher...*: "When I look around this noble circle." Aria from the opera *Tannhäuser* (1845) by Richard Wagner (1813–83). At the Venusberg (in Thuringia, in the vicinity of Eisenach), Tannhäuser is held a willing captive through his love for Venus. (The relationship of the opera to Castorp's view of his own situation is obvious.) Tannhäuser escapes from the spell of Venus (i.e. merely sexual pleasure) and finds himself at the Wartburg Castle, where a singers' competition on the subject of "love's awakening" is to be held. The aria referred to here in the novel is sung by the minnesinger Wolfram (minne-singer = medieval poet-singer). In his aria Wolfram sings of the "pure essence of love" which he imagines as "a magical spring into which my spirit gazes full of wonderment." Pure love is platonic and must never be sullied, and he is always ready to sacrifice himself to this ideal.

Key themes of the opera are the struggle between sacred and profane love, and redemption through love (a theme running through almost all Wagner's mature work). The opera has already been alluded to several times before this in the novel (cf. p. 64, l. 15, p. 83, l. 17, p. 147, l. 11, p. 290, l. 29, & p. 546, l. 35), but here Hans Castorp encounters it more immediately and intimately. Nevertheless, this selection really does not reflect what Castorp has experienced with Chauchat. It is not surprising, therefore that this recording is not one of his favorite selections: Wolfram's aria lacks the erotic element, and Castorp is more like Tann-häuser, subject to the seductive attractions of love. (In the opera Tannhäuser responds: "I know love only through the enjoyment of it.") This is the first indication that Castorp will interpret his favorite record-ings in a highly idiosyncratic way.

ll. 9ff.   *duet from a modern Italian opera*: from *La Bohème* (1896) by Giacomo Puccini (1858–1924). The six lines that describe this selection are filled with highly suggestive associations. The duet, as is stated, begins with "Da mi il braccio, mia piccina" ("Give me your arm, my little one"; with no apostrophe after "Da"). This line is sung by Rodolfo to the tuber-cular Mimi at the end of the first act. Mimi's response ("her answering melodic phrase") is "Obbedisco signor!" ("I obey, sir!"). Rodolfo asks Mimi to tell him that she loves him, whereupon she sings ("with aban-don," according to the stage direction): "I love you!" and the two leave the stage arm in arm. The last three lines of the act are heard off-stage:

Rodolfo: Say that you love me!
Mimi: I love you.

Both: Love! Love! Love!

All this (and the Berghof recording most likely begins earlier in the scene), clearly reflects in Castorp's mind his love for Chauchat: he is Rodolfo, she is Mimi, and when alone, they express their love and exit arm in arm. Castorp finds that there could be "nothing on earth more tender" than Rodolfo's line: "Give me your arm, my little one," and what the narrator call the "intense mingling of emotions" (p. 632, l. 10f.) between the two singers is nothing less than Hans Castorp's own wishful thinking. (N.B. Castorp's fascination with Chauchat's arm; cf. p. 126, l. 24.)

l. 11   *a world-famous tenor*: Enrico Caruso (1873–1921).

ll. 12f.   *a little soprano…*: Nelly Melba (1861–1931).

l. 15   *Hans Castorp flinched*: A delicious piece of irony: immediately after Mimi has sung her line: "I obey, sir!," Behrens enters the room. Just Settembrini had earlier interrupted Hans Castorp's day-dreams about Chauchat, so now his enjoyment of his latest reverie about her is impaired by the unwanted interruption of the Hofrat. His guilty reaction reveals the sensitivity of the operatic allusions in his mind.

l. 18   *lab assistant*: although the literal meaning is that Hans Castorp is Behrens's assistant where the gramophone is concerned, Castorp as Behrens's "lab assistant" makes him an ally with death.

l. 30   *cantabile*: the first half of a double aria.

(633) l. 13   *this little truncated coffin*: death is connoted again. Music and death are inextricably entwined.

ll. 15f.   *head on one shoulder, mouth open…*: his typical attitude when listening to music (cf. p. 109, ll. 39f.).

The five favorite recordings that Hans Castorp listens to constitute, in essence, a reprise of the major themes of the novel. In each case Castorp interprets text and music in a manner that is both selective and distorting: the interpretations are tailored to his personal situation.

ll. 40ff.   *One small group of records…*: the ensuing discussion of the work reveals that it is the opera *Aida* (1871) by Giuseppe Verdi (1813–1901). It suits Thomas Mann's symbolical intentions to accept as truth the common (but false) belief that Verdi wrote this opera to celebrate the opening of the Suez Canal. In fact, Verdi had rejected a request to write a hymn commemorating this event, and it was his opera *Rigoletto* that was performed during the opening ceremonies for the canal in November 1869. But Verdi was also commissioned by the Khedive (i.e. Vice-King) of Egypt to write *Aida*, whose première was performed in Cairo on Christmas Eve 1871 in the new opera house in Cairo. Thus Thomas Mann is able to merge the two facts into an image that suits his purposes: the Suez Canal, a marvel of modern engineering symbolizing the Western ethic of work and progress (and that therefore would win Settembrini's praise) is described in a somewhat cumbersome manner as "a work of technology that would bring nations closer together" (p. 634, ll. 4f.). The circumlocution (it originated with Settembrini; cf. p. 153, l.1) is appropriate, because the symbol of what the Suez Canal stands for is going to be contrasted with the fate of the lovers (Radames and Aida) who in Castorp's mind represent his own fate with Chauchat. The distance that Castorp has moved away from Settembrini's position is made clear by the fact that the opera as a symbol of technological progress means nothing to him, whereas he focuses entirely on the transfiguration of Aida and Radames.

(634) l. 6 *the tragic fate of Radames, Amneris, and Aida*: the Ethiopian Princess Aida is a prisoner of the Egyptians. The Egyptian general, Radames, who is engaged to the Egyptian King's daughter Amneris, is in love with Aida and in conversation with her he reveals some military secrets, thus committing treason. He is sentenced to death by being walled up in a tomb.

(635) ll. 11f. *With downcast eyes, so to speak*: an indication of how personally he is taking the words and music.

l. 18 *Tu—en questa tomba?*: You—in this grave? (This could be viewed as a reference to the Berghof.)

l. 30 *tonic*: first note of the scale.

l. 30 *dominant*: the fifth degree of the scale.

ll. 35 *the underlying situation*: we are now in the realm of fantasy and wishful thinking. Castorp equates the slave-girl Aida with Chauchat. He is listening to the end of Act Four that culminates in the final duet of Aida and Radames. As Aida seeks out Radames in his tomb, "to share his fate in the crypt for all eternity," (p. 635, ll. 37f.), so Castorp daydreams that Chauchat will come to him, so that he, too, might be "united at last with the woman he had assumed he would never see again" (p. 635, ll. 40f.).

ll. 39f. *No, no! troppo sei bella!*: "No, no! You are too beautiful!" This is an abbreviated version of what Radames actually sings: "No, you are not going to die! I loved you too much! … You are too beautiful!" The lines in the opera mean that Radames does not want Aida to die, whereas Castorp is imagining a "Liebestod" with Chauchat. In his *Diary* (10 February 1920) Thomas Mann described the fate of Aida and Radames as a "Liebestod"—a phrase that arouses immediate parallels to Wagner and his opera *Tristan and Isolde* (where the two lovers suffer a similar fate; cf. note to p. 185, l. 23).

ll. 40ff. *It required no effort…*: At this moment Castorp identifies with Radames and with his fate.

(636) ll. 1f. *the little black louvers*: the gramophone and music and death are one.

l. 3   *felt, understood, relished*: the three verbs represent progress: Hans Castorp both feels and understands what the music means for him.

ll. 3f.   *the victorious ideality of music*...: there are echoes in this sentence of the sub-chapter *Snow* in which in similar manner the horrors in Hans Castorp's dream had been overcome by a more sublime vision. Music triumphs—albeit fleetingly—over Schopenhauer's Will.

ll. 5ff.   *You had only to picture*...: The description of the horrors of being buried alive is yet another example of Thomas Mann's ironic undermining of a scene of profound emotion (cf. Joachim's death, p. 528, l. 30). It is also an example of the contrast between the harsh reality of life and the uplifting, ennobling power of art. As such, it is an illustration of Schopenhauer's maxim that art can lift us temporarily above the ruthless and inevitable workings of the Will, that blind force that rules the universe (see "Introduction", pp. 12f.). "The consoling power of beauty to gloss things over..." (p. 636, l. 18) expresses the essence of this philosophy.

ll. 15f.   *their voices sweep in unison*...: the music symbolizes the victory over death.

ll. 21f.   *a second piece*...: the *Prélude à l'après-midi d'un faune* (*Prelude to the Afternoon of a Faun*, 1894) by Claude Debussy (1862–1918).

ll. 29ff. *This was the dream*...: the position he assumes is similar to that of lying on his balcony during the "cure": it connotes lethargy, sexuality and death.

l. 32   *the legs of a goat*: has erotic connotations. It is generally assumed that the painting "Fawn Whistling To A Blackbird" (1864/65) by Arnold Böcklein (1827–1901) was Thomas Mann's model for this scene (see illustration overleaf).

(637) ll. 11ff. *There was no "defend yourself" here*...: The music and the associations it arouses stand in stark contrast to the bourgeois ethic of the Flatlands: he does not have to justify himself, he does not have to be responsible, and no one sits in judgment on him for his having forgotten his duty and "gone missing."

Arnold Böcklein: Faun Whistling To A Blackbird

ll. 13ff. *It was depravity with the best of consciences...*: this sentence summarizes succinctly the contrast between two poles of existence between which Castorp has been torn. The dream is one of total forgetfulness and timelessness. The final scene of Aida had signified for Castorp the apotheosis of forbidden love; this is followed now by the apotheosis of lethargy. The word "depravity" (the German word in the original indicates immoral conduct or debauchery) connotes the sexual undertone: at the first performance of the piece choreographed by Vaslav Nijinsky in Paris 1912 the work had an overtly sexual nature for its time and ended with a scene of simulated masturbation.

l. 15   *Western demands for an active life*: Settembrini's strictures against music ("politically suspect"; cf. p. 112, l. 33) are rejected with a good conscience.

ll. 18ff.   *And there was a third*: the opera *Carmen* (1875) by George Bizet (1838–75). Hans Castorp's willful re-telling of the plot directly mirrors his own fate vis-à-vis Chauchat. Earlier allusions to *Carmen* (see p. 232, l. 28f. & p. 602, 9ff.) have prepared the way for this more extended "analysis." The entire episode, however, is a distortion of the libretto in order that Castorp can see himself as Don José and Chauchat as Carmen.

l. 22   *seen repeatedly in the theater*: we are somewhat belatedly informed that he was very familiar with the opera.

l. 22   *to whose plot he had even alluded once...*: see p. 602, ll. 9ff. The "very crucial conversation" (l. 23) was his conversation with Peeperkorn (pp. 591ff.) in which they had talked about Hans Castorp's relationship with Chauchat and that had ended with Peeperkorn's proposal that they drink to their brotherhood (cf. p. 603, ll. 3ff.).

ll. 23ff.   *It was the music from the second act...*: the Berghof's recording begins with Act 2, Scene iii, which takes place in the café owned by Millas Pastia. In this scene Carmen and Don José reveal the two opposing attitudes to life: freedom versus duty. The plot description that follows (pp. 637–38) is both highly selective (it omits details that do not suit the forced parallel between Carmen/Don José and Chauchat/ Castorp), and it contains alterations and additions to the original text that amplify the psychological connection of the opera to Castorp's own situation.

ll. 28f.   *At the same moment, however, trumpets — bugles*: the translation is unable to reproduce the subtlety of the German: the second word for trumpets in the original is "Clairons" (French for bugles)—and with that the connection to Chauchat is established.

ll. 38ff.   *He is beside himself*: compare the novel's text that follows with the actual lines of the libretto: "You have not understood me ... Carmen, it is the call to barracks. I have to go back to barracks for roll-call." The narrator clearly reads a great deal into those brief lines. In Castorp's mind the opera is dealing with something fundamental: the conflict between the call of duty and honor on the one hand, and the natural inclination to love, irresponsibility and freedom on the other. The operatic example refers not just to Hans Castorp, but it is raised to the level of a universal paradigm.

(638) l. 13   *pretends to lose her head...*: this distortion of the libretto is an ironic echo of those occasions when Castorp "lost his head" despite the warning sound of horns — for example, at the beach (cf. p. 467, l. 29), and when he embarked on his snow journey (cf. p. 466, ll. 19f.).

ll. 21f.   *the principle behind...*: this is the fundamental conflict between the call to duty and the force of love.

l. 22   *French bugles—or Spanish horns*: in the opera they are Spanish military bugles; but the bugle-call is played in the orchestra by French horns—which permits the allusion to Chauchat. Also connoted here is Spain, which serves as a leitmotif of duty, obedience, and rigidity.

l. 32   *"Through every long and lonely hour"*: Don José's aria "La fleur que tu m'avais jetée" ("The flower that you threw to me"; although the novel quotes the German version of the libretto which distorts the original) acquires the profoundest meaning for Hans Castorp. It is quite clear that he sees himself as Don José, fated to love and to suffer. Note

Hans Castorp's reaction when the record comes to an end: "'Yes, yes,' Hans Castorp said in somber gratitude" (p. 639, l. 18). There are also additions here to Bizet's text in order to emphasize the impact that the opera makes on Castorp. (Cf. Thomas Mann in his *Diary*: "I played José's aria three times, while reading the text at the same time. The emotion in it is very strong. The connection to Hans Castorp fascinates me.")

l. 33   *Hans Castorp often played this record by itself*: this preserves his fantasy about the aria, avoiding the unpleasant fact that Carmen rejects Don José immediately thereafter.

(639) l. 7 *was lost for good and all*: not in the original libretto.

ll. 17f.   *and put on the finale*: the "finale" is that of Act 2. Acts 3 & 4 of the opera are omitted, so that the parallel between the opera and Castorp's experiences may be maintained.

ll. 18ff.   *standing up to his officer*...: the German original merely says that "his encounter with the officer had cut off his return." (In the libretto Don José has an argument with an officer who has come to visit Carmen.) This permits the parallel with Hans Castorp's meeting Joachim and as a consequence having no "way back" to the Flatland. Thus Castorp, by staying at the Berghof, has "deserted the colors" and has gone into the mountains with a gypsy woman (Chauchat).

ll. 22f.   *Oh, follow to the mountains fair*...: these lines are deliberately chosen to draw the parallel with Castorp's journey to the mountains at the beginning of the novel.

ll. 25ff.   *To roam and walk*...: The translation is inaccurate and adds a line that Thomas Mann had omitted. It should read:

> The world is wide open—you have no cares;
> Your fatherland knows no limit;
> And above all: the most blessed joy,
> Freedom laughs! Freedom laughs!

These lines offer a concise summary of what Castorp has learned over the past five years.

l. 30   *"Yes, yes," he said once more*: i.e. he believes that he has been listening to his own story. He ignores the tragic conclusion of the opera.

l. 30   *moved on to a fourth piece*: "Valentin's Prayer" from the opera *Faust* (1859) by Charles Gounod (1818–93).

ll. 35ff.   *Someone stepped forward*...: this piece of music has for him very close associations with his cousin Joachim.

(640) ll. 15f. *but all the same it touched Hans Castorp*...: he identifies with Valentin's sister Margaret, thereby connoting his own questionable masculinity and androgynous nature.

l. 23   *it will play a certain role later*: in the next sub-chapter *Highly Questionable* (see p. 670, l. 11 ff.).

l. 30   *Schubert's* Lindenbaum: "The Linden Tree" from the song-cycle *Die Winterreise* ("The Winter's Journey," 1827).

l. 31   *Am Brunnen vor dem Tore*: "By the well near the gate." A song from the song-cycle *Die Winterreise* (*The Winter's Journey*; 1827) by Franz Schubert (1797–1828) that ostensibly follows the travels of a spurned lover. But the cycle is not simply about the lover; it is really about the journey of man towards the grave. In a letter from 1943 Thomas Mann wrote that the song symbolized for him "all the seductiveness of things that we love that harbor the germ of corruption."

Linden Tree

At the well by the gate
There stands a linden tree;
I dreamed in its shadow
Many a sweet dream.

I carved in its bark
Many a word of love;
In joy and in sorrow
I was always drawn to it.

Again today I had to travel
Past it in the depths of night.
There even in the darkness
I closed my eyes.

And its branches rustled,
As if they called to me:
Come here to me, friend,
Here you'll find peace!

The cold winds blew
Right into my face;
The hat flew off my head,
I didn't turn around.

Now I am many hours
Distant from that place,
And I still hear it whispering:
You'll find peace here!

l. 32   *sung by a tenor*: Richard Tauber (1891–1948), whose recording of the song Mann possessed.

(641) ll. 27ff. *an object created by the human spirit...*: the narrator is talking about a symbol that points towards some universal quality or trait. Thus the song has implications beyond the text and beyond the immediate listener: it tells us something about the world at large and about life.

ll. 37ff. *Does anyone believe...*: this paragraph makes it quite plain that the narrator believes that Hans Castorp been "enhanced" during his time at the Berghof, and that he is now able to comprehend the deeper significance of the *Lindenbaum* song. For the first time we are told by the narrator that Hans Castorp has learned something important: the "significance" of this song, which in its essence contains the "sympathy with death" that has emerged as his chief motivator (cf. p. 642, ll. 5f.: "the universal state of mind that this song epitomized so intensely"). He is now "conscious" (and the italics are the narrator's) of the significance of the "Lindenbaum" and why he so loves it. The song denotes for Castorp that world of "forbidden" love and death to which he had always inclined. It was his fate to be predisposed to the world of erotic love and death, but his stay at the Berghof has helped him advance to deeper insights.

(642) ll. 8f. *all of which had matured him...*: the narrator's comments about Hans Castorp's progress could not be clearer: his life has been enhanced and he has gained insights (l. 7), and his regular "playing king" ("taking stock") about his situation has made him into "an intuitive critic of this world" (l. 9), and had ultimately led him to view it "with the scruples of conscience" (l. 11).

l. 20   *It was death*: for Thomas Mann the *Lindenbaum* is the most representative work of German Romanticism (see "Introduction," pp. 17f.). The song expresses the ultimate Romantic desire—which is for death. The Romantic yearning for death is the expression of a fundamental desire for peace—but this ultimate peace can only be found in the grave.

l. 30   *sympathy with death*: this is the central motif of the novel.

ll. 36ff. *The workings of darkness...*: the allusions in this paragraph evoke the world of Naphta and a view of death based on religious piety (cf. Castorp's summary of this p. 495, ll. 26ff.). It is a view that Hans Castorp acknowledges to exist, but one that his own reflections about life and death overcome and supersede. The "pious devotion" of which he speaks subscribes to the Catholic view of death as the transition to heavenly peace. But Castorp's reflections do not concern themselves with heavenly peace after death; rather, they confront death in this life and seek a way to overcome it through a love of humanity.

ll. 40ff.   *Settembrini ... his clear-minded mentor*: no longer the "wind-bag," Settembrini's criticisms of the dangers of "backsliding." are remembered here (cf. p. 97, ll. 8ff.) and applied (critically) to his appreciation of Schubert's song. Hans Castorp recognizes the limited validity of Settembrini's comments—and moves beyond them (see the commentary that follows below).

(643) ll. 10ff.   *this was a fruit...*: the implication of these lines is that music is a powerful force and that it can, indeed, be "politically suspect." Like a fruit, when enjoyed at the right moment (i.e. when it is ripe), it can produce "purest regalement of the spirit" (l. 12), but consumed at the wrong moment it "could spread rot and decay among those who partook of it" (ll. 13f.). In other words, music has the power to lead one down dangerous paths (and Thomas Mann may also have been thinking of Germany's own political future here): in Hans Castorp's case towards an unhealthy preoccupation with death. In the scene, however, he overcomes that danger and moves forward—ironically, onto the battlefield where death presides. Thomas Mann later wrote about this music, specifically *Die Winterreise*: "The Romantic is the National ... for music is the national art of Germany, and more than other arts it can hope to bind and to unite."

l. 20   *he triumphed over himself*: a key concept. Friedrich Nietzsche had declared that "to triumph over the self" was a central goal of life. In the context of *The Magic Mountain* this process entails resisting and overcoming the seductive attractions of death. The *Lindenbaum* embodies an "enchantment of the soul with dark consequences" (p. 643, ll. 22f.): behind the song's seductiveness lurks the Romantic fascination with death.

l. 30   *an enchanter of souls*: Richard Wagner, as Mann admitted.

l. 27   *We were all its sons*: i.e. not just Hans Castorp, but all the readers of the novel.

ll. 31ff.   *One might even found whole empires upon it...*: there is a clearly political dimension here: a political philosophy (e.g. fascism) that seduces the populace with its mystical promises of a blessed future ("very progressive, and not in the least nostalgic"; ll. 32f.) is ultimately promising nothing more than death.

ll. 37ff.   *It was truly worth dying for...*: having overcome the fascination with death, the person who chooses to die for this "song of enchantment" ("Zauberlied" = magic song) is dying for a hopeful vision of the future.

(644) *Highly Questionable*

Readers might be forgiven for wondering what on earth this sub-chapter is doing in the novel. The description of a séance would seem to belong to the more frivolous pursuits of the patients at the Berghof sanatorium, worthy of perhaps no more than a paragraph or two. But Mann devotes an entire, and quite lengthy, sub-chapter to the topic, and we are clearly being asked to take seriously the events that are described, as having considerable importance for our hero. What, then, are we to make of it?

The impetus for this sub-chapter came from Thomas Mann's own experiences in December 1922 and January 1923 at the house of Albert, Freiherr von Schrenck-Noltzing, who was by profession a specialist for nervous ailments. Mann's observations at the séances conducted by Schrenck-Noltzing (aided by two mediums) provided him with the basis for this sub-chapter, as well as for an essay *Occult Experiences* (1924).

Initially, the sub-chapter provides an ironic refutation of Settembrini's earlier emphatic rejection of supernatural phenomena (see p. 443, ll. 38 ff.), which according to him a) could not happen, and b) would only appear to be real to someone who was mentally ill.

But the location of this sub-chapter towards the end of the novel, between *Fullness of Harmony*, and *The Great Petulance*, just before the final sub-chapter *The Thunderbolt*, is clearly meant to be significant. And in fact, if we read the sub-chapter carefully, we can draw further conclusions about Hans Castorp's progress at the Berghof. In this section Mann establishes a connection between myth and the occult—and that in turn has a bearing on politics: the outbreak of War with which the novel ends is a consequence of the unhealthy relationship to Romanticism. Furthermore, we know from Thomas Mann himself that he viewed this subject-matter as an appropriate component of the study of "the mysticism of the body." Nihil humanum me alienum est : Nothing human is foreign to me. The title of this sub-chapter indicates both the nature of the events depicted and the author's own reservations (to say nothing of Hans Castorp's) about occult phenomena. The original uses a superlative ("Most Questionable [Matters]") which even intensifies the doubt.

l. 1.   *Edhin Krokowski's lectures*: see pp. 122ff. and pp. 185ff. The transition of Krokowski's lectures into the realm of parapsychology and "magical arcane matters" (l. 6) is a natural extension of his function in the novel. He belongs to the realm of the East, the subconscious, the libido, eros, the darker side of life. His psychoanalysis is repeatedly referred to as the "dissection of souls" ("Seelenzergliederung"), so it is not surprising that he plays a major role in the conjuring up of souls in this sub-chapter.

ll. 3f.   *a subterranean character, a whiff of the catacomb*: allusions to the connection of the Berghof with the Underworld (cf. Settembrini's comments, p. 56, ll. 1ff.), and of Krokowski's lectures with the "darker" side of humanity.

ll. 7f.   *the sanatorium's main attraction...*: most unlikely at this time (cf. note to p. 9, ll. 32f.)

l. 17   *the very riddle of life itself*: which Hans Castorp himself had investigated, cf. p. 281, ll. 2ff.

l. 36   *an omniscient universal soul*: cf. Naphta's talk of "anonymous and communal" (p. 386, ll. 37f.), and Hans Castorp's "collective memory" in the sub-chapter *Snow* (cf. p. 481, ll. 37f.)

(645) ll. 1ff.   *the "occult" realm...*: if we accept that there are, for example, psychosomatic factors in illness, then we must logically also accept the view that the psyche has the power to affect the material world. The debate continues about "mind" and "matter"—and which came first.

l. 32   *Odense*: main city on the island of Funen ("Fyn" is the Danish name for the island); birthplace of Hans Christian Andersen (1805–75).

(647) ll. 23f.   *this was his native soil—marshy, soggy, unsteady footing...*: the unreliability of the floor beneath one's feet when "uncanny" things are being experienced is a repeated leitmotif; cf. p. 214, ll. 5 & 18. It affects Hans Castorp here as well, cf. p. 648, ll. 2f.: "the ground had shifted under his feet." This all relates to the insubstantiality of all things that are not concrete, tangible, and rational—hence the "boneless" Russian language (which symbolizes the philosophy of the "East"; p. 113, l. 23), the Austrian horseman's cough (the abyss of death; p. 12, ll. 16ff.), and the "soggy ... earth" of the First World War (p. 705, l. 18).

(648) l. 6   *sensations of unmistakable terror*: Hans Castorp is clearly petrified with fear at entering these unfamiliar regions.

ll. 9ff.   *regions to which his mind was forbidden...*: but Hans Castorp's curiosity (cf. "placet experiri"; l. 29) overcomes his reservations.

ll. 14f.   *his clairvoyant great-aunt*: see p. 215, ll. 14ff.

ll. 22ff.   *He could sense in advance...*: Settembrini's influence is clearly at work here.

l. 29   *placet experiri*: Settembrini's tutelage has had consequences the Italian never dreamed of. The pleasure in experimenting now leads Castorp into a world that is totally anathema to his erstwhile mentor.

ll. 32ff.   *the unconditional curiosity...*: his indefatigable curiosity leads him to engage this new and dangerous realm. The "tourist thirsty for knowledge" ("Bildungsreisender") is a repetition of the phrase on p. 565, ll. 40f. & p. 581, l. 14 that implies that this experience, too, is a part of Hans Castorp's education.

l. 34   *tasted the mystery of personality*: i.e. Pieter Peeperkorn. We are asked to believe that the mystery of Peeperkorn's personality is akin to something occult.

ll. 35f.   *something of a military character...*: it is his duty to pursue this new subject, in order to be consistent.

(650) l. 3   *Odense*: see note to p. 645, l. 32.

l. 18   *New Jersey*: U.S. state, adjacent to New York.

ll. 34f.   *twenty-five letters of the alphabet*: presumably because "I" and "J" count as one.

l. 41   *the red-shaded nightstand lamp*: the ever-present leitmotif when a mystery is being probed.

(651) l. 19   *his chatterbox way*: true of Hans Castorp's frequent earlier outbursts; in the latter stages of the novel he becomes less talkative.

(652) l. 19   *never got mixed up in any questions at school*: cf. p. 649, ll. 12ff.

(653) ll. 8f.   *Hastening while...*: this phrase, and its inverse repetition, underscore the sense of time being suspended at the Berghof.

l. 12   *gnomic*: i.e. like an aphorism.

ll. 35ff.   *And then Holger the spirit...*: the major images in the "poem" (for which no source has been found) describe the approach of evening with the setting sun and the passage of time as sand runs through the hourglass – i.e. the end of life.

(654) l. 23   *the hermit's cell...*: this image may derive from the etching *St. Jerome in his Cell* (1514) by Albrecht Dürer (1471–1528).

St. Jerome in his Cell

l. 38   *the Chaldeans and the zodiac*: allusions with special relevance for Hans Castorp (see p. 364, ll. 7ff.).

(655) l. 28   *Across room 34*: a little mystical joke is lost here. The original says literally: "Through 34" (meaning: the sum of the digits). Since the sum of the digits is 7, "Holger" is telling the truth.

(656) l. 21   *the room was bathed in bright clarity*: the remedy for "irrational" activities (cf. p. 189, ll. 37ff., when Settembrini turns on the light in Hans Castorp's room).

ll. 27ff.   *the "souvenir" that had frightened his uncle...*: cf. p. 429, ll. 8ff.

ll. 35f.   *that casual upward fanning of the hand...*: cf. p. 647, l. 31.

(657) ll. 8f.   *those few flakes of brimstone*: sulfur.

ll. 15ff.   *His pupil did not say yes or no...*: Hans Castorp reaffirms his skepticism and independence vis-à-vis Settembrini and takes the position that since we can never be certain that something is real, there is room for intermediate phenomena.

l. 32   *Caro mio!*: My dear!

l. 36   *Man was the measure of all things*: saying ascribed to the Greek philosopher, Protagoras (ca. 490–420 BC).

ll. 39ff. *It were better a millstone were hung...*: Settembrini paraphrases *Matthew* 18, 6: "...it would be better for him to have a heavy millstone hung around his neck, and to be drowned in the depth of the sea."

(658) l. 15 *Wenzel the Bohemian*: at this time Bohemia was a part of the Austro-Hungarian Empire. After the First World War it became the core territory of Czechoslovakia.

l. 18   *a special album*: Hans Castorp has selected some recordings to be played.

l. 31   *"telekinetic"*: literally: "distant movement" (Greek).

l. 40   *ideoplastic*: ideas take on concrete form.

(659) ll. 12f.   *his gushings on love*: Dr. Krokowski's lectures are ironically called into question by the narrator (although the word "gushings" has a slightly more negative connotation than the original).

l. 25   *swampy...*: these images evoke wide associations with the mysterious realms of life and the unfathomable motivation for questionable human actions (cf. the First World War, where the young soldiers, including Hans Castorp, get bogged down in the "squishy mire"; cf. note to p. 704, l. 1).

ll. 32f.   *turned the other cheek*: cf. *Luke* 6: 29: "If someone strikes you on one cheek, turn to him the other also." Paravant's action is, however, for a different purpose.

ll. 33f.   *an alumnus of a dueling fraternity*: cf. note to p. 252, l. 3f.

ll. 34f.   *quite different conduct...*: a slap on the cheek was an insult that would have required a response in the form of a challenge to a duel.

(660) l. 2   *the reddish light of a ceiling lamp...*: evoking mystery.

ll. 18f.   *the miserable, hunchbacked man...*: the reference is to "Das bücklige Männlein" ("The Hunchbacked Little Man") from a famous collection of folk-songs (*Des Knaben Wunderhorn—The Child's Cornucopia*) by Achim von Arnim and Clemens von Brentano, published 1806–08. In the song the hunchbacked little man performs a series of nasty actions that affect the child, and then asks the child to pray for him.

l. 21   *renounce his abstinence*: since the following scene contains strongly sexual components, Castorp's "abstinence" from the séance sessions has sexual connotations.

l. 31   *Valentin*: the brother of Gretchen in Goethe's *Faust* (see note to p. 489: *A Good Soldier*). Hans Castorp identifies Valentin with Joachim. On his reaction to the recording, cf. p. 639, ll. 30ff.

l. 33   *this good soldier*: cf. previous note.

ll. 35ff.   *And if God takes me...*: the lines are from the aria known as "Valentin's Prayer" sung by Valentin before he goes off to battle.

ll. 40f.   *certain possibilities...*: he has decided to try to conjure up Joachim from the dead.

(661) ll. 3f.   *Oh, please go ahead and look*: see p. 214, ll. 17ff.

l. 36   *his experience in the x-ray laboratory*: cf. p. 214.

l. 41   *Sankt Pauli*: district of the city of Hamburg, notorious for its red-light district. This impression of Hans Castorp prepares for the sexual nature of the events that follow.

(662) l. 4   *Hans Castorp and the other nine participants*: with Krokowski, plus the other two women who are out of the room here, there are 13 people at the séance (cf. p. 663, l. 39), the number also present at the Christian Last Supper.

l. 8   *behind Joachim's back*: N.B. Hans Castorp's guilt-feelings.

l. 15   *Hippocrates*: Hippocrates of Kos (ca. 460 BC–ca. 370 BC), an ancient Greek physician considered one of the most outstanding figures in the history of medicine. He is often referred to as the "father of medicine."

l. 16   *Rembrandt's* Anatomy Lesson: the full title of the painting is *The Anatomy Lesson of Doctor Nicolaes Tulp* (1632) by Rembrandt van Rijn (1606–69). Dr. Nicolaes Tulp is pictured explaining the musculature of the arm to medical professionals.

ll. 23f.   *a little red-shaded lamp*: two red lamps to create the aura of mystery (and sex).

The Anatomy Lesson of Doctor Nicolaes Tulp

l. 26   *a few infamous items*: "infamous" because they had played a role in earlier episodes of "telekinetic" occurrences: cf. p. 658, ll. 27f., 660, ll. 3ff., p. 658, ll. 24f.

(663) l. 2   *cincture*: a girdle, usually used in a religious context.

ll. 35ff.   *another, more distant memory...*: see p. 316, ll. 15f.

(664) l. 3   *reddish light*: we are in a bordello.

ll. 22ff.   *reminded him of the gloom...*: cf. p. 213, ll. 24ff.

(665) l. 7   *Millöcker*: Karl Millöcker (1842–99), well-known Viennese operetta composer.

ll. 23f.   *She squeezed...He*: i.e. Elly is Holger—and once again the confusion of the sexes is present.

ll. 34f.   *Then very close to Hans Castorp's ear...*: the implication here is sexual: Hans Castorp is "marrying" Elly/Holger; cf. p. 668, ll. 1ff.: Hans Castorp as the husband, with Elly's knees clamped between his own.

l. 38   *which the director had explained to him*: cf. p. 260, ll. 28ff.

(666) ll. 2ff.   *confused feeling...*: the confusion stems from the fact that he is acting as "husband" to the virginal Elly, assisting in her "birth of Holger," and in the fact that he is talking to Holger (a male) through her.

ll. 27ff.   *despite his once having heard...*: cf. p. 214, l. 17.

(667) ll. 13f.   *although we are not completely sure...*: Hans Castorp's fate in the First World War is not clear (cf. note to p. 702, ll. 5ff.).

ll. 15f.   *the strangest hours he would ever experience*: these strong words indicate the effect that this séance is having on Hans Castorp.

ll. 17ff.   *These were hours...*: the scene, having already had over-tones of the sexual (cf. note to p. 665, ll. 34f.), now takes on elements of a birth (cf. l. 36: "maternity ward"), and later "martyrdom" (p. 669, l. 24). Cf. also p. 669, ll. 33ff.: "The scandalous birthing proceeded."

l. 36 *maternity ward bathed in reddish light*: the sexual implication is clear.

(668) l. 5 *as little Leila's once…*: cf. p. 296, ll. 28f.

l. 11 *Salvation Army revival meeting*: the Salvation Army is an international evangelical movement, founded in 1865 in the United Kingdom and based on a quasi-military structure. Its "revival meetings" were designed to convert people to Christianity.

l. 35 *she reached out her cupped hand…*: cf. p. 528, ll. 5ff., where the dying Joachim makes a similar motion. This strange motion derives from Thomas Mann's own experience at séances where the motion signified the transition from death to life.

(669) l. 38 *eclampsia*: a serious complication of pregnancy, characterised by convulsions.

l. 40 *This magnetization*: the belief that some mysterious power may be passed between human beings by touching (as when Krokowski touches Elly) goes back to the German physician, Franz Anton Mesmer (1734–1815), who believed that there was an "animal magnetism" between human beings (cf. "mesmerism").

(670) ll. 12f. *"Valentin's Prayer"…*: cf. note to p. 639, ll. 30ff.

(671) ll. 2f. *And now since I must leave*: first line of the aria.

l. 8 *gallant, devout, and French*: this aria relates directly to Joachim, but it also connotes Chauchat and Castorp's obsession with her.

l. 10 *O Lord of heaven…*: final lines of the aria.

ll. 11ff. *She reared back…*: the actions might be viewed as those similar to experiencing an orgasm.

l. 23 *the red light*: the erotic connotation here is homoerotic.

ll. 27ff. *It was Joachim…*: cf. p. 529, ll. 8ff.

l. 37 *that strange, unidentifiable thing*: Joachim is wearing—anachronistically—a helmet that was not issued to German soldiers until 1915.

(672) l. 8 *lasquenet*: a German foot-soldier.

l. 18 *the tears came to his eyes*: cf. note to p. 169, ll. 28f. The reference here is also appropriate: in the Bible the phrase occurs in the Lazarus-episode (cf. *John* 11: 35).

l. 26 *he turned on the white light*: just as Settembrini had done long ago when Castorp was day-dreaming of Chauchat (see p. 189, ll. 37ff.).

ll. 32f. *he nodded menacingly…*: Hans Castorp clearly does not approve of what has just happened. Thomas Mann commented (in 1942): "Hans Castorp's exit from the séance room shows clearly that he, too, finds what has transpired to be unworthy, sinful, and repulsive."

The Great Petulance

l. 36   *we have already called...*: cf. *The Great Stupor*, p. 616 ff.

(673) l. 1   *curiosity of the tourist thirsting for knowledge*: cf. note to p. 649, ll. 32ff.

ll. 11ff.   *a love of quarrels*: this entire sub-chapter is a pre-cursor of the biggest quarrel of all: the First World War. The word for quarrel ("Zanksucht") used here is derived from the leitmotif "zanken" (cf. note to p. 274, l. 31).

l. 28   *Minsk*: largest city (and now the capital) of Belarus, a land-locked area surrounded by Russia, Lithuania, Latvia, Poland, and Ukraine.

l. 41   *the student, or former student...*: see p. 74, ll. 22ff.

(674) ll. 36f.   *that was the positive thing about him*: this is equivalent of damning with faint praise.

l. 38   *nothing unclean about his name*: another ironic dig at Weidemann's prejudice (a stress on "his" would make the meaning clearer). Weidemann is the only openly anti-Semitic character in the novel.

l. 38f.   *The Aryan Light*: a fictional name.

(675) l. 1   *Herr Hirsch ... Herr Wolf*: the assumption that these names are "Jewish" is incorrect.

(676) l. 15   *Davos ... Graubünden*: see note to p. 3, l. 2.

ll. 19ff.   *It was a Polish affair...*: this episode is based on an actual affair of honor that had occurred in Munich in 1913. The particulars of the written exchanges reflect some of the diplomatic communiqués that preceded the First World War.

(679) l. 3   *Lemberg*: at this time the capital of Galicia in the Austro-Hungarian Empire. Now Lviv, an important city in Ukraine.

l. 41   *vulnerable to the ... charms of slaps...*: a hint of what is to follow between Settembrini and Naphta.

(680) ll. 2ff.   *the old affirmer of life...*: it is only appropriate that Settembrini's own health would fail as human relations, both local and European, deteriorate.

ll. 7ff.   *the illness that had been the physical cause...*: Naphta, too, is becoming more ill as European politics embraces nihilism.

ll. 38f.   *The unadmitted, secret universal desire for war...*: Naphta has his finger on the pulse of European politics.

(681) l. 5   *the sinking of the* Titanic: collided with an iceberg and sank, 14–15 April 1912. Naphta's appraisal of the event is the opposite of the view of Settembrini who saw the *SS Titanic* as a heroic memorial to human reason (cf. p. 351, l.10).

11f.   *the universal lust for war*: Naphta is both in tune with the mood of the age and recognizes the inherent nature of humanity.

l. 36   *science—in which he did not believe*: Naphta's unambiguous answer to Settembrini's earlier question to him, cf. p. 390, ll. 28f.

(682)   l. 7   *That monistic claim*: i.e. that there was unity in reality.

l. 12   *Haeckel*: Ernst Haeckel (1834–1919), one of the first advocates of evolution in Germany. See note to p. 271, ll. 19f.

l. 13   *Empiricism*: a theory of knowledge that asserts that knowledge arises from experience.

l. 32   *cosmogony*: theory of the origin of the universe (as opposed to cosmology, the study of the universe).

(683)   ll. 7ff.   *what he understood by "freedom"*...: Naphta's idea of freedom is, of course, radically different from that of Settembrini and leads in the direction of irrationalism—hence the latter's fear that Hans Castorp might be all too attracted to it.

l. 23   *Monstein*: mountain village approx. 20 km. west of Davos that had (and still has) retained the character of a very old village.

l. 30   *Frauenkirch and Glaris*: villages immediately to the west of Davos.

l. 32   *the Rhätikon chain*: see note to p. 264, l. 20.

ll. 33ff.   *The road they took*...: cf. Castorp's initial train journey, with its metaphorical associations: "between cliff and abyss" (l. 35).

l. 40   *Zügenstrasse*: mountain near Davos-Monstein.

(684)   l. 2   *Stulsergrat*: a mountain that, in fact, cannot be seen from Monstein. No matter, Thomas Mann wishes to connote an allusion to Valhalla, so this serves his purpose. "The gigantic wall" is probably the "Gipshorn."

l. 5   *Valhalla*: burial place of the Nordic gods.

ll. 6ff.   *Hans Castorp admired it greatly*...: Castorp's attitude is reminiscent of Peeperkorn's, cf. p. 582, ll. 10ff.

l. 12   *Mount Everest*: was not scaled until 1953.

ll. 41ff.   *Romanticism*...: Since Romanticism plays a central role in the novel, it is appropriate that the final, decisive argument between Naphta and Settembrini should be about this topic. Naphta's view of Romanticism is this: While rebelling against the dominant power of reason and the cultivation of humanistic individualism, and rejecting "classical" models, the Romantics embraced emotion and instinct, in alliance with a political nationalism that subjected the individual to the state. In this respect, the "revolution" led to "reaction" and dictatorship.

(685)   l. 5   *Enlightenment*: Naphta denies that it was exclusively the Enlightenment that led to revolution and the emancipation of humanity.

l. 8   *periwigs*: the original word for "wig." The suggestion is that those who clung to "classical" ideals were stuffed shirts.

l. 9   *the German Wars of Liberation*: 1813–15, struggle to drive Napoleon's forces out of Germany.

ll. 9f.   *Fichtean enthusiasms*: Johann Gottlieb Fichte (1762–1814) had written a series of *Speeches to the German Nation* (*Reden an die deutsche Nation*, 1808), which became instrumental in fanning the flames of German nationalism in the struggle for liberation from Napoleon.

l. 10   *song-singing*: songs were a strong unifying and motivating factor in the resistance to Napoleon.

l. 29   *geocentrism*: the theory that the Earth is at the center of the universe. Cf. p. 389, ll. 23ff. where Naphta had first argued in favor of geocentrism.

l. 36   *Arndt*: Ernst Moritz Arndt (1769–1860), one of the leading writers of the German independence movement against Napoleon.

l. 37   *Görres*: Joseph von Görres (1776–1848), another writer of the independence movement. *His Christian Mysticism* (*Christliche Mystik*) appeared in four volumes between 1836 and 1842.

(686) l. 2f.   *the Reformation*: the attempts by certain Protestant leaders, such as Martin Luther, to reform the Catholic Church. Naphta's cynical view—expressed by his laughter: "hee hee"—is that the movement has been misinterpreted and that it was confused about its goals.

l. 5   *Luther*: Martin Luther: see note to p. 374, l. 37.

l. 13   *Kotzebue*: August von Kotzebue (1761–1819) was a prolific and highly successful dramatist who at the same time was employed as a spy by the Russian government, in particular to provide information about the activities of the student associations. The student Karl August Sand (1795–1820) assassinated Kotzebue in the hope that the act would fan the flames of German nationalism. Sand was executed in 1820.

l. 14   *Holy Alliance*: see note to p. 150, l. 1.

(687) l. 37   *Jacobin revolution*: cf. note to p. 389, l. 16.

(688) l. 1   *a pigtail*: this is Naphta's metaphor for the anachronism of humanism.

l. 14   *Distruttore! Cane arrabiato! Bisogna ammarzarlo!*: Destroyer! Mad dog! He has to be killed!

ll. 17ff.   *Hans Castorp was imitating...*: something he has done frequently at emotionally charged moments.

l. 33   *in terms of the law*: dueling was against the law.

(689) l. 1   *insisted on duel with pistols*: any form of dueling was forbidden to Jesuits.

l. 41   *All'incontro*: on the contrary.

ll. 41ff.   Settembrini's argument here completely undermines and contradicts his stance throughout the novel: Reason in the abstract "contains far more profound and radical possibilities for hatred … than are found in social life" (p. 690, ll. 1ff.) and can lead to "bestial deeds" (Castorp's conclusion, p. 690, l. 23). The champion of reason reveals reason's potential for ultimately destructive ends. The fact that Settembrini had been led by Naphta to fight the duel "showed that he, too, was enveloped by the same inner state that had possession of them all" (p. 690. ll. 20f.). The Schopenhauerian Will exerts itself even in the seemingly most rational being. The duel between Settembrini and Naphta is, of course, merely a precursor to the ultimate act of the Will: the First World War. Thomas Mann commented on the duel that it had "not only intellectual hostility as its motive, but also pedagogical rivalry (quasi-erotic)."

(690) l.7   *a return to the primal state of nature*: the rationalist Settembrini admits to the elementary nature of the Will.

ll. 27ff.   *From his fund of memories…*: Hans Castorp realizes the truth about humanity—and his vision forecasts the outbreak of war.

l. 28   *Wiedemann and Sonnenschein*: cf. p. 675, ll. 19ff.

(691) ll. 27f.   *the shiny little revolver…*: cf. p. 77, ll. 27f.

ll. 29f.   *Belgian made … Brownings*: a Browning pistol was used by the assassin Gavrilo Princip to assassinate Archduke Franz Ferdinand of Austria in Sarajevo on June 28, 1914, precipitating the First World War.

(693) ll. 11f.   *first because…*: presumably his obligation to both men as the object of their pedagogical efforts.

ll. 26f.   *The lady from Minsk*: see note to p. 673, l. 28.

(694) l. 26   *while waiting for a nosebleed to end*: cf. p. 117, ll. 20ff.

(696) ll. 12f.   *shot himself in the head*: the logical outcome of Naphta's view of life.

l. 20   *Infelice! Che cosa fai per l'amor di Dio!*: Unhappy man! What in God's name are you doing!

The Thunderbolt

l. 27   *a mythic, romantic bundle of time*: see "Introduction," pp. 27f.

l. 30   *bad Russian table*: the fact that he ends up here is a final indicator of his "progress" away from bourgeois convention.

l. 31   *Bukharan*: former name of Uzbekistan, at this time an emirate under the control of Russia

l. 32   *a little beard*: another symbol of his emancipation from the Flatland—as we are explicitly told below: "a sign of a certain philosophical indifference to his appearance" (l. 10). Cf. also p. 697, ll. 17ff.

(697) ll. 7ff. *like a student...*: as discussed by Albin and Castorp many years earlier, cf. p. 78, ll. 32ff.

l. 10f. *an orgiastic sort of freedom*: i.e. the only form of total freedom with absolutely no restraints (cf. *Herr Albin*, p. 79, ll. 12ff.).

l. 14 *no wild and defiant decisions*: i.e. to leave the Berghof without permission.

l. 26 *even if they did not understand Latin*: the understanding of Latin would imply a commitment to the ideals of the Classical West.

ll. 36f. *The boy named Teddy...*: cf. p. 306, ll. 28ff.

(698) l. 14 *regions of unwholesome barometric pressure*: i.e. Davos high up in the mountains.

l. 23 *prohibited*: Hans Castorp is exploiting his medical condition to release himself from family obligations.

l. 33 *the total abrogation of every emotional bond...*: his emancipation from the Flatland is confirmed.

l. 37 *his former girlfriend*: the sexual nature of the cigar continues.

l. 41 *Oath of Rütli*: a name that connotes both an historical event and a philosophical decision by Hans Castorp. According to legend, the "Oath" taken on the Rütli mountain in 1291 by Swiss freedom fighters (including the iconic Swiss hero William Tell) initiated a war of liberation from their Austrian oppressors. By changing to the "Oath of Rütli" brand, Hans Castorp is signaling his own act of liberation. The metaphor also looks ahead to his return to the Flatland and service to his nation.

The meadow on the Rütli mountain

(699) l. 5 *no longer carried his pocket watch*: a sign that time means nothing to him anymore.

l. 10ff.   *It was his way of honoring...*: Hans Castorp has realized that he has been living in a hermetic world, where time is of no consequence, and his experiences have been in the manner of an hermetic experiment: the "alchemy" of the ideas and experiences he has been subjected to has worked its "magic" and subjected him to "his soul's fundamental adventure" (l. 14). On "stroll by the shore" (l. 10), cf. p. 536, ll. 34ff.

l. 21   *rodomontade*: bragging or blustering speech; a leitmotif that occurs several times (cf. p. 304, l. 23 & p. 703, 24f.).

l. 24   *stupor and petulance*: referring back to events at the Berghof, cf. pp. 616ff. & 672ff. The personal tensions in the world-in-little of the Berghof—at which all the European nations are represented—is a reflection of the political tensions on the European canvas.

l 26   *the magic mountain*: the first direct reference to the novel's title.

l. 27   *its entranced sleeper*: another reference to the "Siebenschläfer" (cf. note to p. 534, l. 39). Hans Castorp, like the figures in the legend, has awakened from a long sleep in a hermetic world.

l. 28   *sheepishly rubbing his eyes*: like someone in a fairy tale who has just awakened after a long sleep.

l. 32ff.   *he had not been given much of a hearing...*: Hans Castorp's break with the Flatland has become so final that he is not even interested in the events leading up to the First World War. His personal concerns are purely philosophical and centered on his own development (cf. "playing king," p. 383, ll. 34f.).

l. 36f.   *an arrogant preference...*: the allusion here is to the philosophical problem posed by Plato: When we contemplate the important aspects of life (e.g. beauty, truth, justice), do we see the things in themselves or merely their shadows, i.e. manifestations of them in operation, but never the thing itself that lies behind the manifestation?

l. 39f.   *after first establishing sudden clarity*: i.e. by switching on the light.

l. 42f.   *It was the other way around now*: with delicious irony the narrator not only indicates the emancipation of Hans Castorp from Settembrini—it is Castorp who sits at Settembrini's bedside—, but also implies that Settembrini's noble ideas have come to naught: he lies sick in bed while the world is about to be engulfed in flames.

(700) l. 3   *Carbonaro chairs*: which Settembrini has inherited from his grandfather, cf. p. 399, l. 10.

l. 16   *He spoke in a weak, but heartfelt voice...*: all of Settembrini's noble plans have been thwarted, and his grandiose hopes for the victory of reason and enlightenment have been swept aside by the outbreak of the

First World War. As he sees all his dreams evaporating, it is only fitting that his own physical strength should be failing.

ll. 18ff.   *dove's feet ... pinions of eagles*: cf. note to p. 375, ll. 31f.

ll. 21ff.   *the politics he had inherited*: cf. p. 154, ll. 9ff.

l. 27   *the principle of obduracy*: cf. note to p. 154, l. 32.

l. 28   *the Holy Alliance*: see note to p. 150., l.1

l. 28ff.   *there were inconsistencies here*: as we have already seen, cf. p. 154, ll. 33f. & p. 375, l. 10,

l. 41   *Recently—a year and a half or two years before*: the narrator has been infected with Hans Castorp's changing sense of time. In the original the word for a year is, in fact, a diminutive, and the text reads literally: "Two little years or one and a half ago."

ll. 41f.   *the diplomatic cooperation...*: Albania had declared its independence (from the Ottoman Empire) in 1911. At the London Conference in November 1913 Italy and Austria had combined against Russian and Serbian resistance to get Albania's independence confirmed.

(701) l. 3ff.   *demi-Asia...*: the references here are to some of the central elements of Naphta's philosophy.

l. 3   *Schlüsselburg*: cf. note to p. 238, ll. 4ff.

l. 6f.   *the immense loan...*: In 1913 France had agreed to make a loan to Russia over the next five years (commencing in 1914) to build railroads in Poland. Since the Congress of Vienna in 1815 Russia had acquired increasing control over Polish affairs. Settembrini's discomfort arises from the simplistic dualism of his world view in the context of pre-1914 European politics: that France (the West, Enlightenment, reason, etc.) would look favorably on Russia (the East, darkness, barbarism, etc.) is bound to offend him.

ll. 9f.   *his grandfather had equated...*: cf. p. 153, ll. 18ff.

l. 10   *July Revolution*: see note to p. 153 ll. 19ff.

l. 11f.   *that enlightened republic and Scythian Byzantium*: Settembrini's characterization of France (the "enlightened republic") and the Ottoman Empire—"Scythian" because in his eyes it was so backward and unenlightened (cf. note to p. 220, l. 17). Byzantium was the name of Constantinople before 330 A.D. (since 1930 Istanbul).

l. 15   *the murder of the archduke...*: Archduke Franz Ferdinand of Austria (the heir to the throne) was assassinated on June 28, 1914 in Sarajevo while on a state visit. This episode is considered to be the proximate cause of the First World War.

l. 15   *our German sleeper*: this is another reference to the mediaeval legend of the seven youths in Ephesus; see p. 534. l. 37.

l. 19   *committed to free a nation*: Austria-Hungary had invaded Bosnia and Herzegovina in 1908 and annexed these two states into its Empire. When the Archduke went on an official visit to Herzegovina in 1914, there was a strong feeling of resentment against Austria (and thus against him as its symbol). Settembrini, while deploring an act of assassination, cannot refrain from admitting that the act was intended to help free a nation from foreign domination.

l. 20   *the citadel he hated*: Vienna.

l. 21   *the upshot of Moscow's schemes*: Russia supported Serbia is its dispute with Austria-Hungary—thus Settembrini believes that the assassination of the Archduke could well have been instigated by the Russian government.

l. 22f.   *the ultimatum…*: after the assassination of the Archduke Ferdinand on June 28, 1914, Austria-Hungary ("the Hapsburgs"—i.e. the Emperor) presented Serbia with an ultimatum on July 23, 1914, containing a lengthy list of demands, and demanded a response within two days.

ll. 29f.   *In the days of the first mobilization…*: Austria-Hungary and Serbia began to mobilize on 25 July 1914; on 28 July Austria-Hungary declared war on Serbia. On August 1, 1914 Germany declared war on Russia and on 3 August on France.

l. 32   *nincompoop*: the translation is a little unfair to Hans Castorp. The implication is that he is ignorant of and naïve about European politics—a simpleton who needs guidance.

l. 35   *But if you think…*: i.e. he would not advocate that Italy join Germany in an alliance against France.

l. 35   *caro*: my dear.

(702)   l. 1f.   *our sleeper…*: see note to p. 701, l. 15.

l. 5ff.   *set free…*: the outbreak of the First World War jolts Hans Castorp out of his "sleep" on the Magic Mountain and frees him from the Berghof's hold over him. The War causes him to return to society, and this—in the tradition of the German Bildungsroman of the nineteenth century—signifies a return to life ("life was to receive back her sinful problem child," l. 10f.). However, the traditional pattern after which the hero henceforth makes a positive contribution to society is thrown into doubt for two reasons: first, Hans Castorp will have to undergo yet another "ordeal" (l. 12)—i.e. fight in the War; and second, he may not survive: "…three salvos fired in his, the sinner's, honor" (l. 13f.)—the latter implies that "perhaps" (l. 13) he dies. Cf. also the narrator's earlier comment: "we are not completely sure as to his later fate" (p. 667, ll. 14f.). Thomas Mann commented in his *Diary* (1919): "Hans Castorp's departure for the war is his departure towards the beginning of the fight for a new world, after having tasted during his education the components of Christianity and Paganism."

l. 11 *her sinful problem child*: "sinful" from the perspective of life (i.e. normal bourgeois society) because he withdrew from its obligations. Cf. also l. 16: "the sinner."

l. 13 *three salvos*: as were fired over Joachim's grave (cf. p. 530, ll. 32f.).

l. 14 *he sank back down in his knees...*: as Tannhäuser does when he is freed from the Venusberg.

l. 15 *a heaven darkened by sulfurous fumes...*: on i.e. the field of battle.

l. 16 *the grotto ceiling...*: the reference is to the love grotto in the opera *Tannhäuser*. The eponymous hero of the opera is captivated by the sins of the flesh that he experiences with Venus in the grotto. The parallel with Castorp and Chauchat is obvious: the Berghof has been a kind of love-grotto for Hans Castorp, and Clavdia Chauchat has been his Venus. Just as Tannhäuser had to escape from the Venusberg, Castorp has to escape from the Zauberberg (the Magic Mountain).

l. 21f. *a wild departure*: he is leaving, as Joachim did, without the permission of Behrens (cf. p. 413, ll. 11f.).

l. 27 *the teeming little station*: Settembrini has accompanied Hans Castorp to the station—as is only fitting: he has for years urged the young man to leave the Berghof.

l. 30f. *a Mediterranean—or perhaps a Russian—kiss*: Settembrini, in embracing Hans and in kissing him the way Chauchat did, is tacitly admitting the validity of Chauchat's world: in a total view of life, the irrational has its place. In Settembrini, too, the Will asserts its power.

l. 34 *the forms appropriate to the educated West*: Settembrini drops the formal form of address in favor of the informal.

l. 36 *E così in giù—in giù finalemente! Addio, Giovanni mio!*: So you're going down there—finally down there! Farewell, my Hans!

l. 40 *you are the one to go...*: the original is more ambiguous: "It was intended that you be the one"—in other words, Hans Castorp is the type to save Germany, not his militaristic cousin. Settembrini also acknowledges life's irony: "The tricks life plays" (l. 41).

(703) l. 3 *Addio!*: Farewell!

l. 6f. *the tip of the ring finger...*: i.e. a tear comes to Settembrini's eye.

l. 8 *Where are we?*: from the description that follows, we are in Hades (cf. "hellhound" [l. 11]; "reluctant shades" [l. 23])—and Hans Castorp has come to Hell without a guide.

l. 8   *Dusk*: in the original the word "Dämmerung" is used, which can
mean either dusk or dawn. On the one hand, the surface meaning is clear: a
cataclysm is approaching, one that connotes the end of the world as
envisioned by Richard Wagner: his great opera *The Ring of the Nibelung*
ends with "The Twilight of the Gods" ("Götterdämmerung"), the end of
the world. This scene in the novel connotes Wagner's vision: "fire
reddening a murky sky that bellows incessantly with dull thunder" (ll. 9f.).
But the ambiguity of the word "Dämmerung" is also intentional, because
the novel's conclusion is ambivalent: the War signifies the end of an era
("dusk"), but the hopeful statement with which the novel ends is a dream
of the dawning of a new day.

l. 20   *a signpost*: one of the later songs in *Die Winterreise* contains
the following final verse:

Einen Weiser seh' ich stehen	I see a signpost
Unverrückt vor meinem Blick;	Fixed before my gaze;
Eine Straße muß ich gehen,	I must travel a road
Die noch keiner ging zurück.	On which no one ever returned.

l. 24   *bombast and rodomontade*: cf. p. 699, l. 21.

l. 26   *troops*: strictly speaking a "troop" is a military unit (consisting
of a number of soldiers), not an individual soldier. The German text calls
them "comrades."

l. 28   *that kindhearted sinner*: see note to p. 702, l. 11.

l. 30ff.   *They have been called up...*: no specific details given, but
the description of the young men on the battlefield recalls the Battle of
Langemarck on 10 November 1914, when 6th Reserve Division of the
German army attacked the enemy lines and suffered severe losses. (The
village of Langemarck was never taken.) This action was later transformed
into a myth that bore little relationship to the reality of the day. That myth,
elaborated and ornamented in every re-telling and creative depiction, told
how courageous student volunteers, singing the German National Anthem
"Deutschland, Deutschland über alles," assaulted the enemy trenches and
suffered grievous losses before occupying them. The "Heroes of
Langemarck" became one of the central myths of World War I.

Note that the narrator's description of the scene (pp. 704–05) contains
little of heroism, and much of the horrors and senselessness of war. N.B.
The description of the helmets places this action in the early stages of the
war.

ll. 37f.   *this was no promenade*: using the same word ("Lustwandel") that had been used throughout to describe the walks of Hans and
Joachim (cf. note to p. 45, ll. 23f.).

(704) l. 1 *the squishy mire*: the physical circumstances in the First World War relate to the metaphorical descriptions of decay and decomposition and the loss of human form, beginning with the sound of the Austrian horseman's cough (cf. p. 12, ll. 21ff.). The dictates of *eros* and the "sympathy with death" result in the dissolution of the individual in sludge and mud.

l. 7   *the marshy wood*: see previous note.

(705) ll. 5ff.   *One might imagine...*: the following descriptions recall the motifs of Hans Castorp's dream in the sub-chapter *Snow*, cf. p. 482, ll. 18ff. The vision of a happy human race contrasts with the ugly reality of war.

l. 18   *the soggy, branch-strewn earth*: cf. note to p. 704, l. 1.

ll. 18ff.   *What's this? He's singing?*: Hans Castorp's recalling of the *Lindenbaum* at this crucial moment indicates his subconscious desire for peace and finding his way "home."

l. 25   *a howling hound of hell*: the hound of hell was Cerberus who guarded the entrance to the Underworld. Hans Castorp has emerged from the "Underworld" of the Berghof only to enter a new Underworld.

ll. 39f.   *And all its branches rustled...*: These lines are from the final verse of the song, which concludes: "Come to me, friend,/Here you will find rest."

(706) l. 2   *life's faithful problem child*: Settembrini's term (cf. p. 303, l. 12) has been taken over by the narrator.

ll. 3f.   *It was neither short...*: the narrator uses the same words that appear in the *Foreword* (cf. p. xii, l. 7) and that have been a leitmotif throughout.

l. 4   *We told it for its own sake*: again echoing the *Foreword*, cf. p. xi, ll. 1f.

l. 8f.   *dab the corner of one eye...*: the narrator is moved at Hans Castorp's departure from the scene, just as Settembrini was (cf. p. 703, ll. 6f.).

ll. 18   *you saw the intimation of a dream of love...*: Hans Castorp's vision in the sub-chapter *Snow* (see pp. 480–87) and his conclusions at the end of *Fullness of Harmony* (cf. p. 643, ll. 21ff) become the ultimate message of the novel.

ll. 19f. `*this worldwide festival of death*: alluding to the *Danse Macabre* (Dance of Death), cf. pp. 281ff.

l. 21   *will love someday rise up out of this, too?*: The "love" in this last sentence of the novel must be of a different kind compared to that which has been at issue before—for the "love" that has consumed Hans Castorp throughout the novel was constantly associated with disease and death. In developing his own concept of the *Homo* Dei, and in moving beyond the erotic in his relationship to Chauchat, he has progressed from *eros* to *caritas*.

Hans Castorp has returned to the Flatland. Does this mean that Settembrini has won? After all, the latter's most fervent wish for his ward was for the latter to return home. But Hans Castorp returns with insights that go beyond any of the positions he has encountered at the Berghof. One of Castorp's chief characteristics was his ability to absorb all the influences and opinions emanating from the other major characters—and to evaluate critically everything he heard and experienced. He never took a position on one side or the other, but remained "the man in the middle." His ultimate stance entails the primacy of the individual, independence in thought and action, and personal autonomy. He learned to adopt an open-minded humanist attitude of loving life in all its varied manifestations and to conquer the dangerous fascination with disease and death. While acknowledging the negative forces underlying existence, he came to realize that one must strive for goodness.

This new view of life is not that envisioned by Settembrini, because Hans has moved beyond Settembrini's simplistic positivistic views to a "higher" position. Hans Castorp returns to the Flatland not as a character who is ready to assume a valuable role in society (as a conventional Bildungsroman would have ended), but rather as a man who has achieved the goal of "self-overcoming" in the Nietzschean sense. Thus the novel does not end with a demonstration of progress, but rather with an expression of hope.

In 1943 Thomas Mann wrote: "The hero of the novel was only seemingly the nice young man Hans Castorp [...]; in reality it was *homo Dei*, mankind itself with its religious question about the self, about its whence and whither, its essence and goal, its place in the universe, the secret of its existence, the eternal dilemma and task of Humanity."

SELECT BIBLIOGRAPHY

Select List of Books in English

Bloom, Harold, ed. *Thomas Mann's* The Magic Mountain. New Haven: Chelsea House, 1986.

Dowden, Stephen, ed. *A Companion to The Magic Mountain*. New York: Camden House, 2002.

Heller, Erich. *Thomas Mann. The Ironic German*. Boston & Toronto: Little, Brown, 1958.

Hollingdale, R. J. *Thomas Mann. A Critical Study*. London: Hart-Davis, 1971.

Kurzke, Hermann. *Thomas Mann. Life as a Work of Art*. Transl. Leslie Wilsson. Princeton: Princeton UP, 2002.

Lehnert, Herbert & Eva Wessell, eds. *A Companion to the Works of Thomas Mann*. New York: Camden House, 2004.

Reed, Terence J. *The Uses of Tradition*. Oxford: OUP, 1996.

Robertson, Ritchie, ed. *The Cambridge Companion to Thomas Mann*. Cambridge: CUP, 2002.

Vaget, Hans Rudolf, ed. *Thomas Mann's* The Magic Mountain. *A Casebook*. New York: OUP, 2008.

Weigand, Hermann J (1971) *Thomas Mann's Novel "Der Zauberberg": A Study*. Chapel Hill: University of North Carolina Press, 1965.

Select List of Books in German

Langer, Daniela. *Thomas Mann* Der Zauberberg. *Erläuterungen und Dokumente*. Stuttgart: Reclam, 2009.

Neumann, Michael. *Thomas Mann. Der Zauberberg*. Kommentar von Michael Neumann. Frankfurt a.M.: Fischer, 2002.

Sprecher, Thomas. *Davos im Zauberberg. Thomas Manns Roman und sein Schauplatz*. Zürich & München: Wilhelm Fink, 1996.